BLOWING UP the BRAND

POPULAR CULTURE & EVERYDAY LIFE

Toby Miller
General Editor

Vol. 21

PETER LANG
New York • Washington, D.C./Baltimore • Bern
Frankfurt • Berlin • Brussels • Vienna • Oxford

BLOWING UP the BRAND

CRITICAL PERSPECTIVES ON PROMOTIONAL CULTURE

EDITED BY MELISSA ARONCZYK AND DEVON POWERS

PETER LANG
New York • Washington, D.C./Baltimore • Bern
Frankfurt • Berlin • Brussels • Vienna • Oxford

Library of Congress Cataloging-in-Publication Data

Blowing up the brand: critical perspectives on promotional culture /
edited by Melissa Aronczyk, Devon Powers.
p. cm. — (Popular culture and everyday life; v. 21)
Includes bibliographical references and index.
1. Branding (Marketing) 2. Brand name products.
3. Imagery (Psychology) 4. Popular culture.
I. Aronczyk, Melissa. II. Powers, Devon.
HD69.B7B575 306.3'4—dc22 2010023360
ISBN 978-1-4331-0866-2 (hardcover)
ISBN 978-1-4331-0867-9 (paperback)
ISSN 1529-2428

Bibliographic information published by **Die Deutsche Nationalbibliothek**.
Die Deutsche Nationalbibliothek lists this publication in the "Deutsche Nationalbibliografie"; detailed bibliographic data is available on the Internet at http://dnb.d-nb.de/.

FSC
Mixed Sources
Product group from well-managed forests, controlled sources and recycled wood or fiber
Cert no. SCS-COC-002464
www.fsc.org
©1996 Forest Stewardship Council

Cover design by Patricia Duque Campos

The paper in this book meets the guidelines for permanence and durability of the Committee on Production Guidelines for Book Longevity of the Council of Library Resources.

Printed in the United States of America

CONTENTS

LIST OF FIGURES

ACKNOWLEDGMENTS

This book began as a conference by the same name held at the Institute for Public Knowledge at New York University on May 8 and 9, 2009. Our goal was to bring together a diverse group of scholars whose work we had admired and whose ideas touched on what we saw as a growing body of critical thinking around issues of promotional culture.

To say the conference was productive would be an understatement. The striking parallels we noted among our colleagues' research findings as well as the phenomenal interest the conference generated among both participants and audience members convinced us of the usefulness of putting together an edited volume to crystallize these elements of a rapidly developing and dynamic area of research and scholarship.

Our sincere thanks go to the conference participants, most of whom are contributors to this volume, for their ongoing commitment to this project; and to the individuals and organizations whose mentorship and support were invaluable: Craig Calhoun, Sam Carter, and the Institute for Public Knowledge; Ted Magder and Marita Sturken in the Department of Media, Culture, and Communication at New York University; the New York Institute for the Humanities; and our own university departments. At various points we received helpful critical feedback from a number of readers, among them the members of the NYLON sociology of culture network at New York University; Andreas Killen; Andreas Koller; Susan Murray; Amber Jamilla Musser; David W. Park; David Parisi; and Marion Wrenn. Finally, we are immensely grateful to Toby Miller, series editor; Patricia Duque Campos, for her excellent cover design; and to Mary Savigar and Sophie Appel at Peter Lang for devoting their time and expertise to this project.

MELISSA ARONCZYK
CARLETON UNIVERSITY

DEVON POWERS
DREXEL UNIVERSITY

CHAPTER ONE

Blowing Up the Brand

Melissa Aronczyk & Devon Powers

"New Branded World" Redux

Only about a decade ago, popular understanding of brands and branding was largely confined to the products and practices of the corporate enterprise. When journalist and cultural critic Naomi Klein wrote the bestseller *No Logo* in 2000, a searing critique of the "new branded world" (3) of industrial influence, the focus of her attack was on how corporations' transnational reach, predatory methods, and tools of exploitation, exclusion, and censorship had impacted a wide range of social and political activities and institutions. The instant recognition and global penetration of "the swoosh, the shell and the arches" (Ch. 16) underlined Klein's account of the creeping corporate encroachment of personal, public, and mental space. Aiming to chart the anticorporate activism on the rise to resist and transform these practices, *No Logo* fed a worldwide movement to foster awareness of "the brand bullies" and challenge their dominance of the status quo.

Even while this consciousness was on the rise, however, other forms of "brand awareness" were taking place. First, and surely disappointing for its author, *No Logo* came to serve not only as a bible for social justice movements, labor rights activists, and environmentalists, but also as a reference point for marketing and branding agencies themselves.[1] Second, in a striking reversal of *No Logo*'s lessons, many anticorporate activists and their causes themselves became "brands," taking the rationalized logic of brand management to the heart of their organization (du Gay 1996; and, e.g., Bob 2002, 2005).[2]

This process mirrored a more general shift toward entrepreneurial forms of governance by a wide range of institutions starting in the 1970s. Transformations in the perceived requirements of organizations at the urban, regional, and national levels to be faster paced, more systematized, and globally competitive began to demand new forms of authority that were more familiar with the requirements of the market (Harvey 2001: Ch. 16; Keating 2003). Crises of legitimacy and relevance in the public sector were met with claims of expertise and tried-and-tested solutions from the private realm. In this context adopting a brand was seen as a symbolic shorthand for market savvy, business acumen, and global competitiveness—whether for urban centers, transnational governance institutions, or nation-states. *New York Times* columnist Thomas Friedman put it bluntly: "As we move into a world where everyone has the same hardware and everybody is being forced to get the same software to go with it, a country's brand, and the unique bond it can build with its foreign investors, becomes even more important" (1999: 244). In an article titled, "No Logo, No Future," brand strategists Fiona Gilmore and Rebecca Rumens decried government aid to developing countries, advocating "brand surgery" instead—the transfer of brand-based training and skills to encourage more entrepreneurial approaches. "We must ask not only what our government can do to alleviate poverty in Africa," they conclude, "but ask what our employers or favorite brands can do" (Gilmore and Rumens 2005; see also Anholt 2005). Overall, it came to seem as though the structures of private ownership and strategic management developed to capitalize products and services in the corporate world increasingly resonated with the renewed aims of a broad range of public, private, and governance institutions; even those hitherto immune from—or at least inured against—the requirements of global capital.

At present we are no longer surprised to hear the term "brand" applied to multiple forms of political, social, and cultural expression and organization: the professional identities of individuals and families—from Tiger Woods to Tyra Banks, Stephen King to LonelyGirl18, the Kardashians to the Novogratzes (Green 2009); politicians and political parties of every affiliation and stripe (Klein 2010; Greenberg 2008; Pasotti 2009); arts, civil society, and advocacy organizations (Wallace 2006; Stallabrass 2006); geographical spaces at multiple scales (Aronczyk 2007; Donald et al. 2008; Jansen 2008); ethnic and kinship groups (Comaroff and Comaroff 2009); philanthropies and charities (Bishop and Green 2008; King 2006; Stole 2008); sports teams and other large-scale entertainments and franchises (Rein et al. 2006); movements for social justice and human rights (Bob 2005); educational and healthcare facilities (Gould 2003; Waldby and Mitchell 2006); privacy and security regimes[3]; the military (Helmus et al. 2007); and religious groups (Einstein 2007). Aesthetic styles, from fashion to music to typography, claim their own brands.[4] Branding is on the agenda of policy centers, transnational agencies, and think tanks, alternately investigated as a strategy for international diplomacy, a matter of public policy, and a source of institutional funding. In university settings it has spilled out of business departments and into the social sciences and media and cultural studies as both a course subject and a self-reflexive planning objective.

What has given rise to *these* new branded worlds? At one level, we can see this sudden brand mania merely as recent public awareness of changes that had been building in the corporate sector for decades. Brand managers, marketing professors, and other members of the professional "persuasional" class have for some time argued for the relevance of brand strategy to other aspects of large-scale organization (e.g., Kotler and Levy 1969; Olins 1979). In its insistence on "effectiveness," "efficiency," and "discipline," branding is advocated as cure for the ailments of a vast range of groups and individuals, whether the ailments stem from financial, structural, or communicational complaints (e.g., Clifton 2003; Anholt 2005; Holt 2004). In a competitive global economy characterized by surfeits of information and hypermediation, and corresponding deficits of time and attention, brands are heralded as the "imaginative genre" (Poovey 2008) that can simplify, differentiate, and narrate a wide range of economic and social values. In the contemporary context, Klein's portrayal of the "international rule of the brands" (2000: 446) resonates at an even greater frequency.

To apply the logic of the brand to these previously unbranded organizations, sites, and forms of subjectivity is not merely to call attention to the thorough marketization and commodification of everyday life. We suggest that the globalized, self-reflexive use of brands and branding to describe and structure these multiple and varied spheres is both symptom and cause of a series of shifts in how social relations, subject positions, and political programs are organized, governed, and articulated.

Blowing Up the Brand represents an attempt to account for these shifts. The fourteen chapters in this volume do not seek to make epochal claims but rather to draw examples from a variety of sites to magnify the ways in which brands have become structuring elements of our everyday lives. Its authors address the contradictory character of brands as forms of self-expression; the "utility of fiction" in political branding; the rise of a "brand-managerial" class of cultural experts, entrepreneurs, and intermediaries; and the extension of brand models along previously unbranded horizons, whether geographic, conceptual, moral, or biopolitical. In this introductory chapter we try to account for some of the changes that have taken place to create these newer contexts of organization and expression. To "blow up" the brand in this book is not necessarily to explode or destroy its structuring logics—though our tools of inquiry are purposively sharp. Rather our aim, as the subtitle of the book suggests, is to develop an arsenal of critical perspectives that can target what is at work in these branded contexts.

We call the ensemble of these contexts *promotional culture*, building in many respects on the insights developed by Andrew Wernick in his seminal volume, *Promotional Culture: Advertising, Ideology and Symbolic Expression* (1991). For Wernick, promotional culture resulted from an environment in which capitalist forms of exchange came to dominate all other forms of exchange; and in which a widening range of cultural phenomena whose primary function was to communicate a promotional message had become "virtually coextensive with our produced symbolic world" (182). These phenomena extend far beyond the obvious category of advertising to encompass 1) "the whole universe of commercially manufactured objects (and services), in so far as these are imaged to sell" (182); 2) the systems of commercial media which constantly link nonpromotional to promotional messages (akin to Raymond Williams' ([1974] 1990) notion of television "flow"); 3) all other communicative activities of not only private but also public institutions, either due to their commodification (as in the case of higher education) or to their analogous relationship to the market form (as in the case of electoral politics); and 4) the commodification of labor power, which engenders "dramaturgical" behavior by individuals via self-promotion and careerism. To this last category Wernick adds related phenomena such as the promotional function of consumption more generally (per Veblen's observations about consumption and status over a century ago); and the strategies of self-presentation and promotion that accompany the "mate/companion/friendship market"—a prescient observation in 1991, before the emergence of the MySpaces, YouTubes, and Facebooks of this world. The circulation of these promotional phenomena over deeper and broader terrain resulted, for Wernick, in a set of historical conditions by which promotionalism infected "all the circuits of social life," becoming the dominant symbolic language, the "communicative substance," of contemporary capitalism (1991: 188).

Though these features are clearly still in play twenty years on, it is equally clear that there have been a number of modifications of these phenomena that require renewed attention if we are to account for the current phase of promotional culture as well as the role of the brand as its emblematic cultural form and structuring element. In what follows we attempt to identify and describe some of these changes as well as account for and integrate recent critical attempts to define the boundaries of the brand.

Putting Communication to Work: Reputation, Value, and the Fact/Fiction Continuum

Though the imaging of commodities for promotion and sale has arguably been part of industrial capitalism since its beginnings (Wernick 1991; Moor 2007) and though scholars have long recognized the role of consumption in meaning-making as well as status, class, and identity formation (and contestation) (Veblen [1899] 1994; Cohen 2003; Fox and Lears 1983; Liechty 2003), the increasingly central role of brands in contemporary culture considerably alters established relationships between identification, commodification, and acts of consumption.

A key change underlying these new relationships lies in the realm of brand valuation. In the late 1970s, corporate brand owners began to seek ways to account for their brands as assets on their balance sheets, over and above the physical assets of the company (Lindemann 2003; Madden et al. 2006). The recognition that the value of such "intangible" or "reputational" capital could match or even exceed the value of material and territorial capital was made poignantly clear by the "zero-risk globalization" maneuvers of corporate firms in the 1980s and 1990s: outsourcing, downsizing, and other strategies of vertical disintegration which encouraged organizations to divest themselves of accountability for their products and forms of production while focusing on their brand images and marketing efforts (Klein 2000). This understanding has become especially relevant in the contemporary context of finance capital, characterized largely by dematerialized, deterritorialized, speculative units of exchange. Among the flexible accumulation strategies of postindustrial capital, in which labor processes, markets, products, and consumption patterns are subject to constant commercial, technological, and organizational change, brands emerge as the ideal rhetorical device to smooth and soften the impact of such change. In the context of market volatility, product failure, or other forms of risk, the brand can be "leveraged" or repositioned to maintain its image and equity among consumers.

In this light it is perhaps not surprising to observe the expansion of branding models to a wide range of previously noncorporatized institutional forms. As several chapters in this volume attest, public institutions have been increasingly adopting the "conceptual apparatus" of neoliberalism and its practices of economic liberalization, privatization, and stabilization (Buck-Morss 2002; Harvey 2005). This has led to new kinds of governance strategies: the rise of public-private partnerships; the replacement of Keynesian welfare-state policies with models of innovation and enterprise; coalitions of academic, government, and business institutions to foster so-called creative economies; and other initiatives that privilege the public purse over the public good. In this context public institutions seek both to maintain a stable identity and to limit the crises of accountability that might follow from such dramatic ideological and material shifts. In the absence of productive activity or, more contentious, the implementation of unpopular policies or practices, the purpose of the brand is to be buoyant enough to float above and beyond its actual practices (Klein 2000; Lury 2004). As Miriam Greenberg describes in her account of New York City Mayor Michael Bloomberg's urban renewal campaign, for example (chapter 6 in this volume), the "co-branding" of politician, place, and policies reveals the now inextricable relationship of image marketing, economic development, and political power. Despite clear opposition to Bloomberg's activities as well as obvious contradictions within his party strategies during his first two terms in office, his third-term reelection was widely seen as inevitable. Similarly, Gabriele Cosentino and Waddick Doyle (chapter 10) chart the rise and rise of Italian prime minister and media mogul Silvio Berlusconi, whose political brand remains steady despite a variety of provocations and scandals, expertly managed as it is through his television network, his advertising agencies, and his soccer team.

As other authors in this volume observe, these tendencies are not limited to government but extend to a variety of forms of organizational identity. Graham Knight (chapter 8) explores the adoption of brand rationalities by social movement and activist groups, who conclude that the strategic communication of brand management has become the only possible means by which to advance their causes; while Alison Hearn (chapter 9) shows how the increasing drive by universities to attract entrepreneurial students and faculty, accumulate high rankings, and promote "market-ready, industry-driven" education has led to a surprising proportion of university budgets being spent on the engineering and marketing of a distinctive brand.

What these examples suggest is that to understand the role of brands and branding in contemporary life is a matter of addressing not merely the commodification and marketization of institutional practices, but the commodification of public discourse itself. The notion that public discourse can become a source of economic value is not new; nor is it unique to the logic of the brand. From the late nineteenth century, Gabriel Tarde (1969: 313) noted the role of public opinion in establishing and standardizing economic value (see also Arvidsson 2006). Mid-twentieth-century concerns about the rise of advertising as the "idiom" and "style" of an increasingly industrialized culture (Horkheimer and Adorno [1944] 1972) also spoke to the marketization of communication, though with considerably less optimism. In 1973, Daniel Bell's prescient forecast of a "knowledge society," in which human capital replaced physical capital as the primary source of economic value, and information, communication, and technology functioned as axiomatic principles of postindustrial capitalism, laid the conceptual foundations for the current setting (see Garnham 2005).

What is specific to contemporary brand logic is the way in which the brand functions in the new media environment, where information and communication are prime sources of capital. From Adam Arvidsson's (2006) perspective, brands are themselves a form of informational capital which produce, govern, and evaluate information and communication. As a form of production, brands are no longer simply promotional devices for products but facilitators of contexts or "platforms" (Lury 2004; Schmitt 2010) for interaction, as the relationship between consumers and brands becomes less about the consumption of a product than about the social relations, experiences, and lifestyles such consumption enables. As a form of governance, brand owners manage these aspects of the social by collecting and harnessing information provided by consumers (for example, via marketing tools such as customized databases, search-engine advertising, and biometric identification; see Turow 2006) and use them to strengthen the relationships between brands and their consumers as well as further determine the range of "acceptable" (because productive of further brand capital) social positions and patterns. As a form of evaluation, brands work both as economic "goodwill" (i.e., intangible capital) and as relational devices to establish, on an ongoing basis, compatibility with existing social values. The brand therefore operates as a source of value in both the moral and the market sense: it simultaneously mediates subjective qualities, tastes, and norms; and it mediates objective financial worth—promoted and protected by legal regimes of intellectual property, trademarks, and copyright (Coombe 1998, 2004, 2005).

The expansion of the brand from its prior role in the promotion of commercial goods and services to its ability to represent and financialize social qualities underlines its productivity as a form of both "fictionalization" and "factualization," in Mary Poovey's (1998, 2008) terms. In *Genres of the Credit Economy*, her treatment of paper credit instruments as genres that mediated value in eighteenth- and nineteenth-century Britain, Poovey demonstrates the importance of fictionalization to the construction of value systems. Forms of representation (such as paper money instead of gold coins) and forms of writing that "embodied, interpreted, or made (what counted as) value comprehensible" mediated value in ways that naturalized and normalized new financial arrangements (2008: 90).

Processes of fictionalization are also at work in the contemporary branding paradigm, as Celia Lury and Liz Moor show in their contribution to this volume (chapter 2). Looking at the current valuation techniques employed by brand consultants and firms, Lury and Moor reveal how such techniques do not only measure but also *create* forms of value for the brand.[5] This is achieved in at least two ways: by adopting creative accounting strategies which admit hitherto unquantifiable social values onto balance sheets—for example, monetizing public goods such as a corporation's environmental impact or corporate social responsibility efforts, known as "triple bottom-line" initiatives; or by using new techniques such as "open-source branding" or "consumer cocreation," where consumers are encouraged to create ads for a brand or otherwise record their brand consumption activities, which can then be absorbed into the valuation process. Such "qualculation" (Callon and Law 2003; Lury 2004) is intrinsic to the brand's ongoing relevance in social settings.

It is not only the fictionalization of capital that enchants and structures credit economies but also its "factualization." That is, the construction of *facts* in the economic realm is a crucial characteristic of the creation of financial systems (Poovey 2008). In Poovey's account of this process in eighteenth-century Britain, developing the necessary conditions of objectivity and belief in the workings of the new financial system necessitated "additional social measures":

> Among these was the creation of the epistemological and social categories...of expert knowledge and the knowledge expert or specialist. The transformation of the previously suspect (because self-interested) merchant into the (disinterested) economic expert was, in part at least, a function of new, authoritative genres by which financial information could be conveyed. Paradoxically, these new genres, including

> political economy itself, were both modeled on and intended to reinforce the ever-elusive distinction between valid and invalid monetary forms (80).

If branding is the genre of the contemporary political economic era, those fluent in the language—branding consultants, market researchers, creative gurus, industrial designers, and ad agencies—have become the experts, and their expert knowledge the frame of reference. Indeed, such "promotional intermediaries" (Moor 2008; Davis 2006) have increasingly manifested their ability to determine the validity or invalidity of both economic and cultural forms. In the process of transforming *values* into *value*, promotional intermediaries displace the work of accountants and others formerly charged with the "monopoly of asset recognition" to create a "social facticity" of their own (see Lury and Moor in this volume). Thus self-styled nation branding consultants like Simon Anholt (2007) create brand indices for cities and countries, where attributes of place such as "levels of immigration," "governance," and "culture" can be measured and ranked against those of other nations; urban-planner-turned-creativity-guru Richard Florida (2002) can chart the "gay index" of urban regions and suggest that a higher proportion of homosexuality in a city indicates its creative and economic potential; and social researchers like Elizabeth Currid and Sarah Williams (2010) can measure the "buzz" or "hype" surrounding cultural events, to ultimately show how this hype can translate into financial returns for the event organizers. Such measures create value not only for their clients but also for the promotional intermediaries themselves (Harvey 2001), whose legitimacy depends on their ability to use their promotional discourse to build and maintain their own reputations. John Corner (chapter 3 in this volume) addresses this last point by offering another perspective along the "fact–fiction continuum" (Poovey 2008: 90), focusing on the "utility of fiction"—that is, the naturalization of deceit—in the communicative practices of the political realm. Drawing on historical examples from Athenian democracy to Arendtian notions of "organized lying" and more recent discussions of political hypocrisy, Corner questions the potential for public action in a political environment embedded in promotional culture.

The act of putting communication "to work"—whether for commercial, political, or other gain—has inspired some theorists to bring renewed attention to the performativity of discourse in capitalist realms. For some, this attention has consisted in expanding the notion of performativity from its origin in speech acts (Austin 1962) to the spaces or contexts where certain discourses take place.[6] Nigel Thrift (2005), for example, describes a "cultural circuit of capitalism," in which professional-managerial rhetoric advocating new management techniques is enacted, promoted, and circulated internationally through spaces of visualization (e.g., business magazines), spaces of embodiment (e.g., management training seminars), and spaces of circulation (e.g., business travel networks or online collaborative work sites). Hongmei Li's chapter in this volume (chapter 7) offers a remarkable account of the cultural circuit of capitalism as it makes its way into Chinese society. By documenting the discursive shift from *chengfen* (family origin or class status) to *shenjia* (personal assets and brand worth) as the primary measure of an individual's rank in society, Li shows how promotional culture is embraced in China and perpetuated in media reports, sport regimes, and celebrity worship.

Other theorists have widened the concept of performativity to accommodate the act of circulation itself. As Benjamin Lee and Edward LiPuma point out, the notion of performativity has traditionally been tied to meaning-making, while circulation and exchange have been set aside as "processes that *transmit* meanings, rather than as constitutive acts in themselves" (2002: 192). Bringing circulation under the rubric of performativity allows Lee and LiPuma to demonstrate how it is the *circulation* of cultural activities, from reading books to the global movement of financial derivatives, that creates "imagined communities" (Anderson 1993) with their own forms of interpretation and evaluation.

The capacity of brands to "perform" a sense of community through the creation and circulation of meaning has been heralded by promotional experts and intermediaries (MacInnis et al. 2009). Marketers argue that the very purpose of nation branding, for instance, is to inspire a sense of collective belonging to the nation-state. As such the brand identity must not only be representative of particular ways of being but actually *lived*—embraced and embodied—by the country's citizens if it is to be effective as a modern version of nationality (Aronczyk 2008).

This is what Arvidsson means when he refers to brands as informational capital: Just as valuation techniques create economic value for the brand, so do the communicative exchanges consumers have about the brand—either face to face or via online networks. This is apparent not only on "brand fan" websites or at clubs for BMW aficionados but also on online platforms that are built specifically to use the social communication of consumers as sources of economic value. Think of travel websites whose "expert" information about where to stay and what to do is provided by the posts of frequent travelers, or computer hardware and software sites where troubleshooting about the product is performed by users, or retail sites that solicit and implement consumers' ideas for new products and services (Schmitt 2010). The properties of new media increase opportunities for collaboration, contribution, and innovation of informational content (Lury 2004; Kember and Zylinska 2010), all of which redounds to the economic value of the brand. Moreover, by communicating with others about the importance of the brand to their lives, *consumers become promotional intermediaries themselves,* working in the service of the brand yet without the financial remuneration that its owners enjoy.

At least two important conclusions can be drawn from this brand logic. First, if the brand's value is determined in circulation, we must recognize that a growing variety of circulating discourses can be mobilized in the service of the brand: all kinds of media attention, whether in the form of product reviews, news stories, or consumer-generated content; word of mouth; and rumor, to name only a few examples (Muniz and O'Guinn 2009; Coombe 1997). Though technically such information is "valuable" to brand users, its economic value accrues primarily to the owners and other financial stakeholders of the brand. The brand therefore remains a controlled and controlling device that limits social and political potential for participation. We discuss this matter in more detail below.

Second, the brand must be seen in its capacity to occupy a particular spatial and temporal zone. The brand's coordinates plot a discursive space that is maintained by a series of relationships—not only between individual consumers and producers but also between them and the product or service itself; the communities of brand users; and a variety of institutions, including the media, retailers, equity markets, government, and nongovernmental organizations (Muniz and O'Guinn 2009). This discursive space is, as we have seen, not determined immediately in the process of production but rather via the brand's circulation throughout these discursive realms. As such the brand is predicated on the future; a brand is, as the multinational branding firm Interbrand puts it, "the promise" of an experience, the making of relationships that "create and secure future earnings by growing customer preference and loyalty" (Interbrand 2007: 14; see also Lury and Moor in this volume). Indeed, as Wernick writes, promotion in general is performative, a "complex of significations which at once represents (moves in place of), advocates (moves on behalf of) and anticipates (moves ahead of) the circulating entity to which it refers" (Wernick 1991: 182).

In this optic the brand works as a "chronotope" (Bakhtin 1981)—a set of temporal and spatial relationships that are intrinsically connected and aesthetically expressed. Mikhail Bakhtin used the concept of the chronotope to describe a literary setting in which space "becomes charged and responsive to the movements of time, plot and history" (84). The chronotope defines not only genre but the very "image of man [sic] in literature," because, following Kant, cognition requires the elementary perceptions and representations of space and time in order to be seen and understood (85). The concept of the chronotope was introduced by Einstein as part of his theory of relativity; and its origin in mathematics is relevant here, as Lury and Moor explain in the second part of their chapter in this volume. Topology is the study of "the properties of…surfaces that are 'spaces in themselves.'" For Lury and Moor, brands operate in a "topological culture"—a "multi-dimensional space of (future) possibility." It is multidimensional because of the sheer scale and scope of its relations as well as its ability to develop non-standard and proprietary forms of economic measurement; and it is a "future" space due to its ability to continually discount present value. The new space created, Lury and Moor argue, "is that of the 'ideal, risk-free brand'" (p. 47 in this volume).

In creating a spatial and temporal setting in which the brand can operate "risk-free," we might ask what role we, as consumers, users, and citizens, are expected to occupy in this new setting. If our ability to communicate in a promotional culture is managed by contemporary systems of informational capitalism, are our public identities—the ones we share on Facebook and retail sites, the ones we use in our professional lives, the ones we put out to the world—now given over to the production of capital? Has the public subject become a promotional subject? It is to this question that we now turn.

Branded (in) Public: Performing Authenticity

> What makes figures of publicity attractive to people?…This question does not ask simply how people are seduced or manipulated. It asks what kinds of identifications are required or allowed in the discourse of publicity (Warner 2005: 176).

The notion of "publicity"—the quality of being in public; the rights and obligations that constitute public life—has a long and complex history, as Western political thought of the last four centuries has revealed (Taylor 2002; Warner 2005). For Charles Taylor (2002), the distinctive character and status of publicity in modern life has emerged via three "social imaginaries" by which individuals conceive of themselves as members of a collective society: the public sphere, the citizen state, and the market economy.

In the popular imaginary of the present, it seems the term "publicity" has come to stand less often for the first two pillars Taylor identified and more often for the third, as the quality of public interactions appears increasingly oriented around self-interested economic gain. In this vision of publicity, being in public takes on a distinct cast, one in which the industries and symbolic systems of commercial promotion are not merely discursive analogues to forms of belonging, behaving, and relating in public, but also actual structuring forces for these actions, as public communication is overwhelmingly mediated by institutions which are sponsored by these industries. In this view the idealized aim of public communication is no longer to circulate vital information, reach reasoned ("rational-critical") consensus, or ensure democratic participation; it is to provide settings for presentation, promotion, and persuasion, with the ultimate goal of economic advantage.[7]

This perspective has dominated theories and critiques since the mid-1940s, when Horkheimer and Adorno ([1944] 1972) famously decried the instrumentalization of culture amid the rise of mass production. Rather than being liberated by mass culture, they argued, we have become dominated by it. Lash and Lury summarize their view:

> Culture took on the same principle of accumulation already widespread in the capitalist economy...now culture, previously associated with the development of human subjectivity, became objective like any other commodity (2007: 3).

Similar currents of thought emerged in the writings of other postwar thinkers: Erich Fromm decried the "marketing orientation" of the bureaucratized individual (1990); his colleague C. Wright Mills worried about the rise of the "competitive personality" (1970). As culture became industry, personhood became personality, and advertising overtook sociality, society was subjected to repression and control, while confectionery distractions and desires functioned as unconscious tools of seduction and manipulation.

While it is impossible to deny the legacy of this current of thought, we find labels of "manipulation" and "seduction" (as well as their frequent partners "propaganda" and "spin") to be unproductive concepts in accounting for the function and impact of promotional paradigms in the current social, political, economic, and technological context. As Warner's above quote suggests, understanding the appeal of publicity in its second-order sense might rather reside in the kinds of identifications and subject positions that are *required* or *allowed* in the contemporary context.

One way to think about subjectivity in the context of contemporary publicity is to consider the increasingly imbricated relationship between culture and the economy. It is not just that culture has been thoroughly commodified, but also that the economy has been culturalized in a variety of ways (du Gay and Pryke 2002; Comaroff and Comaroff 2009). Some theorists have explained the new culture–economy nexus by pointing to the "cultural turn" in studies of economic and organizational life. Such studies demonstrate how the objects of economic analysis—markets, firms, institutions—are inextricable from the analysis itself; that is, the economy is a product of the discourses that constitute, frame, and perform it. In this perspective, aspects of the economy are seen less as rational, objective entities than as cultural forms in their own right (Callon 1998; Callon and Law 2003; du Gay and Pryke 2002).

Another way to think about the renewed relationship between culture and the economy is in terms of the "creative industries," an increasingly popular concept in institutional, urban, and national governance. Creative industry refers to the way creative activities of all kinds—from work in the cultural sector to online networks of collaborative knowledge and information sharing to individual notions of craft—can now be used for economic gain. While we may do these kinds of work *not* as a means to an end but ostensibly for our own personal development, the role of the creative economy is to find ways to monetize such activities. Maurice Lazzarato calls the ensemble of such economically viable creative activities "immaterial labor," a term which expands beyond knowledge and information transfer to encompass "the kinds of activities involved in defining and creating cultural and artistic standards, fashions, tastes, consumer norms, and more strategically, public opinion" (qtd. in Read 2003: 127; see also Lury 2004; Arvidsson 2006).

The origins of the creative economy paradigm are frequently attributed to changes in governance strategies in the United Kingdom. In 1998, a Creative Industries Taskforce was formed by the Secretary of State for Culture, Media and Sport under then-prime minister Tony Blair. The taskforce prepared a report on the role and potential of the creative industries, defined as "those industries which have their origin in individual creativity, skill and talent and which have the potential for wealth and job creation through the generation and exploitation of intellectual property" (Creative

Industries Mapping Document 1998).[8] In addition to the already underwritten categories of cultural expression such as the visual and performing arts, music, publishing, film/video, TV, and radio, the government also deemed creative industries to include advertising, architecture, computer and video games, software, design, and fashion.[9] Establishing the terms of the creative economy therefore involved not only the commodification of cultural practices typically held to be outside the purview of the market but also the expansion of the category of culture itself, to accommodate more technologically oriented and economically productive activities.[10]

Newly entrepreneurialized public institutions around the world have rushed to adopt the creative economy model.[11] This renewed spirit of enterprise demonstrates the "culture of the new capitalism" (Sennett 2006), where temporary work, downsizing, and other "flexible" labor and market conditions have been converted from a liability into a potential breeding ground for cultural liberation and individual growth. Amid the disappearance of bureaucratic corporate structures, the argument goes, one can always go into business for oneself.

It is in this context that the figure of the "cultural entrepreneur" has emerged—or rather, been "semantically recharged" (Corner and Harvey 1991)—to meet the new terms of this creative economy. Taking American street-graffiti artist Shepard Fairey as the ne plus ultra prototype of the cultural entrepreneur, Sarah Banet-Weiser and Marita Sturken (chapter 12) deftly show how the combination of artistic production and self-promotion blurs the boundaries of creativity and commerce. As they explain, "creative autonomy, long considered historically to be in opposition to (and thus threatened by) market forces, is, within this economy, effectively organized and managed by market forces" (p. 267 in this volume).

While a growing number of institutions and individuals celebrate the creative economy and its new possibilities for self-identification, critical theorists are far less optimistic. Angela McRobbie calls creative workers "agents of the neoliberal order," while Andrew Ross calls them the "precariat," arguing that the rise of a "creative class" (Florida 2002) does not represent a new version of autonomy but rather operates as "the post-Fordist successor to the proletariat," subject to the same vagaries of labor exploitation (Ross 2009: 6). As Banet-Weiser and Sturken suggest, even creativity itself has become a brand, "reified and transformed into an object that is marketed, distributed, and exchanged within the contemporary economy, and takes on a particular 'value' as a lifestyle, policy or set of politics" (p. 268 in this volume).

As promotional intermediaries and entrepreneurs become the central actors of contemporary culture, concerns over authenticity have come to the fore. As Jeff Pooley reminds (chapter 4 in this volume), the notion of authenticity as an individual, moral ideal has been examined in depth by a wealth of writers over the course of the twentieth century. In the context of modern life, especially the rise of atomizing work environments, advertising culture and entertainment media, and "the gospel of self-fulfillment," writers like Philip Rieff, Christopher Lasch, and Warren Susman worried about the decline of authentic sources of experience. Faced with this unhappy dilemma, some thinkers conceived of authenticity as a means to the end of promotionalism, a way to overcome the superficiality of the personality market and the pressures of publicity images. Others, however, offered a middle ground, one in which the performative character of authenticity (or as Pooley puts it, "being instrumental about authenticity") might yield a modicum of sincerity.

John L. and Jean Comaroff (2009) take this position to the extreme, documenting a variety of ways in which the branding and marketing of ethnic group identities has productively contributed to new and rich forms of consciousness and empowerment. Genealogical tourism, heritage marketing, the sale of ethnic knowledge, rites, and rituals: such "ethnopreneurialism," they argue, reinforces rather than denies the social constitution of authenticity. "Against the telos of both classical and critical theory," they write, "the rise of ethno-commerce in the age of mass consumerism is having counterintuitive effects on human subjects, cultural objects, and the connection between them" (28):

> It is the case that the intensive marketing of ethnic identity may well involve a Faustian bargain of sorts, leading to self-parody and devaluation. But...it also appears to (re)fashion identity, to (re)animate cultural subjectivity, to (re)charge collective self-awareness, to forge new patterns of sociality, all within the marketplace (26).

Where to situate the sources of the self in all of this? "Enterprise culture" leads to a particular conception of the individual; one which, as Nikolas Rose argues:

> ...links up a seductive ethics of the self, a powerful critique of contemporary institutional and political reality, and an apparently coherent design for the radical transformation of contemporary social arrangements. In the writings of "neoliberals" like

> Hayek and Friedman, the well-being of both political and social existence is to be ensured not by centralized planning and bureaucracy, but through the "enterprising" activities and choices of autonomous entities—businesses, organizations, persons—each striving to maximize its own advantage by inventing and promoting new projects by means of individual and local calculations of strategies and tactics, costs and benefits (1998: 153).

If such "technologies of the self" (Rose 1998) appear in some respects to require and allow greater autonomy, flexibility, and potential for self-discovery, the other side of the coin is more tarnished. Interpellating citizens as consumers or users, kinship groups as "ethno-preneurs," and so on entails a kind of subjectivity in which individuals can no longer assume the entitlements formerly granted by their designation as "citizen," "resident," or "group member" but must now take on personal responsibility to secure their life benefits, advantages, and goals. We can witness this transformation in the marketization of public services, where the outsourcing, downsizing, and technologizing of staff and service provision has been engineered in tandem with an outlook of the citizen as active "user" who, according to market logic, is supposed to inform and educate herself and then demand or "choose" the goods and services she requires (see Moor 2009). A more uncomfortable instance of this process is examined by Mary Ebeling (chapter 11 in this volume): In the pharmaceutical industry, not only does drug branding encourage a patient to become an active consumer who can advocate for the marketed benefits of the branded drug to her doctor; but the branding of medical devices that must be surgically implanted transforms the human body itself into a productive site of financial value. By intervening in the relationship between patient and doctor, branded communications "recruit" patients to influence their doctor's medical judgement. "How, exactly," Ebeling asks, "would a patient enact the brand identity of the defibrillator implanted into her heart?" (p. 242).

As Rose explains, the job of the contemporary categories of experts such as the entrepreneur or the intermediary is to reconcile, or at least smooth over, the inherently contradictory aspects of promotional life:

> For the new experts of the psyche promise that modes of life that appear philosophically opposed—business success and personal growth, image management and authenticity—can be brought into alignment and achieve translatability through the ethics of the autonomous, choosing, psychological self (Rose 1998: 157).

In the shift of address from patient to choosy consumer, citizen to active and autonomous user, body to source of "biovalue," the terrain of promotional culture appears logical, inevitable, and desirable. As the self becomes thoroughly instrumentalized, so do we increase our promotional capital to meet and respond to such instrumentalization. By performing our promotional selves we convert moral values into market value and back again. We allow a singular vision of success to dominate the conversation. And overlaying all of these shifts is the stable narrative of the brand, blown up and extending in all directions to contain, qualify, and erase its multiple contradictions.

Towards a New Media Literacy

The title of this book thus signifies not only the expanded space the brand has come to occupy in contemporary life—an expansion that acquires potency as branding continues to naturalize its presence within a wide range of domains. It also speaks to our belief that by magnifying the work of the brand, we might better perceive its intricacies. The critical perspectives presented within these chapters are in effect both examples of and strategies for such an approach, intended to showcase the increased scope of promotional culture as well as offer tactics with which to interrogate it.

The versatile capabilities of the brand—to frame relationships both economic and social; to represent, communicate, and circulate forms of value; and to create and capture modes of attention—make for striking parallels with the digital technologies that currently dominate and assimilate the mediated environment. Not only does the impact of the brand rely on the technological changes that have destabilized and converged mediated communications, especially over the last decade; the brand is also itself a technology of communication and a product of that changed environment. This is what Lury intends when she identifies the brand as a "new media object," a multifaceted entity that "[is comprised of] a mode of production, a technical or physical support, and a set of conventions that articulate or work on that support" (2004: 6); in other words, the brand functions at once as hardware, software, and protocol (Manovich 2001; Galloway 2004).

Though an array of recent technologies coexist under the label new media—including but not limited to computers, the Internet and World Wide Web, mobile telephony, and social networks—their ability to blend previously distinct media forms, transform methods of distribution, and create new opportunities for sociability renders them similar in their effects. *Interactivity* lies at the core of the revolutionary potential identified for such media, a value that is frequently lauded for its ability to foster peer production and collaboration, enhance democracy and participatory culture, and generate "collective intelligence" (Benkler 2006; Jenkins 2006; Levy 1997). Though the brand per se is not traditionally included in the conception of new media's interactivity in this fashion, it is certainly an interactive site, where consumers maintain social connections, foster identification, and create meaning that not only benefits the brand but also themselves (Muniz and O'Guinn 2001; Bengsston and Firat 2006).

It therefore is not our intention to deny the possibility of meaningful sociality enacted through branded environments nor to discount the potential for productive changes to result within them. Yet a narrow focus on the benefits of interactivity, coupled with uncritical celebration of the media that inspire it, cause us to lose sight of more troubling outcomes. As Lury explains, to the extent that the brand is a point of contact between production and consumption, it can be conceived as "a frame that organizes the two-way exchange of information." But "interactivity" is not the same as "interaction" (Lury 2004: 7): between these two terms lie ongoing power relations between producers and consumers. Moreover, interactivity may be employed as a "strategy for deferring critical reflection" (Andrejevic 2009: 43), standing in for relations that might prove more meaningful or impactful, if less convenient or tidy. This belief is especially consequential in the political realm where, as Dean (2005) argues, it "relieves top-level actors...from the obligation to respond." Interactivity tends to replace the difficult work of politics. It is in this environment that promotional communication—such as joining a Facebook group, wearing a sloganified T-shirt, or staying "on message"—is taken as a political end in itself, whether or not it results in material effects. As Dean (2005) writes, "The circulation of communication is depoliticizing, not because people don't care or don't want to be involved, but because we do!" (see also Barney 2008).

Interactivity may defer critical reflection not only by surrogacy, but also through distraction. Put another way, interactivity can shroud the purpose of interaction, encouraging users to click, play, and share before considering what, how, or why. This is precisely the strategy of emerging practices such as sonic branding, as Devon Powers (chapter 13 in this volume) observes. In applying their expertise to the aural environment, sonic branding professionals frame the immersive nature of sound as a way to integrate consumers into a brand's identity, working under the assumption that musical sound preempts critical reflection. Sound, in this case, becomes elemental to the interface of the brand, an attempt to both solicit consumer response and delimit and depoliticize the territory and range of sensory experience.

One important byproduct of interactivity is feedback, often in the form of valuable consumer information. Consumers may be only vaguely aware of their participation in this process and prohibited from learning what companies know about them or how the information is being put to use (Turow 2006). Andrejevic calls this "the work of being watched"—the labor consumers perform that facilitates their own surveillance (Andrejevic 2002). In later work, Andrejevic makes a more forceful claim, linking monitoring and "feedback-based forms of control" to early cybernetics theories (2009: 43). He warns that "the modality of control can itself shift, in ways that incorporate the very forms of critique that once sought to challenge it by undermining and deconstructing it" (2009: 37).

Such observations highlight the continuing importance of analyzing power relations, which often remain intact even as unidirectional, centralized media forms give way to decentralized, user-oriented ones. Yet they also present us with the difficult challenge of rethinking the purpose of critique itself. This difficulty arises not because critique can lose its hard edge, suffer co-optation or, only slightly better, come to exist as just one perspective among the many on offer (Andrejevic 2009: 39; Dean 2005). Instead, the more pressing concern is *the propensity for critique itself to become promotional;* that is, where critique becomes imagined as an end in itself.

In a context where longstanding separations—between control and feedback, production and consumption, "top down" and "bottom up"—no longer hold, where can we locate the potential for critical reflection? Thinking of the brand as a new media object, in Lury's terms, challenges us to develop innovative tactics of media literacy. In the world of the brand—where consumption is imbricated into production, where the audience becomes the text, where meaning itself is a source of economic and social value—what some call the "holy trinity" of media studies (industry, audience, and text) thoroughly collapses. Media literacy, understood as "the ability to access, analyze, evaluate, and communicate messages in a wide variety of forms" (Hobbs 1998), must therefore become "new," not only by focusing on new media objects, but also by merging insights and methods from various camps of media literacy practice, such as media production, textual analysis, and political economy—not despite the conflicts within these camps, but precisely because of these conflicts (see Hobbs 1998; Lewis and Jhally 1998). What happens, for instance, if we abandon perspectives that understand consumption as either governed by the all-encompassing structure of capitalism or resisted by the cunning agency of consumers? As Arlene Davila demonstrates in her ethnography of Puerto Rican shopping malls (chapter 5 in this volume), what emerges is a more faithful, if less easily categorizable, understanding of consumerism's diverse meanings. Her analysis contrasts the political, economic, and discursive acts that allow the island to be covered with shopping malls with the realities of how consumers navigate these acts for individual and varied needs.

Similarly, we might consider allowing those products that are often considered peripheral to our inquiries to take center stage, as Jonathan Gray does in his inquiry into the promotional texts of film and television (chapter 14). In arguing that "paratexts" such as trailers, toys, promos, and fan-produced content enhance the meaning of the texts on which they are based as well as establish narrative worlds in their own right, Gray critiques the efforts of media literacy which, in focusing narrowly on commodification, voids them of artistic potential and mistakenly divorces the processes of media production from audience interpretation—a practice that contradicts new media's trend toward convergence of these practices.

Our goal is neither to lament this new branded world nor cheer it. The speed with which these dynamics continue to change means that we cannot anticipate their full impact. What's more, we might not yet have adequate analytic tools at our disposal. That promotional culture creates some opportunities for engagement as well as forecloses upon others is certain. What is possible, and what we hope this volume achieves, is a recognition of both these opportunities and foreclosures, along with the willingness to examine the potential of new forms of critique, and the drive to envision new possibilities for our own work.

Notes

1. A European brand strategy firm puts *No Logo* on its recommended reading list, calling it one of several "quick, easy-to-read books that will change the way you think about company and corporate logos and more specifically how effective corporate branding can be" (http://www.e-creation.eu/logo-development-and-branding.aspx) (accessed 7 January 2010). *No Logo* won the Canadian National Business Book Award in 2000, a prize sponsored by PriceWaterHouseCoopers and the Bank of Montreal. Klein was none too pleased about the prize, saying *No Logo* was not a business book but an "antibusiness book" (Posner 2001).
2. Marketing professors Muniz and O'Guinn propose that even political statements can draw community support when expressed in the language of brands: "Revolutionary politics are enacted not through choices of consuming or not consuming, but in identifica-

tion, group sanctioning, and community championing of brands that are deemed by the collective to be the best vessels of the group's 'alternative' politics" (2009: 16).

3. See, for example, the European Commission-funded program, "Privacy Awareness through Security Organization Branding," which since July 2009 has been using brand management techniques to develop and promote privacy standards for certain security organizations. Accessed at http://pats-project.eu/.
4. On typography and brands, see the symposium organized by Concordia University professor Matt Soar: www.logocities.org.
5. Indeed the current slogan for Interbrand, a multinational branding firm, is "Creating and Managing Brand Value."
6. Though as Judith Butler has explained, speech acts *require* a context, "a venue of power by which its performative effects might be materialized" (1997: 12).
7. The ambiguity of the term "publicity" in its capacity to refer either to "publicness" or "persuasion" is not, of course, limited to the activities of the present. As John Corner writes, "the notion has made a long journey from its eighteenth-century use by Kant to indicate the new, enabling possibilities for the exercising of public reason and for the wider 'visibility' of public opinion that followed from the increased circulation of printed publications, through to its present use in many contexts as a synonym for 'hype.' We can see the deformation of the idea of publicity within the institutional contingencies and power relations of modern politics as absolutely central to the problem of modern public communications" (p. 68 in this volume).
8. The relationship of the creative economy to the law is especially acute. The expansion of legal claims to culture in the form of greater protection for "publicly circulating forms of signifying property" (Coombe 1998: 56; see also Garnham 2005; Lury 2004: Ch. 5) has engendered new kinds of authority and authorship in the regime of the brand. Trademarks, patents and copyright laws give brand owners both new terrains of expression and new realms for compensation.
9. See www.culture.gov.uk/what_we_do/creative_industries/default.aspx.
10. In keeping with Daniel Bell's (1973) prognosis, information technologies are increasingly seen as central to innovation and creativity, allowing government funding to be redirected to organizations which aim to develop ICT capacity (National Research Council 2003: 24).
11. See, for example: In Canada: Conf. Bd. of Canada (2008); in South Africa: ulf.gov.za/documents/the-creative-industries-in-south-africa; in Australia: cultureandcreation.gov.au/research-documents/cics.

References

Anderson, Benedict. 1993. *Imagined Communities.* London: Verso, 1993.

Andrejevic, Mark. 2009. "Critical Media Studies 2.0: An Interactive Upgrade." *Interactions: Studies in Communication and Culture* 1 (1): 35–51.

———. 2002. "The Work of Being Watched: Interactive Media and the Exploitation of Self-Disclosure." *Critical Studies in Media Communication* 19 (2): 230–248.

Anholt, Simon. 2007. *Competitive Identity: The New Brand Management for Nations, Cities, and Regions.* Houndmills: Palgrave Macmillan.

———. 2005. *Brand New Justice: How Branding Places and Products Can Help the Developing World*. Rev. ed. Oxford: Elsevier.

Aronczyk, Melissa. 2008. "'Living the Brand': Nationality, Globality, and the Identity Strategies of Nation Branding Consultants." *International Journal of Communication* 2: 41–65.

———. 2007. "New and Improved Nations: Branding National Identity." Pp. 105–128 in *Practicing Culture,* ed. Craig Calhoun and Richard Sennett. London: Routledge.

Arvidsson, Adam. 2006. *Brands: Meaning and Value in Media Culture*. New York: Routledge.

Austin, J. L. 1962. *How to Do Things with Words*. 2nd ed. Cambridge, MA: Harvard University Press.

Bakhtin, Mikhail. 1981. *The Dialogic Imagination*. Ed. Michael Holquist. Austin: University of Texas Press.

Barney, Darin. 2008. "Politics and Emerging Media: The Revenge of Publicity." *Global Media Journal—Canadian Edition* 1 (1): 89–106.

Bell, Daniel. 1973. *The Coming of Post-Industrial Society: A Venture in Social Forecasting*. New York: Basic Books.

Bengsston, Anders, and A. Fuat Firat. 2006. "Brand Literacy: Consumers' Sense-Making of Brand Management." *Advances in Consumer Research* 33: 375–380.

Benkler, Yochai. 2006. *The Wealth of Networks*. New Haven, CT: Yale University Press.

Bishop, Matthew, and Michael Green. 2008. *Philanthrocapitalism*. New York: Bloomsbury Press.

Bob, Clifford. 2002. "The Merchants of Morality," *Foreign Policy* 129 (Mar/Apr): 36–45.

———. 2005. *The Marketing of Rebellion: Insurgents, Media, and International Activism*. Cambridge: Cambridge University Press.

Buck-Morss, Susan. 2002. *Dreamworld and Catastrophe: The Passing of Mass Utopia in East and West*. Cambridge, MA: The MIT Press.

Butler, Judith. 1997. *Excitable Speech: A Politics of the Performative*. London: Routledge.

Callon, Michel. 1998. *The Laws of the Markets*. Oxford: Blackwell.

Callon, Michel, and John Law. 2003. "On Qualculation, Agency and Otherness." *Boundaries,* October 26.

Clifton, Rita. 2003. "Introduction." Pp. 1–9 in *Brands and Branding,* ed. Rita Clifton and John Simmons. Bloomberg Press: New York.

Cohen, Lizabeth. 2003. *A Consumers' Republic: The Politics of Mass Consumption in Postwar America*. New York: Vintage Books.

Comaroff, John L., and Jean Comaroff. 2009. *Ethnicity, Inc*. Chicago: University of Chicago Press.

Conference Board of Canada. 2008. Compendium of Research Papers: The International Forum on the Creative Economy. 253 pp.

Coombe, Rosemary. 2005. "Legal Claims to Culture in and against the Market: Neoliberalism and the Global Proliferation of Meaningful Difference." *Law, Culture and the Humanities* 1: 35–52.

———. 2004. "Commodity Culture, Private Censorship, Branded Environments, and Global Trade Politics: Intellectual Property as a Topic of Law and Society Research." *Blackwell Companion to Law and Society,* ed. Austin Sarat. Oxford: Blackwell.

———. 1998. *The Cultural Life of Intellectual Properties*. Durham: Duke University Press.

———. 1997. "The Demonic Place of the 'Not There': Trademark Rumors in the Postindustrial Imaginary." Pp. 249–274 in *Culture, Power, Place: Explorations in Critical Anthropology,* ed. James Ferguson and Akhil Gupta. Durham: Duke University Press.
Corner, John and Sylvia Harvey, eds. 1991. *Enterprise and Heritage: Crosscurrents of National Culture.* London and New York: Routledge.
Creative Industries Mapping Document. 1998. United Kingdom. http://www.culture.gov.uk/what_we_do/creative_industries/default.aspx (accessed January 2010).
Currid, Elizabeth, and Sarah Williams. 2010. "The Geography of Buzz: Art, Culture and the Social Milieu in Los Angeles and New York." *Journal of Economic Geography* 10 (3): 423–451.
Davis, Aeron. 2006. "Placing Promotional Culture." Pp. 149–163 in *Media and Cultural Theory,* ed. James Curran and David Morley. London: Routledge.
Dean, Jodi. 2005. "Communicative Capitalism: Circulation and the Foreclosure of Politics." *Cultural Politics* 1(1): 51–74.
Donald, Stephanie H., Eleonore Kofman, and Catherine Kevin. 2008. *Branding Cities: Cosmopolitanism, Parochialism, and Social Change.* New York: Routledge.
du Gay, Paul, and Michael Pryke, eds. 2002. *Cultural Economy: Cultural Analysis and Commercial Life.* London: Sage.
du Gay, Paul. 1996. "Organizing Identity." Pp. 151–169 in *Questions of Cultural Identity,* eds. Stuart Hall and Paul du Gay, London: Sage.
Einstein, Mara. 2007. *Brands of Faith.* New York: Routledge.
Florida, Richard. 2002. *The Rise of the Creative Class.* New York: Basic Books.
Fox, Richard, and T. J. Jackson Lears. 1983. *The Culture of Consumption: Critical Essays in American History, 1880–1980.* New York: Pantheon Books.
Friedman, Thomas. 1999. *The Lexus and the Olive Tree: Understanding Globalization.* New York: Anchor Books.
Fromm, Erich. [1947] 1990. *Man for Himself: An Inquiry into the Psychology of Ethics.* New York: Henry Holt.
Galloway, Alex. 2004. *Protocol: How Control Exists After Decentralization.* Cambridge, MA: The MIT Press.
Garnham, Nicholas. 2005. "From Cultural to Creative Industries: An Analysis of the Implications of the 'Creative Industries' Approach to Arts and Media Policy Making in the United Kingdom." *International Journal of Cultural Policy* 11 (1): 15–29.
Gilmore, Fiona, and Rebecca Rumens. 2005. "No Logo, No Future." *Brand Strategy,* 1 October.
Gould, Eric. 2003. *The University in a Corporate Culture.* New Haven: Yale University Press.
Green, Penelope. 2009. "Branding the Family." *New York Times,* 6 May.
Greenberg, Miriam. 2008. *Branding New York: How a City in Crisis Was Sold to the World.* New York: Routledge.
Harvey, David. 2005. *A Brief History of Neoliberalism.* Oxford: Oxford University Press.
———. 2001. *Spaces of Capital.* London: Routledge.
Helmus, Todd C., Christopher Paul, and Russell W. Glenn. 2007. *Enlisting Madison Avenue: The Marketing Approach to Earning Popular Support in Theaters of Operation.* United States: Rand National Defense Research Institute.
Hobbs, Renee. 1998. "The Seven Great Debates of Media Literacy." *Journal of Communication* 48 (1): 16–32.
Holt, Douglas. 2004. *Iconic Brands: The Principles of Cultural Branding.* Cambridge, MA: Harvard University Press.

Horkheimer, Max and Theodor Adorno. [1944] 1972. "The Culture Industry: Enlightenment as Mass Deception." Pp. 120–167 in *Dialectic of Enlightenment.* Trans. John Cumming. New York: Herder and Herder.

Interbrand. 2007. *The Brand Glossary.* Houndmills: Palgrave Macmillan.

Jansen, Sue. 2008. "Designer Nations: Neoliberal Nation Branding—Brand Estonia." *Social Identities* 14 (1): 121–142.

Jenkins, Henry. 2006. *Convergence Culture: Where Old and New Media Collide.* New York: NYU Press.

Keating, Michael. 2003. "The Invention of Regions: Political Restructuring and Territorial Government in Western Europe." Pp. 256–277 in *State/Space,* ed. Neil Brenner, Bob Jessop, Martin Jones, and Gordon MacLeod. Malden, MA: Blackwell.

Kember, Sarah, and Joanna Zylinska. 2010. "Creative Media between Invention and Critique: Or What's Still at Stake in Performativity?" *Culture Machine* 11: 1–6.

King, Samantha. 2006. *Pink Ribbons Inc.: Breast Cancer and the Politics of Philanthropy.* Minneapolis: University of Minnesota Press.

Klein, Naomi. 2010. "Naomi Klein on How Corporate Branding Has Taken over America." Excerpted from *No Logo,* 10th Anniversary Edition (Toronto: Random House). *The Guardian,* January 16. http://www.guardian.co.uk/books/ 2010/jan/16/naomi-klein-branding-obama-america (accessed May 9, 2010).

———. 2000. *No Logo: Taking Aim at the Brand Bullies.* Toronto: Random House.

Kotler, Philip, and Sidney Levy. 1969. "Broadening the Concept of Marketing." *Journal of Marketing* 33 (1): 10–15.

Lash, Scott, and Celia Lury. 2007. *Global Culture Industry.* Cambridge: Polity.

Lee, Benjamin and Edward LiPuma. 2002. "Cultures of Circulation: The Imaginations of Modernity." *Public Culture* 14 (1): 191–213.

Levy, Pierre. 1997. *Collective Intelligence.* New York: Basic Books.

Lewis, Justin, and Sut Jhally. 1998. "The Struggle over Media Literacy." *Journal of Communication* 48 (1): 109–120.

Liechty, Mark. 2003. *Suitably Modern: Making Middle-class Culture in a New Consumer Society.* Princeton: Princeton University Press.

Lindemann, Jan. 2003. "The Financial Value of Brands." Pp. 27–46 in *Brands and Branding,* ed. Rita Clifton and John Simmons. New York: Bloomberg Press.

Lury, Celia. 2004. *Brands: The Logos of the Global Economy.* London: Routledge.

MacInnis, Deborah, C. W. Park, and Joseph Priester, ed. 2009. *Handbook of Brand Relationships.* New York: M. E. Sharpe.

Madden, Thomas J., Frank Fehle, and Susan Fournier. 2006. "Brands Matter: An Empirical Demonstration of the Creation of Shareholder Value through Branding." *Journal of the Academy of Marketing Science* 34 (2): 224–235.

Manovich, Lev. 2001. *The Language of New Media.* Cambridge, MA: The MIT Press.

Mills, C. Wright. 1970. "The Competitive Personality (1946)." Pp. 263–273 in *Power, Politics and People: The Collected Essays of C. Wright Mills,* ed. Irving Louis Horowitz. Oxford: Oxford University Press.

Moor, Liz. 2009. "Designing the State." Pp. 23–39 in *Design and Creativity: Policy, Management and Practice,* ed. Guy Julier and Liz Moor. Oxford: Berg.

———. 2008. "Branding Consultants as Cultural Intermediaries." *The Sociological Review* 56 (3): 408–428.

———. 2007. *The Rise of Brands.* Oxford: Berg.

Muniz, Albert M. and Thomas C. O'Guinn. 2009. "Collective Brand Relationships." Pp. 173–194 in *Handbook of Brand Relationships,* ed. Deborah MacInnis, C. Whan Park, and Joseph Priester. New York: M. E. Sharpe.

———. 2001. "Brand Community." *Journal of Consumer Research* 27: 412–432.

National Research Council (U.S.). 2003. *Beyond Productivity: Information Technology, Innovation, and Creativity.* Washington, D.C.: The National Academies Press.

Olins, Wally. 1979. *The Corporate Personality: An Inquiry into the Nature of the Corporate Identity.* 1st American ed. New York: Mayflower Books.

Pasotti, Eleonora. 2009. *Political Branding in Cities: The Decline of Machine Politics in Bogota, Naples, and Chicago.* Cambridge: Cambridge University Press.

Poovey, Mary. 2008. *Genres of the Credit Economy: Mediating Value in Eighteenth- and Nineteenth-Century Britain.* Chicago: University of Chicago Press.

———. 1998. *A History of the Modern Fact: Problems of Knowledge in the Sciences of Wealth and Society.* Chicago: University of Chicago Press.

Posner, Michael. 2001. "He Wishes to Deklein the Prize," *Globe and Mail,* 5 May.

Read, Jason. 2003. *The Micro-Politics of Capital.* New York: SUNY Press.

Rein, Irving, Philip Kotler, and Ben Shields. 2006. *The Elusive Fan: Reinventing Sports in a Crowded Marketplace.* New York: McGraw-Hill.

Rose, Nikolas. 1998. *Inventing Our Selves: Psychology, Power, and Personhood.* Cambridge: Cambridge University Press.

Ross, Andrew. 2009. *Nice Work if You Can Get It: Life and Labor in Precarious Times.* New York: NYU Press.

Schmitt, Garrick. 2010. "Super Bowl Shuffle: Why Marketers will Shift to 'Platforms.'" *Advertising Age,* 1 February. adage.com/digitalnext/article?article_id=141790 (accessed February 2, 2010).

Sennett, Richard. 2006. *The Culture of the New Capitalism.* New Haven: Yale University Press.

Stallabrass, Julian. 2006. "No Logo." *The Guardian.* 23 November. http://www. guardian.co.uk/artanddesign/artblog/2006/nov/23/nologo1 (accessed January 2, 2010).

Stole, Inger. 2008. "Philanthropy as Public Relations: A Critical Perspective on Cause Marketing." *International Journal of Communication* 2: 20–40.

Tarde, Gabriel. [1898] 1969. "Opinion and Conversation." Pp. 297–318 in *On Communication and Social Influence,* ed. T. N. Clark. Chicago: University of Chicago Press.

Taylor, Charles. 2002. "Modern Social Imaginaries." *Public Culture* 14 (1): 91–124.

Thrift, Nigel. 2005. *Knowing Capitalism.* London: Sage.

Turow, Joseph. 2006. *Niche Envy: Marketing Discrimination in the Digital Age.* Cambridge, MA: The MIT Press.

Veblen, Thorstein. [1899] 1994. *The Theory of the Leisure Class.* New York: Dover Publications.

Waldby, Catherine, and Robert Mitchell. 2006. *Tissue Economies: Blood, Organs, and Cell Lines in Late Capital.* Durham, NC: Duke University Press.

Wallace, Margot. 2006. *Museum Branding: How to Create and Maintain Image, Loyalty and Support.* Lanham, MD: AltaMira.

Warner, Michael. 2005. *Publics and Counterpublics.* New York: Zone Books.

Wernick, Andrew. 1991. *Promotional Culture: Advertising, Ideology, and Symbolic Expression,* London: Sage.

Williams, Raymond. [1974] 1990. *Television: Technology and Cultural Form.* London: Routledge.

PART ONE

Authenticity, Value, and the Utility of Fiction in Promotional Culture

CHAPTER TWO

Brand Valuation and Topological Culture

Celia Lury & Liz Moor

Introduction

In the past thirty years, the functions of brands and branding have undergone substantial shifts. Where they were once used simply to identify and distinguish relatively similar products, they now serve a much wider range of purposes, from providing a framework for new product and service development and guidelines for staff training and recruitment, to driving mergers, acquisitions and joint ventures (Lury 2004; Trevillion and Perrier 1999). As their functions have become more numerous and complex, and their role more important, so systems for measuring the "value" of brands have proliferated. Very often, these systems aim explicitly to translate a brand's reputation into a financial or monetary value, so that brands can be included as assets on balance sheets or used in some of the ways outlined above. Such systems may also serve as promotional tools, providing an indication of the likely value (in terms of return on investment) of branding or rebranding projects to potential clients or to audiences inside an organization, and forging new links between marketing and financial departments. Finally, mechanisms for mapping value may be developed in response to consumer or other external pressures, taking the form of benchmarks or codes of conduct that open elements of the value chain (as well as the "values" of particular organizations) to greater scrutiny. One of the interesting characteristics of such systems is that although they very often involve assessing qualitative features of some kind, this measurement of qualities is usually undertaken to facilitate *quantitative* calculations of the likely impact of particular types of actions and decisions on financial outcomes. Importantly, these mechanisms for *measuring* value are, more often than not, closely linked to processes of *creating* value. As one company puts it:

> Brand valuation in our opinion should not be seen as just a number; the valuation process itself enriches the user with a far more comprehensive understanding of how business generate[s] cash flows through an understanding of their customers, the markets and channels they operate in, the competitive environment, and operational capability to deliver value and growth (Whitwell 2005).

For this reason, we want to suggest that mechanisms for measuring brand value are central to the operation of brands and branding in contemporary societies. It is our aim in this chapter to examine in more depth the combination of social and technical means through which brands are implicated in the measurement and the creation of value. We do this, in the first instance, by outlining some of the newer functions of brands and branding in socio-economic contexts described variously as design-intensive, reflexive, and "knowing" (see Lash and Urry 1997; Thrift 2005). We then go on to examine a number of different ways in which brand values and behaviors are measured and the context in which such measurements take place, starting with better established forms of brand valuation and accountancy, and moving on to more recent developments in which alternative dimensions of value are assessed, and in which a wider range of motivations for valuation are evident. We include in this a discussion of the proprietary technique of Interbrand, a brand consultancy specializing in valuation, as well as alternative forms of valuation devised to promote the services of other consultancies, and new forms of valuation based on the use of information and communications technologies.

We then consider these techniques in the light of debates about changes in the value form in contemporary capitalism, neoliberal government and debates about the space and standards of measurement (or metrology), focusing in particular on this last approach. For us, the consideration of the practices of measurement is a way to investigate how it is that brand valuation schemes measure *and* create value. That is, from our point of view, mechanisms or expert systems that are ostensibly concerned with measuring, describing, or accounting for dimensions of brand value are implicated in the *creation* of brand value, and indeed in the creation of brands themselves as epistemic or complex "objects of knowledge" (Knorr Cetina 1999; Lury 2004). We will suggest that the measurement of value they permit is not limited to the measurement of the value as it is understood to be created in traditional models of value chains (Porter 1998) but also extends to the newer value forms associated with multiple practices of relating—including adding, connecting, associating, linking, mediating, translating, listing and tagging. Such practices, we will suggest, occur in a new space—the space of topological culture.

The Changing Role of Branding

As brands have become more central to the strategic aims of organizations and the social sphere of consumption, a number of scholars have attempted to map and explain the new ways in which branding functions. Thus while classic definitions of the functions of brands describe them in terms of creating the trust necessary for market transactions to take place or providing incentives for companies to maintain certain standards of quality, more recent commentators note the role of brands in driving mergers and acquisitions, shaping and framing corporate strategy and joint ventures, and providing new revenue from licensing and franchising (e.g., Trevillion and Perrier 1999). At the same time, critical authors have made a number of further points to do with branding's role in new forms of capital accumulation and its connection to both the expansion of the role of marketing and its use of new information technologies. Lury (2004), for example, argues that the brand should be seen to have multiple levels and dimensions and that its new productivity is related to its capacities as a "complex object," that is, as an object that is performative, distributed, and relational. It is, in short, because a brand relates to consumers, and they relate to it, that it can operate as a device to manage markets and other collectives.

Arvidsson (2006) focuses more closely on brand management and its efforts, firstly, to guide consumers' social and affective investments in brands in ways that reproduce a distinctive brand image and strengthen brand equity, and secondly, to devise standardized measurement techniques by which this concept of brand equity can be translated into "a quality that is compatible with other qualities" (2006: 130). In both accounts, branding is understood to take place in a context in which consumers' activities have become increasingly valuable for capital and in which marketing has an expanded role in profiling this activity and feeding it back into the production process. Both thus explore the brand as a locus of valorization. In her earlier work, Lury analyzes this in terms of processes of "qualculation" (Callon and Law 2003), while Arvidsson proposes that by making qualities compatible, brands embody the general form of value of informational capital, to be understood in terms of its communicability; that is, its ability to be stored, networked, compiled, and transferred.

In a more recent study, Moor (2007) provides a historical discussion of the growth of branding, exploring the increasingly diverse ways in which it is used and organized. She highlights the significance of the fact that the branding concept is being applied to more organizations than ever before, including governments, cities, faiths, charities, web communities, financial services, education, new media, and the public sector. Sometimes, she notes, brand strategy aims to generate value for shareholders (the "plc" [public limited company] sector in the UK)[1] but sometimes it does not. In charities, for example, branding may be used to recruit volunteers, to attract external funding and government contracts, or to develop stronger and more "licensable" identities that enable a charity to pursue lucrative cause-related marketing agreements. In the public sector, branding may be used to establish the legitimacy of a new department or public body, or to organize citizens' perceptions of their own relationship to government and their responsibility to act in particular ways.

What all three accounts recognize is that branding is assembled or put together differently in different contexts, where it involves diverse forms of representation, diverse techniques and technologies, and diverse kinds of relationships for diverse kinds of strategic purposes. This diversity of purpose places increasing pressure on the branding industry to be able to justify the branding concept, and brand valuation is a key tool in this process. At the same time, the "plc model" has come to be questioned in the private sector[2] as the concept of the "triple bottom line" (see Elkington 1997; and below) places demands on corporations to answer the needs of a range of stakeholders, not just shareholders. This means that brand valuation itself is under pressure to explore new dimensions of value and to establish techniques by which the diverse values of a more diffuse set of "stakeholders" can be measured and connected to the strategic and financial interests of shareholders and, increasingly, other stakeholders too.

Established Forms of Brand Valuation

Before we begin to examine these new dimensions of value and the techniques by which they are identified, let us first consider the more established forms of brand valuation, which seek to translate brand reputation into a financial value. Brand valuation has its origins in debates during the 1980s about the growing role of "intangibles" in value creation in the "new economy" (Power 2007), and more specifically in corporate efforts to find a way of including brands as a type of intangible asset on balance sheets. This was done initially in order to avoid expensive "write downs," in which the discrepancy between the price paid for an acquisition and its tangible assets has to be written off, giving the impression that a company's money had been wasted. An early example of this is the case of Grand Metropolitan (now Diageo), which in 1987 acquired Heublein from Nabisco. In its first set of accounts published after the acquisition, £565m of the £800m ($910 of $1300) paid for Heublein was written off as goodwill, and although this write-down was made against reserves rather than as a charge to profits, it meant that the balance sheet net assets fell substantially (Corbett 1997). Since from Grand Metropolitan's point of view the money spent on Heublein had not been wasted and indeed had brought new (but intangible) "assets" to the company in the form of Heublein's brands, in 1988 it announced its intention to value its brands and set out the key principles through which this valuation would be applied.

Despite the fact that, even as late as 1998, many large corporations still did not value their brands as assets on balance sheets (see Trevillion and Perrier 1999: 13), brand valuation systems have, in recent years, become much more widely accepted and used. This is partly because of changes in the financial reporting guidelines set out by national and international accounting bodies, such as the International Accounting Standards Board (IASB) and the UK Accounting Standards Board (ASB). Thus for example in 1999 the IASB issued International Accounting Standard 38, "Intangible Assets," which explicitly recognized that purchased brands should be capitalized separately from goodwill. This should be done on the basis of "fair market value" and should be checked for "impairment" on an annual basis rather than being automatically amortized. At around the same time, the ASB issued new Financial Reporting Standards, FRS 10 and FRS 11, which also provided guidelines for the treatment of "acquired goodwill" on balance sheets (Lindemann 2004). As Michael Power (2007) points out, these efforts to represent and value brands within traditional accounting frameworks for financial reporting were "part of a mood of experimentation in new systems...[that] sought to bridge disciplinary differences and create new productive relations between accounting, marketing, business strategy and social values" (132).

Valuing brands, then, depends on establishing a "fair market value" for the brand. This can be done in a range of ways. These include: a cost-based approach, which tries to gauge the cost of creating or re-creating the brand from scratch; a market approach, which tries to assess what a brand might be sold for on the open market; and an economic use or income-based approach, which seeks to project likely future earnings from the brand (Haigh 1997). This latter income-based or "economic use" approach is the most common. Thus for example Interbrand's brand valuation tool begins by making a forecast of future revenue and earnings based on previous sales figures. It then strips out the return that would normally be expected from tangible assets, leaving a figure for "prospective earnings from intangibles" (Trevillion and Perrier 1999). This is followed by an attempt to establish the level of earnings that can be directly attributed to the brand, by comparing the role of the brand in driving the business with that of other intangibles such as patents and human resources. To do this Interbrand uses its proprietary "Role of Branding" index, which seeks to identify the factors driving a business and then weigh them according to their relative importance, often making use of independent marketing research as part of this process (Perrier 1997). The final stages of the valuation procedure try to establish the degree of security that the brand adds to future revenue streams, by compiling a "Brand Strength Score." This involves comparing the brand under scrutiny with a hypothetical "ideal, risk-free brand" (Trevillion and Perrier 1999), along dimensions such as type of market in which it competes, stability of the brand over time, investment levels, degree of "internationality" and levels of legal protection (Andrew 1997). In this way, the projected "brand earnings" derived from the Role of Branding index can be adjusted to take account of the brand's relative security or riskiness, thereby providing a figure that can be capitalized and put onto the balance sheet.

Although Interbrand's brand valuation method is now well accepted, and other accounting firms sell similar services, it was initially quite controversial. A report by the London Business School, for example, questioned the validity of Interbrand's valuation methodology, claiming that it was neither "totally theoretically valid nor empirically verifiable" (Barwise et al., cited in Power 1997: 79), and that it was not clearly auditable because auditors would only be able to recheck the process rather than the book values. Yet others have argued that the controversy can more accurately be seen in terms of (lack of) trust in the expertise and credibility of Interbrand. As Power suggests, Interbrand's valuation methodology was no more subjective than any other valuation mechanism that depends on projecting future earnings streams; the problem, rather, was of the "social and institutional acceptability of organizations...who have threatened accountants' monopoly of asset recognition" (1997: 80). Indeed the process of establishing the legitimacy of brand valuation as a practice has involved sustained, and ongoing, disputes between the financial directors of top companies and various national and international accounting standards groups (Blackett 1997). As we suggested at the beginning of this chapter, methods for *measuring* value can also be linked to a process—or the promotion of the process—of *creating* brand value. Thus while the understanding of future value in terms of multiple, interrelated dimensions—such as "leadership," "stability," and "support"—is partly what distinguishes brand valuation from other accountancy techniques (Trevillion and Perrier 1999: 36–7; Andrew 1997), such an understanding may also, in turn, feed in to the business strategy and behavior of highly branded companies.

In the period since these debates took place, we would argue that the "monopoly of asset recognition," so fiercely guarded by accountants at the time, has been further undermined, and for a number of reasons. First, questions about the role of intangible assets in wealth creation are by no means resolved, and debates in this area continue to focus on new ways of measuring and valuing "intellectual capital" (Trevillion and Perrier 1999). Second, and as Power has recognized in a subsequent book, the accounting problem of intangibles was not only an issue of the credibility of Interbrand and accountants' territorial claims but also reflected "more fundamental issues to do with sources of corporate value *arising from relationships*" (2007: 133, emphasis added). These are not limited to those relationships (for example with customers and suppliers) captured, albeit implicitly, in Interbrand's Role of Branding index and Brand Strength Score, but may also include "potentially threatening agents...who possess a growing capacity to construct an alternative 'social facticity' of organizational reputation and challenge it" (Power 2007: 133). These relationships may not be amenable to the "hard" forms of valuation preferred by Interbrand and others, but may instead give rise to "new 'socially sensitive' accountings...such as value-added statements, social indicators, eco-balance sheets, triple bottom line accounting, and sustainability reporting" (2007: 133–4). Third, there has been a considerable increase in the availability and use of transactional data to both flesh out and animate the "key market variables" used in brand valuation, with the greater availability of data making information about these variables less stable and more dynamic. Fourth, as new objects of branding (such as cities, charities, educational establishments, sports organizations, and public sector institutions) are emerging, so new techniques designed to account for and measure these objects come out. Again, these measurement systems do not conform to the "hard" auditing standards demanded by institutions such as IASB or ASB, but instead experiment with novel ways of manipulating data and feedback and making it useful. As social and cultural (not just commercial) entities become objects of branding, brand valuation is more and more about measuring "qualities" as well as quantities, further undermining any monopoly on valuation practices previously held by accounting bodies.

New Forms of Brand Valuation

In what follows we want to briefly highlight three new ways in which the "values" of brands are measured, compared, and made productive. We do not take these examples to represent fixed categories or types of valuation, for they are just a few among many, and there is much variation even within each of the examples we describe. Rather, what makes them interesting for us is that they give some indication of the increasingly diffuse set of ways in which value is recognized in contemporary organizations and of the more multidimensional, topological, space in which brands now operate.

To begin with, let us consider the "European City Brand Barometer" produced by Saffron, a British branding consultancy specializing in place branding (Hildreth n.d.). This example of brand valuation comes from an exercise designed to "compare and contrast place brand strengths" and is based on the use of metrics to compare the strength of cities' "natural" assets—that is, their relatively fixed practical and cultural amenities—with their current "brand strength," that is, the extent to which those assets are recognized by outsiders and exploited by the city itself. As such, it is a key example of the way in which new forms of systematization and measurement have promotional as well as descriptive functions (see Julier and Moor 2009), and of how brand valuation and measurement are directly linked to the use of brands and branding in value creation. Indeed what makes this case intriguing is that, by explicitly focusing on the gap between where a city "is at" and where it "could be," it locates new opportunities for value creation and positions branding itself as an enterprise "focused on identifying, measuring and exploiting sources of value" (see Power 2007: 133).

Saffron's research focused on two key indicators: "city asset strength" and "city brand strength." City asset strength refers to "a city's baseline potential," determined by scoring cities out of 100 in key areas found by a survey of UK citizens to reflect the practical amenities and cultural qualities that were most important to people in choosing a city break. These included sightseeing and historical attractions, cuisine and restaurants, friendly and helpful locals, and good shopping facilities, as well as practical factors such as low cost, good weather, and ease of getting around. A city's "brand strength," by contrast, was calculated using factors chosen by Saffron itself: "pictorial recognition" of a place; "quality and strength of attractive qualities"; "conversational value"; and "media recognition." Again, cities were scored up to a maximum of 100. Perhaps unsurprisingly, the survey found that while in general a high score for asset strength was accompanied by a high score for brand strength, there were also cases where a city's assets were stronger than its recognition or brand value or where a city's brand strength outperformed its apparently more fixed and objective assets. In fact, Saffron went so far as to produce a "brand utilization" score, by calculating brand strength as a percentage of asset strength. Cities such as Sofia in Bulgaria, Lisbon in Portugal, Wroclaw in Poland and Vilnius in Lithuania all emerged as "hidden gems," which, "much like undervalued stocks, seem to have a reality (city asset strength) that is more attractive and of higher quality that is currently accounted for in their brand (city brand strength)" (Hildreth n.d.: 10). In these cases, Saffron suggests, "active branding" could help cities to push their brand utilization score close to, or even above, 100 percent.

This example of brand valuation and measurement is interesting for a number of reasons. Firstly, it uses multiple dimensions of value, most of which do not refer to an externally fixed or shared standard of measurement. The brand strength score, for example, included conversational value as a key variable, which was determined using the hypothetical question, "How interesting would it be at a cocktail party to say, 'Hey, I just got back from_____?'" (Hildreth n.d.: 8). And this variable in turn was combined with other measures derived from surveys, content analysis, and prompted and unprompted consumer "associations." We suggest that such heterogeneity of the dimensions of value, along with the lack of external reference points, is indicative of both the inventiveness of contemporary valuation systems and the fact that brands are very difficult to compare using established forms of measurement. The point of brands, of course, is that they are supposed to be distinctive. Secondly, this system depends in part upon a projection of future value—not only how valuable a brand is now but how valuable it could be. In this respect the Saffron brand valuation tool is comparable to Interbrand's system, which also depends on projecting future earnings. As we will go on to suggest below, projection into the future—or rather, discounting the present—is part of the way in which the problem of the apparent *lack* of comparability between brands is circumvented, but it is also characteristic of the topological culture—that is, the multidimensional space of (future) possibility—in which brands now operate. Finally, Saffron's Brand Barometer clearly serves a promotional function for the consultancy; that is, by highlighting the gap between a brand's current and future value, it identifies an opportunity for Saffron to be employed to narrow that gap. And while the use of quasi-scientific measurement systems in the promotion of creative industries is of interest in its own right (see Julier and Moor 2009), it too provides evidence of some of the limitations of conventional, accountancy-endorsed, methods of valuation, and the gradual opening up of a space in which competing consultancies try to capture the more complex and multifaceted types of value associated with the brand.

This opening up can also be seen in a second example, to do with the uptake of ideas about the "triple bottom line" of contemporary business. This concept was introduced by John Elkington (1997) to describe the ways in which concerns with sustainability—and specifically the social and environmental impact of corporations—could be factored into business decision-making and incorporated into balance sheets or annual reports. As with corporate social responsibility initiatives more generally, debates about "triple bottom line" accounting are characterized by disputes about the extent to which businesses should be allowed to self-regulate, and how far governments should intervene to establish sustainability concerns as public goods that can be enforced through law or through economic instruments of various kinds. What interests us about such systems is what they tell us about contemporary forms of measurement and the attempt to map new dimensions of value and value creation. Interestingly, Elkington links the emergence of sustainability concerns to what he calls a "transparency revolution," which is driven by the "coming together of new value systems and radically different information technologies" (1997: 7). But this meeting of social or political values and technical possibilities does not simply involve rendering previously hidden qualities visible but rather is productive of new value-creating behaviors,[3] which may evolve without reference to external measurement standards or benchmarks. In this context, we suggest, social and environmental values may themselves emerge as dimensions of brand value.

We can pursue this further by noting that in the absence of a formal or compulsory system of sustainability reporting for private companies, triple bottom line measurement systems take a variety of forms. Indeed organizations of various types and sizes have experimented with ways of measuring and representing these additional dimensions of value. And here the role of visualization in the new forms of measurement is especially interesting, since different visualizations themselves provide distinct articulations of a brand in relation to values. They also show that there is often a lack of consistency of use of measurement standards in brand valuation exercises carried out by a single agency, much less any reference to the measurements of other organizations. So although representations that emerge from these experiments evidence a widespread aspiration to identify and measure a more diffuse set of values, they also illustrate the difficulty of doing so in the absence of external standards or shared indicators. As we will suggest below, contemporary forms of brand valuation, in addition to seeking to extend the range of value dimensions that can be measured and compared, may also involve a kind of internal self-calibration in which the brand becomes its own reference point.[4] Furthermore, we would suggest that in the absence of such indicators, the adoption of triple bottom line systems represents both an opportunity for companies to reflect upon their own activities and the wider set of ways in which they produce value, and a potential space in which external values of social or environmental responsibility may be claimed as dimensions of the brand itself.

This project is complicated, however, by the fact that there are multiple systems for measuring social and environmental values, and that in some cases these are emerging—or are likely to emerge—with little or no direct involvement by companies themselves (see also Elkington 1997: 7). This can be seen in the rankings, auditing, and "league tables" of different companies made by activist groups or nongovernmental organizations, as well as in more experimental forms of "silent" or "shadow" accounting, in which outside parties or stakeholders mimic the official annual reports of public companies but include more critical information about the company's social, economic, and environmental activities than is found in the official versions.[5] This means that, even though the "symbolic power to classify and name no longer lies with the state in the last instance" (Burrows and Gane 2006: 807) and instead lies increasingly with private capital, it does not reside *solely* and exclusively with those private corporations. And what follows from this, in turn, is that the process of creating and measuring value may often be mediated through relationships with groups, publics and environments that are external to the company as such. Indeed, this is at the heart of an understanding of branding in terms of the building of relationships[6] or what has come to be called "open-source branding" (Pitt et al. 2006), "consumer co-creation," or "collaboration" (Zwick, Bonsu and Darmody 2008; Prahalad and Ramaswamy 2004).[7] Importantly, the recognition and management of such relationships by brand managers does not necessarily require the alignment of intentions, creating common aims, or sharing ownership of outcomes between collaborators. Indeed, as Michael Power (2007) notes, experiments with new forms of accounting (including triple bottom line reporting) are often part of an effort to engage with the issue of sources of corporate value that arise from relationships not only with customers but also with threatening or adversarial agents who seek to challenge the brand.

The significance of relationships to new techniques for measuring and creating (brand) value can be seen most clearly in our final example, to do with the use of transactional data. Transactional data typically refers to data collected from consumers (sometimes without their knowledge) as a by-product of their doing something else; for example, shopping at the supermarket or making a purchase on a credit card. This data may be valuable because it may help companies to predict future behavior, illuminate consumer tastes and preferences (and therefore be used in marketing), or provide information that can be used to calculate the potential value (or lack of value) of a person's custom (see, e.g., Turow 2006). It is in this sense that some authors argue that the value form is expanding to include "life itself" (see Thrift 2005, 2007),[8] or that brand management, and "informational capitalism" in general, increasingly involves the private exploitation of social knowledge and communication (Arvidsson 2006). Media and electronic technologies are argued to have greatly enhanced the productivity of social communication, in part because of their ability to generate and store new types and volumes of information, but also to cross-reference it with other types of data produced or collected elsewhere. Such developments provide the possibility that dimensions of brand value may be created through processes of linking, adding, tagging, and cross-referencing, and through the process by which brands are taken up in new contexts and given a new significance (Barry 2001). At the same time, brands themselves are deemed to become valuable through their ability to organize, and even program, the types of social communication that unfold in electronic environments and to appropriate the "ethical surplus" thus produced (Arvidsson 2006).

There are now quite well established ways of measuring the "engagement" of users with a website, using "web analytics" tools that measure things like number of unique visitors, page views per visitor, time spent on site, total time spent per user, frequency of visits, depth of visits and "conversions" (into sales). These tools include Omniture and WebAnalytics, as well as the free service Google Analytics (www.google.com/analytics). However, with the rise of blogs and other social media, both as part of and beyond the corporate website, the focus is now turning towards tools that can generate "community insights" and measure, track, and compare them using "community analytics." So-called "listening platforms," for example, allow organizations to track discussions between users, identify key participants, and even understand, albeit at a fairly simple level, the "sentiments" being expressed. For example Harvest Report Server 2.0, one of the key tools of this type, claims to "deliver...value to your business by helping [you to] understand the value and sentiment of customer conversations...to analyze what they are saying and understand their tonalities."[9] It includes a dashboard that provides scores on key indicators, as well as the "data values" for particular dimensions of interaction and overall trends. Its "sentiment detection" feature provides details about the "overall tonality" of social media discussions on the site, identifying the key words or phrases producing the strongest positive or negative sentiment, as well as who is saying them. This can be done using either "system-driven" words and phrases (for example, words used in a marketing campaign) or user-driven words and phrases (that is, those that come up frequently in user-generated conversation). Using this information, it can also identify and measure the activities of different "user types"—that is, the ways in which different users do or do not contribute to a "community" over time. These types might include those who typically ask questions, those who answer them, those who initiate new topics, and those who merely "spectate" or follow discussions generated by others.

In terms of the themes we have identified above, it is significant that these tools are aimed primarily at individual companies and brands, allowing them to set their own key words and phrases and thus "self-calibrate" in the sense of setting—and modifying—the parameters by which they wish to measure their users' activities. Such tools therefore provide brands with a means of exploring the value of particular relationships and, potentially, of identifying areas for improvement and intervention in order to make those relationships more productive or valuable. On the other hand, new products of this type have also sought to provide more general standards for measuring what they call "community health." Lithium Technologies, for example, has produced a "Community Health Index," which is a tool for tracking aspects of an online community's behavior, but is also grounded in research that has compared the metrics of many different types of community in order to identify "the diagnostic and predictive metrics that most accurately represent key attributes of a healthy community: growth, useful content, popularity, responsiveness, interactivity and liveliness" (Lithium Technologies 2009: 1). Its aim in doing this has been to provide "a common standard for the industry," by which different communities may be compared over time.[10]

Elsewhere, a number of other companies now sell services that track and measure the ways in which brands are discussed across a wide range of social media, not just those hosted by a company itself. For example, Nielsen Online offers a "BuzzMetrics" service that seeks to "uncover and integrate data-driven insights culled from nearly 100 million blogs, social networks, groups, boards and other CGM platforms." It also has an "online threat tracker" that tries to "identify and assess online rumors and threats" and "monitor known and unknown threat sources and topics." Another company, Metrica, specializes in tracking and measuring the impact of PR campaigns across online, social media, and user-generated content (UGC) as well as traditional print and broadcast. Such technologies mean that the kind of social knowledge and communication generated by brands (and mentioned by Arvidsson, above) is not only available to be exploited privately by brands but may also have a wider valence. In 2008, for example, Portfolio Communications in the UK used a similar set of technologies to create league tables that ranked British higher education institutions according to the "volume and tone of online buzz." Based on the idea that "social media, such as blogs and online reviews, are just as, if not more, important [as official websites]," the league tables were not commissioned by any particular institution but rather served primarily as a form of promotion for Portfolio itself (which is part of Metrica). At the same time, the league tables were widely taken up by universities as a means of promotion, in some cases coming into conflict with other, better established, metrics for measuring university output and quality such as the government-sponsored Research Assessment Exercise.

Analyzing Brand Valuation Mechanisms

How should we understand the significance of these different types of brand valuation systems? Firstly, it is important to note that the general context is one in which value creation increasingly takes place beyond the commodity form. The argument here is that there has been a general change in how and what constitutes the economic value form. As we noted at the beginning of our chapter, brand valuation itself has its roots in debates during the 1980s about the growing significance of "intangibles" in the economy, but this shift in economic value is also dealt with by a number of critical scholars. There are a variety of different perspectives here. So, for example, Lazzarato (2004) proposes that the material or physical and mechanical aspects of formally productive labor are increasingly giving way to communicational, cooperative, and relational forms of work. The forms of value associated with this kind of work confound classic measures of productivity (where the value of the finished product is related to the costs of production, including the costs of labor and machinery) because their live, qualitative, and heterogeneous dimensions exceed and escape such attempts. Alternatively, Thrift (2005) argues that the value form is no longer restricted to labor at work, but encompasses "life itself," with consumers trained from an early age to participate in the creation of value by using all their capabilities. Brand valuation techniques—particularly those that make use of transactional data derived from consumer activity—may be seen as attempts to measure and exploit these new value forms.

Secondly, it is also significant that debates about intangibles and about the types of value arising from relationships take place in the context of a form of governance that, according to some authors at least, actively encourages and facilitates an "entrepreneurial" approach to measurement and a "market" of authorities and expertise in social and economic life (see, e.g., Barry 2002; Strathern 2000; Shamir 2008; Power 2007). In one example, Andrew Barry (2002) describes the case of Serco, a private company that manages the UK government's laboratory responsible for measurement standards (in areas such as pollution), but which may potentially compete with other companies to provide such services. Elsewhere, Ronen Shamir (2008) notes that neoliberal governance facilitates "private" forms of authority such as professional associations, accountancy and credit-rating agencies, and standard-setting organizations, which may increasingly assume regulatory roles or experiment with "novel forms of legality" (2008: 7). Developments such as these help us to understand how it is that the authority of accountants and accounting standards boards came to be challenged by private corporations such as Interbrand but also how it is that new types of value measurement, such as "triple bottom line" scores, have developed with no external regulation and with a variety of measurement techniques. Indeed, in light of the links we identify between techniques for measuring value and opportunities for creating value, it seems as if these techniques are judged in terms of their *efficacy*[11] as much as their accuracy or reliability. In other words, there is a change in the criteria used to assess valuation techniques *themselves* as part of the shift to forms of neoliberal governance.

To these accounts, we would like to add another, which stresses the importance of a new space of what we have been calling topological culture for these emerging systems of measurement and calculation. First, let us outline some of the conventions in the established field of metrology, the science of measurement.[12] A core concept in this field is *traceability*, which is defined by the industry association as "the property of the result of a measurement or the value of a standard whereby it can be related to stated references, usually national or international standards, through an unbroken chain of comparisons, all having stated uncertainties." The level of traceability establishes the level of comparability of the measurement: whether the result of a measurement can be compared to the previous one, whether it was obtained a year ago, or somewhere else in the world. Traceability is most often obtained by *calibration*, which is the process of establishing the relation between the indication of a measuring instrument and the value of a measurement standard.

What we want to suggest—on the basis of the examples outlined above—is that brand valuation techniques extend the chain of comparisons upon which its metrology depends, so that it includes relations that extend in many (differently organized and heterogeneous) directions simultaneously. It is in this sense a multidimensional metrology, and is sustained by the use of multivariate statistical analysis. However, the standards by which the chain of comparison is calibrated are not shared within the industry but are often singular, established on a case-by-case basis. Here we would draw attention again to the importance of recent developments in information and communication technology including linked databases and the growth of informatics infrastructures that allow for a much greater range of measurements to be made, recorded, coded, and associated with each other through database mining, correlation, and analysis. What is involved here is the extension of traceability as a consequence of a multiplication of indices and a proliferation of techniques for establishing continuity or traceability. Indeed, there is a kind of internal self-calibration at work in brand valuation. That there is no external standard or measuring unit was the basis of some of the critiques of early techniques of brand valuation, but the appropriateness of attempts to establish external forms of comparability is explicitly challenged by many of those in the brand valuation industry, on the basis of the special characteristics of the brand. Interbrand, for example, notes that although one might arrive at a value for a brand on the basis of something comparable,

> ...comparability is difficult in the case of brands as by definition they should be differentiated and thus not comparable. Furthermore, the value creation of brands in the same category can be very different, even if most other aspects of the underlying business such as target groups, advertising spend, price promotions and distribution channel are similar or identical. Comparables can provide an interesting cross-check, however, even though they should never be relied on solely for valuing brands (Lindemann 2004: 6).

As we outlined above, in place of—or alongside—a comparative approach, Interbrand relies in part on a (multidimensional) space of possibility in which a new kind of measure-relation is established. The space is that of the "ideal, risk-free brand" (Trevillion and Perrier 1999), whose multiple dimensions include the type of market in which it competes, stability over time, investment levels, degree of "internationality," and levels of legal protection (Andrew 1997). It is in relation to this singular future space of multiple dimensions that the Interbrand measure of brand strength is established. In this case, the future is not an extension of the present situation of the brand but is rather the ideal basis from which the present value is discounted. As Interbrand put this, "The financial principle relates to the net present value of future expected earnings, a concept widely used in business. The brand's future earnings are identified and then discounted to a net present value using a discount rate that reflects the risk of those earnings being realized" (Lindemann 2004: 7).

We want to suggest that these characteristics of brand valuation metrology—the putting of multiple, heterogeneous dimensions into relationship with each other, the adoption of internal calibration or internal measure relations, and the projection of a space of future possibility against which the present is discounted—are indicative of the emergence of what we are calling a topological culture.

What do we mean by topological? In classical mathematics, a geometrical object such as a curved line or a surface was described by the rate at which some of its properties change, such as the rate at which its curvature changes between different points. In the early nineteenth century, for example, a curved two-dimensional space was studied by embedding the surface in a three-dimensional space with its own fixed set of axes (in which, conventionally, time was represented as extension in space). Then, using those axes, coordinates would be assigned to every point on the surface; finally, the geometric links between points determining the form of the surface and its dynamic properties would be expressed as algebraic relations between the numbers (this is the basis of calculus). This was, historically, the mathematical basis of techniques for predicting change. But in the nineteenth century mathematicians Friedrich Gauss and Bernard Riemann developed methods that allowed the study of (n-dimensional) surfaces without any reference to a supplementary embedding of space/time. The field of topology has since developed through the study of the properties of these surfaces that are "spaces in themselves" (Klein, qtd. in DeLanda 2005), and, in doing so, it makes use of a different understanding of measure.

So, for example, Riemann notes, [classical, Euclidean] measurement consists of the superposition of the magnitudes to be compared: "It therefore requires a means of using one magnitude as the standard for another" (1873: 15). But this arbitrary logic of measurement, and the selection of one standard measure, which is externalized and used as a unit of measurement for another, was not adequate to understand the multiply extended magnitudes or manifolds which he wished to investigate. In such spaces, Riemann proposed, two magnitudes can only be compared when one is a part of the other, as regions in manifoldness. More than this, multiply extended magnitudes are capable of different measure relations or metrics as they unfold in a space of constant curvature. Following this insight, topological approaches[13] have since been developed and widely applied to analyze, intervene in, and occupy this dynamic space in, for example, the modeling of financial markets, the mapping of the Internet and, we suggest here, the valuation of brands.

At the same time, topology—along with the rest of modern mathematics—deploys new ways of working. It tends not, as did classical mathematics, to begin with the task of finding, for given equations, exact solutions associated with precise coordinates in a Euclidian space but rather starts with an equation and then explores the properties of the space in which it has a solution. So while geometry has classically been understood as the perception and organization (that is, the representation) of a static, homogenous space that might be projected reliably into the future, topology offers a set of (postrepresentational) tools for thinking about processes of actualization in n-dimensional spaces. With the use of such tools, numbers do not just represent but construct and take on virtual properties, making it possible to build generalized spaces of calculation and opening up new ways of mapping possibility, identifying innovation and creating dimensions of value. What is interesting from our point of view is that brand valuation techniques deploy a similar relation to the future: they are not confined to the extension of the present into a certain future but are designed to enable the actualizing of virtual possibilities in the present.

This strategic occupation of a relation to a future that is modeled as a dynamic space is, we suggest, critical to the capacity of brand valuation techniques to measure *and* create value. In the examples we outline above, it is the ability of brand valuation techniques to calibrate ratios of value in a dynamic space of possibility that enables them to function simultaneously as tools of measurement and as innovation systems.[14] Whether or how the value of the relations they measure and create is or should be understood as collaboration—as many of those working in the brand valuation business suggest they should—is a key question, given that many of these relationships do not depend on the alignment of intentions or interests, or necessarily lead to shared ownership of what is created. We would suggest that the future of such techniques depends in part on the ability of "enunciatory communities" or "recursive publics" (Kelty 2005) to challenge the instrumental notions of owners, stakeholders, and interests.

Conclusion

In this chapter we have tried to demonstrate the significance of brand valuation systems, and other ways of measuring brands, for understanding how brands create value in contemporary economies. We began by outlining the brand valuation tool used by Interbrand and noted that it has evolved both in collaboration and in conflict with more established accountancy systems. On the one hand, it has gradually accrued legitimacy through a process of mutual accommodation between its own system and the established business reporting standards and forms of measurement developed elsewhere. On the other hand, the singularity and distinctiveness of brands—and indeed the issue of "intangible assets" more generally—continues to pose problems for these more established systems and opportunities for new, more entrepreneurial agencies.

We then discussed three alternative systems that are currently used as additional ways of measuring brand values, highlighting their multidimensionality, lack of internal consistency and reference to external measurement standards, and relation to a dynamic future space of possibility. We show that these experiments in alternative forms of brand measurement are indicative of both an aspiration to identify and represent new dimensions of value beyond the strictly financial (and often to claim these as properties of the brand itself, rather than as distributed, shared or social values) and to find ways of accounting for and managing the sources of value that emerge from relationships—relationships which, we have suggested, do not necessarily involve alignment of aims or shared values and goals. We have analyzed these developments in terms of a more general set of changes in economic productivity and the value form, and also in terms of contemporary forms of governance, in which an "entrepreneurial" approach to measurement and authority is actively encouraged. Our argument here is that the development of valuation techniques in these ways means that the brand—as an instance of an object that is specifically organized to be open, reflexive, and defined by its distinctiveness or singularity—is made to function as an epistemic object of experimentation for new practices of measurement that are emerging simultaneously with new spaces of exchange. Both of these perspectives—the economic and the political—highlight a changing context in which brands are able to experiment with new ways of creating and measuring value. We then introduced the view that this context might also be seen as the space of a topological rationality or culture.

To situate this last perspective in more general cultural terms we will conclude by recalling the "turn to the surface," noted as long ago as the 1920s by the critic Siegfried Kracauer ([1927] 1995) in his analyses of the mass culture of the Weimar Republic. To develop an understanding of what he calls the mass ornament, Kracauer pays special attention to the cultural forms of his day—the hotel lobby, arcades, the Tiller girls, and bestsellers as well as cinema and photography. The turn to the surface is understood by Kracauer in terms of the penetration of mass culture by *ratio*: famously, he describes what he calls the mass ornament as "the aesthetic reflex of the rationality to which the prevailing economic system aspires" (79). He describes the ratio at work as having a mathematical logic—a "Euclidean geometry"—that organizes the mass. This is the logic of a "linear system," and the "elementary components" of physics, such as "waves and spirals," training "the broadest mass of people to create a pattern of undreamed-of dimensions" (77). But the logic to which the prevailing economic system aspires now is neither Euclidean nor linear. Rather—as a number of writers argue (Adkins 2002; Lash 2002; Thrift 2005; DeLanda 2005; Lazzarato 2004; Urry 2002; Lash and Lury 2007)—the logic of contemporary societies is complex and nonlinear. And, so we propose, it is to the topological reflexivity of this logic that that we must look to understand the measuring and making of contemporary forms of value.

Notes

1. The "plc" sector in the UK is similar to the US Corporation (Corp.).
2. See for example Caulkin (2009).
3. We might also note here that Sherry Turkle's ethnography of the early stages of personal computers (1995) describes the emergence of a new form of transparency in computer interfaces which, rather than allowing a user to see through to what makes a computer work, enables him or her to find out what can be done by trial and error, experimentation, and play.
4. For example the UK supermarket Tesco, as part of its efforts to adopt a "balanced scorecard" approach, has devised its own "customer value metrics," derived from internal market research with its own customers about what they considered valuable (Parker and Heapy 2006). In 2007 it was reported that Tesco was exploring the idea of creating stickers with "carbon footprint" information on every single product in its stores. Both cases illustrate the brand's effort to "self-calibrate" in terms of its relationship to social and environmental values, and to claim those values as dimensions of *brand* value.
5. See for example www.st-andrews.ac.uk/~csearweb/aptopractice/index.html.
6. An early exponent of this view is Cova (1997; 1999) who argues that brands have a "linking value" for identity construction. According to Cova and Pace (2006), several approaches now exist towards the making of communities in marketing theory, such as "consumer subcultures," "consumer tribes," and "situation based communities," each of which is to be distinguished by different forms of attachment.
7. So, for example, Lego invites customers to develop new models in its Lego-Lab; American Apparel invites consumers to apply to be models; Dove provides a platform for contributors to reflect on the effects of beauty norms; Apple encourages consumers to send them self-made commercials; and Starbucks has launched a drink "created" by consumers.
8. It is interesting in this regard to note that one of the reasons brands are seen to require special forms of valuation is that they are potentially immortal. Thus Interbrand notes:

"Intangible assets such as brands that can claim infinite life do not have to be subjected to amortization. Instead, companies need to perform annual impairment tests" (Lindemann 2004: 4).

9. See www.telligent.com/products/harvest-report-server.
10. Interestingly, Lithium has also tried to use its research to assess the interdependence of different variables affecting "community health."
11. See Jullien (1999).
12. The science of measurement, embracing both experimental and theoretical determinations at any level of uncertainty in any field of science and technology is, according to the International Bureau of Weights and Measures (BIPM), known as metrology (http://search.bipm.org/bipm/en/). The term has been widely taken up and adapted in social studies of science and technology.
13. Topological algorithms are the curve or interface of a surface that has no inside or outside but is a space in itself.
14. Parallels may be drawn with developments in biomedical, bioscientific, and bioengineering domains, including, for example, statistical strategies for clinical trials that ideally enroll everyone as "patients-in-waiting" and objects of "surplus health" extraction, pioneered by cholesterol lowering drugs such as Lipitor (Dumit 2002).

References

Adkins, Lisa. 2002. *Revisions: Gender and Sexuality in Late Modernity*. Buckingham: Open University Press.

Andrew, David. 1997. "Brand Strength Analysis." In *Brand Valuation*, ed. R. Perrier. 3rd edition. London: Premier Books.

Arvidsson, Adam. 2006. *Brands: Meaning and Value in Media Culture*. Abingdon: Routledge.

Barry, Andrew. 2001. *Political Machines: Governing a Technological Society*. London: Athlone.

———. 2002. "The Anti-Political Economy." *Economy and Society* 32 (2): 268–284.

Blackett, Tom. 1997. "Foreword to the Third Edition." In *Brand Valuation*, ed. R. Perrier. 3rd edition. London: Premier Books.

Burrows, Roger, and Nicholas Gane. 2006. "Geodemographics, Software and Class." *Sociology* 40 (5): 793–812.

Callon, Michel, and John Law. 2003. "Qualculation, Agency and Otherness." Paper presented at Economics at Large Workshop, New York University, 14–15 November.

Caulkin, Simon. 2009. "It's Time to Explode the Myth of the Shareholder." *The Observer*, 29 March.

Corbett, Gerald. 1997. "The Benefits of Valuing Brands." In *Brand Valuation*, ed. R. Perrier. 3rd edition. London: Premier Books.

Cova, Bernard. 1997. "Community and Consumption: Towards a Definition of the "Linking-Value" of Products or Services." *European Journal of Marketing* 31 (3–4): 297–316.

———. 1999. "From Marketing to Societing: When the Link Is More Important than the Thing." In *Rethinking Marketing. Towards Critical Marketing Accountings,* ed. D. Brownlie et al. London: Sage.

Cova, Bernard, and Stefano Pace. 2006. "Brand Community of Convenience Products: New Forms of Customer Empowerment—The Case 'My Nutella the Community.'" *European Journal of Marketing* 40 (9–10): 1087–1105.

DeLanda, Manuel. 2005. *Intensive Science and Virtual Philosophy*. New York: Continuum.

Dumit, Joseph. 2002. "Drugs for Life." *Molecular Interventions* 2: 124–127.

Elkington, John. 1997. *Cannibals with Forks: The Triple Bottom Line of 21st Century Business*. Oxford: Capstone.

Haigh, David. 1997. "Accounting and Forecasting for Brands." In *Brand Valuation*, ed. R. Perrier. 3rd edition. London: Premier Books.

Hildreth, Jeremy, n.d. *The Saffron European City Brand Barometer*. www.saffron-consultants.com/news-views/publications (accessed July 14, 2009).

Julier, Guy, and Liz Moor. 2009. *Design and Creativity: Policy, Management and Practice*. Oxford and New York: Berg.

Jullien, François. 1999. *The Propensity of Things: Towards a History of Efficacy in China*. Trans. Janet Lloyd. New York: Zone Books.

Kelty, Christopher. 2005. "Geeks, Social Imaginaries and Recursive Publics." *Cultural Anthropology* 20 (2): 185–214.

Knorr Cetina, Karen. 1999. *Epistemic Cultures: How the Sciences Make Knowledge*. Cambridge, MA: Harvard University Press.

Kracauer, Siegfried. [1927] 1995. *The Mass Ornament: Weimar Essays*. Trans. Thomas Levin. Cambridge, MA: Harvard University Press.

Lash, Scott. 2002. *Critique of Information*. London: Sage.

Lash, Scott, and Celia Lury. 2007. *The Global Culture Industry: The Mediation of Things*. Cambridge: Polity.

Lash, Scott, and John Urry. 1997. *Economies of Signs and Space*. London: Sage.

Lazzarato, Maurizio. 2004. "From Capital-Labor to Capital-Life." *Ephemera: Theory and Politics in Organization* 4 (3): 187–208.

Lindemann, Jan. 2004. "Brand Valuation." http://www.brandchannel.com/papers_ review.asp?sp_id=357 (accessed July 7, 2009).

Lithium Technologies. 2009. *Community Health Index for Online Communities*. www.lithium.com/community/resources (accessed April 24, 2009).

Lury, Celia. 2004. *Brands: The Logos of the Global Economy*. London: Routledge.

Moor, Liz. 2007. *The Rise of Brands*. Oxford and New York: Berg.

Parker, Sophia, and Joe Heapy. 2006. *The Journey to the Interface: How Public Service Design Can Connect Users to Reform*. London: Demos.

Perrier, Raymond. 1997. *Brand Valuation*. 3rd edition. London: Premier Books.

Pitt, Leyland F. et al. 2006. "The Penguin's Window—Corporate Brands from an Open-Source Perspective." *Journal of the Academy of Marketing Science* 34 (2): 115–127.

Porter, Michael E. 1998. *Competitive Advantage: Creating and Sustaining a Superior Performance*. New York: Free Press.

Power, Michael. 1997. *The Audit Society: Rituals of Verification*. Oxford: Oxford University Press.

———. 2007. *Organized Uncertainty: Designing a World of Risk Management*. Oxford and New York: Oxford University Press.

Prahalad, C. K., and Venkat Ramaswamy. 2004. *The Future of Competition: Co-creating Unique Value with Customers*. Boston: Harvard Business School Publishing.

Riemann, Bernhard. 1873. "On the Hypotheses Which Lie at the Bases of Geometry." Trans. W. K. Clifford. *Nature* VIII (183, 184): 14–17, 36, 37. http://www.maths.tcd.ie/pub/HistMath/People/Riemann/Geom/ (accessed July 11, 2009).

Shamir, Ronen. 2008. "The Age of Responsibilization: On Market-embedded Morality." *Economy and Society* 37 (1): 1–19.

Strathern, Marilyn, ed. 2000. *Audit Cultures: Anthropological Studies in Accountability, Ethics, and the Academy.* London: Routledge.

Thrift, Nigel. 2005. *Knowing Capitalism.* London: Sage.

———. 2007. *Non-Representational Theory: Space, Politics, Affect.* London: Routledge.

Trevillion, Kylie, and Raymond Perrier. 1999. *Brand Valuation—A Practical Guide: Accountants' Digest 405.* London: Accountancy Books.

Turkle, Sherry. 1995. *Life on the Screen: Identity in the Age of the Internet.* New York: Simon and Schuster.

Turow, Joseph. 2006. *Niche Envy: Marketing Discrimination in a Digital Age.* Cambridge, MA: The MIT Press.

Urry, John. 2002. *Global Complexity.* Cambridge: Polity.

Whitwell, Stuart. 2005. "Understanding Brand Equity and Brand Valuation." http://www.intangiblebusiness.com/Brand-services/Financial services/News/ Understanding-brand-equity-and-brand-valuation~464.html (accessed July 7, 2009).

Zwick, Detlev, Samuel K. Bonsu, and Aron Darmody. 2008. "Putting Consumers to Work: "Co-creation" and New Marketing Govern-mentality." *Journal of Consumer Culture* 8 (2): 163–193.

CHAPTER THREE

Promotion as Institutionalized Deception

Some Coordinates of Political Publicity

John Corner

In this chapter I want to contribute to the broader critical inquiry into practices of promotion and of branding in contemporary politics and society, into the continuing development of "promotional culture," by examining a selection of issues around what I have termed "institutionalized deception." I mean to indicate by this term a very wide range of activities, many of them "professionalized," through which deceit is planned and executed as part of routine institutional business, often as part of broader corporate or governmental strategies of promotion. My interest is also in exploring at least some of the pragmatic aspects of deceit *as a practice*, not just its character as a pressing normative issue in many different contexts.

In pursuing my exploration, I want to connect with a number of reference points, both historical and cross-disciplinary, which seem useful for productive intellectual engagement with institutionalized deception today. Hence, the "coordinates" of my title, indicating the different lines of relationship that might help to establish positions within what is a rather wide and varied territory. I also want to consider some of the concepts and assumptions through which questions of deceit have been addressed, particularly those concerning the political sphere. Often this has been with the intention of condemning deceitful practice and outlining, if only by sketchy implication, alternative and more ethical routes to public communication, political claims-making and media reporting. Towards the end of my account, I want to give some attention to this question of alternatives.

Deception: Definitions and Dimensions

Tightly defining what is meant by "deception," and certainly what is meant by a charge of "lying," is a challenging task and I shall not attempt it here. Something along the following lines will be sufficient for my own analytic purposes: I am looking at various ways of encouraging faulty understanding (including the acceptance of falsehoods) in order to promote institutional interests and—perhaps—to reduce institutional damage. Not all promotion involves deception, of course, but it seems that increasingly, a wide range of promotional activity has recourse to it in different ways, as do some of those often more subtle, complex and indirect strategies of appeal characteristic of branding.

Although in the main I shall be concerned with specifically political practices of deceit, I would like at the outset to note the deep embedding of deceitfulness, of the "utility of fiction," in many areas of everyday life. These range from the private sphere, where deception is a regular problem of personal life (sharply brought out in fictional narratives, both classic and modern), to the activities of different types of corporate and public enterprise.[1] Here, investment banking has recently provided us with some high-profile, high-impact instances (particularly but not exclusively in the form of fraud) to join those of governments, with which their strategies of public relations are occasionally interwoven. Sometimes these practices of deception are constrained at least notionally by explicit codes of practice, as in those regulating the advertising industry; sometimes they enjoy a relatively free run against assumptions about norms of "professional" or "public service" behavior and the trust that can be placed in them. Not surprisingly, these norms have been the subject of increasing skepticism in many parts of the world. In the United Kingdom, for example, the invasion of Iraq and its aftermath provided a range of instances (notably, about the existence of weapons of mass destruction) where a degree of institutionalized deception was not only suspected but ultimately revealed to have taken place.

Contemporary political promotionalism varies in its nature, including some of those practices now broadly classified as "political marketing" that extend across a wide span of the politics–public interface. Most prominently, there is the deceptive work of "spin," a broad and loose term indicating activities increasingly regarded by many, albeit with resignation, as a routine part of contemporary politics. This routine character, sometimes given an affirmative projection, comes through, for instance, in the presentation of political publicity in the television series *The West Wing*.[2] Close to the negative end of the spectrum, there is what still frequently gets called, despite the looseness of the term, "propaganda." This is often seen to be based on major falsehood and, in the strength of its desire to misinform, to move significantly away from any acceptable model of democratic communication. In relation to no point on this array of practices, however, should the emergent skepticism I noted above be regarded as any kind of satisfactory antidote. It is quite possible to exaggerate the scale and depth of its presence in popular political culture as well as its efficacy. Writing pessimistically about the positive public perceptions surrounding President Obama's campaign promises regarding the way through and beyond the economic crisis, Mike Davis (2008) has observed that deception might be "the mother's milk of American politics." Gloomy readings don't come much more fundamental than this!

Political deception has a lengthy and rich history. It is an activity contextualized by myriad other examples of the centrality of deception in human affairs, ranging from the most intimate to the most corporate-strategic. To say this is not to try to excuse it or minimize its consequences but merely to place the phenomenon in perspective, even if we then want to argue that recent years have seen a growth in its scale and intensity, as well as in the damage it has done to the principles and practices of democracy.[3] At several points in what follows I shall refer to the impact of commercial developments in promotion and branding upon political and public communication. This impact, too, has a long history; but there is good reason to believe that the twentieth century, with its transformations in media technology, both accelerated and intensified such influence. However, my main focus will be on forms of governmental communication as they deploy deceptive practices and the ways in which these practices are variously relayed, amplified and sometimes questioned and exposed for what they are by the media.

In the analysis of political deception, historically or internationally or both, the general relationship of the political elite to the media system at any given time is an important variable. It is obvious that where there is clear and extensive alignment between the two (sometimes guaranteed by direct and explicit control), then strategies of deception can use the media as an agency of relay and dissemination with relative confidence and ease. Where tension or conflict exists between them, on the other hand, strategies will have to take account of this and will also have to regard the media as an agency of risk as well as opportunity. It is not at all surprising that both academic and public debate about the relationship between elite and media in given national contexts, particularly in cases where neither obvious control nor regular overt opposition can be identified, is lively and heated in character and hard to resolve, not least because of possible internal variations in the media profile.

Political deception is, I have noted, highly differentiated in its scale and kinds internationally. At the broadest of levels, I think it is possible to divide it up in relation to its basic contexts and goals. In any serious analytic scheme, this might require further subdivision to take account of more specific circumstances.

First of all, there is deception that is part of communication designed primarily to increase positive evaluation of the "sender" by either a target group or the public in general. This is the most directly "promotional" form of approach, often linked directly to shifting commercial practices of marketing, branding, and advertising. It is routine and often the result of lengthy preplanning.

Secondly, there is deception as a part of communication designed to increase negative evaluation of opponents or competitors. This also employs promotional and brand differentiation (brand superiority) approaches drawn from the commercial sector, although political strategies often have a scope for "attack advertising" beyond that of conventional commercial activity. Again, this is a routine kind of deception and may often be the product of lengthy planning.

Thirdly, there is deception that is part of communication that is essentially reactive and that often has short planning periods, even to the extent of being spontaneous. This is often designed to decrease negativity following from either a) real world events or b) strategies as described in type two above, carried out by an opponent or competitor. Practices here are defined by their immediate link with the situation to which they are responding. They are a key area of deceptive work in modern politics, particularly in the form of denial. Denial embraces the various phrased (written or spoken, implicit or explicit) attempts to counter what has been suggested by others and which, were it to be true, would be damaging. Such suggestions include those regarding, for instance, personal relationships, policy agreements and disagreements, or knowledge of a specific circumstance or event. Denial of "knowledge of" is a widespread, established practice in many political systems.

In the case of all three of these broad "types," any deception may be preceded by a clear and considered appraisal of 1) the chances of the deception being detected and 2) the scale of the consequences of this detection, particularly if the charge of lying could cogently be lodged. However, the practices in type three run special risks of under-appraisal in both respects, given their likely character as short notice responses to occurring events or political moves by others. All three types have been encouraged in their intensity and scale of practice by the growing density and frequency of media-political relations, especially as conducted through political interviews and press statements. As politicians have been called upon to fill more media space more often with comments about their own and rivals' values, actions, and policy implications, the lure of deception has not only exerted a stronger pull but has become more deeply naturalized.

It is clear that the precise forms deception can take in all the instances above will vary widely. Elsewhere I have discussed the concept of propaganda and identified some of the more obvious modes through which almost all types of promotional behavior slide—perhaps sometimes plunge—into forms of deceit (Corner 2007). Following this model, the key modes seem to be as follows:

1. Lying. This is the deliberate construction and circulation of information known to be false, although it can be practiced across a scale ranging from the directly explicit statement to the merely suggestive implication. Of course, the term itself raises acute definitional issues around self-consciousness and intentionality that may complicate considerably attempts to "prove" a lie and certainly to win acceptance of this charge from the liar.

2. Exaggeration. This involves a distortive presentation of either positive or negative facts in a way that fits the position being promoted. What does and does not count as "distortion" will frequently be disputable against other accounts but in some cases it will be identifiable against verifiable data.

3. Strategic selectivity. This is the omission from an account of important information that works against the viewpoint being promoted. It can also involve the inclusion of material of questionable relevance that might nevertheless appear to lend support to the position being advanced. Nearly all promotional work involves strategic selectivity.

4. The withholding of information from public circulation. This can be part of a more systemic policy of censorship when exercised by public au-

thorities. It clearly overlaps with lying where denial is involved, as it frequently is in politics.

5. Explicit or covert affective appeals to desire or to fear, exerting persuasive force outside the terms of any logical argument. This is, of course, a defining feature of the language of advertising from its origins to its contemporary stylings.

6. Use of rhetorics of visual display and/or linguistic structure that seek to manage phatic contexts (e.g., those relating to trust through interpersonal relationships) and to organize the flow of meaning and value in ways not arising directly from the content of the communication. Again, this is a developed feature of advertising, although common in a range of interpersonal settings in which self-presentation is at issue.

It is possible to view this list in terms of a descending order of seriousness and possible consequences, although the categories of practice are frequently found in combination and can be seen to occur in cases both of spin (a category tending to give primary focus to exaggeration and selectivity) and propaganda (in which lying is often perceived to be a core practice, although not strictly a necessary one for the term to be applied). In relation to this, it is clear that while some of the practices listed above are so routine in everyday public promotional work as hardly to be noticeable (inside the relevant institutions, by journalists, or even by the public that gets to know about their use), the charge of lying is still considered in many contexts to be a serious one, grave enough in certain circumstances to cause irreparable political damage, as a range of cases in different countries would quickly illustrate.[4] It will be noticed that the last two items on my list are essentially stylistic practices, while the earlier ones are essentially substantive insofar as they involve management of the core information flow.

I think a list of this kind is an aid in helping us both to analyze and to judge examples of deception and to think about ways forward. Particular instances will require it to be both adapted and elaborated to provide a more refined reading, but it has a basic usefulness when combined with my earlier typology of three broad contexts for political deception. I shall discuss it further when I examine the different normative judgements made about current practice and the related issue of possible reform.

Before I turn from this analytical coordinate to another, historical one—that of practice in ancient Athens—I want to note how practices of political deception in electoral systems, particularly but not only around elections themselves, develop a particular and distinctive intensity. The interparty campaigning and the closeness of strategic planning that figure in nearly all political communication during these periods become much more obviously aligned with commercial practice as the competitive advertising of the political product becomes focal. This widely observed and commented-upon situation is one in which a license is extended, *de facto* if not *de jure,* to certain kinds of deception as part of the "fair game" of competitive pitching.[5] One dimension of the problem of deception in many countries has been the extension of this competitive, interparty framework for discourse to a much wider range of government-public communications outside of electoral periods (the widely used idea of the "permanent campaign" is relevant here) and its increasing naturalization across this range. Again, recognition of this factor would have to feature in any discussion of alternatives.

The Classical Example: Democratic Athens

I want briefly to draw on scholarship here in order to connect back to what is a key reference point for many writers on democratic deficit, albeit one routinely subject to "mythic" simplification: the political protocols of Athenian democracy. In his book, *Deception and Democracy in Classical Athens* (2000), Jon Hesk provides an illuminating account of political discourse in the shift from predemocratic to democratic contexts, in both cases exploring the character of elite–mass tensions and ways of resolving these.

In a fascinating note on Demosthenes, a fourth-century politician, Hesk observes how this leading figure regarded deceit by elites ("official deceit") as a major threat to democracies because these systems require mass debate and decision-making in a way that tyrannies do not (Demosthenes called democracy "a system based on speeches"). Hesk examines the way in which deception (*apate*), lies (*pseude*), and trickery (*dolos*) all appeared in Athenian texts as issues for discussion in relation to democratic practice. While in the pre-democratic period resorting to these tactics was seen as "an admirable facet of cunning intelligence" (Hesk 2000: 10), they are tactics increasingly put under pressure by the principles of democratic culture—despite the fact that many writers on the subject of propriety of discourse in democracy and the dangers of sophistry do not actually practice what they preach.

One of the most valuable points Hesk makes concerns the extent to which a continuing recognition of the benefits of military trickery complicates and impedes the debate about deceit within politics. This passage is worth quoting at length:

> The problematization of military trickery at Athens perhaps stems from the way in which the city put deceit to work ideologically. The Athenian is to define himself in opposition to the enemy who is "other" because the enemy trains and prepares for military deceit. How is this opposition to be maintained if the "ideal" Athenian citizen entertains such training himself? ...And yet the need to entertain military deceit did become more pressing because of the changed operational demands thrown up by the Peloponnesian War... (Hesk 2000: 292).

In addition to the "operational demands" in which deception designed to secure military advantage against the "other" becomes used as part of internal political communication, Hesk also notes attempts to identify kinds of "good lying" or "good fictions." These often focus on situations where deceit occurs in order to sustain and perhaps to boost civic morale and pride. So, for instance, when referring in public pronouncements to the earlier history of Athens, all skepticism about its long-abandoned and widely criticized religious practices is omitted in favor of a positive sense of continuity with the noble past. In a reference to the "nuance, anxiety and debate" that surrounded these practices, Hesk remarks that there was an attempt to distinguish "between a deceptive use of rhetoric which is centered on winning at all costs" and the use of persuasive tactics "in the service of responsible, honest advocacy which benefits the polis" (2000: 293). Again, this is a strikingly familiar idea across the ages, even allowing for the need not to be seduced into imagining too great a continuity across radically different political circumstances. Hesk himself draws clear conclusions:

> The Athenian representation of deceit has the potential to be politically instructive for modern Western democracy. Like Euripides' Hippolytus, our own citizens have been wrongly convicted by lies or the misapprehension of *who* is doing the lying. Like Demosthenes, our government ministers have attacked the dishonesty of some and yet justified deceit in certain contexts. Like Pericles, our representative elites do construct our national identity with reference to notions of "honesty and openness" and contrasting stereotypes of duplicitous "foreign" nations. And this construction helps to justify all manner of dubious adventures in foreign policy and to conduct even well intentioned adventures in an imperious manner (Hesk 2000: 295, emphasis in original).

Hesk's account helps further to demystify the idea of Athenian democracy as an exemplary model of practical virtue and, in the process, gives us a useful sense of the deeper problems surrounding politics, language, and truth.

Contemporary Deception: Analytic and Normative Commentary

I want now to return to the present and to examine some of the more recent ways in which political deception has been theorized and discussed. This has involved varying approaches to separating out the different kinds of deception, their relative levels of seriousness and the possibilities (if any) of moving beyond them.

In earlier writing on aspects of promotional culture, I noted the important contribution of Hannah Arendt to any serious analysis of lying in politics (Corner 2007). In particular, I cited from her essay on the Pentagon Papers, a body of official documents on the history and conduct of the Vietnam War (Arendt 1973). Developing points from her earlier ideas about political deceit (particularly Arendt [1961] 1993), she condemns the "non-truthfulness" which the Papers show to have been pervasive but sets this within a more general and complex sense of political deceit:

> Truthfulness has never been counted among the political virtues and lies have always been regarded as justifiable tools in political dealings. Whosoever reflects on these matters can only be surprised by how little attention has been paid, in our traditions of philosophical and political thought, to their significance... (Arendt 1973: 10).

With an eye for questions of political contingency and the pragmatic, she notes how "the lie did not creep into politics by some accident of human sinfulness. Moral outrage, for this reason alone, is not likely to make it disappear" (1973: 11). However, Arendt differentiates between the "ordinary lying" familiar to politics since ancient times and what she calls "organized lying." She regards the latter "industrialized" and often "professionalized" practice as introducing a new scale of political problem. For while ordinary lying seeks to conceal certain facts (including by denial, as I noted earlier) within the context of specific circumstances, allowing them perhaps to become available at a later date, "organized lying" seeks destruction rather than concealment. Its tendency is towards a major modification of, indeed a displacement of, reality, and she judges its rise with great concern.

Arendt offers an intellectually rich engagement with the dynamics of lying within political systems, including an examination of the links between core forms of political action and political subjectivity (the forms of political consciousness). Her account is clearly a critical one—she is appalled by the abuse of power which political deception involves—but it is also one that recognizes a certain level of the inevitable in relation to her topic. This recognition is historical as well as systemic. Its sense of the endemic connects back to the long history of politics as well as to its organizational and processual specificity as an area of human action.

Other writers have also identified the "inevitable" character of deception and addressed it with varying degrees of composure or disquiet.[6] Some, like Arendt, move on from this position to note levels of seriousness and to separate that deemed "inevitable" from that which is either partly remediable or (within certain conditions) open to elimination altogether, whatever its contemporary pervasiveness. The British political philosopher Glen Newey has conducted his own investigations into the political lie. In a 2003 report, he looks closely at incidents around British arms sales and foreign policy, specifically, the "Arms to Iraq" trade of the 1980s and the subsequent public inquiry into this. He extends his discussion beyond these points of reference to the general question of standards of truthfulness in public life. Newey works with a strong sense of the alienation of the public from political processes (a situation he calls *ressentiment*). This produces circumstances in which a culture of political deception flourishes, and "electoral competition between politicians or political parties generates expectations in the electorate, not all of which can be met" (Newey 2003a: 3.3). A paradoxical context emerges in which "demands for openness and accountability create a culture of suspicion and make it more likely that politicians will resort to evasion, misrepresentation and lies" (Newey 2003a: 3.31). In a phrase resounding with suggestiveness, he observes that the overall situation becomes one in which "discontent with democratic politics is both the cause and the consequence of political deception" (Newey 2003b). While he calls for greater critical attention to the principle of accountability and to the systems for applying it, in one of his most controversial comments he goes on to note that:

> Truthfulness is a contingent rather than absolute value in democracy. It is sometimes justifiable for a democratic polity to engage in collective acts of self-deception, because deceiving (including lying to) the public is sometimes justifiable... (Newey 2003a: 3.6).

And so:

> The public sometimes has a right to be lied to when legitimate democratic expectations place an obligation on the authorities to provide goods which can be secured only via mendacity (Newey 2003a: 3.6).

This proposition is not, of course, a blanket justification for political lying, but it is hardly surprising that it became a focus of attention when Newey's work was reported in the press following a news release by his funding agency.[7] Like Arendt, Newey cannot work comfortably with the idea of a politics in which deceit plays no part at all because such an idea is far too unrealistic in its grounding. His close analysis of political instances discounts total abolition as a serious aspiration and questions any proposed arrangements that would seek to achieve it. He is, however, absolutely clear that there are many examples of unacceptable deceptive behavior to which measures of control if not eradication should be applied. For instance, he calls for action to be taken against the tactical ambiguity employed by both politicians and public servants in situations where the speaker knows the (wrong) meaning the public is likely to take (he classifies this as a form of lying). Although he examines a range of ethical objections to present practice, however, he does not present his case within the framework of a general political critique, like Arendt, but as part of a more "objective" analytic inquiry into political behavior within a given system and its normative contradictions.

More recently, another writer has provocatively raised not only the "inevitability" factor in deception, but also the (selective) case for "desirability." This is the Cambridge political scientist David Runciman. In his study, *Political Hypocrisy* (2008), he concentrates on a specific form of deception, focusing on the personal "hypocritical" behavior of leading politicians rather than on the institutionalized practices that I have been reviewing here. Runciman points to the complexity of his central term: it might involve saying one thing and doing another (a familiar charge against the political elite), or it might involve saying different things according to specific contexts (and therefore according to "role"). Hypocrisy, he notes, always consists of an "element of pretense" and a "kind of lie" (2008: 9), though not a lie explicitly rendered in the manner of institutionalized misinformation. It is essentially theatrical and can be seen to involve the use of a "mask."

Runciman shares with Newey, and to a certain extent with Arendt, a recognition and acceptance of how the specific contexts of politics as a practice, including the play of discourse across antagonisms and mutually incompatible settings, will necessarily involve deception. He regards 24/7 media as inevitably encouraging more hypocrisy since politicians are required to account for themselves and to justify past, current, and future actions in greater detail, more frequently, and through more intensive spoken interaction with various interlocutors (including professional interviewers) than in the past. Like the two other writers, he thinks identifying the most "harmful" forms is more important than blanket condemnation and attempts at total eradication. He aligns far more strongly with Newey than Arendt in his willingness to claim the functional benefits of certain kinds of deception or insincerity within democratic politics, and to note the risks of imposing the idea that politicians must be entirely consistent in their views and expressed values across all their various roles and contexts of operation. A "role performance" involving inconsistencies of account that are identifiable as hypocrisy can actually serve democratic political effectiveness, Runciman argues. At its lower levels (perhaps, for example, at the level of the routine gathering of support for policy initiatives across diverse constituencies or of addressing issues to different interest groups), it is a necessary feature of successful political performance and even of practical democratic accountability. Only at a certain point, assessable in relation to the issue concerned and to the scale of the deception involved, does it become a matter for criticism and for alternatives.

I have not done justice to Runciman's careful study of the history of commentary on hypocrisy "from Hobbes to Orwell" nor to the subtlety by which he explores variations in "the masks of power," but I think it is useful to bring his work into my discussion. It is a recent, striking example of an approach that neither quietly ignores the magnitude of the problem of political deception nor handles it by categoric denunciation.

Continuities and Changes: Some Key Issues Outlined

From the main themes discussed above, it is possible to draw up an inventory of points. First of all, I present an inventory of the present situation that might be generally accepted (if only in broad terms) as indicating some key features of institutionalized deception. These might then connect with a further set of points about the principal issues of continuing disagreement, issues that will inform further research and debate as well as political and social critique and calls for change.

Key Features of Institutionalized Deception

- Political and public agencies have increasingly drawn from the full range of advertising and commercial promotional practices (including marketing and branding strategies) in their approach to communicating with the public. This has occurred not only at the level of practices but also of the recruitment and training of communications personnel.

- Political claims-making and related institutional publicity have increasingly played into intensive systems of media relay within the 24/7 profile, some elements of which have been (in different national settings) compliant and supportive of these strategies and some of which have been critical. The pitch to the media has started to become of greater importance than the pitch to the public directly, even though the web may be marginally changing this situation. Strategies of "winning," and indeed of "forming," public opinion (sometimes only to the minimum levels necessary for political decisions to be "carried") have become dominant over attempts to protect and use public space for the full deliberation of policy issues.
- A certain level of deception and hypocrisy is seen by some commentators to be endemic to the business of politics, particularly within the realm of high politics itself and in the conduct of interparty competition. For instance, democratic elections are aligned closely in their communicative profile with commercial advertising campaigns. There has been a tendency in many countries for the campaign frame to become installed as the permanent frame not only for interparty exchange but also for communications from the political elite to the public.
- One consequence of the factors identified above has been frequent resort to forms of deception in public life, with the use of forms of denial become virtually naturalized as a dimension of political discourse. Deception has not only occurred in elite-public communications, it has also been a feature of inter-elite communications (as, for instance, between various departments and agencies of state including, notoriously, between intelligence agencies and other areas of executive power).

What Problems Has This Posed for Critique or Change?

- One problem for critics has been deciding where "to draw the line." This is a line between conduct that might be considered either inevitable or excusable (even if regrettable) and conduct that is unacceptable to the democratic process and therefore must be restricted and perhaps penalized. The term "propaganda" has been widely used to signal a self-evidently unacceptable form of public communication (although it also has a history of positive usage within developing modernity).[8] By contrast, it is clear that across many areas of public and corporate life, the word promotion (often linked with the idea of publicity) signals what is judged to be a necessary dimension of the routine seeking of advantage and opportunity. When subject to close communicational analysis (drawing on a typology similar to the one I sketched earlier), in many instances it is not at all clear what the difference might be between the practices gathered under these two headings.[9] The word "spin" has over the last two decades often been applied to political communication by commentators and journalists in order to indicate forms of devious practice, not quite conforming to desired levels of integrity. Applied to corporate publicity it would be a superfluous term, since what it implies about selectivity and the relentless, strategic prioritizing of the positive are largely admitted to be accepted imperatives of communication in that sphere. However, even in the political sphere, spin has now become increasingly naturalized as routine, with only gross instances of it receiving critical media attention.

- Uncertainty over where to "draw the line" leads to problems not only at the level of practical intervention (an obvious and longstanding obstacle) but also at the level of formulating a more coherent ethics of public discourse. Such an ethical code, in order to be cogent and effective, has to be robust in relation to the possibilities of compromise, inconsistency and contradiction that follow from its positioning within the contexts of societies extensively defined by their competitive commercialism and related discursive standards and habits.
- Close to the heart of the issue are continuing difficulties surrounding the idea of "publicity." This notion has made a long journey from its eighteenth-century use by Kant to indicate the new, enabling possibilities for the exercising of public reason and for the wider "visibility" of political opinion that followed from the increased circulation of printed publications, through to its present use in many contexts as a synonym for "hype." We can see the deformation of the idea of publicity within the institutional contingencies and power relations of modern politics as absolutely central to the problem of modern public communications. However, in noting this deformation, as in using Habermas's idea of the public sphere to plot deficits in political communicational space (Habermas 1989 provides the key reference here), we must remember that we are placing a political idea against a political reality and that the reali-

ties of Kant's political contexts and the realities of the eighteenth-century British society whose intellectual culture was found so suggestive by Habermas were not self-evidently preferable to our own. In fact, the reverse judgement is firmer. Moreover, it is a much remarked paradox that in the eighteenth-century point of reference it was precisely the mechanisms of the market and of competitive exchange that were seen to give public discourse a new freedom from the distorting controls of sovereign privilege and established state interests.

Where to from Here?

I have attempted to offer some diverse points of reference with the aim of positioning current political deception within its history and within the much larger map of contemporary promotionalism. If there is a danger, and many believe that there is, in the way that political and public practice now reflects so much of contemporary promotional culture, its dynamics of competitive marketing and its attitudes towards its addressees, how can we best go about identifying this danger in ways which engage public attention and carry the possibility of action? How far can the structures and processes of democracy be insulated from the crosscurrents of strategic publicity within which they are currently embedded? I have pointed to the continuity of deception as a feature of many different political cultures historically. I have also drawn on theoretical writings in which the question of the levels and types of deception is raised in the context of the recognition that politics as a sphere of activity involves a certain irreducible level of untruthfulness. Runciman, in quoting the eighteenth-century philosopher Jeremy Bentham on the "utility of fiction" in politics, notes that "Bentham's struggles suggest an important truth about democracy, that it has some necessary fictions at its heart, and if we try too hard to circumvent them, we will end up talking cant" (2008: 141). However, even if agreement could be reached on this provocative point, separating out what we might be prepared to view as areas of "necessary fiction," of "allowable" rhetorical excess, from the damaging strategic deceptiveness of much current political claims-making would still be an important task.

I have identified interparty rivalry as a major source of the dynamics of deception in many political systems. But it is also an important source of control, insofar as the imperative of unmasking your opponent, of revealing the inconsistency and the untruth of their claims, is a key strategy of political competition. Nevertheless, it seems clear that, in many political systems, other mechanisms for the public audit of political claims-making need now to be introduced, even if devising them in such a way as to make them practical and effective presents a major challenge. The media still play an important audit role in many countries, although their nature as variously propagandist agencies of the state and as branches of the entertainment industry complicate and sometimes displace this function. Whatever the specific pattern here, the performance of both old and new media in their reporting and discussion of political publicity (including forms of policy-related and personalized "branding") will continue to be a crucial part of both the projection and the blocking of deception as a strategy of political discourse. The reporting, on both sides of the Atlantic, of the financial crisis of 2008—its origins, trajectory, and management—gives a further opportunity to survey this performance and set it alongside other recent major areas of coverage, notably the "war on terror" and climate change, in which deceptive strategies of different kinds are playing a major role. Steady intensification of the media coverage of politicians and political claims-making has introduced increased requirements upon politicians to account for their actions in different media modes and thereby increased the opportunities for, and both the attractiveness and the risks of, deceptive practice of varying kinds.

It is worth remarking here on the distinctive nature of the promotionalism–product relation as it works in politics, in order to note the differences from other forms of publicity and branding as well as the connections. It has often been remarked that promotional strategies can only be successful in conjunction with a "good product," since consumer experience will work to counteract these strategies in the case of faulty or poor exemplars. In relation to some products, particularly those involving health risks, this is by no means as clear-cut as it can be made to sound (i.e., the widespread perception of specific product deficits cannot be guaranteed). In relation to politics, the idea is even more open to question, since determining precisely what the "product" of politics is, in a way that makes it open to clear consumer judgement against established criteria, immediately becomes a complex and uncertain business in most instances. Policy outcomes, unless they are unanimously judged to be disastrous, are products of a much less clearly assessable kind than, say, cars, refrigerators and computers. In that sense, political promotion has weaker lines of consumer accountability than those which, in the commercial world, follow directly from product use.

What is absolutely certain, however, is that a normative shift in current practice brought about by indignation or by repeated calls for politicians to "tell the truth" will not occur. Just as deception is institutionalized into the structures of political systems it afflicts, so institutional changes will have to be a key part of any reform. This is a matter which requires urgent public attention. In the meantime, researchers must continue the vigorous exposure and critique, the "blowing up," of those many examples of deception which serve to undercut core democratic values, enforce wrong decisions both in domestic and foreign policy, and bring politics into ever closer alignment with commodity marketing.

Notes

1. Recognition of this broader background against which the analysis of forms of political lying has to be carried out is also usefully made in Alterman (2004).
2. The kinds of promotional practice seen to be at work in this series show considerable "artfulness" in producing positive presentations and responses for the White House, sometimes against the odds, but very little significant deceit of the public. See Richardson (2006) for detailed examination of particular examples from selected episodes in relation to the ethical and professional world portrayed.
3. See Peter Oborne (2005) who, as well as arguing for the significance of its impact upon democratic culture, sees the recent growth of political lying almost exclusively in terms of the practice of Britain's New Labour government since 1997. This may finally be too partisan a perspective, since the continuity with episodes in the life of previous Conservative governments, particularly concerning foreign policy, also deserves attention.
4. In the UK, the example of Tony Blair in relation to the doubtful intelligence information upon which he made the case for the invasion of Iraq in 2003 has continuing resonance. At one point, the deliberate misspelling of his name as "Bliar" was widespread in sections of popular culture, including on T-shirts. In the United States, both Nixon and Clinton, in very different circumstances, saw consequences follow from the judgement that they had resorted to deliberate deception when questioned on matters of significance. Many European countries (including Italy, France, and the Irish Republic) have had recent scandals involving serious deceit by senior political figures that has been damaging, if not always fatal, to the careers of those involved.
5. The way in which electoral competition encourages ideas derived from commercial marketing about "how far you can go" in positive and negative claims-making is discussed in a number of academic studies. See Kavanagh (1995) on the British situation and Thurber and Nelson (2009) on American contexts.
6. Among those writers, apart from those mentioned in the main text, who have given the issue a primary focus, Macintyre (1994) is worth noting as a broad and suggestive philosophical treatment; Cliffe, Ramsay, and Bartlett (2000) and Oborne (2005) are useful critical studies concerning UK politics; and Alterman (2004) provides a detailed, comparative examination of presidential deception.
7. An example here would be Hinsliff (2003) in *The Guardian* newspaper.

8. See, for instance, the assessments of Harold Lasswell (1934), much influenced by the thinking of John Dewey.
9. Corner (2007) provides a more extensive discussion of this point.

References

Alterman, Eric. 2004. *When Presidents Lie: A History of Official Deception and Its Consequences.* New York: Viking Books.

Arendt, Hannah. [1961] 1993. "Truth and Politics." Reprinted in H. Arendt, *Between Past and Future.* Harmondsworth: Penguin.

———. 1973. "Lying in Politics." Pp. 9–42 in H. Arendt, *Crises of the Republic.* Harmondsworth: Penguin.

Cliffe, Lionel, Maureen Ramsay, and Dave Bartlett. 2000. *The Politics of Lying: Implications for Democracy.* London: Palgrave Macmillan.

Corner, John. 2007. "Mediated Politics, Promotional Culture and the Idea of 'Propaganda.'" *Media, Culture and Society* 29 (4): 669–677.

Davis, Mike. 2008. "Can Obama See the Grand Canyon? On Presidential Blindness and Economic Catastrophe." TomDispatch.com, October 15. http://www.tomdispatch.com/post/174989/mike_davis_casino_capitalism_obama_and_us (accessed June 2009).

Habermas, Jurgen. 1989. *Structural Transformation of the Public Sphere.* Cambridge: Polity.

Hesk, Jon. 2000. *Deception and Democracy in Classical Athens.* Cambridge: Cambridge University Press.

Hinsliff, Gaby. 2003. "Truth Is, Politicians Just Can't Help Lying." *Observer,* September 18. http://www.guardian.co.uk/politics/2003/may/18/research.highereducation (accessed January 2010).

Kavanagh, Denis. 1995. *Election Campaigning: The New Marketing of Politics.* Oxford: Blackwell.

Lasswell, Harold. 1934. "Propaganda." Pp. 521–528 in *Encyclopedia of the Social Sciences,* ed. E. Seligman and A. Johnson. Vol. 12. New York: Macmillan.

Macintyre, Alasdair. 1994. *Truthfulness, Lies, and Moral Philosophers: What Can We Learn from Mill and Kant?* Princeton University Tanner Lectures on Human Values. http://www.tannerlectures.utah.edu/lectures/documents/macintyre_1994.pdf (accessed January 2010).

Newey, Glen. 2003a. *Full Report on Research Activities and Results.* Report on "Truth and Deception in Democratic Politics." United Kingdom: Economic and Social Research Council.

———. 2003b. "Politicians Being Economical with the Truth Is the Price of a Healthy Democracy?" Press Release on "Truth and Deception in Democratic Politics," May 18. United Kingdom: Economic and Social Research Council.

Oborne, Peter. 2005. *The Rise of Political Lying.* London: The Free Press.

Richardson, Kay. 2006. "The Dark Arts of Good People: How Popular Culture Negotiates Spin in NBC's *The West Wing.*" *Journal of Sociolinguistics* 10 (1): 52–69.

Runciman, David. 2008. *Political Hypocrisy.* Princeton, N.J.: Princeton University Press.

Thurber, James A., and Candice J. Nelson. 2009. *Campaigns and Elections American Style.* 3rd Edition. Boulder, Co.: Westview Press.

CHAPTER FOUR

The Consuming Self

From Flappers to Facebook[1]

Jefferson Pooley

This chapter argues that we ought to revisit a rich, half-neglected tradition of thinking on the twentieth century consuming self. This includes figures like David Riesman, Philip Rieff, Daniel Bell, Warren Susman, Erich Fromm, Jackson Lears, and Christopher Lasch. Their accounts overlap; they clash too, but in revealing ways. They do not form anything like a self-conscious school, but there are family resemblances among them. At the very least, this body of work is good to think with, but it is my stronger claim that when read charitably, in an imagined conversation with one another, they have identified the contradiction that is at the core of the modern American self. That contradiction could be summed up as: Be true to yourself; it is to your strategic advantage.

In describing this self, some of the thinkers—Lears, Rieff, Bell, and Lasch especially—stress the new yearning for individual self-fulfillment through authentic experience. We are called on, say Lears and the others, to embark on quests of self-discovery that promise to affirm our uniqueness. This deeply felt demand is tapped into, but also intensified and rechanneled, by the self-improvement industries and especially advertising. For Lears and the others, the consumer-culture form that self-fulfillment takes on is shot through with contradiction. It is shallow, narcissistic, and not at all authentic.

Some of the other thinkers invoked here—notably Fromm and Riesman—place the accent elsewhere: on performance. They show how we are called upon to stage-manage the impressions we give off to others as the essential toolkit for success. Whether a passing conversation or the lifelong stewardship of one's "brand," we face an injunction to present our selves in a flattering light. As Fromm draws out most vividly, this involves a certain detachment from oneself, as a project to be managed and promoted. To Fromm and Riesman, we are all marketers and salesmen.

There are obvious tensions between these two injunctions: to find and express your true self but also to carefully curate your impressions. Each of the thinkers invoked above—whether they stress performance or self-fulfillment—registers this tension. Perhaps Warren Susman's account of what he calls the "culture of personality" best captures the self's Janus-faced aspect: as early as the 1920s, Susman (1979) argues, the new "personality" ideal joined yearning for authentic experience to calculated self-promotion, with a focus on the conscious staging of an attractive exterior.

Promotion and authenticity are deeply interwoven into the fabric of the ideal American self, even if they make for an oxymoronic coupling. The thinkers referred to above do make this point, but they do not really trace the "prehistory"—nor the ongoing dynamism—of these dueling injunctions. For that prehistory, we might turn to Charles Taylor's (1989) account of the self's sources; and to Lionel Trilling (1972) for the dynamism.

The contradiction between self-promotion and expressive distinction, bound up as it is with a highly adaptive market economy, is in fact self-feeding. That is, the pervasiveness of what might be called "calculated authenticity" leads, as Trilling shows, to rejectionist forms of authenticity—*real* authenticity, untainted by the professional smile and the glad hand. These flights to deeper kinds of authenticity are, however, marketed in turn—returned, that is, to the promotional fold. The result can be thought of as an "authenticity bind," as I discuss below.

In the conclusion, this analysis is applied to Facebook, the social networking site founded in 2004. The self that is performed on Facebook is beset by the same dueling injunctions that Lears and the rest identify with the rise of a consumer culture. Facebook is especially fit for the arts of expressive self-performance; indeed, this chapter highlights some of its distinct aspects, including the fact that performer and audience are mutually aware of the performance *as* performance. On Facebook, self-disclosure is by definition managed, and we all know it. It's the song of myself, but with the lyrics tapped out very carefully. It is, with apologies to Lewis Hyde, extroversion with a motive. In the artful profile photo, in the status update witticism, we find the same contradiction between authenticity and promotion—only intensified.

The Cultural Contradictions of Consumerism

There is something absurd about the sheer number of adjectives that scholars have affixed to the word "self": commodity, therapeutic, other-directed, plural, postmodern, protean, empty, belabored, branded, performing, market, minimal, narcissistic. There are others: punctual, expressive, dramatized, homeless, consuming. It's a messy, cross-disciplinary literature, and the temptation to fasten yet another adjective onto that inviting word can be overpowering—if only to impose some order on a topic of extraordinary complexity. The half-neologisms abound, each new one getting lost in a Babel-like din—which, paradoxically, offers a license for thesis overreach.

This chapter isolates just two strands of an impossibly tangled yarn of selfhood. Even *that* twisted mess, if it could be untangled, is particular—a product of a specific history, the modern West's, and, in the form under discussion here, the United States. To take the point further: this mode of selfhood wasn't lodged in each and every American's head from birth. Most of the figures referred to here describe the ways that particular aspects of this self emerged first among the relatively well off, and then trickled down unevenly over the course of the twentieth century. The chapter mainly discusses the self in an ungendered way, without reference to other kinds of difference—and without considering the effects of migration and contact with non-Western modes of selfhood.[2]

Qualified in this way, the history of American consumer culture helps to explain some of the contradictions of self-fulfillment. In particular, there is that body of literature produced from the late 1940s to the early 1980s: Erich Fromm's *Man for Himself* (1947), David Riesman's *The Lonely Crowd* (1950), Philip Rieff's *The Triumph of the Therapeutic* (1966), Daniel Bell's *The Cultural Contradictions of Capitalism* (1976), Christopher Lasch's *The Culture of Narcissism* (1978), Warren Susman's "'Personality' in the Making of Twentieth Century Culture" (1979), and Jackson Lears's *No Place of Grace* (1981). These authors are nearly all sociologists and historians, whose books were very often bestsellers though unevenly influential. With the partial exceptions of Susman and Lears, none of them is much read anymore. They advance broadly resonant arguments, though they are not anything like a self-conscious school. If it's a tradition, it is a partially invented and fractious one. But there are traceable lines of influence.

What the authors have in common is a loosely overlapping argument about the emergence, in twentieth-century America, of a "therapeutic ethos."[3] An older culture—normally placed in the nineteenth century—had emphasized thrift, restraint, and self-control. It was a "bootstrapist" ideal of delayed gratification—the Protestant ethic so aptly summarized in Benjamin Franklin's ([1793] 2003) list of 13 virtues. By the 1920s, a new individualism had supplanted the denialist ideal, one focused on self-realization and expressions of vitality. This "gospel of self-fulfillment," as Rieff (1966: 251) called it, preached release and psychic health.

Common to all these works is the claim that social structure and character are bound up with one another—a major theme of the undergraduate University of Chicago course that Rieff, Bell, and Riesman taught together in the late 1940s and early 1950s.[4] The shift, in particular, from an economy oriented around production to one dependent on consumption—nineteenth-century scarcity to twentieth-century abundance—is crucial for each account. A new, aspirational advertising culture adopted and adapted the spirit of self-fulfillment for its promotion of consumer goods. The drive to realize oneself was not confined to consumption as such but found expression across a range of twentieth-century cultural phenomena: in pop psychology, liberal Protestantism, entertainment media, celebrity worship, and self-help literature. The authors writing in the 1970s and early 1980s saw the self-fulfillment ideal in aspects of the New Left, in the counterculture, in the human-potential movement, in management literature, and in the spread of New Age spirituality. The old producerist ethic had long since been replaced by the credit card and the bikini.

This "therapeutic ethos" tradition is very keen to point to the ways that our twentieth-century questing for self-fulfillment is shot through with contradiction. As Lears and the rest want to say, so much of our seeking after personal meaning ends up in the consumption of "fulfillment" that's prepackaged, mass-produced, and shallow. We assemble our identities with the colorful, store-bought baubles of the consumer culture and channel our energies into prettifying our exteriors. What's worse is that much of this self-absorption is taken up as a strategic command: you will succeed if you carefully cultivate a charming persona. As Bell, Susman, and the rest see it, we are very far indeed from the authentic self-realization that is the culture's stated ideal.

Yet there is one glaring mismatch among these works, on the important question of explanation. That is, what exactly brought about the transition from self-denial to self-gratification? The weakest accounts rely on an underarticulated functionalism—the idea that new social and economic orders somehow generate just that modal self that suits them best. Rieff blames errant, libertine intellectuals. Riesman points to large-scale demographic shifts. Some of the authors—notably Lasch and Bell—aren't even internally consistent about what has driven the shift. Nearly all of them, however, at least gesture toward the experience of rapid and disorienting social change in the late nineteenth and early twentieth centuries; for Lears and Susman, especially, this is the primary factor.

They have in mind the whole bundle of social changes often summed up as the transition from *Gemeinschaft* to *Gesellschaft*. The rise of the bureaucratic state, with its rational-legal tentacles. The late industrial revolution, with the uprooting of primary communities—"whole populations conjured out of the ground," as Marx put it—bound for the city and the factory floor ([1848] 2002]: 225). Social life increasingly governed by contract, exchange, and expediency—Carlyle's "cash nexus" ([1839] 1971]: 199). The sped-up pace of life, helped along by rapid technological change from the railroad to the telegraph. The explosion of visual stimuli brought on by new image technologies like the photograph and the motion picture—Daniel Boorstin's (1962) "graphic revolution." A new national market, populated by transcontinental corporations, financial institutions, and department stores. Though with much longer and more complicated histories, the claims, too, of scientific rationality and the decline in religious certainty—what Max Weber referred to as the "disenchantment of the world" (1946: 155).

It is the *experience* of living through these changes that Susman, Lears, and the others count as significant. Especially the pace of change itself: the ceaseless flux of modern life generated by a world without clear limits yielded disorientation, anomie, and unease. The new prominence of impersonal exchange and faceless bureaucracy gave rise to a sense of impotence, amplified by the jostle of urban life. As Georg Simmel observed, the city brought on an "intensification of nervous stimulation," and with it "swift and uninterrupted change of outer and inner stimuli" ([1903] 1950: 410). To Lears especially, these conditions, along with the loosening grip of religion, generated a sense of weightlessness and unreality, mainly among the upper classes.

The claim by Lears et al. is that the older, fixed ethic of self-control could not cope with the new anxiety. A yearning for intense, vital experience—often but not always articulated in personal terms—was expressed around the turn of the century in a number of places, including liberal Protestantism, the new therapeutic professions, and (in the early years of the twentieth century) on film screens and in the dance halls. A growing consumer economy harnessed itself to this longing for personal fulfillment, in part by speaking to public anxieties in the language of story-driven advertising. The result was the "democratization of desire," as William Leach calls it (1993: 4–5)—a kind of unfulfilling fulfillment in which felt needs are only momentarily sated, and require still more short-lived relief in endless cycles of consumption and surface-level reinvention.

It is worth talking about this "therapeutic ethos" tradition because I believe they got it mostly right. Lasch and the others are correct, in part, that we have been rolling around in a more or less shallow mud-pit of debased self-fulfillment for almost a hundred years.[5] They are also right in their claim that the anxieties and weightlessness of turn-of-the-century life produced a yearning for personal meaning—and they are right, too, that a consumer-driven market economy responded, in profitable ways, to those intensely felt needs.

But the "therapeutic ethos" tradition also got it wrong; in certain respects they went too far, and in others they did not go far enough. They went too far because they largely ignore the way in which that nineteenth-century ethic of self-denial, and the twentieth-century drive for self-fulfillment are both genuine moral ideals. These ethics have a long history, and they continue to resonate as moral ideals—not as the products of a J. Walter Thompson bull session.

The "therapeutic ethos" theorists did not go far *enough* because they did not consider key implications of the self-fulfillment culture's contradictions. In his 1989 magnum opus *Sources of the Self*, Taylor provides a sweeping and astonishingly rich account of the development of the Western self. His method is perhaps too dependent on exemplary thinkers—Montaigne shouting, across the valley of centuries, to Rousseau—but he insists, and mostly follows through, on his claim that the currents he is following are often generated in, and manifest themselves at, the level of everyday life (see Taylor: Ch. 12).

Taylor identifies two powerful moral ideals that have evolved out of the history of the modern West, especially since the seventeenth century. The two ideals—self-responsible freedom and expressivism—map on very nicely to that nineteenth-century ethic of self-mastery and the twentieth-century self-fulfillment imperative, respectively.

Taylor traces the first ideal, of self-responsible freedom, to Rene Descartes and his crucial detachment of the self from the body and the rest of the material world. Only by looking inward, to the rational mind, can we secure knowledge and proof of God's existence. To Taylor, the next important step was John Locke's and involved extending disengagement and control to one's own self. This ideal of self-objectification is what C. B. Macpherson (1962), in a nastier tone, refers to as "possessive individualism," which he also finds exemplified in Locke. This ideal of disengaged, self-responsible freedom informed the radical Enlightenment and various strands of liberal thought and stresses our dignity as self-transforming agents.

The other ideal, expressivism, depended too on the turn inward, but emerged in the late eighteenth and early nineteenth centuries in part as a reaction *against* disengaged rationality. The ideal, anticipated by Rousseau but fully articulated by German Romantics like Johann Herder, depends on the idea that we have inner depths that are unique to each of us. In order to discover my originality, I need to explore these depths and express—give voice to—what I find there. "Being true to myself means being true to my own originality," summarizes Taylor, "and that is something only I can articulate and discover" (1992: 28–29). Taylor calls this "expressivism," or the ethic of authenticity—and in his view that ideal animates the twentieth-century culture of self-fulfillment, including what he calls its "most degraded, absurd, or trivialized forms" (29).

There is a reason—or really a pair of reasons—why this back story matters. First, thinking about authenticity as a pre-existing moral ideal fills a hole in the story told by the therapeutic ethos tradition: in those accounts, the drive for self-fulfillment comes off as always already debased and seems—despite impressive intellectual gymnastics—to come out of nowhere. A more convincing explanation is that an already resonant moral ideal, expressivism, was adapted to cope with the wrenching social change that Lears and Susman describe. The expressivist ideal—giving voice to one's uniqueness—offered a solution to the problems of anonymity and the cash nexus. What's missing in Taylor is what Lasch and the rest provide: an account of how and why the drive to realize oneself came, in fact, to be trivialized.

The second reason why the back story matters is that, as Taylor points out, reports of the Protestant ethic's death have been greatly exaggerated, certainly by Lasch and the others. We are indeed, as Bell himself concedes with puzzlement, "workers by day and swingers by night" (1979: xxv).

It is my view that the two ideals—the expressivist and the possessive—are locked in a tight embrace, and that the market has a bear hug around both. The result is that we are asked to find ourselves but at the same time to work on ourselves. The injunction to explore and realize one's true self is hopelessly mixed up with the demand to treat oneself as an object. There is an obvious contradiction here. The culture's advice often takes this form: the best way to work on yourself is to consciously cultivate an authentic persona. Authenticity, in other words, is presented as a means to the end of promotion. The result is a potent and contradictory cocktail of self-promotion and expressive distinction, stirred by the self-improvement industries, the therapeutic professions, and especially advertising. This is why, everywhere we look, we see instances of what I call *calculated authenticity.*

If this is right, it helps explain an otherwise puzzling tension in the "therapeutic ethos" tradition. Many of the authors, notably Lears, Bell, Rieff, and Lasch, highlight self-absorption and even solipsism—the "pursuit of happiness to the dead end of a narcissistic preoccupation with the self," in Lasch's words (1978: 21).

But another strand in the tradition, best represented by Fromm and Riesman, points instead to a heightened sensitivity to *others*—not to one's self. Fromm (1947) calls it the "marketing orientation," and he means that we are called on to sell ourselves on the "personality market"—to develop those features which "can best be sold" (69, 77). This quality results from our experience of ourselves, Fromm says, as "the seller *and* the commodity to be sold" (70). Riesman's concept of "other-direction" is an admitted reformulation of Fromm's "marketing personality," though shorn of its Marxist roots.[6] Riesman's "other-directed" type, who he takes to be dominant, has a finely calibrated radar to pick up others' signals, and adjusts his behavior accordingly.

These two strands of the "therapeutic ethos" tradition reflect the two sides of that tight embrace mentioned above: to promote oneself, but as an attractive and sincere being. Warren Susman, alone among the "therapeutic ethos" scholars, brings these two strands together in his classic 1979 article. He contrasts a nineteenth-century "culture of character" with a twentieth-century "culture of personality," by comparing what we would call self-help literature from the late 1800s with the teens and twenties. In the first period he finds words like "work," "duty," and "integrity" throughout the advice manuals, but by the 1920s a new vocabulary—"fascinating," "glowing," "creative"—had taken its place. The new self-help literature instructed readers to stage-manage an attractive front, through grooming, dress, and a charming personality. Susman summarizes the new message: "One is to be unique, be distinctive, follow one's own feelings, make oneself stand out from the crowd, and at the same time appeal—by fascination, magnetism and attractiveness—to it" (289). It is, of course, a contradictory message, but a pervasive one—and arguably the main theme of twentieth-century advertising.

Calculated Authenticity and Its Discontents

Nowhere is the blend of strategic performance with the trappings of authenticity on more vivid display than in Dale Carnegie's 1936 *How to Win Friends and Influence People*, which remains in print today after 16 million sales. Under the banner "Six ways to make people like you," Carnegie instructs readers to "Become genuinely interested in other people," and to "Make the other person feel important—and do it sincerely" ([1936] 1982: 105). This is what I have been calling calculated authenticity. It's the glad hand; it's what David Foster Wallace called the "professional smile" (1996: 43n15). It's the off-the-cuff joke that's rehearsed. It's being, in short, instrumental about authenticity. Think of Apple's "Here's to the Crazy Ones" ads,[7] or Pepsi's Obama-knock-off bus wraps, complete with "Hope" and "Together" in the proper font. Calculated authenticity is marketing Burt's Bees as mom-and-pop long after it's part of Clorox (Whitfill 2009). It's Tom Peters exhorting his readers to imitate the black church. It's Steven Covey imploring managers to recognize employees as "whole persons" rather than as "things"—because things take time and money to motivate.[8] It's the normalization of plastic surgery. It's what Arlie Hochschild (1983) has called "emotional labor"—training employees to act perky, for example. It's promoting already signed artists on YouTube with grainy, living-room video, as Hollywood Records has done recently (Smith and Lattman 2007). It's stealth person-to-person marketing. Even the "benign fabrications" (Goffman 1974: 87) that we are compelled to make in everyday interaction—the shifting, audience-dependent performances that we enact dozens of times a week—force us all, arguably, into the role of bit-part gladhanders.[9]

Here's where Trilling comes in. His 1972 book *Sincerity and Authenticity* is a brilliant meditation on *deep* authenticity, which he sees as a flight from the inauthentic sort. As he writes,

> Society requires of us that we present ourselves as being sincere, and the most efficacious way of satisfying this demand is to see to it that we really are sincere, that we actually are what we want our community to know we are. In short, we play the role of being ourselves, we sincerely act the part of the sincere person, with the result that a judgment may be passed upon our sincerity that it is not authentic (10).

What Trilling captures is the disgust that all the bad faith provokes. Deep authenticity, he argues, is a rejectionist ideal—a "cosmic defiance" of the "coercive inauthenticity of society" (99, 168). His view is that the reaction can take two distinct forms. The first is to reject society outright—to deal "aggressively with received and habitual opinion" (94). He points to the "mocking laughter" (130) of some modernist art, as well as the extremist offshoots of New Left protest. There is something nihilist and violent—a psychopathic and Promethean isolation—in the repudiation that deep authenticity calls for (167–168).

Trilling is much more accepting of the second kind of response, an ultimately serious form of irony. He calls it the "doctrine of masks," which he reads in Oscar Wilde's playful dismissals of sincerity (118–120). "Man is least himself when he talks in his own person," said Wilde. "Give him a mask and he will tell you the truth" (qtd. in Trilling 1972: 119). The idea is that irony, with its engaged disengagement, is more authentic than the sincere expression of insincerity.

Trilling's account of deep authenticity helps us to understand the range of responses to what we might think of as the colonization of the apparently earnest. We can build on his insights without assuming, as Trilling seems to, that the rejectionist impulse need issue in the Weathermen or the embrace of insanity. Softer forms of rejection are all around us, most notably in various youth subcultures. Indie college radio, or the rave scene that Sarah Thornton (1996) studied, draw on a vocabulary of deep authenticity—identities contingent on a contrast with a mainstream "sellout" culture. There is a "community of the saved," last remnant character to many subcultures but without the cult of holy madness that Trilling fears.

Trilling also helps us to re-interpret the pervasive ironic stance in American cultural life in deep authenticity terms. The irony we encounter isn't necessarily as high-minded as Oscar Wilde's, but even the "air quotes" sarcasm, as Joshua Glenn (1998) calls it, of much hipster culture can be read as a defensive gesture—a fear of being taken in by the apparently earnest.

For all of Trilling's insight, it is perhaps less important to fret over rejectionist nihilism than over the market's uncanny ability to incorporate these softer forms of deep authenticity. As Thomas Frank (1997a, 1997b, 2000) has shown in his hilarious and sobering send-ups of "liberation marketing," capitalism rides these waves of dissent because restless innovation and the great refusal, properly filtered, bolster the bottom line. Dionysus is welcomed with enthusiasm into the boardroom, mainly because apocalyptic moods and antirational modes of behavior sell emphatically well. Frank has repeatedly documented the widespread uptake of what he calls the "countercultural idea" in marketing and the rest of mainstream popular culture. The hip versus square contrast with gray-flanneled, 1950s-styled organization men is a well-established advertising trope. In his essay "Why Johnny Can't Dissent," Frank (1997a) concludes:

> The people who staff the Combine aren't like Nurse Ratched. They aren't Frank Burns, they aren't the Church Lady, they aren't Dean Wormer from *Animal House*, they aren't those repressed old folks in the commercials who want to ban Tropicana Fruit Twisters. They're hipper than you can ever hope to be because hip is their official ideology, and they're always going to be there at the poetry reading to encourage your "rebellion" with a hearty "right on, man!" before you even know they're in the auditorium. You can't outrun them, or even stay ahead of them for very long: it's their racetrack, and that's them waiting at the finish line to congratulate you on how outrageous your new style is, on how you shocked those stuffy prudes out in the heartland (44–45).

In some respects, the market is merely answering our yearning for the authentic in an inauthentic culture. It's also true, as Marshall Berman (1982) argues, that the very logic of competition and profit seeking has an antinomian character. Capitalism, he writes,

> ...requires constant revolutionizing, disturbance, agitation; it needs to be perpetually pushed and pressed in order to maintain its elasticity and resilience, to appropriate and assimilate new energies, to drive itself to new heights of activity and growth. This means, however, that men and movements that proclaim their enmity to capitalism may be just the sort of stimulants capitalism needs (1982: 117–118).

If deep authenticity is all about "dealing aggressively with received and habitual opinion," as Trilling (94) claims, we can't ignore that the market is singularly good at melting solids into air.

The ironic stance, too, is susceptible to market repackaging, in the form of Old Navy ads and celebrity fare like *Best Week Ever*, or even the humble Snuggie. As the *New York Times* revealed (Newman 2009), the company behind the wearable blanket deliberately deployed the Chia Pet–style cheesy infomercial. It was, in other words, a self-conscious attempt to trigger hipster parody and ironic uptake. Its sales figures suggest the tactic has worked brilliantly. In a similar vein, David Foster Wallace's essay on television and postmodern fiction salutes the idealistic irony of an earlier generation of postmodern novelists but despairs that the hip irony of younger novelists has been "absorbed, emptied and redeployed by the very televisual establishment that [the first generation] had originally set themselves athwart" (1993: 184). Wallace finds himself glancing back, wistfully, at what he calls "single-entendre values" (192).

The result of these contradictions is an "authenticity bind." What I mean is that the tension between the self-fulfillment ideal and the injunction to work on oneself as an object is a *productive contradiction.* That tension, as we've seen, yields a calculated authenticity that is then amplified by the market, in advertising and self-help culture. The felt need for authenticity remains unmet and leads at least some of us to go deeper in search of the real thing. But the coolhunters are never too far behind, and the rejectionist strands of authenticity get peddled back to us—thereby rendering those deeper strands inauthentic too. One can imagine the pattern repeating, as a kind of self-feeding cycle. As Hochschild wrote, "the more the heart is managed, the more we value the unmanaged heart" (1983: 192).

This talk of authenticity and the unmanaged heart may appear hopelessly naive. To refer to "calculated" authenticity is to imply that there is a meaningful opposite in the form of "real" authenticity, a claim that can bring out sighs of frustration. To be clear, I am not claiming that "real" authenticity exists nor that the ideal is written into the human soul. Expressivism is the product of a specific history; if it has a hold on us, it is not because of some universal human need. Academics are often driven by a denaturalizing zeal, quick to unmask the putatively natural as historical and contingent. This is all for the good, but there's also a corrosive edge to that unmasking, which implicitly discredits the thing that has been revealed as historical and contingent. Yes, the ethic of authenticity is a product of history, but that does not mean that we should dismiss its claims on us. It has become a widely resonant moral ideal; it is part of who we are. Admitting this much allows us to develop an immanent critique—to point to the ways that our culture of self-fulfillment contradicts the moral ideal it purports to express. We can point to internal contradictions but also to contradictions between expressivism and other deeply felt ideals, like the strand of self-governing freedom discussed above. As we have seen, the picture is made more complicated because the market has a parasitic relationship with both ideals, which in the case of authenticity leads to increasingly desperate forms of expression.

Facebook and the Consuming Self

All of this is a prelude to a brief, concluding discussion of Facebook. The rapidly growing social networking site recently added its 350 millionth member, and its estimated value is more than $6 billion (Oreskovic 2009). If you do not already have a Facebook account, you have no doubt been exhorted to sign up by friends and family. It is, at this point, nearly impossible to hold out; Farhad Manjoo (2009), writing recently in *Slate*, even accused non-Facebookers of an affectation—akin to the cellphone holdouts of a few years back.

In my view, the expressivist/self-promotional cocktail is a fundamental aspect of the Facebook experience. The site may also be a great platform for activism, a site for new kinds of interaction, and certainly an efficient way to reconnect with old friends. But it is also a calculated authenticity machine, where we are asked to carefully curate our identities.

All social interaction is performative; there is no such thing as a nonperformative, "authentic" self-disclosure, on Facebook or in person. Rather, I am interested in the ways that Facebook provides a new space for a particular *kind* of performance, expressed by Susman's "culture of personality"—that unhappy blend of authenticity, self-promotion, and the modern experience of anonymity. This chapter intends to argue against the claim, made by danah boyd and others, that Facebook and social media have ushered in a *new form* of sociality. Instead it stresses the continuities in the performance of identity throughout the modern American consumer culture. At the same time, it points to features of Facebook that serve to *amplify* the already potent "culture of personality" ideal.

Facebook has evolved dramatically over the last few years, but its invitation to present a magnetic, distinctive self has remained an open one. The most obvious space for this on the site is the profile itself, the place for various kinds of personality disclosures: favorite music, interests, TV shows, quotations, and so on. In a straightforward way, we populate these fields to project the identity that we want others to take in. When we list *Little Miss Sunshine* as our favorite movie or *Catcher in the Rye* as the book we most treasure, we are creating a literal "personality" profile, in a series of inescapably self-conscious acts. The implicit demand is to present oneself as interesting and distinctive.

The static profile has, however, been largely displaced by the newsfeed—the fast-moving stream of status updates, tagged photos, quiz results, clip postings, and mafia results. The newsfeed is a much more dynamic, real-time perfomance, a frequently refreshed advertisement for oneself. All of this represents, as many others have noted, the Twitterization of Facebook, up to and including the newer option to take one's page public.

Consider the care with which users tap out their status updates. The *Times* video critic calls them "spontaneous bursts of being" (Heffernan 2009). Instead it seems that there is a kind of wittiness imperative. Or witness the speedy cycle of profile photo replacement, and the virus-like spread of the "25 random things about me" chain postings. Or Facebook's most intriguing aspect: the conversations that take place on users' "Walls" in response to a status update—in which one-to-one or one-to-a-few chats are broadcast to the whole community of friends. On Facebook, close to two thirds of communication between users takes this "pubversational" form, as opposed to private chats (boyd 2007).

Even the profile photo has taken on the character of a status update. Many users replace their profile shots regularly, often as an allusion to a recent event or as a visual proclamation of fun-loving zaniness. Photos, more broadly, have become the indispensable vehicle for self-disclosure on the site. Isn't it true that parties are, first and foremost, photo opportunities? Forty-five years ago, Daniel Boorstin wrote about pseudo-events: gatherings staged for the press that, he claimed, were only ambiguously real. Like Boorstin's politicians, revelers sometimes seem less interested in fellow partygoers than in the snapshot-viewing Facebook audience to come.

Two aspects of Facebook in particular have the practical effect of intensifying its self-consciously performative character. Both can be drawn out by comparing the site to Erving Goffman's analysis of face-to-face interaction. Goffman observes that we are called on to present ourselves in a number of distinct contexts in our everyday lives (1959: 48–49). Such "audience segregation" requires that we tailor our performances according to the current audience; that is, our roles shift when we leave a job interview to hang out with friends. He also proposes a contrast between *frontstage* and *backstage* regions (106–140). The backstage is inaccessible to the audience; it is the space where performers can step out of character. For Goffman, this is a relative distinction, since any backstage with two or more people has a performative aspect.

It is clear that Facebook, to some extent at least, disrupts these features of everyday performance. In *No Sense of Place* (1985), Joshua Meyrowitz made a parallel argument about television. On Facebook, the audience is no longer neatly segregated; your boss, your mother, and your best friend are all reading your status updates and viewing your photos. It is true that the site enables you to manipulate its privacy settings to prevent your mother from clicking on the keg-stand photo, but most Facebook users do not take advantage of these settings (Debatin et al. 2009: 85–86; Tuunainen et al. 2009). As danah boyd (2006) has observed, there is now one big audience containing hundreds of spectators from every corner of your life; but it is in effect invisible. On Facebook, we are all invited backstage—or at least to a loosely patrolled middle-stage.

There is another important difference between Facebook and everyday interaction offline. In face-to-face settings, there is a great deal of apparent spontaneity—what Goffman calls "presumably uncalculated behavior" (1959: 8). Facial expressions, hand gestures, and even certain kinds of speech are typically treated as unrehearsed—even if, as Goffman notes, they may well be. On Facebook, by contrast, there is no apparent spontaneity. We are all—newsfeed reader and status-updater alike—aware that each update is a conscious act. There is, in other words, a mutual awareness of performance *as performance*.

Some of this comes out in the advice to be a careful custodian of your online brand—because if you don't then Google will (see, for example, Tugend 2009). More to the point, the mutual awareness factor means that, even if you *are* interesting and distinctive, you are still forced to self-consciously present those traits. Everyone knows that everyone else asks the question, "How is that going to look on Facebook?"

Both of these features—the mutual awareness factor and audience desegregation—help to awaken that rejectionism and refusal that I have referred to as "deep authenticity," if only because they make the contradictions between authenticity and self-promotion more palpable. Obscure band references can signal membership in subcultures, for example, and some users populate their profiles—or update their status—with nonsensical, or deliberately mystifying phrases. Then there are the internal émigrés, the ones who have joined Facebook but are gripped by a kind of expressive paralysis, who leave their profile fields empty and rarely if ever post a status update. This is a much larger group than we normally acknowledge. The problem is that Facebook obscurantism, Facebook irony, even Facebook refusal are all susceptible to commercial repackaging.

It was inevitable that viral marketers would turn to Facebook, with paid status updates, phony Facebook groups, and sponsored, paid-for gift-giving. A small industry of firms, like PayPerPost and Magpie, pay Facebookers and Twitterers to post ads as status updates. In a tip for posters, PayPerPost (2009) advises: "Advertisers often appreciate personalized experiences as they relate to the topic of the post, too...readers are smart folks—if your content seems insincere, it loses meaning and will lead to lower traffic long term." And the cycle continues: the more the heart is managed, the more we value the unmanaged heart.

Notes

1. I want to thank the editors, Brooke Duffy, Heidi Khaled, Brett Bumgarner, and Joel Penney for helpful criticism.
2. This is not to hide something particular in universalist packaging. My neglect of difference is, in part, a product of space constraints but also grounded in the fact that most of the broad historical changes I invoke below were experienced across lines of difference, producing similar (if not identical) dilemmas of self-understanding. No doubt the distinct positions that women, or African Americans, or working-class Americans brought to epochal, turn-of-the-century social change led to distinct experiences, but it is my view that most of these relate to timing and the pace of diffusion. Women, for example, were addressed (and imagined) as consumers first and more regularly, so that many of the tensions between authentic expression and self-promotion were, and continue to be, more deeply felt. Even so, Americans of diverse backgrounds have been, over time, recruited unevenly into the same culture of performative self-fulfillment.
3. The "therapeutic ethos" phrase first appeared in Rieff (1966: 254).
4. The class was the legendary "Social Sciences 2" (or "Soc 2"), part of the required social science sequence at the College of the University of Chicago. See the many excellent essays, including Riesman's own reflections, in MacAloon (1992).
5. I say "in part" because, depending on the author, the indictment is stretched too far and made to include too much.
6. In a footnote, Riesman (1950) credits Fromm: "This picture of the other-directed person has been stimulated by, and developed from, Erich Fromm's discussion of the 'marking orientation' in *Man for Himself*" (22).
7. Under the long-running "Think Different" campaign, created by TBWA/Chiat/Day in 1997, two "Crazy Ones" television commercials were widely aired and featured black-and-white images of prominent iconoclasts, including Albert Einstein, Bob Dylan, Martin Luther King, Jr., John Lennon, and many others. The voiceover for the one-minute version begins, "Here's to the crazy ones. The misfits. The rebels. The troublemakers.

The round pegs in the square holes. The ones who see things differently. They're not fond of rules. And they have no respect for the status quo. You can praise them, disagree with them, quote them, disbelieve them, glorify or vilify them" (see Shields 2001).

8. Peters, in *The Pursuit of Wow!* (1994: 113): "Typically dull white folks (of any denomination) could learn a lot from the best inner-city African-American churches, starting with Reverend Cecil Williams's inspiring, energetic Glide Memorial Church in San Francisco. (Hint, for starters: Glide doesn't have 'services', it has 'celebrations'" (quoted in McGee 2005: 168). Covey (2004: 23): "The point is if you neglect any one of the four parts of human nature, you turn a person into a thing, and what do you do with a thing? You have to control, manage and carrot-and-stick them in order to motivate them" (see 21–25).
9. In *The Presentation of Self in Everyday Life*, Goffman observes: "...there is hardly a performance, in whatever area of life, which does not rely on the personal touch to exaggerate the uniqueness of the transactions between performer and audience" (1959: 50).

References

Bell, Daniel. 1976. *The Cultural Contradictions of Capitalism*. New York: Basic Books.
———. 1979. "Foreword." Pp. xi–xxxii in *The Cultural Contradictions of Capitalism*. London: Heinemann.
Berman, Marshall. 1982. *All that Is Solid Melts into Air: The Experience of Modernity*. New York: Simon and Schuster.
Boorstin, Daniel J. 1962. *The Image; Or, What Happened to the American Dream*. New York: Atheneum.
boyd, danah. 2007. "danah boyd on Myfriends, Myspace." MediaBerkman: Berkman Center for Internet & Society Podcast.
———. 2006. "Friends, Friendsters, and Myspace Top 8: Writing Community into Being on Social Network Sites." *First Monday* 11 (12). http://www.firstmonday.org/issues/issue11_12/boyd/index.html.
Carlyle, Thomas. [1839] 1971. *Selected Writings*. Harmondsworth, UK: Penguin Books.
Carnegie, Dale. 1936. *How to Win Friends and Influence People*. New York: Simon and Schuster.
———. 1982. *How to Win Friends and Influence People*. Rev. ed. New York: Pocket Books.
Covey, Stephen R. 2004. *The 8th Habit: From Effectiveness to Greatness*. New York: Free Press.
Debatin, Bernhard, Jennette P. Lovejoy, Ann-Kathrin Horn, and Brittany N. Hughes. 2009. "Facebook and Online Privacy: Attitudes, Behaviors, and Unintended Consequences." *Journal of Computer-Mediated Communication* 15 (1): 83–108.
Frank, Thomas. 2000. *One Market Under God: Extreme Capitalism, Market Populism, and the End of Economic Democracy*. New York: Doubleday.
———. 1997a. "Why Johnny Can't Dissent." Pp. 31–45 in *Commodify Your Dissent: Salvos from the Baffler*, ed. Thomas Frank and Matt Weiland. New York: Norton.
———. 1997b. *The Conquest of Cool: Business Culture, Counterculture, and the Rise of Hip Consumerism*. Chicago: University of Chicago Press.
Franklin, Benjamin. [1793] 2003. *The Autobiography of Benjamin Franklin*. 2nd ed. New Haven, CT: Yale University Press.
Fromm, Erich. 1947. *Man for Himself: An Inquiry Into the Psychology of Ethics*. New York: Rinehart.

Glenn, Joshua. 1998. "Camp: An Introduction." *Hermenaut* 11/12. http://www.hermenaut.com/a28.shtml

Goffman, Erving. 1959. *The Presentation of Self in Everyday Life*. Garden City, N.Y.: Doubleday.

———. 1974. *Frame Analysis: An Essay on the Organization of Experience*. New York: Harper & Row.

Heffernan, Virginia. 2009. "Being There." *New York Times Magazine*, February 15, p. 15.

Hochschild, Arlie R. 1983. *The Managed Heart: Commercialization of Human Feeling*. Berkeley: University of California Press.

Lasch, Christopher. 1978. *The Culture of Narcissism: American Life in an Age of Diminishing Expectations*. New York: Norton.

Leach, William. 1993. *Land of Desire: Merchants, Power, and the Rise of a New American Culture*. New York: Pantheon Books.

Lears, T. J. Jackson. 1981. *No Place of Grace: Antimodernism and the Transformation of American Culture, 1880–1920*. New York: Pantheon Books.

MacAloon, John J. 1992. *General Education in the Social Sciences: Centennial Reflections on the College of the University of Chicago*. Chicago: University of Chicago Press.

Macpherson, C. B. 1962. *The Political Theory of Possessive Individualism: Hobbes to Locke*. Oxford: Clarendon Press.

Manjoo, Farhad. 2009. "You Have No Friends: Everyone Else is on Facebook. Why Aren't You?" *Slate.com*, January 14.

Marx, Karl, and Friedrich Engels. [1848] 2002. *The Communist Manifesto*. New York: Penguin Books.

McGee, Micki. 2005. *Self-Help, Inc.: Makeover Culture in American Life*. New York: Oxford University Press.

Meyrowitz, Joshua. 1985. *No Sense of Place: The Impact of Electronic Media on Social Behavior*. New York: Oxford University Press.

Newman, Andrew Adam. 2009. "Snuggie Rode Silly Ads to Stardom over Rivals." *New York Times*, February 27, B6.

Oreskovic, Alexei. 2009. "Investor Values Facebook Common Stock at $6.5 Billion." *New York Times*, July 13.

PayPerPost. 2009. PayPerPost University: Best Practices. http://www.payperpostu.com/bestpractices.html (accessed July 16, 2009).

Peters, Thomas J. 1994. *The Pursuit of Wow!: Every Person's Guide to Topsy-Turvy Times*. New York: Vintage Books.

Rieff, Philip. 1966. *The Triumph of the Therapeutic: Uses of Faith After Freud*. New York: Harper & Row.

Riesman, David. 1950. *The Lonely Crowd: A Study of the Changing American Character*. New Haven, CT: Yale University Press.

Shields, Ronald E. 2001. "The Force of Callas' Kiss: The 1997 Apple Advertising Campaign, 'Think Different'." *Text and Performance Quarterly* 21 (3): 202–219.

Simmel, Georg. [1903] 1950. "The Metropolis and Mental Life." Pp. 409–426 in *The Sociology of Georg Simmel*, ed. K. H. Wolff. Glencoe, IL: Free Press.

Smith, Ethan, and Peter Lattman. 2007. "Download This: YouTube Phenom Has a Big Secret." *Wall Street Journal*, September 6, A1.

Susman, Warren. 1979. "'Personality' in the Making of Twentieth-Century Culture." Pp. 212–226 in *New Directions in American Intellectual History*, ed. J. Higham and P. K. Conkin. Baltimore, MD: Johns Hopkins University Press.

Taylor, Charles. 1989. *Sources of the Self: The Making of the Modern Identity*. Cambridge, MA: Harvard University Press.

———. 1992. *The Ethics of Authenticity*. Cambridge, MA: Harvard University Press.

Thornton, Sarah. 1996. *Club Cultures: Music, Media, and Subcultural Capital*. Hanover, NH: University Press of New England.

Trilling, Lionel. 1972. *Sincerity and Authenticity*. Cambridge, MA: Harvard University Press.

Tugend, Alina. 2009. "Putting Yourself Out There on a Shelf to Buy." *New York Times*, March 28, B6.

Tuunainen, Virpi Kristiina Pitkänen, Olli, and Hovi, Marjaana. 2009. "Users' Awareness of Privacy on Online Social Networking Sites—Case Facebook." *BLED 2009 Proceedings*. http://aisel.aisnet.org/bled2009/42.

Wallace, David Foster. 1993. "E Unibus Pluram: Television and U.S. Fiction." *Review of Contemporary Fiction* 13 (2): 151–194.

———. 1996. "Shipping Out: On the (Nearly Lethal) Comforts of a Luxury Cruise." *Harper's Magazine*, January, 33–56.

Weber, Max. 1946. "Science as a Vocation." Pp. 129–156 in *From Max Weber: Essays in Sociology*, ed. H. H. Gerth and C. W. Mills. New York: Oxford University Press.

Whitfill, Andrea. 2009. "Burt's Bees, Tom's of Maine, Naked Juice: Your Favorite Brands? Take Another Look—They May Not Be What They Seem." *AlterNet*, March 17.

PART TWO

Branded Space, Branded Citizens

CHAPTER FIVE

A Nation of "Shop 'til You Drop" Consumers?

On the Overspent Puerto Rican Consumer and the Business of Shopping Malls[1]

Arlene Davila

> Yes, Puerto Rico is in deficit, but have you seen how Plaza (las Americas) is always full?
>
> I'll leave and go to New York...but Puerto Rico can't really be that bad, if the stores are always full!
>
> I'll shop less. The clothing *compraera* (shopping sprees) are over, no more *lujos* (luxuries). I'm going to buy the TV before it goes up in price.

These are three common responses to the Puerto Rican government's announcement of a series of emergency measures to address the island's economic deficit, which in 2009 was worsened by the global crisis (Muriente-Pastrana 2009). The sentiments contained in these statements include disbelief that Puerto Rico could in fact be in such bad economic shape when the shopping malls are always full, and evidence of two common economic coping strategies: emigration, to improve one's financial situation, or more consumption, as in, "Time to go purchase that discounted TV." The view that things can't be that bad because people are shopping is at the core of Puerto Rico's economic deficit/consumption puzzle. How can the island appear to maintain a strong retail profile when it is mired in unemployment and underemployment? Why are shopping malls always full? Where does the money that drives all this consumption come from?

That Puerto Ricans like to shop is a common cliché. While conducting research on the island, whenever I described my work on Puerto Rican shopping culture I was met with a similar response, often voiced with a mixture of pride and embarrassment. "Of course shopping is our national pastime," one said. "Puerto Rico is the country that consumes the most throughout Latin America," said another, who reminded me that Puerto Rico has one of the largest shopping malls (Plaza Las Americas) and the greatest number of shopping centers per square mile in the United States. People were quick to recall such statistics, but no one could point me to the source for their "facts" about Puerto Rican shoppers. These "facts" have become ingrained common knowledge. Puerto Ricans describe themselves as the most avid of conspicuous consumers, with impulse shopping, *novelistas* (easily swayed by the new), and *despilfarrador* (money squandering) among the adjectives most easily summoned. In sum, consumption is seen as the greatest cause of Puerto Rico's economic ills but also as an important sign of Puerto Ricans' sense of humor and optimism—the feeling that another day will come.

As a Puerto Rican anthropologist who has lived for over 20 years in New York, returning to the island on a repeated basis, I have grown accustomed to this dominant myth of the Puerto Rican "shop 'til you drop" consumer as well as quite skeptical of it. Despite Puerto Ricans' vehement self-characterization as the most avid of consumers, the discourse of overconsumption as constitutive of national character is common among modern and modernizing citizens around the globe. It is also increasingly central to consumers' general critique of and engagement with consumer society. Additionally, research on American consumer culture has long documented the ways in which consumption by marginal groups in society, be they African American, Latino, or female, is often pathologized as aberrant, irrational, and out of control, in reference to an imagined rational consuming subject who is thrifty, savvy, and immune to the seductions and deceptions of the market. In other words, while consumption has long served as a primary medium for the assertion of modernity, progress, and national identity both in the United States and in many modernizing countries around the world, it has always been a contested territory in which societies debate status, merit, class, and identity around notions of proper and improper types of consumption (Cohen 2003; Miller 1995; Liechty 2002).

In particular, ever since Veblen's late nineteenth-century discussion of women's role in fueling conspicuous and wasteful consumption, scholars have attested to how consumption by marginal groups in society is often the most policed, scrutinized, and disparaged. These groups are not only purchasing goods but rather compensating for status, belonging, and even identity itself (Chin 2001; Halter 2002; Veblen [1899] 1994; Zukin 2004;

Zukin and Maguire 2004). And, one may ask, why shouldn't we police the overspending of those most marginal among us? Doesn't it make sense that they should be chastised for their overconsumption and, especially in times of economic crisis, deterred from shopping in the first place? This chapter argues that we don't know enough about the consumption practices of Puerto Rican consumers, or of any consumer for that matter, to be summoning such quick generalizations about them. When we do so, we may be veiling the larger political and economic trends that shape and profit from the myth of the "shop 'til you drop" consumer. In particular, subscribing uncritically to this view masks the contextually specific uses of the global discourse of overconsumption in particular locations as well as the multiple political and economic interests this discourse may be designed to serve. As I will document in detail below, this discourse distorts the realities and strategies Puerto Ricans use to shop at the same time that it absorbs that activity in order to produce and expand the branded spaces in which this shopping takes place.

The growing recognition of consumption as a central practice and discourse for modernity has yielded few ethnographic studies that account for consumption practices in the so-called developing world. Nor do they account for the trends fueling a boom in shopping mall construction in places like China, Latin America, and Russia at the very same time as the American retail sector is in decline.[2] This chapter attempts to address this quandary. I suggest that when offering generalized notions of Puerto Ricans as uncontrolled ultrashoppers, Puerto Ricans may be subscribing to dominant discourses often circulated about groups perceived to be less "modern" or less equipped for modernity, in not dissimilar ways to how colonized groups blame their subjugated status on their own indolence and lack of entrepreneurship.

There is evidence of contestation over the role of consumption in Puerto Rico (Ortiz-Negron 2007; Davila Santiago 2005). Ortiz-Negron's work, in particular, has documented the rise of a dominant anti-consumption discourse in Puerto Rico, most strongly represented by state institutions and the church, which posits consumption as an amoral activity that destroys local culture as well as social and family ties. In contrast to this view, local scholars have noted the numerous ways in which individual practices of consumption such as shopping and visiting the mall provide possibilities for social interaction and crucial opportunities for claiming identity (Davila Santiago 2005; Ortiz-Negron and Guilbe Lopez 2005). My own work draws from and contributes to contemporary research on shopping and consumption by anthropologists, geographers, and cultural studies scholars who have critically probed this realm of practice to expose some of the ways in which people resignify consumption and the shopping mall as a space of sociality (Miller 1995, 1998; Wilson 2004; Zukin 2004). It is important to exercise caution when pursuing this line of inquiry, however. At times these narratives reinforce some of the dominant local discourses on shopping that reinstate the consumer as an active agent, while losing track of the subordination that is also experienced at the mall. In other instances, they further a romanticized view of consumption and consumption sites as democratic spaces that are open to everyone, whether they come to shop, browse, or hang out. Uncritically embracing this view hinders our full examination of the existing social inequalities that are actively reproduced in these spaces. A poignant example is the common re-signification of the shopping mall as the new version of the public square, a site for an array of social activities. Such a view overlooks a number of problematic features of the mall, such as its ongoing sanitization and policing, as well as its purposeful exclusion of informal vendors, beggars, vagabonds, and the homeless, among other characters who are not so easily kept at bay in the public street (O'Dougherty 2006; Ortiz-Negron and Guilbe Lopez 2005; Zukin 2004).

My research draws from observations and interviews at shopping malls in the metropolitan area of Puerto Rico. I conducted the majority of my ethnographic fieldwork in Plaza Rio Hondo, a 538,442-square-foot shopping center located in Bayamon, a municipality in the metropolitan area. The mall is situated in a central hub of retail activity, surrounded by six other shopping malls within five miles of the site. Rio Hondo is anchored by Big Kmart, Best Buy, and Marshalls Mega Store and has a representative mix of stores that one would find in most shopping malls throughout the island—namely, a mix of tenants selling moderately priced and average-to-low-quality women's attire, such as Click, Kress, Payless, Rave, and Infinito. The more "upscale" stores, such as Banana Republic, Ann Taylor Loft, and Gap are found at Plaza del Sol, the shopping mall nearest to Rio Hondo. Rio Hondo opened in 1982 and was purchased in 2005 by Developers Diversified Realty Corporation (DDR), an American company that acquires, develops, leases, and manages shopping centers. DDR's corporate overview indicates that the company "owns and manages approximately 720 retail operating and development properties in 45 states, plus Puerto Rico, Brazil,

Russia, and Canada," making it one of the largest managers of shopping malls in the world (Developers Diversified Realty 2009).

My research involved observations of retail activity and interviews with shoppers throughout the mall and in the food court. I literally went shopping on a daily basis, browsing through racks of merchandise alongside other customers, which allowed me to probe them about their shopping experiences, their assessments of prices, their shopping techniques, and so forth. I also offered a $10 Kmart gift card as an incentive to ten respondents who agreed to provide longer interviews about their shopping habits. My questions revolved around people's consumption habits, including how frequently they visit the mall; how often they buy something; what other activities they engage in at the mall; whether they dress up or undertake other preparations before coming; with whom they visit at the mall; their debt/income status; their views about Puerto Rican consumer culture; and lastly, how they were affected by and coping with the economic crisis. These observations were complemented with research on the retail industry on the island and how this industry is marketed to the Puerto Rican shopper.

The Welfare State Goes Shopping

By all economic measures, Puerto Rico's economic profile could not be more dire. Annual income per person on the island is less than half that of Mississippi, the poorest state. More than forty-eight percent of island residents live below the federally defined poverty line, while with over twelve percent unemployment, a large percentage of the local population remains idle. An article in *The Economist* newspaper estimates that "half the working age men in Puerto Rico do not work" and that "federal transfers make up more than 20 percent of personal income." It goes on to note that federal transfers coupled with a little income from informal work surpass the wage one would get in the open market, though with far less work.[3]

This situation has led numerous scholars to describe Puerto Rico as the colonial welfare state par excellence. In particular, economists have noted the island's dependency on an extremely vulnerable and increasingly indebted public sector and a declining manufacturing sector for jobs, which has rendered it unable to function without federal social welfare funds and other direct forms of aid (Morrissey 2006; Grosfoguel 2003). Most pressing, the island's dependency and economic vulnerability have made it extremely susceptible to the U.S. economic recession. Indeed, Puerto Ricans have experienced the effects of the recession more severely than in the continental United States. For instance, while Americans were complaining of rising living costs when the consumer price index rose by two or three percent, in Puerto Rico the consumer price index was up fifteen percent by 2006, with basics such as water, electricity, food and fuel becoming more out of reach for the Puerto Rican consumer (Dougherty 2007). In particular, the rise in fuel costs directly affected the price of most consumer products, which already carry high transportation costs to import into the island. The result has been growing inequality as the middle class increasingly shrinks, leaving behind, as one informant put it, "the rich, the poor, and the even more poor."

Tellingly, on the morning of January 9, 2009, in the midst of my research, the government declared a state of emergency on the island, announcing the freezing of all new government hires, the firing of over 11,000 government workers, and a proposal for new taxes on consumption goods like cellular calls, cigarettes, gasoline, and alcohol. Shock waves were felt throughout the island. Cries of foul play were voiced by listeners on the AM live-talk radio circuit. Callers and local economists were especially outraged that consumers would bear seventy-five percent of the proposal's impact, versus the fifteen percent the government would bear, and the mere ten percent directed at the private sector, the richest sector of the island, despite the recently elected government's new platform that it would not raise nor impose new taxes and would place residents' interests first (Diaz 2009: 30).

In sum, the average Puerto Rican consumer is largely overspent and in debt. This dire situation has been documented by the Center for the New Economy, a nonpartisan economic think tank, which carried out a study showing that average resident spending and debt far supersedes what s/he generates in income, a pattern that is unsustainable in the long term. This was evident in my interviews where almost everyone I talked to admitted to being in debt, primarily credit card debt. Tellingly, not a single interviewee imagined being entirely free of debt in the foreseeable future. Some spoke of the common practice of managing to stay afloat through the practice of *barajeo,* which literally refers to the shuffling of playing cards but here refers to the payment of credit cards and bills in an alternating fashion or paying off one credit card with another.

Despite this dire economic portrait, the retail industry continues to promote Puerto Rico as a paradise of riches, since it is well aware of the particularities of the stretched and indebted Puerto Rican consumer. Puerto Ricans, like other Hispanic consumers, have larger households that facilitate the pooling of resources, such as using funds from *abuelita*'s (grandma's) pension and saving rent and household costs. Economists have also accounted for the role played by the informal economy, both the drug trade and other more socially sanctioned types of informal work; the pooling of resources from remittances from relatives in the United States; and the easy availability of credit and loans as measures to help make ends meet and keep up consumption levels (Duany 2008; Enchautegui 2008). Puerto Rico's economic situation is additionally buffered by the island's political status as a U.S. commonwealth, providing residents the safety nets of federal transfers and welfare benefits that help maintain consumption levels. Then there's the fact that the island's high population density almost guarantees good numbers for retailers, as higher population density is more easily translatable to higher sales per square foot.

Indeed, since the 1990s, the island has undergone a retail revolution, with half of the shopping centers on the island built after this time (Gigante 2000). This growth has been primarily led by acquisitions from stateside investors. The largest of these involves the purchase of fifteen local malls, among them the Plaza Rio Hondo shopping center, by Developers Diversified Realty (DDR). DDR's statement to investors about their move to Puerto Rico confirms the "business friendly" qualities that attract retailers to the island:

> [Puerto Rico is a] densely populated island whose economy is fueled by consumerism; combined with physical barriers constraining new supply this creates a highly productive retail environment...developable land is limited due to physical barriers of mountains and floodplain; as a result the major retail trade areas are mature and very dense (qtd. in Martinez 2005).

Other attractive factors for the DDR were malls' occupancy rates, which average over 95 percent; consumer spending that is more than double that of the mainland U.S.; and a business-friendly approach to investment, offering businesses faster permits, less regulation, favorable taxes, and lower operating expenses than on the mainland (Rosa 2006).

In other words, Puerto Rico is attractive because its physical containment, high population density, consumer culture, and lenient regulatory practices make it an obvious destination for major retailers. This does not mean that the retail sector has been unaffected by the economic crisis. Even the most confident business sources acknowledge that Puerto Rico's consumer spending has started a recessionary phase, and that it is not expected to expand or to grow significantly in years to come (Business Register 2009). In 2007, Puerto Rico remained among the top ten retail markets in the United States mainly because of the sales at large retailers like Wal-Mart, Sam's Club, Walgreens, Marshalls, Pitusa, KB Toys, and Best Buy, which are able to slash prices to keep sales competitive so they can remain strong (Ryan 2009). Yet the retail industry's practice of measuring the island's retail status on the basis of sales at *mega tiendas* like Wal-Mart is deceptive. Such measurements yield high numbers in sales for megastores, while masking the declining rate of purchases at most other retail stores, especially the small merchants who are unable to compete with comparable prices. In other words, mega-sales at Wal-Mart imply not that Puerto Rican consumption is growing at a limitless rate, but that consumption is simply shifting from more expensive local venues to the cheaper discounted megastores, the only sector experiencing steady and rising sales.

Lastly, it is noteworthy to point out the trend in real estate speculation in the business of shopping malls. The business of building and opening malls and purchasing land with government incentives renders shopping malls a highly profitable investment on the island, irrespective of actual sales, evoking the make-believe qualities in neoliberal capitalism, where the mere illusion of profits becomes a source of value (Comaroff and Comaroff 2001). What is more, in 2007, the Puerto Rican government sweetened the pot still further when it approved House Bill 3540, which extended pass-through tax exceptions at the corporate level to retail real-estate investment trusts (REITs) to stimulate investment (Ryan and Carmona 2007). Tellingly, DDR, the company behind the largest shopping mall deal on the island, was among the first self-administered and self-managed REITs to benefit from the new legislation. Sergio Marxuach, policy director at the Center for the New Economy, was unwavering in his criticism of the new policy. In his view, it simply did not make sense. As he noted in an interview with me, "You grant tax exemptions to attract new industries or to economic sectors that require incentives for growth, but it's not like we have a scarcity of shopping centers on the island!" He was also concerned about the lack of guarantees that new shopping malls would in fact produce new jobs and growth, despite the handsome government incentives. A list of U.S. shopping malls on Wikipedia, while obviously not the most exhaustive source, helps corroborate Marxuach's concern. Puerto Rico's territory, which is approximately one hundred miles long and thirty-five miles wide, is listed as having twenty-eight malls; whereas the state of Connecticut, which approximates the island's size, has a mere twelve.[4] The "Walmartization" of the island's retail sector raises concerns that extend from its effects on the survival of local merchants to fears of its likely impact on the island's physical landscape (Alvarez Curbelo 2005).

Not surprisingly, the ongoing speculation in the business of shopping malls and the involvement of stateside investors are largely hidden from public view by marketing strategies that help to "Puertoricanize" investors' shopping mall ventures. A stellar example here is the media and marketing campaign that DDR commissioned from Cohn Marketing, a Denver-based marketing agency, after its purchase of fifteen shopping malls. Its object was to re-signify and unify the malls into a single brand: the "Isla" shopping centers—shopping centers "of the island." The campaign involved the launching of events and promotions, such as the contest *Chicos con Corazón* (Kids with Big Hearts), a contest to select the children who contribute the most to their communities and their *isla*; the *Mi Isla* gift card, which can be used in any of the malls; and the magazine *Isla Estilo,* promoting events and sales throughout the malls (Gonzalez and Hermilla 2008). The campaign's visual imagery used an *Amapola*, a popular flower on the island, and depicted local scenes and imagery, including the *coqui*, (a local tiny frog) beach and shore scenes and an Old San Juan *garita* (a Spanish colonial guard post).

The extension of tax exceptions to shopping mall developers implies that we are likely to see the continuation of the retail frenzy and the proliferation of even more shopping malls throughout the island. And, most likely, each will be an identical white concrete copy of another, as architecturally uninteresting and unsightly as the next. Writing on why shopping malls tend to be so ugly, consumer behavior analyst Paco Underhill (2005) notes the existing disconnect between the real estate developers who make and invest in malls and the retailers and "merchants of style" that are meant to be housed there. Consequently, unless it is purposefully developed as part of a tourist or cultural "destination," a mall's design has always been secondary to the building's function and price. Constructions have minimal architectural value and are made up of clusters of stores organized around flagship stores at distance from each other to maximize traffic and exposure. Exposure is also aided by escalators that force shoppers to move across halls to reach their destination and bathrooms that are inaccessible and/or hard to find. Most noteworthy, their design and location prevent them from being the accessible, open spaces that malls purport to be. For one, they tend to be inhospitable to public transportation; one has to drive to get to the mall, and throughout the U.S., hindering a mall's access to public transportation is a common measure to exclude minorities and the poor from accessing the mall (Chin 2001).

This was the case at Rio Hondo, where the customer service kiosk attendant looked puzzled when I asked for the public bus routes that came closest to the mall. She did not know, and from the look on her face I could tell that she had never been asked this question. Granted, in Puerto Rico, where there is a lack of viable and dependable public transportation, owning at least one car per household is not a luxury but a necessity to participate in public life. Nevertheless, car ownership is one of the necessities most affected by the recession, the expense most informants had either cut, reduced, or eliminated as part of their cost-cutting measures. That Puerto Rican malls are packed should therefore never be regarded as proof of the island's economy or of the total population's economic health but rather as a sampling of those who have access to transportation and money—which can be simply the same percentage of the population that regularly goes to the malls, whether to shop or not. Indeed, browsing through Rio Hondo and its sister mall Plaza del Sol on a Sunday afternoon, one would think that Puerto Ricans are the most upscale and best dressed people in the world. Well-dressed and well-coiffed people predominate, whether entire families, women with children, or women with other women and youth. At the mall, everyone seems to be either doing well or at least well enough to have paid the necessary "symbolic dues" to assert their right to belong at the mall by performing the role of potential consumers (Zukin 2004; Zukin and Maguire 2004). In contrast, people "out of place" were very easy to spot, as was the vendor of Christian wares I encountered on a Monday morning, within five minutes of entering Plaza Las Americas. The heavyset dark-skinned woman, dressed in sandals, a T-shirt, and a long skirt, quickly stood out from the mostly professionally dressed Puerto Ricans who enter the mall in the morning. In particular, her "out of place" status was easily signaled by the overstuffed bright yellow bags she carried—the type that need to be reinforced, and have "Cash and Carry" written on them, rather than the stylish logo of a Plaza Las Americas establishment. She's often asked to leave, but she's not easily deterred. It's part of her religious mission to persevere, she tells me, while adding that she has become quite savvy in avoiding the guards.

The point is that people's symbolic performances at the mall, such as dressing up and looking good, should not be interpreted as signs of their economic health or ability to spend. Shopping, after all, is an ancillary activity and not always the primary reason to come to the mall. Meeting friends, browsing, breaking the day's routine, access to free air conditioning—all were mentioned as common draws to the mall. The work of Ortiz-Negron (2007) is relevant here. It shows that the mall is never adequately considered a monocultural space. It is used by a variety of activities and events that would once take place downtown or in the township but have now moved to the mall. Each mall has its own character and cultural rhythms, and class and generational markers are not uncommon, highlighted as they are by the types of events that are marketed and the social and cultural activities that are held there.

In fact, retailers are not unaware of the multiple activities that shoppers engage in at the mall besides shopping. These activities are in fact encouraged by an entire industry of mall marketers and interior designers whose job is to transform the mall from a generic white box into an enticing destination accommodating everyone's needs. In particular, Puerto Rican malls have seen the development of built environments and what geographer Jon Goss has termed "pseudospaces" that encourage the "fantasized dissociation from the act of shopping," by fostering other activities and events (Goss 1993). Throughout U.S. malls, similar pseudospaces involving the commodification of space have been built that either exploit the nostalgia for an authentic community—the recreation of Old San Juan architecture in the Plaza Las Americas movie theater corridor is a perfect example of this strategy—or add attractions and displays, such as carousels, art exhibits, entertainments, plants, and sculptures that involve the thematic imagining of space (Goss 1993).

Rio Hondo is lacking in pseudospaces—there are no carousels, fountains, or special decorations to be found. But it has a well-lit, 20,000-square-foot food court, El Embarcadero, that serves as a draw. Retailers design food courts like El Embarcadero to help convert "the inefficient"—in retail lingo, those with the "lowest conversion rates" or who are least likely to buy—into prospective buyers, at least of snacks and drinks at the food court (Underhill 2005). For everyone else, however, the food court is far from a "conversion" space. Instead, they are spaces up for grabs. A group of teenage girls who bought drinks but shared goodies and junk food they had bought elsewhere (such as candy that was not sold anywhere near the vicinity of the food court) and had their "bounty" spread out at a food court table comes quickly to mind. At the same time, people's strategies to "retake" the mall via other social activities beyond consumption do not negate their understanding that they are occupying a space of consumption and that their re-appropriation of this space needs to be qualified in retail terms.

A well-documented group of mall users are the *caminantes*, a group of senior residents who have appropriated the Puerto Rican malls as a safe space for exercise, as they have in many malls throughout the United States (Ortiz-Negron and Guilbe Lopez 2005). It took me just one visit to discover a group of senior citizens fitting that description in Rio Hondo's Embarcadero Food Court. Meet the Rio Hondo Rascals, a group of retired men over 60 who were easy to spot around the buzzing crowds of families and youth. The Rascals come to the mall every other day. One told me that he had been visiting the mall for over 20 years. They don't come to exercise but rather to socialize; they sit at the same table, and make a point of distinguishing their group as the best group in the mall, particularly by drawing distinctions between their table and the nearby table, "*la de los Medicare*," or the Medicare table, so named because they always get sick.

The Rascals are all retired from well-paid professions, by Puerto Rican standards—the post office, the Bacardi Rum Distillery, the telephone company—and they now enjoy relatively good pensions. They come to chat, to converse, to joke with one another, and sometimes to eat lunch, and they spend somewhere between four and twenty dollars each per visit; they were not certain of the exact amount because they take turns paying for one another, whether it's coffee or a full meal. My observations, however, suggested that they consume a lot less than they let on: their table was always clean and empty without a trace of food whenever I saw them, and they seemed delighted when I offered them a complimentary round of coffee.

Yet once again, and returning to the symbolic performances that are part of people's claims to the mall, the Rascals insisted on being consuming subjects, on spending money. "There are no senior citizens' discounts here. We're like everyone else," one noted. As such, they gave evidence of being fully aware of some of the distinctions apace in determining who can access the mall as a space of leisure and who cannot, or should not. These distinctions included not only the ability to purchase items but also extended to codes of behavior. One explained: "We only allow people with good manners to sit at our table. We don't want to be called *viejos verdes*... We're professionals; we don't socialize in *plazas publicas* (public squares). We come to the mall." For them, "good manners" means refraining from addressing women inappropriately, speaking in loud voices and the type of banter that in their view belongs to a *plaza publica,* not the mall. The Rascals told me that they had had T-shirts printed with their name, "Rio Hondo Rascals," but they would only wear them under the button-down shirts that they regularly wore to come to the mall.

In this way, as Sharon Zukin (2004; Zukin and Maguire 2004) tells us, the act of "dressing up" is best seen as part of consumers' self-disciplining in order to appropriately participate in the not-so-public space of mass consumption. This act entails considerable stress—one must pay to look good, determine what would look good and so forth—but also considerable joy, the joy of asserting one's upward mobility, one's status, one's respectability, and for these qualities to be recognized by others. As one of my interviewees explained, "I dress up, because I may bump into someone I know...seeing fashion live is different from the TV, here in person you can tell if something will suit you." She went on to explain how much she loves to people-watch, and to see how people dress at the mall, fully aware that while she was engaged in people-watching, she too was being put on display for others to see.

Finally, it is important to note that conducting research on shopping malls is already a self-selecting process, since it involves only those sectors of the population that are more likely to participate in this realm of consumption—either because they have money to shop, or because they maintain the social and cultural capital to feel comfortable and welcome to browse the mall or to use it for leisure and fun. Mall goers are undoubtedly a highly diverse population. But generalizing about the totality of the Puerto Rican population from those who come to the mall is misguided. So is drawing larger patterns about people's consumption habits from one or two purchases observed or recalled by informants, without first contextualizing them within the particular social and cultural norms in Puerto Rico.

I recall my own ethnographic research with Hispanic consumers in the United States and how it directly contradicted dominant images circulated about them by Hispanic marketers. Marketers described them as the most brand loyal, most traditional, and least likely to try new brands, while my informants revealed that it was price and availability that mostly guided their shopping selections (Davila 2001). Similarly, Elizabeth Chin's ethnography on black kids and consumer culture in New Haven showed that while these kids are regularly stereotyped as poor yet conspicuous consumers—willing to die or kill for a pair of brand new sneakers—the kids she worked with were tempted but did not succumb to logos and brands; they simply could not afford them. Instead, Chin found that they made rational and calculating choices in their purchases and spent money (given to them by Chin as part of the ethnography) on practical items or gifts for the family (Chin 2001). My observations with Puerto Rican shoppers showed similar contradictions between the discourse and the practice of consumption. It is to these dynamics that I now turn.

Going Shopping: "*Nada de eso de que tengo calor y estoy aburrida*"("Never because I'm hot or bored!")

Despite the intense desires of retailers and shopping mall investors and the dominant folklore, Puerto Ricans are not a homogeneous mass of consumers. Even within a single mall like Rio Hondo, which is considered a more modest and accessible mall, there were visible distinctions among customers as well as evidence that impulse and leisure shopping characterized only a select group of visitors at the mall. Customers entering Kmart, primarily mothers accompanied by their children and families or shopping alone buying "*lo necesario,*" differed from the more upscale shoppers—often pairs of women friends who limit their visit to Marshalls (a store considered more upscale because of its discounted designer ware). Many young women flocked to the sales racks. They restricted their browsing to sale items displayed in store entrances, refraining from entering stores altogether. Others carried shopping supplements as a guide to find the best sales. These are the type of glossy and colorful flyers, or "shoppers" as they are locally called, from Wal-Mart, Kmart, and other establishments that in the United States would be limited to weekend newspaper editions but here are a regular complement to local papers.

In particular, the women whose husbands' working hours had been reduced or eliminated altogether took pains to clarify that they were at the mall to buy only "*lo necesario,*" as opposed to "*la compraera*" or the free-style shopping that they attributed to others, never to themselves. Elsa, a 26-year-old mother of two who works at home, and whose husband's hours at work had been cut, described having to return all the clothes and materials she had purchased for her kids; they were no longer going to a private school as there was no money for school dues or uniforms. She used the Kmart card I gave her strictly for her children's back-to-school purchases. In this way, over and over, shoppers gave more signs of being calculating rather than compulsive. There was the fitting-room chatter about whether one had checked prices at Click or Rave before purchasing the item at Kress; and many women walked into stores carrying shoppers and coupons. At times, especially before lunchtime, the stores seemed desolate. In this regard, I should note that I conducted the bulk of my fieldwork in January, in what is regarded a commercial *tiempo muerto* (down time) when people are outspent after the holidays. Puerto Rican consumption is fueled largely by holidays, and this too brings attention to the social aspects of consumption, and to the seasonal patterns of gift giving and reciprocity that serve to spur, but also to deter, shopping throughout the year.

People recalled the last *gusto* or treat they bought themselves with joy and glee: the $80 Chanel perfume from Sears that a retired woman purchased for herself; or the two pairs of shoes with rhinestones, $49.99 each, bought by a nurse working at a government medical clinic in Barrio Obrero, a working class neighborhood. These were the first shoes she had purchased, rather than inherited from her sister, in years. There was also the single mother who bought herself a pair of shoes when she learned they were half price with the purchase of another pair of shoes she had come to buy for her daughter. She was excited about this special deal because she shared her daughter's shoe size; between them, they now had two new pairs of shoes. Far from being characterized as impulse shoppers, these customers represent women who buy treats for themselves with great calculation and who recall their shopping adventures at the mall with relish, because while visiting the mall may be a common occurrence, buying something for themselves was considered a special treat.

Even young working women, who emerged as the most frequent and enthusiastic shoppers, gave signs of thriftiness and calculation. Claudia, a 24-year-old university student I met at the women's clothing store Rave, was purchasing two shirts on sale at $8 each. She works in retail and lives with her parents, a common pooling resource and cost-cutting measure among young people on the island. Her parents pay most of her living expenses, leaving car payment as her biggest expense. She comes to Rio Hondo for lunch and browses the clothing stores almost daily, frequently leaving with a shopping bag. She dressed fashionably, and her makeup and hairstyle were carefully done. "We're *gastadores compulsivos,* and I'm one of them," she noted, admitting that the bulk of her income is spent on clothing. Yet she too was also paying for the price of maintaining her *gustos.* She skipped this year's vacation, which she regularly takes, a necessary strategy to maintain her weekly shopping trips.

This informant's response brings attention to the type of expenses that people will regularly give up in order to maintain whatever consumption level they may be accustomed to. It also highlights the values and cultural meanings that we regularly impart to different ways of spending money for "leisure" (Chin 2001; Zukin 2004; Zukin and Maguire 2004; O'Dougherty 2002). Vacationing and travel, entertainment (going to the movies, to the theater, to a concert), taking a course, and home repairs are some key leisure expenditures that are rarely frowned upon in society, even though they can incur more costs and debt than a shopping spree at the mall. Unlike a shopping spree, the above expenses are regarded as constructive for personal growth or for the greater benefit of society. But the fact is, in moments of economic hardship, it is far easier and more significant to anyone's budget to give up visiting an aunt in Florida than to do without a trip to the mall. In other words, equating shopping with money squandering, without taking consideration of people's larger economic decisions and invisible calculations to stay afloat, can lead to misguided assumptions of their consumption.

I was especially impressed with the bargain shopping skills of the average Puerto Rican woman I interviewed. Often when I asked about people's latest purchase I was met with stories of elaborate footwork and research carried out before making a purchase. Brenda, who had lost her phone and could not replace it, was thankful to her sister who sent her to Wal-Mart to buy a phone for ten dollars, and then to AT&T to purchase a replacement chip for $26.99. The women I talked to were savvy shoppers and had ample references to what constitutes a real sale, such as the woman who immediately walked away from a 50-percent-off sale rack because a shirt originally priced at fourteen dollars read ten dollars on the price tag. I myself take great joy in using my bargain shopping skills, and was quite proud of the ten-dollar dress I found at Plaza del Sol, until I met Yvette in Plaza Rio Hondo. A 45-year-old single mother, she visits the mall four times a week, to shop and "to get rid of stress," a statement that readied me for accounts of "*compradera*" sprees. But she quickly surprised me with a matter-of-fact discussion of her budget: "If there's money in the budget I buy something small, usually less than ten dollars, but if there's no money in the budget I don't buy, or simply buy something listed in the shopper." Yvette works as an accounting clerk in the purchasing department of a pharmaceutical company, and took great pride in her savvy with numbers and budgets. Her shopping sprees, it turns out, are mainly research trips to look around; she makes a purchase only when money is available. She went on to evidence her vast insider knowledge of where the deals are: shoes for $10 at Wal-Mart; dresses discounted by 80 percent at a "very special store" in Plaza del Sol, which she did not name though she laughed when I guessed "Group USA."

Yvette was not the only respondent who brought up her budget and shared tips for finding the best deals. Jose, a hairstylist in his 40s, was one of the few respondents who described himself as debt free. He had been in debt in his youth and had learned to budget from hardship. Now he divides his monthly pay in four payments to determine well in advance how much he can spend on the movies, his greatest *gusto.* Jose had purchased a new car last year and was keeping up with the payments by refraining from purchasing clothes. His last purchase was Christmas gifts, toys for his nephews. Then there was the "Kmart woman," as I called her, because she buys everything at Kmart: her husband's clothes, the family's shoes, her home decorations, and so on. Yolanda works at home, and her husband works at the post office, which is considered a good job by Puerto Rican standards because it is a "federal" position, not a more vulnerable local government job. She comes four times a week to shop, which she loves to do to "get out of the house." In fact, she admitted purposefully pacing her purchases, buying one item today, leaving another for the next day to ensure that she always has "an excuse to leave the house" for a shopping errand. Her errands were limited, however, to buying detergent and household supplies advertised in the Kmart shopper she faithfully reads. She skips most other stores, she told me, so she's not tempted to buy. She too talked about budgets and prioritizing household expenses before anything else.

Finally, my informants' most effective cost-cutting measure was simply to abstain from going to the mall altogether. This is a common practice among the most marginal groups as documented by a study of the economic practices of unemployed women who had been fired after the closing of manufacturing plants throughout the island (Colon et al. 2008). I too came across women who told me they had stopped going to malls or who said it had been months before their last visit to a shopping mall. In turn, this cost-cutting strategy sheds light on yet another aspect of Puerto Rico's high economic deficit/consumption puzzle: namely, that going shopping is still largely a spatial practice, requiring the bulk of the Puerto Rican population that lives in suburban and rural settlements to leave their homes and communities to go shopping.

More specifically, Puerto Rican society is organized around the automobile. Pedestrian opportunities to access stores and purchase goods are generally limited for those not living within the immediacy of a town center, unlike many major cities where one need only walk a block before encountering a store. Consequently, people in need, such as the women fired from their factory jobs, can limit consumption by eliminating the practice of "going out shopping" altogether. This means that that the image of the overflowing Puerto Rican shopping mall that is so often discussed on the island needs to be tempered by the high physical density and excessive concentration of shoppers resulting from the island's urban planning and its segregation of domestic and commercial spaces. This physical concentration of retail activity assures that shopping centers appear constantly packed, providing a far more skewed picture of retail than if stores were evenly distributed throughout the island's physical landscape.

The Modern Overspent Consumer: Some Local Thoughts on a Global Discourse

Where does all this deliberation about Puerto Rican consumption practices leave us? To summarize, though Puerto Ricans described the average Puerto Rican consumer as *comprarero y gastador* (a compulsive shopper and wasteful), few included themselves in this characterization or admitted partaking in carefree shopping behavior. Perhaps this is because of the political symbolism involved in the act of shopping on an island where economic woes are at the forefront of public debate. O'Dougherty's (2002) work on consumption among Brazil's middle classes in times of high inflation is relevant here. She describes how consumption intensified as a practice of class differentiation but not without a discourse of morality enveloping consumption around the "right" ways to consume and be a good Brazilian. For instance, using cunning to get the cheapest goods was socially accepted and encouraged, but not if it appeared to overstep society's larger needs.

I believe that a similar discourse of shopping morality may be at play among my Puerto Rican informants. Admitting that one over-shops is to announce out loud that one is well-to-do. But in times of economic hardship it also implies that one may be profiting from something or someone at the cost of others, whether one is *riquito* (independently wealthy) or, worse still, stealing from the government, evading taxes, hiding income, or engaged in illicit activities such as in the drug economy. At the same time, reveling in a generalized view of Puerto Ricans as conspicuous and limitless consumers is to believe that while I may not be able to shop, others can and continue to do so. This position allows Puerto Ricans to protect and project an optimistic image of the island as a modern country with high living standards in reference to an imagined "third world" beyond the island that truly suffers. It is to believe, in the words of the "Kmart woman" quoted above, that Puerto Rico is in fact a *pueblo bendecido*, a blessed country, because "Puerto Ricans cry broke but they always find money to make a purchase."

This strategy may prove comforting, but it comes with a price. It involves reproducing the myth of Puerto Ricans as "shop 'til you drop" consumers who are impulsive and wasteful; in other words, it is a self-subjugation that further stereotypes Puerto Ricans as irrational consumers when in fact, as I have shown, they are regularly quite calculating and smarter in their purchasing than retailers would have us believe. Unfortunately, this strategy directly benefits the unabated growth of the shopping mall industry—the most direct beneficiary of the view that Puerto Ricans will always find a buck to make a purchase. In particular, shopping mall investors and real-estate speculators revel in the view of the limitless consumer, which allows them to rationalize the need to build even more shopping malls while benefiting from government tax-free passes that help buffer their losses and investment risks, whether there are shoppers or not. In this regard, we may imagine a not-so-distant future where the shopping mall business may not even need shoppers to make a buck; the illusion will do. And as we have seen, Puerto Rico provides a good illusion. Yet the recent selection of Plaza Las Americas as the main gathering point for a national strike against privatization in the fall of 2009 may suggest that Puerto Ricans may be ready to move beyond the illusion. The strike showcased a key predicament of neoliberalism: if there are no jobs, there can't be shopping. Much can be said about the takeovers of shopping malls by strikers, but to me, they represent a hopeful challenge to the uncritical celebration of an unlimited world of consumption. When the prerequisite for a consumer society disappears—a job, a salary, the type of job security that allows people to make big purchases—only social strife and inequalities remain. It remains to be assessed whether what we're seeing is the emergence of a new type of social movement that links our diminished and limited opportunities in the realm of consumption with the demands for the structural factors that make people's consumer lifestyle possible; demands for the conditions that allow all citizens to fully enjoy and gain access to the dreams and aspirations of our contemporary world. For now, the lesson here is that notions of overconsumption, so widely circulated across modernizing societies, require critical probing for the work they do and the interests they are made to serve in historically and culturally specific contexts. As we have seen, the retail industry accrues value through the myth of the Puerto Rican shopper as a consumer who's inclined to over-shop. This so-called overconsumption allows branded shopping corporations to continue to expand, with considerable encouragement via government incentives. Another lesson is the need to push beyond the seeming "sameness" of the mall. Far from their standard characterization as structures that despatialize localities and level out middle-class identities across the globe, they should be seen as territories that breed symbolic performances and visible acts of distinction by the way they are marketed as well as by their use by shoppers and browsers alike.

Notes

1. Marisol Lebron, Louis-Philippe Michel Romer, Elizabeth Chin, and Maureen O'Dougherty provided useful comments. Thanks to Blowing Up the Brand conference organizers and book editors Melissa Aronczyk and Devon Powers.
2. See Segal (2009) on the decline of America's love affair with shopping malls. See also the International Council of Shopping Centers, a trade organization for shopping malls which traces the development of the industry, and the rise of emerging economies in its monthly "Shopping Center Today": http://www.icsc.org/sct/sct_article.php?i=sct0508&s=1&d=21.
3. See "Trouble on Welfare Island," *The Economist*, May 27, 2006, D12; and Center for New Economy 2006.
4. See http://en.wikipedia.org/wiki/List_of_shopping_malls_in_the_United_States and Puerto Rico's Convention Bureau, http://www.meetpuertorico.com/

References

Alvarez Curbelo, Silvia. 2005. "Las Nuevas Murallas: La Walmartizacion de San Juan de Puerto Rico." Pp. 55–84 in *Ciudades Translocales: Espacios, Flujo, Representacion*, ed. R. Reguillo and M. G. Anativia. New York: Social Science Research Council.

Business Register. 2009. Commercial Trade. http://www.businessregisterpr.com/search?comercialTrade=true

Chin, Elizabeth. 2001. *Purchasing Power: Black Kids and American Consumer Culture*. Minneapolis: University of Minnesota Press.

Cohen, Lizabeth. 2003. *A Consumers' Republic: The Politics of Mass Consumption in Postwar America*. New York: Knopf.

Colon, Alice, Maria Maite Mulero, Luis Santiago and Nilsa Burgos. 2008. *Estirando el Peso: Acciones de ajuste y relaciones de genero ante el cierre de fabricas en Puerto Rico*. San Juan, University of Puerto Rico: Centro de Investigaciones Sociales.

Comaroff, Jean and John Comaroff. 2001. *Millennial Capitalism and the Culture of Neoliberalism*. Durham, NC: Duke University Press.

Davila, Arlene. 2001. *Latinos Inc: The Marketing and Making of a People*. Berkeley: University of California Press.

Davila Santiago, Ruben. 2005. *El Mall: Del Mundo al Paraiso*. San Juan, PR: Ediciones Callejo.

Developers Diversified Realty. 2009. http://www.ddr.com/site.php?center_id=929&state_path=puertorico (accessed January 10, 2009).

Diaz, Marian. 2009. "Medicina peor que la enfermead. Economistas advierten porpuestas del CAREF empeoraran la recesion." *El Nuevo Dia*, January 14, 30–31.

Dougherty, Connor. 2007. "Global Economy: Puerto Rico's Economic Slump Weighs Hard on Consumers." *Wall Street Journal*, August 14, A6.

Duany, Jorge. 2008. *A Transnational Migrant Crossroads: The Circulation of People and Money in Puerto Rico*. San Juan, PR: Center for the New Economy.

Enchautegui, Maria. 2008. *Por debajo de la mesa: Una mirada a los trabajadores informales de Puerto Rico*. San Juan, PR: Center for the New Economy.

Gigante, Lucienne. 2000. "Meet Me at the Movies." *Caribbean Business*. March 1. http://puertorico-herald.org/issues/vol4n10/CBMovies-en.html (accessed January 11, 2009).

Gonzalez, Francis Xavier and Martha Hermilla. 2008. "Bienvenidos a la tercera edicion de Isla Estilo." Isla Estilo. Isla Centros comerciales, December, p. 8.

Goss, Jon. 1993. "The Magic of the Mall: An Analysis of Form, Function and Meaning in the Contemporary Retail Built Environment." *Annals of the Association of American Geographers* 83 (1): 18–47.

Grosfoguel, Ramon. 2003. *Colonial Subjects: Puerto Ricans in a Global Perspective*. Berkeley: University of California Press.

Halter, Marilyn. 2002. *Shopping for Identity: The Marketing of Ethnicity*. New York: Schocken.

Liechty, Mark. 2002. *Suitably Modern: Making Middle-Class Culture in a New Consumer Society*. Princeton, N.J.: Princeton University Press.

Martinez, Marialba. 2005. "Buy, Buy, Buy…" *Caribbean Business*, March 3. http://www.puertorico-herald.org/issues2/2005/vol09n09/CBSalesPR.html (accessed 10 May 2010).

Miller, Daniel. 1998. *A Theory of Shopping*. Ithaca, NY: Cornell University Press.

Miller, Daniel, ed. 1995. *Acknowledging Consumption: A Review of New Studies*. London: Routledge.

Morrissey, Marietta. 2006. "The Making of a Colonial Welfare State." *Latin American Perspectives* 146 (33): 23–41.

Muriente-Pastrana, Aurora. 2009. "Sorprendido el Pueblo." *Primera Hora*, January 10, p. 7.

O'Dougherty, Maureen. 2006. "Public Relations, Private Security: Managing Youth and Race at the Mall of America." *Society and Space* 24 (1): 131–154.

———. 2002. *Consumption Intensified: The Politics of Middle-Class Daily Life in Brazil*. Minneapolis, MN: University of Minnesota Press.

Ortiz-Negron, Laura. 2007. "Space Out of Place: Consumer Culture in Puerto Rico." Pp. 39–50 in *None of the Above: Puerto Ricans in The Global Era*, ed. Frances Negron Muntaner. New York: Palgrave.

Ortiz-Negron, Laura, and Carlos Guilbe Lopez. 2005. *Arcadas de las Estaciones 20–21. Visiones de los centros comerciales en Puerto Rico.* San Juan, University of Puerto Rico: Centro de Investigaciones Sociales.

Rosa, Taina. 2006. "DDR Not Scared of Economic Woes in Puerto Rico." *Caribbean Business* 34 (24): 40.

Ryan, Frances. 2009. "Dismal Roller-Coaster Ride in Retail Shows Glimmers of Hope for Future." *Caribbean Business* 37 (1), January 8. http://www.caribbeanbusiness pr.com/search_news02.php

Ryan, Frances, and Jose Carmona. 2007. "Birth of a New Investment Era." *Caribbean Business* 35 (34): 1; 20–24.

Segal, David. 2009. "Our Love Affair with Shopping Malls Is on the Rocks." *New York Times*, January 31.

Underhill, Paco. 2005. *Call of the Mall: The Geography of Shopping.* New York: Simon and Schuster.

Veblen, Thorstein. [1899] 1994. *The Theory of the Leisure Class.* New York: Penguin Books.

Wikipedia. List of Shopping Malls in the United States. http://en.wikipedia.org/wiki/List_of_shopping_malls_in_the_United_States (accessed January 2009).

Wilson, Ara. 2004. *The Intimate Economies of Bangkok: Tomboys, Tycoons, and Avon Ladies in the Global City.* Durham, N.C.: Duke University Press.

Zukin, Sharon. 2004. *Point of Purchase: How Shopping Changed American Culture.* New York: Routledge.

Zukin, Sharon, and Jennifer Smith Maguire. 2004. "Consumers and Consumption." *Annual Review of Sociology* 30: 173–197.

CHAPTER SIX

Branding, Crisis, and Utopia

Representing New York in the Age of Bloomberg

Miriam Greenberg

On November 3, 2009, New York City mayor and multibillionaire media magnate Michael Bloomberg narrowly won reelection to his third term in office. The circumstances of his reelection were controversial: in order to run for a third term, Bloomberg used his political and financial muscle to pressure the city council to overturn a popular term limits law. When in 2001 previous mayor Rudolph Giuliani tried to use the 9/11 terrorist attacks to justify remaining in office, Bloomberg, then in his first run for mayor, vociferously supported term limits. Yet in 2009, Bloomberg cited another crisis—the Wall Street financial collapse—to justify his own third-term bid, arguing that "a leader of his business acumen" was needed to keep the city on track (Honan 2008). This reversal cost him support across the political spectrum (Edroso 2008; Siegel 2008). Complicating these claims was the fact that Bloomberg's personal and political fortunes as founder of Bloomberg LP and as a prodevelopment mayor were intimately tied to Wall Street and New York real estate, the two industries that many argued precipitated the economic crisis (Brash 2011; Barbaro and Chen 2009).

But perhaps the most controversial aspect of his reelection was the astounding amount of money Bloomberg spent on the campaign. Drawing on a personal fortune of $16 billion, Bloomberg spent $108 million, or more than $200 per vote, surpassing his publicly financed opponent William Thompson by a rate of twelve to one ("World's Billionaires" 2009; NYC Campaign Finance Board 2009a, 2009b). Not only did this figure shatter previous records for municipal races; it was the most ever spent in a self-financed campaign, at any level, in United States history (Barbaro 2009c).[1]

Notably, the bulk of this amount, some 85 percent, was spent on marketing, advertising, and branding—a striking figure given Bloomberg's status as an incumbent with universal name recognition.

News reports eventually uncovered the impetus for such exorbitant spending. Bloomberg's extensive internal polling operations had revealed a growing backlash against him among the city's majority nonwhite, nonwealthy, and Democratic voters. To counter this, Bloomberg hired consultants with a record of "attack-dog politics,"[2] who effectively developed a two-tiered branding strategy. The "campaign on the surface" involved advertising across every major media platform, combining utopian, postcrisis scenes of New Yorkers coming together alongside portrayals of Bloomberg as a populist figure and pragmatic "self-made man" with the smarts to get the city back on its feet. Meanwhile, the "campaign that really mattered" was conducted behind the scenes, ensuring that "through money and muscle...Mr. Bloomberg faced no serious obstacle to winning a third term" (Barbaro 2009b). The latter effort was dubbed the "Powell Doctrine": a "sky-is-the-limit ethos" on spending combined with an "intimidating... even brutal" mix of political threats and financial incentives. The effect was to scare off the opposition, silence potential critics, and depress voter turnout in opposition districts.[3] This underground campaign was an ingenious, if ruthless, form of branding: "Sell the inevitability" of a Bloomberg victory, and blanket the media with the message that "opposition was futile" (Barbaro 2009b). The strategy was a remarkable success. It was not until November 4, 2009, the day after Bloomberg eked out a victory of less than five percent rather than the "blowout" so many predicted, that the realization dawned on the pundits and the press: the "King of New York" was "no longer invincible"—and indeed, never had been (Powell and Bosman 2009).

Bloomberg's reelection campaign provides insight into the intersection between branding and political power, one that is becoming more prevalent in cities and regions around the world. It suggests that branding is not only, or even mainly, a matter of generating publicity, as older forms of urban and political boosterism once were. Rather, branding may be seen as a broader social formation, one in which an emphasis on image and media integration is tied to the extension of market priorities into new social and political realms. We can see the symbolic/material dualism of branding in Bloomberg's canny combination of media and marketing with political and economic muscle: overturning term limits and exerting financial and political pressure to reshape the electoral map. Significantly, these branding strategies were deployed during a period of financial crisis. Bloomberg saw the opportunity for the "creative destruction" of existing political and economic arrangements that moments of crisis often generate—opportunities that have catalyzed "neoliberal," or market-oriented, forms of restructuring over the last four decades (Brenner, Peck, and Theodore 2010). Meanwhile, his branding campaign sheds light on the cultural dimension of this creative destruction. Bloomberg's market-oriented platform was narrated through postcrisis, utopian imaginaries of urban solidarity and community, effectively humanizing the private sector while privatizing many aspects of city operations.

Political and marketing campaigns are brief, intensified examples of branding in times of crisis. Yet they should also be seen as manifestations of a phenomenon with deeper structural and cultural roots and ramifications. In this chapter, I seek to trace out the latter, using the period of Bloomberg-era New York City as my case study. Long a global media and marketing capital, New York is also a city that since the 1970s has been at the forefront of urban branding initiatives (Greenberg 2008). Meanwhile, in the post-9/11 period, Mayor Bloomberg became a leading figure in the move to political branding for a new generation of "CEO-politicians." This chapter will first theorize the co-evolution of urban and political branding and the strategies of representation and restructuring that both employ. I then explore the dominant ideological framework of this branding, namely the appeal to postcrisis, utopian desire. Finally, I turn to an empirical analysis of recent branding campaigns, drawing on interviews with leading figures in the Bloomberg administration.[4] I focus on three areas of innovation in these rebranding initiatives: the development of marketing infrastructures and technologies; the globalization of the city's image; and the integration of urban branding into internal political governance.

The Co-Evolution of Urban and Political Branding

The origins of contemporary branding may be traced to the onset of economic crisis in the late 1960s and 1970s. It was then that corporations based in Western industrialized nations faced a combination of pressures—including global competition, recession, and the critique of the consumer rights movement—that pushed them to embrace a new form of valorization and self-preservation, called at the time "reputational capital" (Arvidsson

2004; Greenberg 2008; see also the introduction to this volume).[5] At the same time, the attempt to quantify, and ultimately produce, this new form of symbolic capital expanded from the private to the public sector. In the midst of recession and ongoing fiscal crisis, cities and regions began to brand themselves as business- and tourist-friendly global capitals. Much like the model of corporate branding upon which this process was based, the new urban branding entailed a two-pronged approach, combining marketing and image-making, on the one hand, with political and economic restructuring, austerity measures and pro-business reforms, on the other (Greenberg 2008). These practices helped shape, and were shaped by, the rise of the "neoliberal city," and with this, "entrepreneurial" forms of urban governance (Brenner and Theodore 2002; Hackworth 2006; Harvey 2001). In conjunction with this market-oriented shift, branding practices enabled the more thorough commodification of the city's symbolic as well as material assets.

Urban branding also altered the interconnected spheres of "promotional culture" in profound ways (Wernick 1991). In essence, urban brands created a powerful place-based promotional umbrella that could extend to other commercial entities—from corporations and industries based or doing business in the city; to products produced in or associated with the place; to movies, television programs, and magazines shot on location; to individual celebrities or entrepreneurs living and working within its borders (Molotch 2003: chapter 6). Branding coalitions, meanwhile, sought to exploit the secondary media coverage, "brand extensions," and actual "cobranding" that came about through the representation of the city via these commercial entities (Keller and Aaker 1992; Chang 2009).[6]

Since the 1990s, politicians have sought to take advantage of this urban brand umbrella. Aspiring and sitting mayors in particular have begun to brand themselves in association with the branded images of their cities in an effort to mobilize citizens as voters and constituents. This shift towards urban and political branding is part of a broader "postparty" and "postmachine" trend in urban politics around the world, through which the political party and its patronage-based machinery no longer hold sufficient power to sway elections and govern effectively (Pasotti 2009). In place of old voter-mobilization governance models, political branding has arisen as a putatively fairer system that emphasizes the figure and "vision" of the individual candidate or official and this individual's capacity to efficiently manage the "business" of the city.

The branding of cities and their politicians are now integrally intertwined, with an urban brand influencing the marketability and image of the mayor, and the branding of the mayor influencing the image and marketability of the city. This conjunction speaks to the ongoing merging of public and private spheres. In 1970s New York City, branding was introduced by private sector-led coalitions based outside City Hall, working in concert with entrepreneurial city and state officials and temporary crisis regimes. Today, by contrast, the branding of New York is centrally managed by a "CEO-mayor," in concert with private sector leaders working inside City Hall, with the goal of furthering both the city's and their own political and economic interests. Such privatization, it is argued, provides a crucial tactical and competitive advantage in times of crisis, when the national and global position of the city is challenged. In a context of increasing market deregulation and volatility, in which crises of various types—fiscal, environmental, security, housing, etc.—occur with greater frequency and impact, this centralized branding regime becomes a kind of rapid response system for gauging and building support, internally and externally, for the city and its leadership. Yet this powerful and profitable new strategy also raises old questions, long central to urban sociology and political science: who governs, and who benefits from, this branded city?

Branding, Crisis, and Utopia

In the neoliberal era, urban brands and branded politicians assist local governing strategies, becoming the most publicly visible aspect of an increasingly privatized restructuring process. This strategy has been particularly useful in periods of crisis, which, by producing profound ruptures in the social system, provoke widespread contestation over the future direction of the city. It is during these periods that brands play their most active role: presenting an imagined consensus that transcends class, race, and neighborhood. In so doing, branding campaigns aim to soothe the trauma of crisis, legitimize new leadership, as well as aestheticize and distract critical attention from highly politicized processes of urban recovery and rebuilding. I propose two interrelated ways of conceptualizing this ideological power. One applies Fredric Jameson's theory of the "utopian aspect of mass culture" (Jameson 1992); the second draws on the expanding field of "crisis communications," specifically the "rhetorical approach" to management and branding in times of crisis (Millar and Heath 2004). These approaches allow us to consider the cultural dimensions and historical and political contexts in which branding campaigns most often arise.

Jameson's theory, from his 1979 essay "Reification and Utopia in Mass Culture," argues against the Frankfurt School model of mass culture. Rather than "empty distraction or 'mere' false consciousness," the ideological aspect of mass culture should be seen, at its root, as utopian. He describes this utopian dimension as that which conveys "our deepest fantasies about the nature of social life, both as we live it now, and as we feel in our bones it ought rather to be lived" (Jameson 1992: 34). This fantasy entails the "optical illusion of social harmony," the "ritual celebration of the renewal of the social order," and "the ineradicable drive towards collectivity" and social solidarity (26, 27, 34). But, he cautions, it is commonly used as a "fantasy bribe," for which empty consumerism is exchanged.

While Jameson doesn't mention it explicitly, the context of crisis is highly relevant to his theory, developed as it was in reference to popular films of the 1970s. By design, crisis-era branding is saturated with utopian themes. The aspirations of targeted groups are researched and responded to by marketing consultants, designers, brand managers, and experts in "crisis communications" who collectively craft these campaigns. Indeed, it might be argued that crisis communications is the *Ur*-form of contemporary brand management, as corporations, cities, and political figures become acutely aware of the need for branding when their image and reputation are most at risk. Crisis communications emerged as a specialization within the fields of brand management and public relations in the late 1980s, prompted by the economic crisis of 1989–1992, a rash of corporate scandals, and the pressures of responding to criticism within the new Internet and cable TV-driven "24-hour news cycle."[7] Leaders in the field argue that effective communications can "[make] crisis an opportunity rather than a calamity," generating "positive outcomes" like renewed customer/constituent loyalty and economic growth (Ulmer, Sellner, and Seeger 2007: 3–4).

The notion of crisis-as-opportunity has been seized upon in another, less publicized sense. High profile rebranding campaigns have almost invariably been accompanied "behind the scenes" by new ways of doing business through political and economic restructuring. In the case of urban and political branding this has entailed policies that spur real estate development and attract tourism and corporate relocation while cutting public spending, minimizing public oversight, and privatizing public space. This sets up the highly contradictory dynamic that Jameson warned us against, in which projections of social solidarity obscure and help reproduce processes of social exclusion.

Rebranding New York City Post 9/11 and the Wall Street Crisis

From 1975, when fiscal crisis pushed the city to the edge of bankruptcy; to 2001, when the attacks of 9/11 sent its economy into a tailspin; to 2008, when its financial firms set off a global financial meltdown, New York has loomed large in the history of urban crisis. The city's stature reflects three main factors: the scale of New York's financial industries, and thus the outsized impact of crisis on the local, national, and global economy; the city's role in the public imagination—dominant in the 1970s, and still prevalent today— as an untamed "asphalt jungle" and "ungovernable city"; and the power of the city's own local media industry to broadcast spectacular images of local crisis around the world. In the context of an image-sensitive global economy, New York has become trapped in a dynamic of image crisis followed by renewed and intensified calls for rebranding.

New York's first branding effort was launched in the mid-1970s by public-private partnerships in response to the city's epic fiscal and image crisis. High-profile tourism campaigns like I♥NY became the publicly visible, populist face of a more controversial process of pro-business economic restructuring (Greenberg 2008). This process has evolved considerably in contemporary New York City, during the period bracketed by the crises of 9/11 and the current Wall Street-led economic collapse. Under the business model of the Bloomberg administration, profound efforts to transform the image and political economy of the city have been undertaken in concert with campaigns by powerful public private partnerships. More than any mayor in New York history, Bloomberg has sought to take "direct coordinated custody of [the city's] image," and to transform this image into a global brand (Bloomberg 2003).

As he did at Bloomberg LP, the Mayor has "vertically integrated" the city's marketing operations, creating a complex hierarchy that controls all aspects of the production and distribution of the brand. This involved hiring the best and the brightest from Wall Street, Madison Avenue and the New York design world, and taking the job of branding New York "in house." In the 1970s, the main groups in the branding coalition were public-private partnerships and state agencies that were independent of and operated outside City Hall. Under Bloomberg, the campaigns are created by public-private partnerships appointed and overseen by the Mayor's office. These partnerships include, primarily, the New York City Economic Development Corporation (NYC EDC), which is charged with stimulating business development for the city through corporate retention and attraction, and NYC & Co, the city's official tourism marketing arm.[8] Both the NYC EDC and NYC & Co operate as "quasigovernmental agencies," funded largely through public monies though free from public oversight. In the aftermath of 9/11, and during his first two terms in office, Bloomberg enlarged these agencies in both size and purview: increasing their funding, expanding their operations, and hiring an upper tier of management that enables both agencies to work directly with the mayor's office at the cabinet level.[9] This restructuring made possible a degree of brand integration for both external and internal political operations that is unprecedented in New York City history, and that is testing the outer limits of what urban branding can accomplish for the city and for the mayor.

The political elevation of these agencies challenges notions of democratic governance. While funded largely by taxpayers, these agencies are primarily beholden to their powerful corporate clients, including some of the city's—and the world's—biggest real estate developers, credit card companies, media conglomerates, hotel chains, and financial firms. Mayor Bloomberg, a longtime member of the city's corporate elite, was himself a board member of these same partnerships prior to assuming office. The elevated political status of these partnerships represents a new degree of political access and influence by powerful business interests.

Three major shifts underlie the Bloomberg-era transformation of the New York brand. The first is the establishment of the organizational base, including technological infrastructure and professional capacity, used to rebrand the city on a global scale. The restructuring and retooling of NYC & Co and NYC EDC have enabled this shift, as I will detail below. The second shift is in the redesign of the representational universe of the city's brand post 9/11. Moving away from more generic city marketing campaigns, branding agencies developed a two-pronged approach: targeting tourists, recent transplants, and locals with utopian images of "authentic New York," an inclusive city of grittiness, creativity, and diversity, while targeting real estate developers, buyers, and businesses with utopian images of "luxury New York," an exclusive city of elite residences, high finance, and high-end consumption. The final shift is in the use of branding as a tool of internal political governance. "NYC," the city's first official brand logo, and www.nyc.gov, the city's revamped website, now provide a common corporate identity and customer service link for all 126 city agencies, projecting a image of City Hall's transparency, accessibility, and efficiency to residents and visitors alike. As we shall see, these three interrelated shifts also underlie the mayor's own carefully crafted political brand, and were central strategies in his costly bid for a third term.

City as Business: Infrastructure, Expertise, and Technology

Over the past eight years, the Bloomberg administration has quietly and expertly constructed a massive new branding apparatus under the aegis of City Hall and modeled it on a vertically integrated, global corporation. The administration has restructured agencies and created new ones; staffed these agencies with professionals from the private sector; ensured that the efforts of these agencies are guided by strategic planning and market research; and integrated all of this via Bloomberg LP's hallmark, state-of-the-art computer terminals, commonly known as "The Bloomberg." As an NYC & Co senior marketing official emphasized, "Bloomberg is a master at creating brands and an extraordinary businessperson. He really knew that if you're going to do the best that you can do for the city—*and that is his goal*—you have to create the city in the likes of how you would create a successful business..." (NYC & Co interview).[10]

At NYC EDC, this restructuring took place internally and outside the public gaze. This is not surprising for this famously opaque organization, which was created in the 1970s to develop private channels through which to stimulate economic activity. Nonetheless, Bloomberg's impact on the scope of such operations has been profound. It entailed hiring an entirely new "C-Suite" of upper management (chief executive, financial, and marketing officers) to guide the city's development priorities. Unlike the previously varied corporate backgrounds of EDC leadership, almost all of these new managers came from investment banking, primarily from powerful firms like Goldman Sachs and JP Morgan. It entailed spinning off the EDC's small business unit, which has become a fully public city agency, so as to focus on deals with big business. It also involved a "5-Borough Economic Opportunity Plan" through which some 80 different pieces of city-owned property would be redeveloped. This scale of urban development has not been seen since the post-WWII era of Robert Moses—though, in its push towards privatization and high end development, it is distinct from the mainly public aims of that earlier period.

Along with this restructuring of the EDC came a new approach to marketing the agency and its activities. The position of Senior VP of Marketing and Communications (SVP) was created, for which a seasoned marketing executive with an extensive background in corporate brand management was hired. The SVP's first tasks were to rebrand the agency as "NYC EDC." This involved the creation of a main brand logo and tagline, the creation of some twenty "sub-brands" to market commercial enterprises on city-owned properties, the hiring of new design staff, and the construction of a state-of-the-art website via the creation of a new interactive media department. These efforts were necessary to communicate the greatly enlarged scope and ambitions of the EDC's development operations under Mayor Bloomberg. They were also essential to SVP's job of reaching an expanded audience. Previously, EDC communications were basic and targeted at one main, albeit segmented, audience: the local and global business community. Now, in an indication of the expanded economic and political role of the agency, EDC's brand campaigns were also targeted to agency employees themselves, as well as elected officials, businesses, and the residents of New York City.

The other epicenter of restructuring was NYC & Co, previously the city's tourism marketing arm. In 2003, with his pursuit of the 2012 Olympic Games as a cornerstone of his post 9/11 plan for economic recovery, Bloomberg created two new marketing groups: NYC Big Events and NYC Marketing. In 2006, in a highly publicized move, he merged these two groups with the city's tourism marketing arm and moved the entire operation to large, new midtown offices (NYC & Co 2006). Bloomberg doubled NYC & Co's city funding to $22.5 million—more than five times what the agency received under the previous administration of Mayor Giuliani. This largesse diluted the funds from member dues from sixty percent to ten percent of the total and, for the first time in the agency's history, shifted control of the city's promotional efforts from travel and tourism industry leaders to the mayor's office itself (McGeehan 2007). Finally, the mayor placed two veteran advertising executives with backgrounds managing some of the world's biggest luxury brands—including Godiva chocolates, Remy Martin cognac, and Cunard cruises—in the newly created positions of Chief Executive Officer and Chief Marketing Officer, respectively (McGeehan 2007). Now, for the first time, NYC & Co had the organizational structure, funds, and expertise to operate as a full-fledged marketing department for the city.

With the aid of the global branding firm Wolff Olins, NYC & Co began operations by creating the city's first official "corporate identity," or logo: three heavyset block letters spelling "NYC." The logo was conceptualized as an "open frame" to be filled with New York's diverse people and infinite forms of cultural expression. To oversee the filling of this frame, the agency hired a new Senior Vice President and Creative Director, a young Yale University graduate in fine arts and a brilliant designer in his own right. Previously this kind of design work was outsourced—as with the commissioning of Milton Glaser to design the I♥NY logo in 1977. Now, in an indication of how seriously culture was taken as an economic engine, an in-house designer was put in charge of maintaining the aesthetic sensibility, pop cultural relevance, and "brand essence" of everything produced by the agency in the name of "NYC."

The notion that New York City's cultural diversity and expression had economic value expanded far beyond the design of a logo. As the mayor indicated in his 2003 State of the City Speech, New York's "cultural attractions" constituted a "competitive advantage" that the city should "imaginatively, aggressively, and relentlessly market" in order to "win us attention from businesses around the world" and "realize additional city revenues immediately" (Bloomberg 2003). His goal in creating the position of Chief Marketing Officer in 2003 was to do precisely this: sell the image and culture of New York—its skyline and landmarks, its famous movies and songs—to corporations interested in co-sponsorship and partnership deals, product and advertising placement, cobranding and naming rights. Once NYC Marketing was folded into NYC & Co in 2006, this branding initiative merged with traditional tourism and convention marketing, transforming NYC & Co from a marketer into a media maker and revenue-generating arm of city government.

The final stage of restructuring involved the creation of ten distinct departments, modeled along the lines of a professional marketing firm. The new Media Department expanded beyond the production of brochures and guides to launch a full service website, complete with original content, updated hourly, written and photographed by an in-house staff of thirty, and translated into nine different languages by another staff of five. In this way the site could compete with established online guides like *Time Out NY* and *New York* magazine. It also enabled the Advertising Department to sell advertising space on the site. Behind the scenes, a new Partnerships Department was put in charge of cobranding and partnering opportunities with external companies that benefit from the tourist and convention trade—from global billboard display companies to credit card companies. The Entertainment Department was charged with pursuing product placement opportunities, seeing that New York City and its logo were shown prominently and positively in television and films. As the NYC & Co official explained, "We just treat the [NYC] brand how other brands are treated. If [a TV show is] going to put an Apple [brand] computer on someone's desk—why shouldn't someone say something about NYC?"

The economic advantage of these massive restructuring efforts were clear. NYC & Co leveraged the $22.5 million it receives from the city to earn some $35 million through direct revenues and partnerships, saving taxpayer dollars. When combined with member dues, the NYC & Co budget now approaches $60 million, a 500 percent increase over the budget of just a decade ago (NYC & Co interview). It also places New York in the top three among city marketing agencies nationally and exceeds the marketing budgets for the entire states of Florida ($33.6 million) and California ($50 million). For the NYC & Co official, however, these national comparisons are not the point: "How do you compete against Dubai, which has a budget of $273 million? That's where our heads are at" (NYC & Co interview).

Luxury and Diversity: Representations of the New Urban Brand

In the year following the attacks of September 11, 2001—the first year of Bloomberg's first term—New York City was branded as a patriotic destination. Advertisements, events, and conventions—notably the Republican National Convention of 2004—directly referenced the disaster, highlighted the city's triumphant strength and ability to rise again, and invited tourists and conventioneers to demonstrate their loyalty by coming to New York City, visiting Ground Zero, and shopping (Greenberg 2003). Studies from market research firms and crisis communications consultants, however, taught the Bloomberg administration that this rhetorical strategy was wearing thin amongst the city's most valued demographic: wealthy business travelers and corporations considering relocation (Wirthlin 2002; Shifflet 2001–2002). Even an oblique reference to patriotic symbols, let alone direct mention of the events of 9/11, made New York City appear "desperate," and repelled affluent travelers (Wirthlin 2002). It was time for the city to "move on" and show that it was back to "business as usual." NYC & Co and NYC EDC were enlisted to achieve this goal, targeting different segments of the city's desired consumer base—tourists and corporations, respectively—and repositioning New York City as a distinctive commodity in the global urban marketplace.

This Is NYC

The city's first official brand campaign, "This Is NYC," was designed in 2006 by the London-based branding firm Wolff Olins. The campaign was then adopted in-house by a newly assembled creative team. The hiring of cutting-edge designers in a period of crisis has its precedent in 1977, when New York State, on the brink of default, hired the advertising agency Wells, Rich, Greene and pop-art graphic designer Milton Glaser to create the I♥NY campaign. In both cases the goal was to harness avant-garde promotional culture to demonstrate the city's youthful vigor and still healthy business climate. In the Wolff Olins campaign, the designers emphasized the uniqueness and diversity of New Yorkers:

> There's only one New York City. But within that one city are five boroughs, approximately 191 neighborhoods, nearly a million buildings and over 8.2 million people. Each individual has their own New York. Within the mind of every single New Yorker resides a different version of New York City. It's a city loved in 138 different languages and viewed through an almost infinite mix of cultures, ideologies, and ways of life. Everyone living side by side. This kaleidoscopic quality is one of the greatest things about this city. It's the very thing we love. But it also makes it difficult to represent. There is no one symbol, no one logo or brand that means New York City to everyone (Wolff Olins 2007).

Indeed, the very impossibility of isolating a single image of New York became the conceit of the campaign:

> Wolff Olins made sturdy letterforms that are thick, rugged—a little on the tough side—just like a New Yorker. The mark is durable and will represent New York for a long time. And the mark functions as a window into infinite complexity. Imagine what you'd see peering in a typical masonry façade—perhaps a fashion designer, a recording engineer or someone crusading for social justice. Like a window this symbol can reveal images of every culture, profession and activity of this city. The NYC brand is a transparent pane of glass that offers a view of real New Yorkers and real NYC neighborhoods. It's a venue for the very ideas that make NYC strong—8 million brands (Wolff Olins 2007).

The campaign celebrated New York's "urbanity," "diversity," even its iconoclasm and historic "crusading for social justice" through a montage of faces and cultural practices. In this way the campaign embodied the urban-centered utopian desires of this charged period; a period during which the very possibility of modern urban existence seemed under threat. Making the subtlest possible reference to 9/11, the shape of the letters and slant of the campaign emphasized the city's "sturdiness," "toughness," "ruggedness," and "durability," responding with attitude and solidarity to the trauma of that event while putting it squarely in the past. The bulky letterforms were then filled with race- and class-diverse snapshots of "authentic" New York-specific references—including hotdog salesmen, designer shoes, hip hop performers, and fashion models.[11]

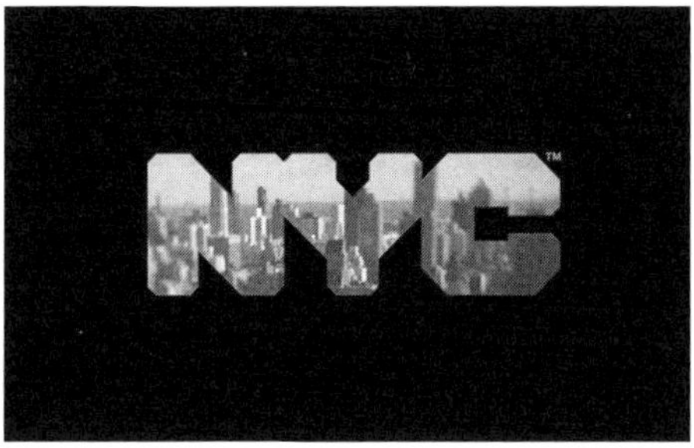

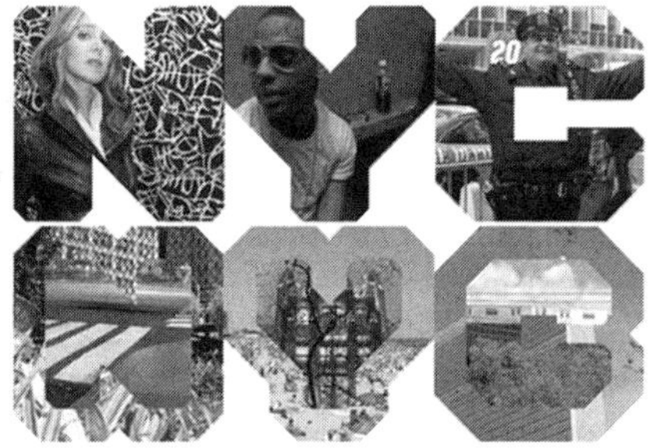

Figure 6.1 (left) The NYC logo, designed by Wolff Olins for NYC & Co in 2006. The bulky letterform evokes a tough, postcrisis New York attitude.
Figure 6.2 (right) The logo is used as a frame to contain images of urban diversity.

A short commercial created for the "This is New York City" campaign used similar montage techniques, juxtaposing historical periods and pieces of New York geography. With the soundtrack of Billy Strayhorn's "Take the A-Train" in the background, recently landed tourists—a white American mother and daughter—look out their cab window at a Manhattan skyline that has been transformed through animation into bobbing lipsticks, ice-cream cones, and Ferris wheels. Jazz-era jubilance is further invoked through clips of the Rockettes dancing and saxophone players swinging atop midtown spires while biplanes circle overhead. Borrowing the emotional charge of the Harlem Renaissance while keeping safe distance from its critical edge, the montage seemed to exorcise the ghosts of the city under attack, turning New York City from a terrorist haven into a shoppers' paradise once again.

The other key element of this representational strategy was to extend the brand through what the senior NYC & Co official referred to as "perception-changing big events," and the free, secondary media coverage such events receive by being covered as news and entertainment across the media spectrum (NYC & Co interview). First events are carefully chosen that will challenge "negative" perceptions of NYC held by important demographics of visitors and/or locals, and that will strategically push the NYC brand in a more "positive" direction. Then the NYC & Co and NYC EDC spend large sums to court, host, and market these events—which now number in the hundreds annually. Examples include the Republican National Convention of 2004 and the Latin Grammys and Country Music Awards, both held in New York for the first time in 2005. This strategy was also behind the multimillion-dollar and ultimately failed effort to bring the 2012 Olympics to New York City.

A similar, "perception-changing" approach was launched to respond to the current Wall Street-led economic crisis and its impact on New York's image. The frontline of attack is an ingenious low-budget, offer-filled program called "New York: The Real Deal," which features *Sesame Street* characters atop tour buses. This was combined with a citywide celebration of the 40th Anniversary of *Sesame Street,* replete with the naming of a street and a holiday after the show, a limited-edition DVD box set, a new "Google doodle," and coverage by all major news outlets (NYC & Co 2009). As the NYC & Co official explained:

> Essentially we're saying, "This is not just the city of Bernard Madoff." So you have Big Bird. While it doesn't say "everyone is not Bernie Madoff"—who could do that?—you say: "We're a family friendly environment. Look at the ambassadors of the city." It opens up the dialogue, the narrative to a new audience. Wrong would be to have a luxury campaign at this time. Right would be to have a family friendly, offer-driven program.

Luxury City

In contrast to the funky, family-friendly diversity of "This is NYC" and "New York: The Real Deal," the Bloomberg administration's approach to overall economic development was branded through a backstage business marketing campaign. Led by the mayor in coordination with the NYC EDC, the campaign was based on a research report by corporate consulting firm McKinsey and Co.[12] The report identified "high-impact industries and functions within industries" that the city should and could successfully attract to New York—namely finance, information technologies, biotechnology, and media—all of which were high margin/high value-added industries. These industries, the report stated, "should be in New York City" and were "ripe for the picking" but would not be enticed on the basis of price. Rather, target marketing should emphasize class-specific perks: the city's highly skilled labor pool, high quality education, as well as high-end cultural and lifestyle amenities for the professional and executive class (Brash 2011).

"Exclusive" and class-specific branding strategies were therefore adopted to spur business development in New York—strategies that seemed diametrically opposed to the city's populist tourism marketing celebrating

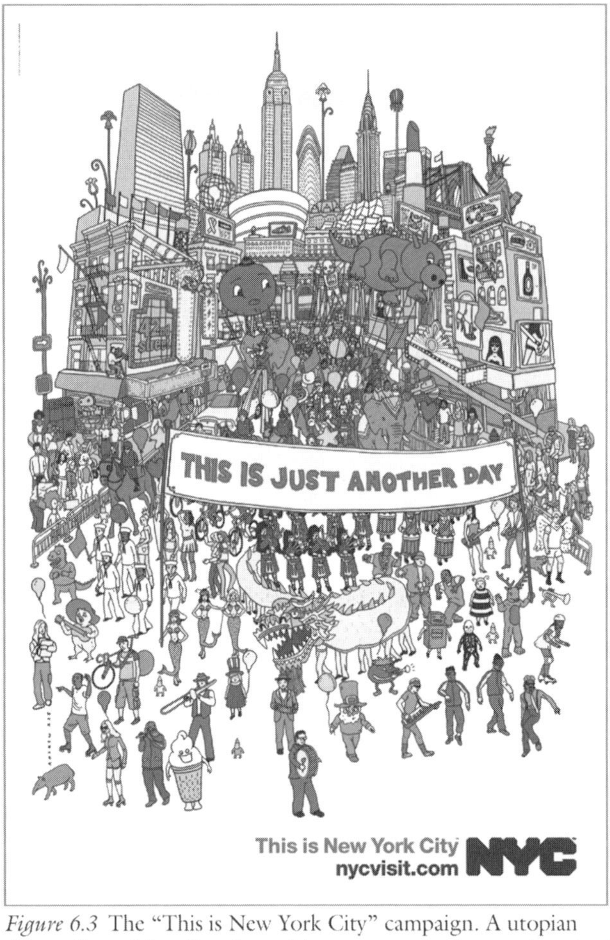

Figure 6.3 The "This is New York City" campaign. A utopian vision of creativity, diversity and harmony set against a reimagined New York skyline.

its "diversity." The strategy was announced in a January 2003 Economic Development Summit, a private, invitation-only event. The summit was attended by the mayor and "100 of the city's top businesspeople and civic leaders," and chaired by Robert Rubin, former secretary of the treasury under President Clinton, and then-chairman of Citigroup (Cardwell 2003). Bloomberg used the summit to assure his audience that his experience as a CEO had shaped his approach to both economic and urban development policy: "I've spent my career thinking about the strategies that institutions in the private sector should pursue... and the more I learn about this institution of New York City, the more I see the ways in which it needs to think like a private company...New York City is never going to be the lowest priced place to do business; it is just the most efficient place to do business. You have to get value for the money that you're going to spend." The ideal target was affluent workers and employers who would be able to take advantage of this high value/high cost environment. "If New York is a business, it isn't Wal-Mart—it isn't trying to be the lowest-priced product in the market. It's a high-end product, maybe even a luxury product."

The Luxury City campaign exploited the fact that global elites could pay a premium to live and work in one of the most expensive cities on earth. It was also part of a broader development agenda to build a physical city that appealed to these global elites, by attracting high-end retailers, hotels, stadiums, and residential towers. Ultimately, this agenda promised to thoroughly transform the face of New York City in a decade, much as the efforts of the public authorities did under Robert Moses in the three decades following WWII.

The Luxury City approach has been tested since the 2008 economic and image crisis. When pressed, the mayor acknowledges he is an advocate of classical "trickle-down" regressive taxation, and against raising income taxes for the city's highest earners: "A very small percentage of people do account for a big part of our income," he said on March 6, 2009, during his weekly radio show. "The first rule of taxation is...you can't tax too much those that can move." Ultimately, the luxury city should be maintained by raising taxes on middle and lower-income New Yorkers, if necessary by raising the sales tax. "You know, the yelling and screaming about the rich—we want rich from around this country to move here. We love the rich people" (Lisberg 2009).[13]

The Promise of Transparency: Neoliberal Governance and the Branded City

The final shift occasioned by the use of urban branding in Bloomberg-era New York is in the realm of governance. The city is not only branded externally, as a place to be consumed by tourists, but also internally, as a product to be consumed by its own residents, as the legitimacy of the Bloomberg administration is reinforced by the political branding of Bloomberg as mayor. Mirroring his enormously successful corporate branding strategy at Bloomberg LP, Bloomberg cobrands his "product" with his own personal brand to mobilize support, whether in the form of new customers or new votes. This approach has served Bloomberg well in both the corporate and the governmental setting. It has helped him coordinate highly complex organizations and to associate himself with the myriad benefits these organizations produce—Bloomberg terminals, Bloomberg News, Bloomberg LP, and now New York City government. It is connected in the public eye with his other highly publicized corporate management practices and technologies, including corporate training for civil servants; statistical, "results-based" performance reports and targets; and most famously, the transfer of the open, "bullpen" layout of his corporate offices, and of Wall Street trading floors, to City Hall.[14] It is embodied by the multi-tiered, "merit-based" pay structure—to which he contributes massive bonuses and charitable donations out of his own pocket to provide added incentives to his inner circle (Barbaro 2009a).[15] In addition, Bloomberg has advanced a model of effective governance linked to technological proficiency and customer service, incorporating Bloomberg terminals into hundreds of city offices, introducing a "311" phone help line, and overhauling the city's official website, www.nyc.gov.[16] Collectively, these practices and technologies have been popularly embraced, serving to legitimize the import of corporate culture into the public sector. The new model sees constituents as consumers rather than clients and promises them access to, and efficient delivery of, high quality services and information—as long as they vote to keep this governance model in place.

As with the urban brand targeted at consumers, this political brand is crafted "in-house" through the work of the Mayor's own branding apparatus: his communications office—which arranges the frequent interviews with the mayor in the "bullpen"—as well as NYC EDC and NYC & Co. Rather than feature the mayor explicitly in their promotions, these firms helped create an overarching brand umbrella, encompassing government agencies and urban development projects, and enabling them all to speak with a "unified voice." It also promotes the idea of "transparency" and "built-in accountability" (NYC & Co interview). In this framework, the mayor's leadership role as pragmatic, technocratic CEO-mayor is implicit.

As an indication of how integrated these external and internal branding strategies are, the senior official at NYC & Co informed me that the unification of governmental messaging was actually a leading motivation behind the creation of "NYC"—the corporate identity associated with the city's break-through post-9/11 tourism marketing campaign:

> The *real* mission [behind "NYC"]—and we were with City Hall when we were discussing this and why this was so important—is that it's the sum of the parts speaking stronger, bigger, better than all the individual parts. So when you see a van going out to help the homeless and it says "NYC," you understand that that is laddering up to the bigger initiatives that are working on behalf of the city, and all the way up to the mayor. And taxpayers can understand where their dollars are going to. And it feels like there is a plan in place, and not just that you don't know what's happening. And there is a lot of pride in that (NYC & Co interview).

Integrating all aspects of city government behind a common identity has not been without conflict. Some of the 126 city agencies have resisted replacing their old logo with "NYC"—much as they have resisted other aspects of neoliberal restructuring under the Bloomberg administration.[17] The NYC & Co official sees such resistance as somewhat irrational: "they think it's important to have their own identity" and don't want to be "oppressed" by the new "*Uber*-brand." The official has arrived at a compromise of sorts, one drawn from her experience managing brands for corporate clients like AT&T and FedEx: the creation of "sub-brands" within the "major brand." Thus some agencies may have personal logos redesigned to more easily connect with the overarching NYC logo. Eventually, however, the goal is to move all agencies under the NYC umbrella: "It's just a process of education, conversation, and working slowly over the coming years." Increasingly, they and the mayor hope, branding will penetrate and link all aspects of urban governance.

Like NYC & Co, NYC EDC has also undertaken the complicated task of developing an urban brand that doubles as a tool of political governance. Here, too, it has done so in the name of promoting the "transparency" of the agency. Under the leadership of its SVP, a sleek, modern "NYC EDC" logo replaced the cumbersome "New York City Economic Development Corporation" insignia, launching a new "NYC: Make It Here" campaign targeting global corporations. The new identity is distinct in look and feel from the bulky and gritty "NYC" campaign, and operates outside of it. (NYC EDC, a public-private partnership, is not counted among the 126 city agencies, and has not been asked to adopt the NYC logo.) Nonetheless, the political aim of the two campaigns is remarkably similar. As underscored by their common embrace of the colloquial "NYC" abbreviation, both emphasize transparency and accessibility for their target audiences in the private sector, as well as the wider benefits to local residents of the work that they do. As a senior EDC official explains, this was key to countering a common perception of the agency's elite orientation:

> When I first came here, we redesigned our whole look and feel, because we looked very bankerish and very exclusionary and very like a "Big Black Hole" kind of company. And what we tried to do was to become a lot more transparent and business friendly and invite people to understand more about what we do and why it was beneficial. The Corporation was doing so many incredible things, and nobody really knew about it. I think partly this was the strategy way back when, that nobody *needed* to know a whole lot about what we did. And anybody that needed to know were [real estate] developers and already knew us. But we are so broad in everything we do that if people don't know us, and what we do, they don't have a sense that the city's under good control and good things are happening. Meanwhile, the media takes lots of cracks at all the projects, and it's really a one-way dialogue. So we try to make sure that people understand that the development that's being done by the city and by the mayor benefits *everybody* (EDC interview).

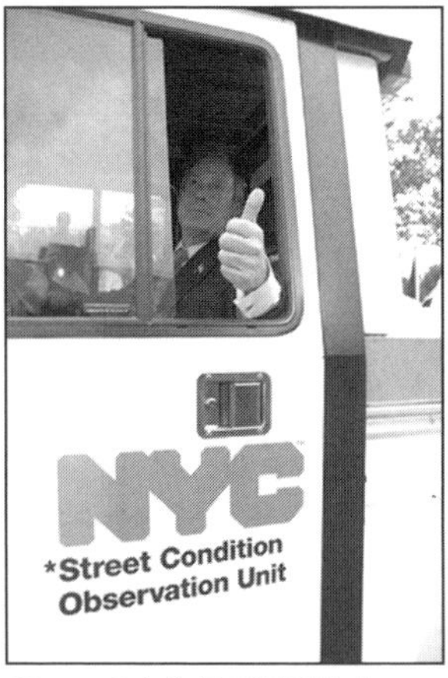

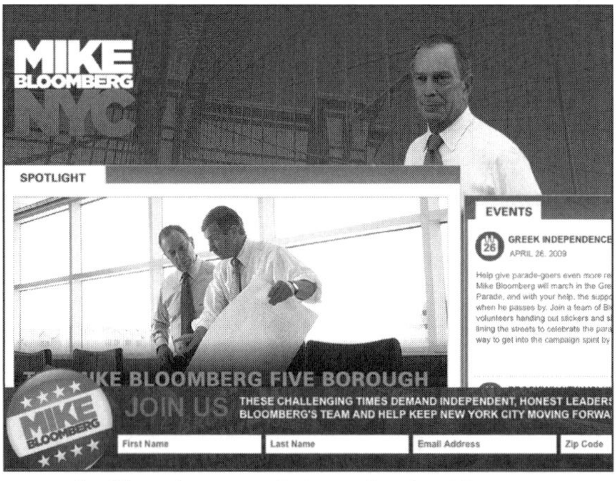

Figure 6.4 (left) "NYC" also promotes the Bloomberg association to local residents.
Figure 6.5 (right) "NYC" (in a different font) used for the mayor's reelection bid, bringing with it the symbolic capital of the broader campaign.

The EDC official's description reinforces the point made by the official at NYC & Co: a new mode of communication and representation was necessary to coordinate and legitimate a new mode of governance under Mayor Bloomberg. In this case, the aim was to help sell and oversee the physical and economic redevelopment of New York City through the Mayor's 5-Borough Plan and its corollary, long-range PlaNYC. These plans, as noted above, overlapped with the expanded 5-borough tourism marketing effort and became pillars in Bloomberg's recent, 5-borough reelection campaign, dubbed "Mike NYC." Unprecedented in scale and scope, these efforts have led to the redevelopment of 80 pieces of city-owned or city-claimed property, including the 125th Street and the Essex Street Markets in Manhattan, Atlantic Yards and Coney Island in Brooklyn, Yankee Stadium and the Hunt's Point Market in the Bronx, Long Island City and Willets Point in Queens, and Fresh Kills in Staten Island.

Meanwhile, these projects have met with organized resistance from neighborhood groups opposed to an element common to most of them: the transformation of previously working class, mixed-use neighborhoods into market-rate real estate development, generally for the purpose of building shopping malls, high-end retail strips, entertainment destinations, and/or central business districts, with the effect of evicting or pricing out current residents and businesses. Thus, a major new job for the creative department at NYC EDC is to use project-specific campaigns to confront political opposition. This has entailed a "huge effort," connecting marketing with business development, and coordinated by the Deputy Mayor of Development (NYC & Co interview). Together, this group has created some 80 new sub-brands for individual neighborhoods targeted for redevelopment as well as hundreds of "pitchbooks" designed for each of the businesses that will have to move out. These books contain utopian renderings of the greener and more affluent future affected communities will enjoy, along with information on how to move out and where to move to. As an EDC official from the creative department explained:

> All of these companies have to move. It's very controversial. So we make these pitchbooks, and we go around to all of these businesses, giving them all of these options of where they could move their business. Nobody wants to move, but eventually they are going to have to move anyway. This helps make people visualize it, and makes it easier.

In an indication of the political lengths to which such branding has gone, these pitchbooks have been given to paid lobbyists to sell particularly controversial developments—e.g., Willets Point, Long Island City, and Coney Island—to local elected officials. The New York City Conflict of Interest Board halted this practice in August of 2009, pointing out that the use of public funds for lobbying purposes is illegal (Rivera 2009; "Bloomberg and Developers" 2009).[18]

As the 2009 election revealed, political branding has its limits when it comes to actually swaying voters. New Yorkers were divided over numerous moves Bloomberg made—e.g., his autocratic style, his multimillion-dollar campaign spending, and his overthrow of a popular mandate on term limits—all of which undermine the "transparent" image of his administration and threaten to undermine his brand.

Nonetheless, it seems that such branding carries with it a significant "return on investment" for the politicians themselves. By contributing to Bloomberg's overall "brand value" as both CEO and mayor, it has been argued that his time in office has added value to the Bloomberg LP brand, and in so doing, fueled the growth of Bloomberg's personal fortune, which is based in his 85 percent share of stock in Bloomberg LP (Loomis 2007). In eight years after taking office, this fortune was quadrupled from $4 billion to $16 billion, making him the city's wealthiest man in New York City and the 17th wealthiest person in the world ("World's Billionaires" 2009).

Bloomberg has not been alone in his good fortune. The number of billionaires in the city has doubled during his tenure, as Wall Street profits have continued to climb alongside recession, "jobless recovery," and the significant increase in the ranks of New York City's poor and low income population, particularly among people of color (Fiscal Policy Institute 2009). Bloomberg-era political and urban branding has helped reproduce and legitimize this class divide. One of the major effects of Bloomberg's political brand has been to represent the meritocratic basis of wealth and corporate profit, the technical superiority of corporate culture, and the natural, even necessary connection of elites to political power. Urban branding helps reinforce these notions, producing the city itself as an engine of wealth, profit, and pleasure-seeking.

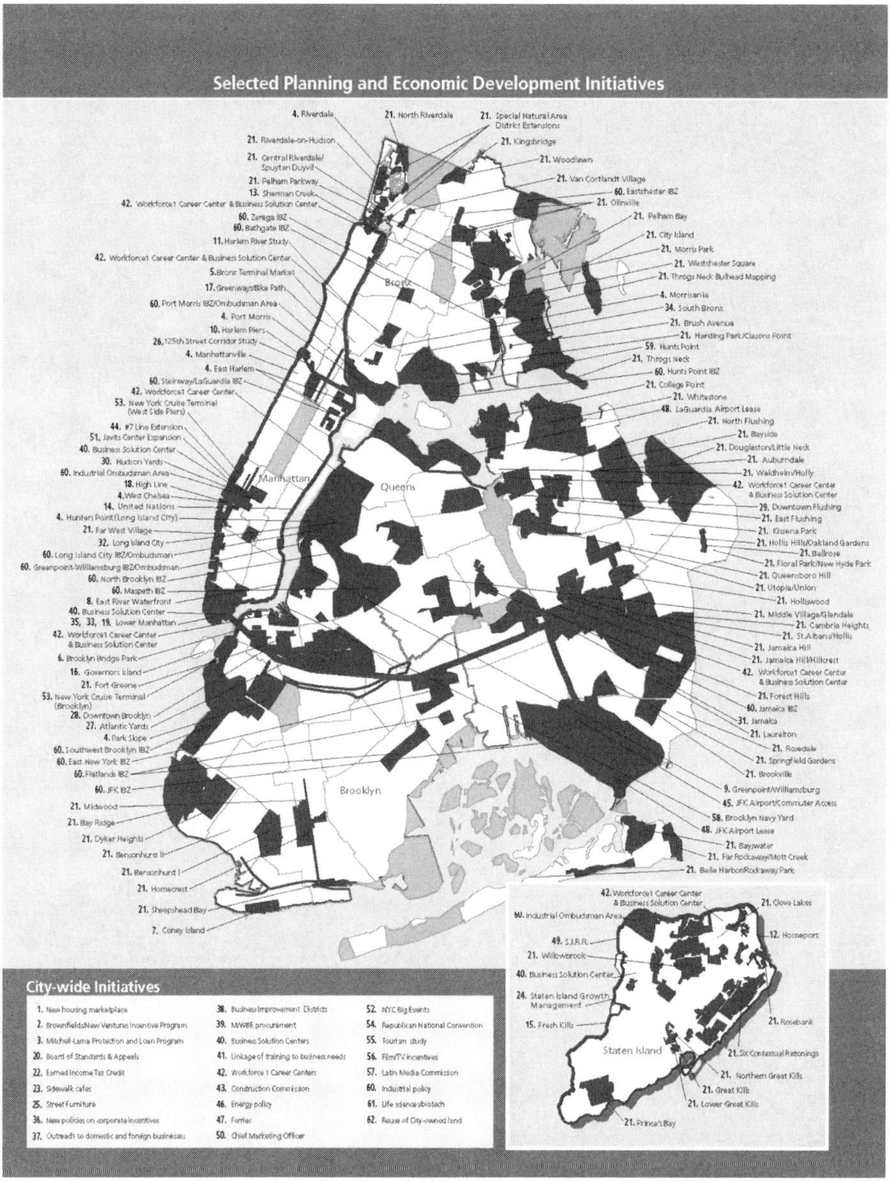

Figures 6.6 (this page) and 6.7 (next page) NYC EDC promotes 5-Borough Economic Development Initiatives in 2007. Most involve transforming working class/industrial neighborhoods into market-rate residential, shopping and business districts.

Transforming New York City

Greenpoint

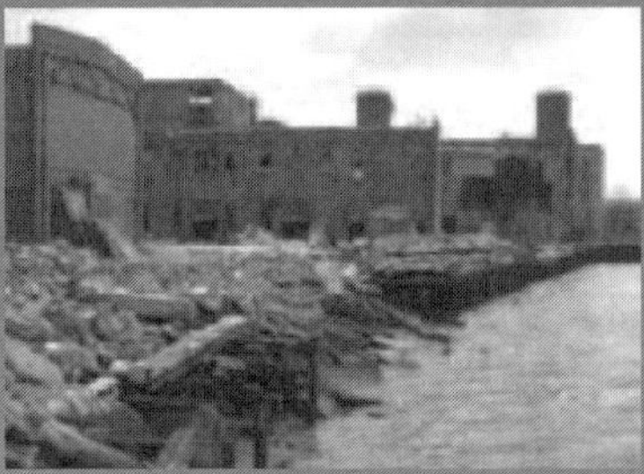

Existing

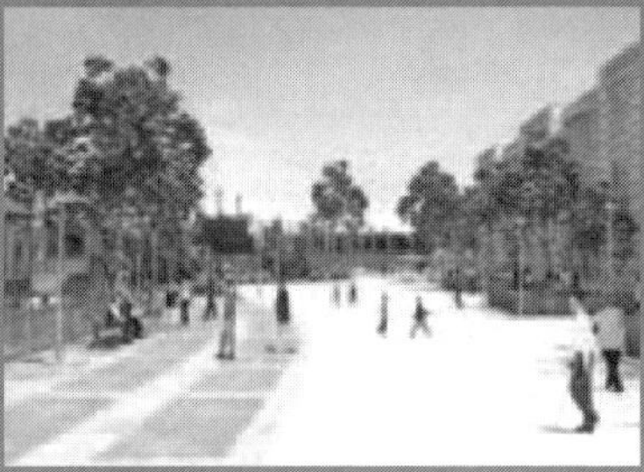

Future

Flushing

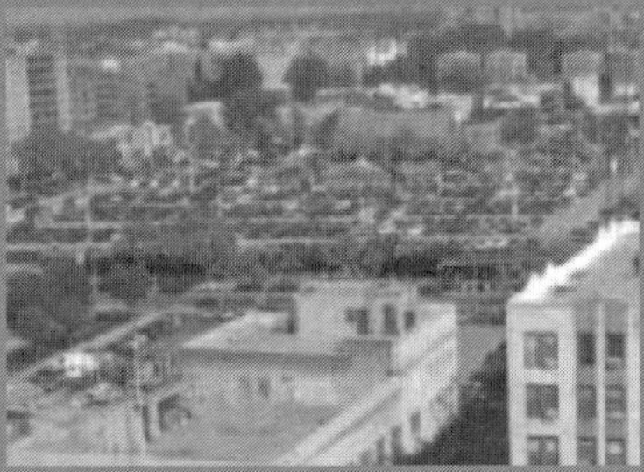

Existing

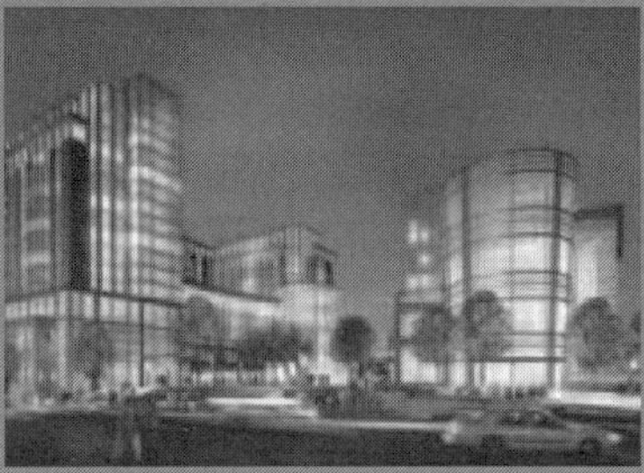

Future

Fresh Kills

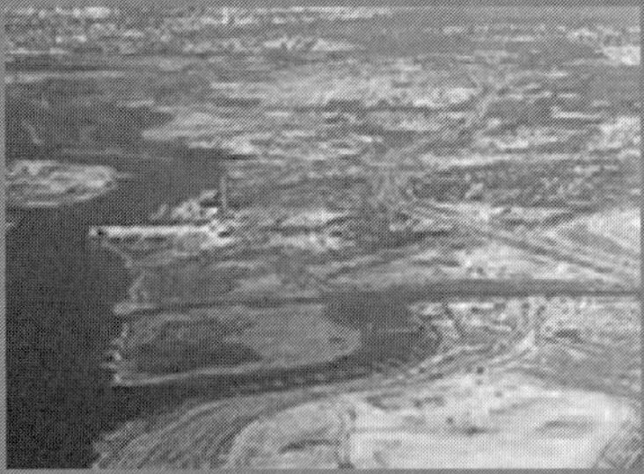

Existing

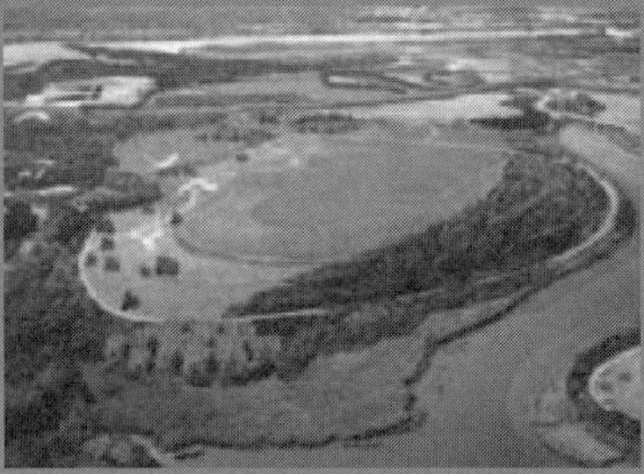

Future

Conclusion

How are we to understand the contradictory discourse contained within New York's new brand? What broader implications does such branding have for cities? I argue that it serves to reinforce a utopian urban imaginary that has emerged globally in the neoliberal period. The utopian notion of governance, as well as of the city itself, is as a transparent consumer democracy that is postclass, postrace, and postpolitical party. The new Utopia is a cosmopolitan capital and a creative city in which divisions are based solely on lifestyle choice, consumer niche, and neighborhood vibe. It is also a resilient city, able to weather grime, crime, and terrorist attacks, to say nothing of the inevitable ups and downs of the stock market. These portrayals reinforce, and are reinforced by, the rebranded image of urban politicians, as evident in Bloomberg's efforts to position himself as a technocratic yet down-to-earth CEO-mayor. "Behind the scenes," other branding strategies are at work to restructure and privatize city agencies, expand market-rate development across the five boroughs, and aggregate power.

Such representations, however contradictory, resonate with popular fears in the midst of crisis, as well as profound desires for authentic and inclusive urban experience, a safe and healthy urban environment, democratic participation in urban politics, and affordable urban space. In short, they help us imagine the "right to the city" to which so many aspire. Embedded within the broader social formation of the neoliberal city, however, urban and political brands may accomplish the opposite of this dream, reproducing the uneven class politics of urban restructuring. The scale and pace of market-rate, "luxury" real estate development under Bloomberg, alongside regressive tax policies that favor businesses and "workers that can move," have led to increasing dependence on volatile and crisis-prone industries like finance and real estate and helped to produce a city with the most unequal incomes and highest levels of unemployment in the nation. Successive waves of gentrification and increases in the cost of living have pushed out mixed-use, working class districts—from Harlem to Willets Point to downtown Brooklyn. Ironically, these neighborhoods have historically been the true home of the grittiness, resilience, and ethnic, racial, and class diversity celebrated in the "This is NYC" campaign. While that campaign represents the utopian fantasy of the city's branding effort, Luxury City is a more accurate representation of the material and ideological transformation of the city and its power structure during the Bloomberg era.

Notes

1. Added to his previous two record-setting campaign budgets, the total amount Bloomberg spent on winning public office came to $250 million.
2. Consultants included Howard Wolfson, who ran Hillary Clinton's notoriously aggressive presidential campaign, and Bradley Tusk, the Deputy Governor in charge of communications for Illinois Governor Rod Blagojevich, until the latter was arrested on federal corruption charges.
3. Campaign pressure was successfully exerted on an extremely wide range of individuals and groups—from local community organizations and non-profits to popular Democratic Congressman Anthony Weiner, who dropped out of the race; to President Obama himself, who, according to the *Times* exposé, agreed to not overtly support Bloomberg's Democratic challenger.
4. I conducted in-depth interviews with a number of key figures, including senior marketing officials at both NYC EDC (interviews conducted on 27 July 2009) and NYC & Co (interviews conducted on August 20, 2009).
5. Of particular significance is the work of Yankelovich, Skelly, and White. See Greenberg (2008).
6. "Brand extension" refers to situations where the urban brand is attached to the corporate brand through advertising campaigns; in "cobranding," the city joins forces institutionally with corporations in the planning and production of joint branding campaigns.
7. Some note that an "essential" precedent was set by the "rapid response capability" pioneered by the 1992 Clinton–Gore campaign and refined during Bill Clinton's eight years under attack by his political adversaries while in the White House.
8. The NYC EDC was originally called the New York City Office of Economic Development (OED), and was created in 1976 by then Mayor Abraham Beame in response to the fiscal crisis. The Convention and Visitors' Bureau was created in 1934, along with thousands of CVBs created in the 1930s cities across the country to stimulate commerce during the Depression.
9. The context of 9/11 was central to this shift in another way: both groups were integral to the creation of the Lower Manhattan Development Corporation, the private sector-led group that drove the redevelopment of Lower Manhattan from 2002–2006.
10. In making this comment, the CMO referenced a Bloomberg quote from a *New Yorker* article that had come out the week prior to the interview. See McGrath (2009).
11. On the desire for a cross-class New York authenticity, see Zukin (2009).
12. See Alper (2002) and Bloomberg (2003). For an excellent discussion on this report, see Brash (2011).
13. Bloomberg added: "People say, 'Oh, well, you know, if the income were redistributed throughout the system more fairly'… I don't know what fair means. You can argue that if you make more money, you deserve more money."
14. A cursory search for references to the "Bloomberg bullpen" calls up tens of thousands of academic and journalistic articles. For the first reference to this, see Nagourney (2001). As the article notes: "The open configuration [of the bullpen] has become a symbol of Mr. Bloomberg's management style in the corporate world."
15. In addition to providing bonuses in the hundreds of thousands to staffers, Bloomberg donated over $1 million to his deputy mayor Patricia Harris' alma mater in her name.

16. See, e.g., Gimein (2002) and Lowry (2007).
17. An example is the Board of Education, which has resisted reforms such as school rankings and merit pay for teachers along with the new corporate identity.
18. The case that has gotten the most press attention is that of former Queens borough president Claire Shulman, who received $250,000 from NYC EDC to lobby city council to endorse the transformation of Willets Point, an industrial area in Queens, into a corporate office park.

References

Alper, Andrew. 2002. "Testimony." Hearing on Corporate Subsidies, Committee on Economic Development, New York City Council.

Arvidsson, Adam. 2004. "On the 'Pre-History of the Panoptic Sort': Mobility in Market Research." *Surveillance and Society* 1 (4): 456–474.

Barbaro, Michael. 2009a. "A Mayor Prizing Loyalty Pays Costly Tribute to His Top Aide." *New York Times*, September 1, A17.

———. 2009b. "Chief Factor in Mayor's Race: Bloomberg Influence." *New York Times*, November 3, A24.

———. 2009c. "Bloomberg Spent $102 Million to Win 3rd Term." *New York Times*, November 27, A1.

Barbaro, Michael, and David W. Chen. 2009. "Bloomberg Sets Record for His Own Spending on Elections." *New York Times*, October 23, A1.

"Bloomberg and Developers." 2009. *The Daily Gotham*, August 21.

Bloomberg, Michael R. 2003. "State of the City Address." Mayoral Press Release, January 8.

Brash, Julian. 2011. *Bloomberg's New York: Class and Governance in the Luxury City*. Atlanta: University of Georgia Press.

Brenner, Neil, and Nik Theodore. 2002. *Spaces of Neoliberalism: Urban Restructuring in North America and Western Europe*. New York: Blackwell.

Brenner, Neil, Jamie Peck, and Nik Theodore. 2010. "Variegated Neoliberalization: Geographies, Modalities, Pathways," *Global Networks* 10 (2): 182–222.

Cardwell, Diane. 2003. "Mayor Says New York Is Worth the Cost." *New York Times*, January 8.

Chang, Wei-Lun. 2009. "Roadmap of Cobranding Positions and Strategies," *Journal of American Academy of Business* 15 (September): 77–84.

Chen, David, and Michael Barbaro. 2009. "Bloomberg Wins 3rd Term as Mayor in Unexpectedly Close Race." *New York Times*, November 3, A1.

Edroso, Roy. 2008. "After Term Limits Overthrow, Era of Bad Feelings Commences." *Village Voice*, October 23.

Fiscal Policy Institute. 2009. *The State of Working New York: Unemployment and Economic Insecurity in the Great Recession*. New York: Fiscal Policy Institute.

Gimein, Mark. 2002. "Mayor Mogul: Mike Bloomberg Wants to Be New York City's CEO. Too Bad He's Only Mayor." *Fortune*, April 1.

Greenberg, Miriam. 2002. "The World Trade Center, Fiscal Crisis, and the Marketing of Recovery." *International Journal of Urban and Regional Research* 27 (2): 386–416.

———. 2008. *Branding New York: How a City in Crisis Was Sold to the World*. New York: Routledge.

Hackworth, Jason. 2006. *The Neoliberal City: Governance, Ideology, and Development in American Urbanism*. Ithaca, N.Y.: Cornell University Press.

Harvey, David. 2001. "From Managerialism to Entrepreneurialism: The Transformation of Urban Governance in Late Capitalism." Pp. 345–368 in *Spaces of Capital: Toward a Critical Geography*. New York: Routledge.

Honan, Edith. 2008. "NYC's Bloomberg Says to Seek Third Term as Mayor." *Reuters News Service*, October 2.

Jameson, Fredric. 1992. *Signatures of the Visual*. New York: Routledge.

Keller, K. L. and D. A. Aaker. 1992. "The Effects of Sequential Introduction of Brand Extensions." *Journal of Marketing Research* (February 29): 35–50.

Lisberg, Adam. 2009. "Mayor Bloomberg: 'We Love the Rich People'; Doesn't Want to Over-tax New York's Wealthy." *New York Daily News*, March 6.

Loomis, Carol. 2007. "Bloomberg's Money Machine: There's Power in that Name." *Fortune*, April 5.

Lowry, Tom. 2007. "The CEO Mayor: How New York's Mike Bloomberg Is Creating a New Model for Public Service that Places Pragmatism Before Politics." *Business Week*, June 14.

McGeehan, Patrick. 2007. "Remaking the City's Image, with 50 Million Tourists in Mind." *New York Times*, February 27.

McGrath, Ben. 2009. "The Power of Michael Bloomberg: Can a Good Mayor Amass Too Much Power?" *New Yorker*, August 24.

Millar, Dan P., and Robert L. Heath, eds. 2004. *Responding to Crisis: A Rhetorical Approach to Crisis Communication*. London: Lawrence Erlbaum.

Molotch, Harvey. 2003. *Where Stuff Comes from: How Toasters, Toilets, Cars, Computers, and Many Other Things Came to Be as They Are*. New York: Routledge.

Nagourney, Adam. 2001. "Bloomberg Vows to Work at the Center of Things." *New York Times*. December 25, A1.

New York City Campaign Finance Board. 2009a. "Michael R. Bloomberg: Campaign Finance Summary." New York City Campaign Finance Board, November 30.

———. 2009b. "William C. Thompson Jr.: Campaign Finance Summary." New York City Campaign Finance Board, November 30.

NYC & Co. 2006. "Mayor Bloomberg and NYC & Company Chairman Tisch Announce City's Plan to Create Single Marketing and Tourism Organization." Press Release, June 8.

———. 2009. "New York City Proclaims November 10, 2009 'Sesame Street Day' 40 Years after Show's Television Debut." Press Release, November 9.

Pasotti, Eleonora. 2009. *Political Branding in Cities: The Decline of Machine Politics in Bogota, Naples, and Chicago*. Cambridge: Cambridge University Press.

Powell, Michael, and Julie Bosman. 2009. "Bloomberg No Longer Seems Invincible." *New York Times*, November 4, A1.

Rivera, Ray. 2009. "New York City Paid to Lobby Itself." *New York Times*, August 20.

Shifflet and Associates. 2001–2002. *USA Travel Recovery/Monitor: A Blueprint for Rebuilding Travel*. New York: D. K. Shifflet & Associates Ltd, December 3, 2001–February 15, 2002.

Siegel, Fred. 2008. "King Bloomberg: Mike Is a Mayor Run Amok." *New York Post*, November 22.

Ulmer, Robert Ray, Timothy L. Sellner, and Matthew W. Seeger. 2007. *Effective Crisis Communications: Moving from Crisis to Opportunity*. Thousand Oaks, CA: Sage.

Wernick, Andrew. 1991. *Promotional Culture: Advertising, Ideology, and Symbolic Expression*. London: Sage.

Wirthlin Worldwide. 2002. "Post 9/11 Assessment of E.D.C. Communications: San Francisco." New York: Economic Development Corporation.

Wolff Olins. 2007. New York City Case Study. http://www.wolffolins.com/clients/newyorkcity (accessed May 10, 2010).

"The World's Billionaires: #17: Michael Bloomberg." 2009. Forbes.com, March 11. http://www.forbes.com/lists/2009/10/billionaires-2009-richest-people_Michael-Bloomberg

Zukin, Sharon. 2009. *Naked City: The Death and Life of Authentic Urban Places.* Oxford: Oxford University Press.

CHAPTER SEVEN

From *Chengfen* to *Shenjia*

Branding and Promotional Culture in China

Hongmei Li

Introduction

This chapter examines the transformation of Chinese culture from *chengfen*, meaning class status or family origin, to *shenjia*, which literally means the body/corporal price and figuratively refers to the monetary and non-monetary assets of an individual, a brand, or a corporation, as an entry point to study the profound social, political, and cultural changes in Chinese society over the past six decades. While *chengfen* can be understood as partly based on the Marxist concept of class that promotes solidarity, *shenjia* is more about the celebration of global neoliberalism and consumer culture, which have taken roots in China in the past three decades. Materials drawn upon in this chapter include media reports from a dozen of the most influential Chinese newspapers, articles from China Academic Journals Full-text Database, and related materials obtained through Google and Baidu search engines.[1] Secondary research is also cited in this study.

It is important to study the shift from the *chengfen* discourse to the *shenjia* discourse because of the pervasiveness of each discourse in its own time. However, no scholars have attempted to compare and contrast them, though researchers have studied either the strong influence of the *chengfen* discourse in the pre-reform era or within the *shenjia* discourse in consumer culture at present.[2] The *chengfen* discourse was propagated in official Chinese media as progressive and as leading China to a more advanced stage of social development and revolution. It was later discredited by the government and the media and replaced by a *shenjia* discourse that is generally celebrated in Chinese media as a positive force in China's social and economic development. As a social marker for the rising middle class, especially for the nouveau riche, the *shenjia* discourse is a media-centered phenomenon situated in the broader context of China's endorsement of neoliberalism and consumer culture that celebrates the hegemony of the market and a one-dimensional notion of success. It symbolizes the hierarchical commercial culture embedded in China's state-supported market economy that aims to integrate itself into the international market.

I argue that the shift from *chengfen* to *shenjia* is not an improvement as many would claim but is rather about a shift in the conceptualization of the individual from a political being to a commercial being in terms of his or her relationship to the state and the economy, and about the production and legitimization of gender, class, and sometimes age hierarchies by a variety of combined forces at work in China's transformation into a consumer society.[3] The two hegemonic discourses are nurtured in specific political environments and thus serve the ruling ideologies of their time.

The *Chengfen* Discourse in China

In the first three decades after the founding of the People's Republic of China in 1949, the most fundamental factor that determined a person's social status and prestige was one's *chengfen,* which literally means "component parts" or "ingredients" of a product but actually refers to one's "class status or family origin." The Chinese Communist Party started to apply *chengfen* to villagers in the Land Reform Movement from 1946 to 1952 (Billeter 1985; Huang 1995; Lu 2008). *Chengfen* was used by the state to refer to "the exact economic condition of each peasant family and hence to its relative position on a socioeconomic scale which included, in ascending order, agricultural workers, poor peasants, middle peasants, rich peasants, and landlords" (Billeter 1985: 128). The state issued specific guidelines about how each villager should be classified. Decisions were often made in four steps: villagers first reported their own class labels, which were subsequently reviewed and passed respectively by the village's Poor Peasant Association, the Peasant Association meeting in full session, and a general meeting of all villagers (Lu 2008). Decisions were made public by announcements and posters at each stage so that people could contest or confirm their own or others' class labels. Thus, villagers knew their own and others' *chengfen*. Even though democratic components were built into the procedure, the state applied a strict system that required every village to identify landlords and rich peasants, even in places where none existed according to the Party's own criteria (Huang 1995). A lot of mislabeling occurred, but little effort was made to correct mislabels especially for landlords and rich peasants because of the accompanying political consequences.

Later, methods were created to label city residents based on their means of production: "peddler," "craftsman," "worker," and "capitalist" (Billeter 1985: 128). Other categories such as "revolutionary fighter," "family of a revolutionary martyr," "cadre," and "soldier" were also coined to grant prestige, rights, and status to contributors to the new regime. While there was a lot of arbitrariness, literally every Chinese citizen was assigned by 1952 to a system that included "over sixty designations" (Billeter 1985: 128). In subsequent political movements, further categories such as "rightist" and "counter-revolutionary" were created to capture one's subjective attitude and behavior toward the new regime. Such a classification system distinguished between the enemy camp and the friendly camp and further determined how to redistribute the confiscated properties and benefit the formerly exploited classes (Watson 1984a). Those with good *chengfen* such as cadres, workers, soldiers, and poor peasants were by definition full of class feelings and revolutionary zeal, but those with bad *chengfen* such as landlords, capitalists, rich peasants, and those connected with the previous nationalist government were by definition enemies and outsiders. At the top of the good classes, family heads who had participated in the preliberation revolution as People's Liberation Army (PLA) officers or party officials were assigned the privileged label of "revolutionary cadre" and their children were given the special title of "revolutionary-cadre children" (Chan, Rosen, and Unger 1980). People of good *chengfen* were later lumped together into five red categories (*hongwulei*), including prerevolutionary workers, poor peasants, lower-middle class peasants, families of revolutionary cadres, and families of revolutionary martyrs. People of bad *chengfen* were later lumped into five black categories (*heiwulei*), including pre-liberation landlords, pre-liberation rich peasants, counter-revolutionaries, "bad elements" (a special term that described people who were considered dangerous or morally corrupt toward the new regime), and rightists.

The *chengfen* system had at least three characteristics (Billeter 1985). First, it was hereditary, especially along the male line. Even though state policy indicated that no class status would be attributed to children under eighteen years old (Billeter 1985; Lu 2008), in practice children enjoyed all the advantages or suffered all the disadvantages related to the father's social status. Children of bad class origins were constantly denied membership of the Party and the Youth League, educational opportunity, promotion, the opportunity to join the military, and (in the case of men) access to desirable marriage partners (Schram 1984: 30). The hereditary nature of *chengfen* was succinctly summarized by a then-common saying: "When the father is a hero, the son is a brave man. When the father is a reactionary, the son is a scoundrel." Second, the *chengfen* system was made permanent, a state that lasted for three decades. Once one's *chengfen*, especially bad *chengfen*, was determined, it was difficult if not impossible to change it. In cities, one's *chengfen* was entered into the household registration book, one's dossier, and other documents, which greatly shaped the fate of each individual in a society where the state monopolized all resources for jobs, education, promotion, and even daily necessities. Various political movements made the despised classes and their children repeated scapegoats of class struggles and public humiliation.[4] Third, the *chengfen* system was arbitrary to some extent because an individual could belong to two or more categories simultaneously. In such cases, it was up to the Party authorities to determine a person's *chengfen* (Billeter 1985). In the countryside, there were also specific quotas for each village to identify class enemies, which resulted in a lot of mislabeling. In cities, many innocent people were labeled as "rightists" simply because each work unit needed to fulfill the quota.

The privileged classes such as cadres, party members, and government officials enjoyed power, special prestige, better salaries, welfare benefits, and even more marital choices, despite the official ideology of egalitarianism that treated all jobs as equal (White 1978–1979). People of good *chengfen,* for example, had more opportunities for desirable marriage partners, while men of bad *chengfen* could only marry within their own categories or marry downward (Billeter 1985; Croll 1984; Unger 1984). Of course, marriage choice was influenced by a combination of one's *chengfen* and one's economic status, and the latter bore a direct association with one's *chengfen.* During certain highly political periods, such as the Cultural Revolution and its aftermath, more attention was given to people of high political status (Croll 1984). Poor or lower-middle class peasants were still placed on the lowest rung as marriage partners, despite their good *chengfen*, largely because of their low economic status and harsh living conditions, mainly resulting from a rigid divide between the town and the countryside and from the state policy that favored industrialization in the city. Peasant girls preferred to marry cadres and military officers to get out of the countryside. Generally speaking, a man and his children were less likely to be affected if he married a woman from a bad family background than a woman marrying a man of bad *chengfen,* since *chengfen* followed the male line. It must be pointed out that the state and Chinese media made serious efforts to promote egalitarianism as an official ideology. Indeed, China was among the most egalitarian countries in the world at that time, and the status of peasants was greatly improved in the first few decades after the establishment of P.R. China (White 1978–1979).

The *chengfen* system primarily focused on the notion of the class struggle between the proletariat and the bourgeoisie, which was largely blind toward issues of femininity and age. While beautiful women were used as promoters for the Communist revolution (Ip 2003), attention to feminine beauty was generally looked down upon as petit bourgeois (Honig and Hershatter 1988: 42). Instead, "iron girls" (*tie guliang,* meaning strong women), peasant workers, and soldiers with rosy cheeks and revolutionary zeal who were wearing androgynous clothing with little self-adornment were advocated as role models for women's liberation from traditional patriarchy and feudalism. Women were said to "hold up half the sky." The media were always critical of women paying attention to their external beauty and stressed that women should focus on political correctness and ideological compatibility when finding partners (Ip 2003). The Cultural Revolution was, in particular, defined as "masculinization" and "puritanical asceticism" (Honig and Hershatter 1988: 11; Yang 1999: 35–67). Seniority in China's Communist revolution was also generally rewarded through the graded wage system.

Under such a system, new values were produced in the Socialist regime. Producing and saving were the two core values. Ideal socialist Chinese cities, stated Whyte and Parish (1984), were "spartan and productive places with full employment, secure jobs with a range of fringe benefits, minimal income and lifestyle differences, an end to conspicuous consumption and lavish spending, and with decent consumption standards for all" (16). Capitalism was severely criticized as a decadent system and class struggle was the guiding principle. This attitude reached a peak during the Cultural Revolution, resulting in an almost complete negligence of economic development and near total isolation from the capitalist West. Under this system, individuals enjoyed a certain degree of agency, but one's fate was largely determined by one's class status and family origin.

China's Transformation into a Consumer Society and the Rise of Neoliberalism

In 1978, Deng Xiaoping, programmatic leader and chief architect of China's reform, made a historic decision for China to shift from class struggles to economic development. Deng made his famous statement that China should "let some people get rich ahead of others" and that material achievement and science and technology advancement should be emphasized. Deng also made one of his oft-cited remarks: "It doesn't matter whether a cat is white or black, as long as it catches mice." In other words, Deng was not concerned with the debate over the capitalist or socialist nature of a policy; as long as it could develop the Chinese economy, it was acceptable. While there were still discussions in Chinese media about whether certain policies or social phenomena were capitalist or socialist in the 1980s, such debates have rarely been heard since the 1990s. In 1989, after the government cracked down on the Tiananmen Square Student Movement (a movement aiming to fight against corruption and promote democracy), resulting in the deaths of hundreds of protesters, the government encountered an enormous legitimacy crisis. Since the 1990s, the Chinese government has totally immersed itself in market reforms and utilized economic development to maintain its legitimacy (Wang 2003).

Neoliberalism has become a hegemonic discourse in China's economic and social development, with mainstream intellectuals, economists and officials actively supporting the privatization of state-owned enterprises, market reforms and foreign investment, often at the expense of workers' rights, environmental protections, social justice, and equality (Zhao 2008). Wang Hui (2003), a prominent scholar and professor at Tsinghua University, points out that neoliberalism has become *the* official ideology in the past two decades. While neoliberal scholars are outspoken advocates for the propertied class, left-leaning economists and scholars, who advocate for social justice and more government control over resource distributions, have long been marginalized and excluded from mainstream academic, media, and public policy forums (Zhao 2008). Material development has become the most important criterion to measure social development in China. On July 1, 2001, former Chinese President Jiang Zeming in his formal speech invited capitalists to join the Chinese Communist Party, and the Party revised its constitution in 2002 at the 16th Party Congress accordingly, suggesting that the Party-state has fully embraced global capitalism. The passing of property rights law in 2003 further indicates that China's policies have shifted to protect private property under the pretence of Socialism with Chinese characteristics. Thus, there has emerged a "power, money, and knowledge regime" (Zhao 2008: 298).

The market-oriented Chinese media, especially business papers, often demonstrate their staunch support for neoliberalism. They have formed an interdependent relationship with neoliberal economists and entrepreneurs largely because of their rapid growth[5] and transformation in the past three decades from pure government propaganda organs to commercial entities that are required to obey the government's "bottom line" and simultaneously make profits (Zhao 1998, 2008). The government has gradually reduced state subsidies to media since the 1980s and, except for a few official party organs, all media now rely exclusively on advertising and subscription fees for survival. Rich entrepreneurs have the power to influence media content through their advertising money. Indeed, Chinese media have become the ally of the rich, giving them extensive positive coverage often with a complete lack of attention to the affairs of common people (Wang and Mou 2002).

The rapid growth of Chinese media also dramatically boosted consumerism in China. China ranks among the world's most lucrative advertising markets. Program ratings, started in 1997 by China Central Television (CCTV), the only centralized TV station in China, have thus become the most important criterion to judge the values of most media programs on CCTV as well as most other TV stations. Interdependent networks that involve media programs, corporate sponsors, advertising agencies, public relations firms, and rating agencies have been established to measure, rank, and produce celebrities, including but not limited to entertainment stars, sport stars, fashion models, economists, entrepreneurs, and TV hosts.

Rapid economic development in China has produced an emergent middle class in China. Discussions of the rising middle class are abundant in popular literature and academic research. Terms like "white collar" (*bailing*), "gold collar" (*jinling*), "bohemians" (*Bobozu*), "yuppie," and "hippie" have entered the Chinese language and are now constantly used in Chinese media to refer to the Chinese middle-class lifestyle. Different criteria are used to define the middle class; depending on the criteria employed, the percentage of Chinese occupying the middle class can vary from less than five percent to 47 percent.[6]

Accompanying such shifts were widening gaps between the rich and the poor, between urban residents and country dwellers and between eastern coastal areas and inland regions. According to the Boston Consulting Group's global wealth report in 2006, the number of millionaire households in China reached 250 thousand, making China number six globally (Boston Consulting Group 2006). According to the 2009 World Wealth Report released by Merrill Lynch and Capgemini, an IT services and business consultancy, China's population included, as of 2007, four hundred and thirteen thousand individuals worth more than one million U.S. dollars, ranking the country fourth in terms of numbers of wealthy individuals in 2008 (Merrill Lynch and Capgemini 2009). With an increasing number of "nouveau riche," the Ministry of Commerce predicts China will become the world's largest luxury market by 2014, accounting for 23 percent of global luxury business (*China Daily* 2009).[7] Pleasure in and pursuit of consumption has become a dominant value among Chinese youth (Zhang 2000; Rosen 2004). While role models for pre-reform China were revolutionary heroes and model workers and peasants, Chinese youth are now inspired to become white-collar professionals, private entrepreneurs (Rosen 2004), and, I would add, wealthy celebrities. Money is increasingly used both as a marker to judge a person's social status and worth, and as the yardstick for success in education, employment, marriage, and healthcare, a finding which has been confirmed in surveys as well as academic and media reports (Rosen 2004). Sun Liping (2003), an oft-cited scholar and professor at Tsinghua University, argues that increasing inequalities have produced a "fractured" Chinese society. Hu Angang (2004), a prominent Chinese scholar, contends that there exist four worlds in China based on the gross domestic product (GDP) per capita (adjusted by purchasing power parity). The "first world" includes Beijing, Shanghai, and Shenzhen, whose GDP per capita has reached a level that is comparable to the developed world, but the population of the three areas comprises only 2.2 percent of the total Chinese population. The "second world" refers to other coastal areas, including Tianjin, Guangdong, Zhejiang, and Jiangsu, where GDP per capita has reached a level comparable to the world average, and its population takes up 22 percent of the total Chinese population. The "third world" refers to 26 percent of the national population, whose GDP per capita has reached the lower-middle level of the world. The "fourth world" refers to the vast poor remote rural areas in midwestern China, whose GDP per capita is at the bottom compared to other countries, but which forms approximately 50 percent of the total Chinese population. Of course, the geographical distinction is a rough estimate because even in the same area, enormous gaps exist between the rich and the poor. Thousands of millionaires in big cities coexist with tens of millions of the poor who are struggling for basic survival.

The Chinese government has openly embraced and even celebrated China's shift into consumer culture (Rosen 2004). Since 1986, China has begun to observe the yearly international Consumer Rights Day, and since the 1990s, the state has actively encouraged domestic consumption and consumer rights (Li 2006). The Chinese Consumer Association and its branches nationwide regularly sponsor national campaigns to educate Chinese consumers about their rights and various laws have also been passed to protect consumer rights, private property, and intellectual property, while Chinese citizens' political rights are not seriously protected. Consumerism seems to have become a new ideology (Tang 2000). In addition, the Chinese government has initiated a branding movement for Chinese national brands to compete internationally (Wang 2008). The Ministry of Commerce has especially encouraged Chinese corporations to pay attention to branding their products globally. In addition, a number of self-help and motivational works have been published since the 1990s to advise people on how to improve themselves and manage their own lives.[8] Branding experts in China such as Li Guangdou and Ye Maozhong constantly advise white-collar professionals and college students on how to brand themselves in the labor market, largely because people can no longer expect lifelong employment but have to face ferocious competition in the Chinese economy that is increasingly integrated with the international labor market. It is against such a backdrop that we can observe the shift from the *chengfen* discourse to the *shenjia* discourse.

The *Shenjia* Discourse in Contemporary China

The concept of *shenjia* was rarely used before the 1980s. Since the 1990s, however, as China started to fully immerse itself into the market economy, it has been widely used in Chinese media and by researchers.[9] Featured prominently in the *shenjia* discourse are sport players, entertainment stars, TV hosts, entrepreneurs, and economists, largely because of their celebrity or celebrity-like status.[10] White-collar professionals, managers, and college students are also sometimes discussed in terms of *shenjia*. According to the *Modern Chinese Dictionary* published by the Commercial Press in 1973, the most authoritative Chinese dictionary, *shenjia* has two meanings: 1) A person's social status; and 2) the price paid for a human slave before the founding of P.R. China. Significantly, the Commercial Press's 2005 dictionary reversed the order of the two meanings. In Chinese media, the word is also specifically used to refer to the appearance fees, advertising incomes, and salaries of celebrities, and also to describe the consumption and lifestyles of the moneyed classes. Educated young people, who are the backbone for and beneficiaries of Chinese economic reforms, particularly like to use this term to describe one's money-making capacity in the current Chinese market economy.[11]

Shenjia is not unique to China but must be situated in relationship to China's entry into the global marketplace and in parallel to similar dynamics in other regions. It has important local characteristics, pertaining to both internal and external standards, and it manifests itself differently for different audiences within China. There is no consensus about how *shenjia* is calculated; rather it is used as a floating term that describes one's market value, often in a tautological way. Sports and entertainment are the two most common categories covered in the media in *shenjia* terms, as I will discuss below. In the following section I will also demonstrate how the *shenjia* discourse is characterized by gender, age, and class hierarchies.

Within the sports industry, soccer players' *shenjia* is the most often discussed in Chinese media, followed by discussions of the *shenjia* of basketball players and Olympic medalists. For soccer players, *shenjia* refers to their salaries or their transfer fees, based on their performances of previous seasons (similarly to the situation in Europe). Soccer started to emerge in China at the turn of the twentieth century. Initially it was considered suitable for males alone. Only after China started economic reforms in 1978 did women's soccer begin to gain popularity and earn support from local governments. Despite this, the women's national team has consistently obtained much less state support, less media coverage and less corporate sponsorship than men's soccer teams, and has consequently developed more slowly (Fan and Mangan 2003). China started the men's league system in 1994 and the women's league system in 1996. Winners, coaches, and officials who helped teams participate in international medal competitions have since been handsomely rewarded by government agencies and corporate sponsors. However, while female soccer players have achieved huge international success, they receive much lower wages than male players who failed miserably internationally. There is a huge wage gap between male and female players.

For example, on the national men's team, which receives both corporate sponsorship and state support, players could earn a monthly salary of up to 160,000 yuan (approximately 20,000 USD) in the mid-1990s, while women could only receive 700 yuan (about 87 dollars, the average Chinese income) (Fan and Mangan 2003). In 1998, the annual income of each division 1A male player was at least 100,000 yuan (approximately 12,000 USD), 20 times the average citizen's income (Dong and Mangan 2001). A star player, who is always male, could earn one or two million yuan a year. Well-known Chinese male players sign contracts with foreign clubs and transnational corporations, and men's teams have imported foreign coaches and players. Chinese men's soccer has thus become an international business, actively participating in player transfers, agents, sponsorship, TV rights, international club networks, and merchandising. However, female players rarely appear in large domestic or foreign advertising campaigns, and no foreign coaches or players have been part of the women's national team. It is thus not surprising that whenever *shenjia* is discussed in Chinese media, it always refers to male players; female players are seldom discussed in *shenjia* terms.

When female athletes' *shenjia is* discussed in Chinese media, it usually refers to something beyond their athletic performance. Their sexuality and beauty are always part of the discourse. While female sexuality was not that important for female sports players in the 1980s (Brownell 1996), the pursuit of the "beauty economy" since the 1990s has influenced how female players are viewed and evaluated (Hopkins 2007; Xu and Feiner 2007). Female players' beauty is regularly emphasized by the Chinese media; "beautiful players" thus have much higher *shenjia* than others. Guo Jingjing, for example, is China's best-branded female athlete not only because she has won more Olympic gold medals than any other female diver in the world, but also—and more importantly—because she is associated with a sport considered appropriate for women. Female diving in the Chinese context is often associated with elegance, softness, and femininity. She is a spokesperson for many Chinese and international brands. She also frequently appears at various corporate-sponsored events along with entertainment celebrities. However, many media reports about her are really about her beauty and graciousness when wearing expensive brands. Her love affair with Kenneth Fok, grandson of a Hong Kong tycoon with high official titles in China, is often a top media story. Other female athletes, such as gold medalists for weightlifting, are rarely covered after the Games and are rarely sought out by corporate sponsors largely because they are not models for Chinese femininity and beauty.

In the entertainment industry, gender hierarchy is even more pronounced. Chinese media often discuss unspoken and unwritten rules (*qianquize*) in the entertainment industry, which is characterized by paid news, bribery, corruption, and sex–money transactions. Numerous media reports have reported that newcomers, especially females, often become victims of such unwritten rules, using their gender and their bodies to win roles and opportunities. For example, one famous model wrote on her blog about how to succeed in the modeling industry:

> You need personal connections, money and media hype. You need to know how to conform to current ways and opinions for personal advantage. You should know how to observe others' behaviors and expressions and act accordingly. For a show, you must expose your bodies before your clients and accept their unhesitating wanton comments; sometimes for an award, you must disregard your own self-esteem…and even sacrifice your pure smile and body.[12]

Her remarks are just the tip of the iceberg in the entertainment industry that is still dominated by males. Even though male entertainers sometimes state that they are victims, it is generally believed that these rules are directed against females.

Generally speaking, Chinese celebrities get more *shenjia* if they are recognized internationally and are projected in Chinese media as representatives of a successful global China. Their *shenjia* is not only measured by their own success but also by the market values they represent both domestically and internationally, as I will discuss in the following section. For the Chinese market alone, celebrities' *shenjia* is often measured by their popularity and (in the case of entertainment stars) box office performances, which are further reflected by their advertising incomes, appearance fees for any specific brand, yearly advertising revenues, or their total assets.

In the realm of soccer, top European players' *shenjia* is constantly discussed, often in reference to players' salaries, transfer fees, or advertising incomes, in sharp contrast to China's restricted market model. Foreign players and coaches are often discussed in the Chinese media as having more *shenjia* than Chinese players largely because they are paid more by their clubs and by global corporate sponsors. In the past twenty years, the Chinese media have demonstrated a particularly strong interest in and benefited from reporting on soccer games and players in England, Italy, Spain, and Germany. In 1989, CCTV signed a broadcasting contract with Sportfive, a broker that controls the broadcasting rights of strong European teams. CCTV not only profited heavily from this deal by selling advertising airtime during the broadcasts but also dramatically popularized soccer games and foreign players in China. Since the launch of the CCTV sports channel in 1995, CCTV has obtained even more broadcasting rights for world top-level sports games and has given more airtime to soccer. In 2005, CCTV launched a 24-hour sports broadcasting channel. In the past few decades, CCTV has provided weekly live coverage of European championships. AC Milan, International Milan, and Chelsea have established Chinese websites for Chinese fans. The Chinese Football Association began in the 1990s to export Chinese soccer players to play in European premier league clubs so that they could gain more "advanced experience." The Chinese media pay close attention to such Chinese players and those who achieve international success are considered to have much higher *shenjia* when they return to China.

Professional basketball player Yao Ming is a good example of the close association of one's *shenjia* in China with the international market and global consumer culture. Yao Ming was signed as the first overall draft pick by the Houston Rockets in 2002. Yao is not the first Chinese player to play for the National Basketball Association (NBA), but his timing was much better than that of his predecessor Wang Zhizhi, largely because of the recent importance of the Chinese market for the NBA. The NBA has heavily marketed Yao to expand its influence in China and to attract Asian American fans (Wang 2004). Information about Yao Ming's salaries and advertising incomes has always been reported in the Chinese media. The *Forbes China* celebrity list ranked Yao the richest of Chinese celebrities for six straight years (Flannery 2009). Oates and Polumbaum argue that Yao Ming is at the center of "an entrepreneurial machine, generating wealth for himself as well as for his agents, handlers, managers, sponsors, team, league, and, broadly speaking, the institutions of commercialized sport" (2004: 193). Indeed, Yao signed advertising contracts with Nike, Reebok, Apple, Visa, interactive game developer Sorrent, Gatorade, McDonald's, Coca-Cola, Garmin, Toyota, and other transnational corporations. Chinese companies such as China Unicom and Yanjing Beer also paid enormous advertising fees for Yao's global celebrity. Team Yao, a group of advisers established in 2000 for Yao Ming who handle public relations, corporate sponsorship, media relations, and legal affairs, "has set out guidelines for the most desirable associations of his persona and image with commercial products"

(Oates and Polumbaum 2004: 206). Team Yao portrayed the basketball player not only as a young, ambitious, hard-working, and responsible individual but also as a middleman who can allow foreign brands to enter the Chinese market and Chinese brands to enter the U.S. market. Yao was featured in a 2004 documentary, *The Year of Yao*, and has occupied a prominent place in the Chinese Basketball Association that is closely associated with China's national honor. For example, he played for China in the 2000 Summer Olympics and carried the Chinese flag at the opening ceremony for the 2004 Olympic Games. For the 2008 Beijing Olympics, Yao carried the Olympic torch into Tiananmen Square, carried the Chinese flag, and led the Chinese delegation at the opening ceremony. Yao thus not only enjoys the freedom to sell his labor to the highest bidder in the international market but also has "the values of national pride, loyalty and entitlement" (Oates and Polumbaum 2004: 203). Wang Chih-ming (2004) argues Yao is made to embody "China, Asian Americans, and the Chinese market simultaneously." Yao's success can therefore be interpreted as the success of global China. As an "export commodity," Yao Ming symbolizes China's unique success in integrating into the global capitalist system while still maintaining an authoritarian regime. The Chinese and global media's active production of Yao Ming's stardom, his "Chinese-ness" and his recognition by high-level Chinese officials further confirm and reinforce Yao's *shenjia*. Yao Ming is celebrated as a cultural and political ambassador. As a cultural figure, he is also viewed as having taught Chinese cultural values to the West. In the U.S.-China Strategic and Economic Dialogue held in Washington, D.C. on July 28–29, 2009, U.S. President Barack Obama quoted Yao Ming, stating: "As a new President and also as a basketball fan, I have learned from the words of Yao Ming, who said, 'No matter whether you are new or an old team member, you need time to adjust to one another.'"[13] Yao Ming's *shenjia* is thus viewed in terms of his performances, his economic success, and his cultural significance in the international market for China.

The Chinese government has actively participated in producing athletes' *shenjia* by awarding sport players and celebrities with monetary and non-monetary assets. In contrast with the pre-reform era when sport players and entertainers only received average wages as ordinary workers, since the 1980s the Chinese government has steadily increased monetary compensation for athletes with outstanding performances. For example, China's National Sports Commission (the current General Administration of Sport of China) awarded each gold medalist 6,000 yuan in 1984. However, for the

2008 Beijing Olympic Games, each gold medalist earned at least 250 thousand yuan from the state, in addition to awards from various centers, provincial governments, and corporations. The award was tax-free. Each gold medal was estimated to be worth 1.5 million yuan; the official award amount was higher than that of the U.S., Japan, and Germany.[14] Prominent sport players and celebrities are also given official titles such as Representatives of the National Committee of the Chinese People's Political Consultative Conference, a political advisory body in China, and thus enjoy a platform to voice their opinions on policy issues. Since sport players are often young, privileging such a *shenjia* discourse also means that older people who cannot profit from the sport economy are mostly excluded.

As stated above, the *shenjia* discourse of international superstars indicates the triumph of global neoliberalism. The *shenjia* of sports players and entertainers is also closely related to the emergence of millionaires and billionaires in China. Sports clubs and entertainment companies are often owned by entrepreneurially minded individuals, who determine whether and how to promote certain players or entertainers. Entrepreneurs often have to develop business and personal ties with sport stars and entertainers for promoting their products and services. Chinese officials are also beneficiaries of the current economic model. They may work closely with entrepreneurs for personal benefits and to benefit their specific work units. Thus, an interdependent network between Chinese economic, political, and cultural elites and transnational capitalists are formed to exploit the Chinese market (Zhao 2008). In this sense, the production of celebrities' *shenjia* is closely related to the production of the *shenjia* of local and global capitalists.

Shenjia as a Media Phenomenon

The *shenjia* discourse is essentially a media-centered phenomenon. While there are discussions about how to calculate one's *shenjia*, there is no numerical formula for ascertaining it. Instead, media use this term very casually as if there is no need to specify it. One's *shenjia* is often discussed in numerous lists such as the top ten, fifty, or one hundred most famous, valuable, popular, or wealthy celebrities, fashion models, personal brands, brokers, movie stars, TV anchors, writers, and entrepreneurs. Even CCTV has produced annual lists of top Chinese TV anchors and top TV programs since 2004 aiming to produce closer linkages between images of anchors with their programs.[15] The *Forbes* list of the wealthiest Chinese individuals published since 1995 and the Hurun Rich Chinese List, compiled by Luxemburg native Rupert Hoogewerf since 1999, are among the most well-known. Such lists are circulated endlessly on Chinese media, especially over the Internet. They serve a self-fulfilling prophecy and function as guidance for advertisers and their agencies to determine the amounts of payment to certain celebrities. A mutual interdependence between media and celebrities is thus produced. On one hand, media exposure has arguably become most important to measure one's publicity in particular and one's *shenjia* in general, but on the other hand, Chinese media also need celebrities to raise their program ratings for profits. Daniel Boorstin argues that celebrities' "chief claim to fame is their fame itself" ([1961] 1985: 60). Celebrities are made by news and they make news. Their familiar names thus become assets for celebrities and for corporate sponsors. In producing the *shenjia* discourse in China, the media have successfully turned many entrepreneurs, entertainers, TV anchors, sport stars, and fashion models into celebrities and simultaneously capitalized on their fame. Celebrities whose *shenjia* are underestimated reportedly threaten to sue the media.

The media use various strategies to produce celebrities. One is called *chaozuo*, a word coined in the 1990s to describe ways to draw attention to specific stocks and raise their values. *Chaozuo* would be impossible under the *chengfen* system because one's *chengfen* was fixed through an extensive dossier system. It can only occur under the *shenjia* system where the value of one's brand depends on media attention and the media economy, and constantly fluctuates. More recently, the term has been used to broadly describe the use of any media hype as a promotional strategy to place a target at the center of media attention. New or existing products, services or individuals can be used to produce media hype through extensive media exposure for a certain period of time. Celebrities' connections with other celebrities, their sexual scandals, and their love affairs are commonly used to produce media hype for films and media-related products. *Chaozuo* has become such a phenomenon that many recent events in China are suspected of being media hype. The Internet plays a particularly important role in generating, distributing, and consuming media hype. Choi and Berger argue that the Internet has contributed to "a global addiction to fame and celebrity" (2009: 193). Both the famous and those dreaming of becoming famous use the Internet to promote themselves. Celebrities and people with celebrity status are then invited as spokesmen for commodities and services, which generates more publicity. Indeed, corporations in China have used celebrity endorsement extensively in advertising campaigns. When I interviewed over forty advertising professionals in China in 2005, many of them pointed to the prominence of celebrity advertising in China. Celebrity worship is common among Chinese young people (Yue and Cheung 2000).

CCTV and many provincial media have played important roles in producing instant celebrities. For example, as the most watched Chinese TV program since 1983, CCTV's annual Spring Festival Gala has turned many hosts and entertainers into household names. For example, Liu Qian, an unknown magician, was reported by many media outlets to have his *shenjia*, calculated by his estimated advertising income and ticket prices, increased to ten million yuan after his appearance in the 2009 CCTV spring gala event.[16] Not only is there increasing demand and higher admission fees for his shows, but he has also recently acquired corporate sponsors. It is thus not surprising that the annual gala is often suspected of bribery, corruption, and sex–money transactions. In 2003, *People's Daily* reported that Zhao An, who had been director of the annual gala for seven years, was sentenced to ten years in prison for accepting bribery, an incident which formally exposed the corruption and dark side of CCTV to the public. Thus, Chinese media are deeply embedded in the neoliberal economic model and are implicated in producing the *shenjia* discourse in China.

While the general tone of Chinese media is to celebrate the *shenjia* discourse as an endorsement of neoliberalism, there have also been minority voices in left-leaning media that criticize the promotion of the rich (Rosen 2004). Sport star Yao Ming has also been criticized as being too materialistic in comparison with past basketball players who only received regular state wages (Oates and Polumbaum 2004). Recently, there have been critical media reports about rich kids (*fu erdai*) who show off their wealth in China and in foreign countries and violate Chinese laws in many cases. There have also been critical reports of rich Chinese not having shouldered enough social responsibility in cases such as the Sichuan earthquake in 2008. However, such voices are still marginal.

Who Has No Shenjia?

What is especially intriguing in the discussion of *shenjia* is that the vast majority of Chinese do not have *shenjia*, including peasants who comprise eighty percent of the Chinese population and workers who were treated as the backbone of Chinese society in the Maoist era. While peasants and industrial workers were granted good *chengfen* in the Maoist era, they are now marginalized and made irrelevant in the *shenjia* discourse. Laid-off workers are particularly marginalized in Chinese society. Migrant workers are sometimes discussed in terms of *shenjia* in comparison with college students, precisely because the former are viewed as having no qualifications for *shenjia*.

The *shenjia* label is rarely used to describe Chinese officials, even though they benefit enormously from the current economic model. Indeed, powerful officials, especially high-ranking officials with real power, are often suspected of having amassed huge personal wealth, and they have numerous opportunities to obtain monetary and other assets through under-the-table transactions. It is no secret that officials collude with Chinese and global capitalists to exploit the vast majority of the Chinese population (Zhao 2008). However, because of the non-transparency of Chinese politics, there is no way to quantify Chinese officials' and their relatives' private assets. Chinese officials often avoid publicizing their salaries and incomes. Nevertheless, they benefit from both the *chengfen* system and the *shenjia* system. While the former system made it explicit that cadres enjoyed better benefits and higher salaries under the pretence of egalitarianism, the current system rewards bureaucrats secretly.

In its extreme form, *shenjia* can be attached to prostitutes who exchange their bodies for monetary return, but the Chinese media rarely, if ever, use *shenjia* to talk about prostitutes. Thus, the concept of *shenjia* is about the legitimating of power relations. It is produced and controlled by media and serves media interests. As a symbol of commercial culture, it is embedded in China's current market economy as it aims to integrate itself into the international market. *Shenjia,* a term that celebrates neoliberalism, naturalizes inequalities along the lines of gender, age, and lifestyle as if it were the ultimate measure and a fundamental means of one's success in the Chinese market. As a marker for social stratification, it objectifies human beings, reifies the "eyeball" economy, and symbolizes the pervasive influence of commercial culture in China that produces what Herbert Marcuse (1966) called the one-dimensional man. In China, a country that welcomes and celebrates global capital, s*henjia* has thus become a signifier of the global middle class and an emergent national identity. China has become a "cool" place and a new frontier for global capitalism. However, *shenjia* represents an uneasy relationship between the majority of the Chinese population and the rising middle class and the superrich. While well-paid stars, celebrities, and entrepreneurs are hailed as part of the new China, the *shen-*

jia discourse excludes the vast majority of the Chinese population, which does not have *shenjia* and thus cannot be commodified.

Conclusion

While *chengfen* describes political beings embedded in a system that prioritized class struggles, *shenjia* refers to commercial beings entrenched in complex networks of individuals, corporations, the market, and the state. Both systems, however, are supported by the state, with the former having more direct state involvement and the latter more indirect state involvement. *Chengfen* underscores an effort to produce social egalitarianism with the unintended consequence of producing another system of social hierarchy; *shenjia* consciously produces economic, social, political, and cultural hierarchies that are fully supported by the current hegemonic discourse of neoliberalism. What is common to both systems is that no one can escape from being labeled. Under the *chengfen* system, everyone had a *chengfen* label; currently individuals are judged in terms of how much *shenjia* they have. Both systems are predicated on the objectification of human beings into something that can be labeled and measured. However, the two systems work under different logics. While the *chengfen* system is more about the prioritizing of class, *shenjia* is more about one's capacity to earn money and nonmonetary assets in a rapidly globalizing Chinese market. While *chengfen* is characterized by its hereditary, arbitrary, and timeless nature, *shenjia* is always changing and is produced in interdependent networks made up of national and transnational capitalists, the Chinese media, and the Chinese state. While gender was not a prominent feature under the *chengfen* system, the new *shenjia* system features it prominently. Female bodies are now valued as objects for consumption, and people and commodities that can reach out to the West are more highly valued than their Chinese counterparts. What is especially interesting is that capitalists, landlords, and intellectuals who were discriminated against under the *chengfen* system are actually favored in the new *shenjia* system, while workers and peasants who obtained good class labels under *chengfen* are marginalized according to *shenjia*. Both *shenjia* and *chengfen* include and exclude, destroy old boundaries and establish new ones simultaneously.

While commercial culture is often celebrated as having the capacity to produce multiple values, my analysis of the transformation from *chengfen* to *shenjia* indicates that commercialization can instead produce a kind of hegemony that dictates individuals' values and behaviors. The transformation from the one-dimensional measurement of Chinese citizens from political beings through *chengfen* to commercial beings through *shenjia* reflects the replacement of one kind of hegemony with another. I contend that the shift from *chengfen* to *shenjia* results in new social hierarchies that are produced by a variety of combined forces in the process of China's marketization.

A crucial question here is whether there is any room to resist such a pervasive *shenjia* discourse in China. While the paradigm of *xiaokang* ("small rich") and moderate consumption was heavily discussed in Chinese media as an alternative development model, now the Chinese media focuses more on the extravagant consumption of the richest in China and globally. There is thus little hope that the *shenjia* discourse will fade away in Chinese media. The only alternative is to raise Chinese citizens' consciousness about the inhumanity and alienation of such discourse.

Notes

1. The 57th World Newspaper Congress in 2004 held in Istanbul released a list of the top 100 daily newspapers in terms of circulation (Sina.com 2004). Eleven of the nineteen newspapers listed in mainland China were analyzed in this study, including *Cankao Xiaoxi*, *People's Daily*, *Yangzi Evening News*, *Yangcheng Evening News*, *Guangzhou Daily*, *Xinmin Evening News*, *Chutian doushi bao*, *Beijing Evening News*, *Jinwan Bao*, *Huaxi dongshi bao* and *Xinkuai Bao*. The other eight newspapers (*Nanfang Ribao, Nanfang Dushi Bao* and *Qilu Wanbao*, *Dahe Bao*, *Nanfang Ribao*, *Qianjiang Wanbao*, *Wuhan Wanbao* and *Beijing Youth Daily)* did not have working search functions and were thus not included in the study. I conducted a keyword search of "shenjia" on all the searchable newspaper websites and analyzed the first 200 hits of each newspaper. If the search yielded fewer than 200 results, all results were then analyzed. For Baidu and Google, the first 200 results were analyzed.
2. For sources documenting the *chengfen* system in China, see Gordon White's (1976) monograph on the notion of class status during the Cultural Revolution; Richard C. Kraus' (1977) and Anita Chan, Stanley Rosen, and Jonathan Unger's (1980) essays on class conflict in China; James L. Watson's (1984b) edited book on social stratification; and Philip C. C. Huang's (1995) essay on class struggles in rural China which formed part of China's *chengfen* discourse. Sources documenting the rise of consumer culture in urban China include Davis (2000); Li (2006); and Wang (2008).
3. Although no scholar has specifically claimed that *shenjia* is a progressive discourse, it is directly related to the Chinese market reforms since 1978 that have been generally celebrated in popular literature and scholarly works in China and the West.
4. The political movements include the Great Leap Forward (1958–1960), the Siqing Movement in the countryside (to clean up politics, ideology, organization, and economy), the Five Anti Campaign in the city (anti-bribery, anti-theft of state property, anti-tax evasion, anti-cheating on government contracts, and anti-stealing of state economic intelligence), and the Cultural Revolution.

5. For example, China's newspapers at the provincial level and above increased from fewer than 200 in the early 1980s to 1922 in 2004. Radio stations increased from 38 in 1980 to 1400 in the 1990s; TV stations increased from 202 in 1985 to 2000, in addition to 1300 cable TV operations; and magazines increased from a little over 2,000 in the early 1980s to 9490 in 2004 (Li 2006).
6. For example, a research team from the Chinese Academy of Social Sciences (CASS) surveyed people aged 16–70 in twelve provinces, special municipalities, and seventy-three districts and countries between November and December 2001 and defined the Chinese middle class using four criteria, including professional status, income, patterns of consumption and lifestyle, and subjective identification. Around 15.9 percent of those surveyed were classified as middle class by profession, 24.6 percent were viewed as middle class by income, 35 percent were middle class by standards of consumption and lifestyle, and 46.8 percent surveyed viewed themselves as middle class. When a comprehensive index for the middle class was created, the percentage dropped to 4.1–6.0 percent. The National Bureau of Statistics in 2005 set the yearly household income for a three-member middle-class family between 60,000 yuan (approximately $7,300 USD) and 500,000 yuan (approximately $80,000 USD) and according to this criterion, only 5.04 percent of middle-class families in urban China qualified (cited in Wang 2008). Lu Xueyi, former director of the Sociology Institute of CASS, defines the middle class as those "who earn salaries and wages mainly through their mental labor," who enjoy "a high capacity to earn high income and work in good work environments and conditions," and have "a certain level of quality leisure time" with corresponding purchasing power and some degree of control over their own labor and work (Xu 2003: 8–9).
7. For example, Yan Jun, managing director of Beijing-based Ecole Fashion & Luxury Consulting Ltd., says that the expanding Chinese middle class constitutes an important group of consumers who desire and can afford luxury goods and that "China has surpassed the United States to become the second largest luxury market after Japan."
8. Since the late 1990s, self-help and motivational literature (*lizhi lei tushu*) has arguably occupied the most important place in the Chinese publishing industry. Translated works are especially popular, including Dryden and Vos 1997; Johnson 1998; and various editions of works authored by Dale Carnegie and published by dozens of publishing houses including the People's Daily Publishing House, the Chinese International Radio Press, Chinese City Press, Chinese Material Press, World Press, Chinese Women Press, Beijing Press, and Inner Mongolian Press. At the 2006 Beijing Book Fair, self-help and motivational works were heavily promoted by various publishers. The number of motivational books in the economics and management category—that is, the ones that purport to teach people how to be successful and make a fortune—was close to ten thousand (Wenhui 2008).
9. I searched "*shenjia*" in Chinese in China Academic Journals Full-text Database that includes magazines, academic journals, and comments from 1950 to the present and obtained 2587 articles on July 13, 2009. Among them, one article was published in the 1960s, four were published in the 1970s, 145 were published in the 1980s, 604 were published in the 1990s, and 1834 were published in the 2000s. Searches of this term on Google and Baidu, the largest search engine in China, on September 9, 2009 resulted in over 9 million and over 13 million hits, respectively.
10. A keyword search of "shen jia" on July 8, 2009 on *People's Daily* website resulted in 22793 entries. The top six categories were sports (3847), economy (1709), entertain-

ment (1654), IT (1501), media (1000), and automobile (964). The first 20 search results were all about sports, including 19 items about male football players and their clubs (17 of which were concerned with foreign players); one item was about the NBA.

11. In my field research in China during the summer of 2008, I constantly heard people talking about others' *shenjia*. Those who most often mentioned *shenjia* were adults between 20 and 50. I rarely heard people over 60 discussing *shenjia*, which might indicate that the *shenjia* discourse is a discourse about and by young people.
12. See Jinwai Bao (2009).
13. See US-China Institute (2009).
14. See Sina.com (2008).
15. See Liu Qiong (n.d.).
16. See Xinmin Net (2009).

References

Billeter, Jean-François. 1985. The System of "Class Status." Pp. 127–169 in *The Scope of State Power in China*, ed. S. R. Schram. New York: St. Martin's Press.

Boorstin, Daniel J. [1961] 1985. *The Image*. New York: Atheneum.

Boston Consulting Group. 2006. Taking the Client's Perspective: Global Wealth 2006. http://www.bcg.com/impact_expertise/publications/files/Taking_Clients_Perspective_Global_Wealth_2006_Dec2006.pdf (accessed September 15, 2009).

Brownell, Susan. 1996. "Representing Gender in the Chinese Nation: Chinese Sportswomen and Beijing's Bid for the 2000 Olympics." *Identities* 2 (3): 223–247.

Chan, Anita, Stanley Rosen, and Jonathan Unger. 1980. "Students and Class Warfare: The Social Roots of the Red Guard Conflict in Guangzhou (Canton)." *China Quarterly* 83 (Sept.): 397–446.

China Daily. 2009. "Battered Luxury Brands Eye Chinese Market for Growth." April 11. http://www.chinadaily.com.cn/bizchina/2009-04/11/content_7669126.htm (accessed Aug. 23, 2009).

Choi, Ju Chong and Ron Berger. 2009. "Ethics of Global Internet, Community and Fame Addiction." *Journal of Business Ethics* 85: 193–200.

Croll, Elizabeth. 1984. "Marriage Choice and Status Groups in Contemporary China." Pp. 175–197 in *Class and Social Stratification in Post-Revolutionary China*, ed. J. L. Watson. Cambridge: Cambridge University Press.

Davis, Deborah S., ed. 2000. *The Consumer Revolution in Urban China*. Berkeley: University of California Press.

Dong, Jinxia and J.A. Mangan. 2001. "Football in New China." *Soccer and Society* 2 (3): 79–100.

Dryden, Gordon and Jeanette Vos. N.d. *Learning Revolution*. Trans. and published by Shanghai Sanlian Publishing House and Kelihua Cultural Firm in 1997.

Fan, Hong and Mangan, J.A. 2003. "Will the 'Iron Roses' Bloom Forever? Women's Football in China: Changes and Challenges." *Soccer & Society* 4 (2/3): 47–66.

Flannery, Russell. 2009. Forbes China Celebrity List. http://www.forbes.com/2009/03/18/chinese-celebrities-beijing-olympics-yao-ming-business-media-chinas-top-celebrities.html (accessed January 13, 2010).

Honig, Emily, and Gail Hershatter. 1988. *Personal Voices*. Stanford, CA: Stanford University Press.

Hopkins, Barbara E. 2007. "Western Cosmetics in the Gendered Development of Consumer Culture in China." *Feminist Economics* 13 (3/4): 287–306.

Hu, Angang. 2004. *Zhongguo Zhanlue Gouxiang (Thoughts on Chinese Strategy)*. Foreword. Jiangsu: Zhengjia Renmin Chubanshe.

Huang, Philip C. C. 1995. "Rural Class Struggle in the Chinese Revolution." *Modern China* 21 (1): 105–143.

Ip, Hung-Yok. 2003. "Fashioning Appearances." *Modern China* 29 (3): 329–361.

Jinwai Bao. 2009. "Revealing the Models for the Automobile Exhibit" (*Jiemi Zhantan Beihou de Chemo Men*). Reprint from *Xinhua News Agency* and *Law Weekly*. May 7. http://www.jwb.com.cn/jwb/html/2009-05/07/content_309487.htm (accessed June 17, 2009).

Johnson, Spencer. 1998. *Who Moved My Cheese? An Amazing Way to Deal with Change in Your Work and in Your Life*. G.P. Putnam and Sons. Trans. and pub. Zhongxin Publishing House, 2007.

Kraus, Richard Curt. 1977. "Class Conflict and the Vocabulary of Social Analysis in China." *China Quarterly* 69 (March): 54–74.

Li, Hongmei. 2006. *Advertising and Consumer Culture in Post-Mao China*. Ph.D. Dissertation. University of Southern California.

Liu Qiong. N.d. "An Analysis of the Increase of Brand Value of TV Hosts through the CCTV Evaluation" (*Cong Yangshi Ceping Kan Zhuchiren Pinpai Jiazhe de Tisheng*). http://www.people.com.cn/GB/14677/21963/22064/2958545.html (accessed July 18, 2009).

Lu, Xinmin. 2008. "Class Status" (*Jieji Chengfen*). *The Archive* (*Dangan Tiandi*) 5: 26–31.

Macartney, Jane. 2005. "TV Talent Contest 'Too Democratic' for China's Censors." *The Times* (UK). Aug. 29.

Marcuse, Herbert. 1966. *One-Dimensional Man*. Beacon Press.

Merrill Lynch and Capgemini. 2009. World Wealth Report. www.ml.com/media/113831.pdf (accessed 13 January 2010).

Oates, Thomas and Judy Polumbaum. 2004. "Agile Big Man: The Flexible Marketing of Yao Ming." *Pacific Affairs* 77 (2): 187–210.

People's Daily. 2003. "Zhao An Was Sentenced to Ten Years in Prison for Bribery and Zhang Jun was Sentenced to Six Years in Prison for Two Crimes" (*Zhao An Fan Shouhuizui Panxing Shinian, Zhang Jun Yi Liangzui Bingfa Pan Liunian*). Dec. 13. http://www.peopledaily.com.cn/GB/yule/1082/2246472.html (accessed July 23, 2009).

Rosen, Stanley. 2004. "The Victory of Materialism: Aspirations to Join China's Urban Moneyed Classes and the Commercialization of Education." *The China Journal* 51: 27–51.

Schram, Stuart R. 1984. "Classes, Old and New, In Mao Zedong's Thought, 1949–1976." Pp. 29–55 in *Class and Social Stratification in Post-Revolutionary China*, ed. J. L. Watson. Cambridge: Cambridge University Press.

Sina.com. 2008. "The Award Level of the Chinese Olympic Team Is Expected to Create a Precedent, and They Are Likely to be Exempt of Income Tax" (*Zhongguo Aoyun Juntuan Jiangjin Jiang Chuang Xin Gao, Geren Suodeshui You Wang Quanmian*). March 14. http://sports.sina.com.cn/o/2008-03-14/11593531394.shtml (accessed July 17, 2009).

Sina.com. 2004. "20 Chinese Newspapers Are Among 'the Top 100 Most Circulated Dailies in the World'" *(20 Jia Zhongguo Baozhi Jishen "Shijie Ribao Faxingliang Qian 100*

Ming") June 3. http://www.gdass.gov.cn/CIC/xwcb02.htm (accessed September 23, 2009).

Sun, Liping. 2003. *Duan Lie* (*The Fractured China*). Beijing: Social Sciences Documentation Publishing House.

Tang, Xiaobing. 2000. *Chinese Modern: The Heroic and the Quotidian*. Durham: Duke University Press.

Unger, Jonathan. 1984. "The Class System in Rural China." Pp. 121–141 in *Class and Social Stratification in Post-Revolutionary China*, ed. J. L. Watson. Cambridge: Cambridge University Press.

US–China Institute. "I Have Learned from the Words of Yao Ming." http://china.usc.edu/ShowArticle.aspx?articleID=1557#Strategic (accessed July 30, 2009).

Wang, Chih-ming. 2004. "Capitalizing the Big Man: Yao Ming, Asian America, and the China Global." *Inter-Asia Cultural Studies* 5 (2): 263–278.

Wang, Ding and Mou Jianqiu, 2002. "Who Is Ignoring the Lower Rungs" (*Shei zai moshi dicing*). *Gaige neican* 2 (20 January): 2–5.

Wang, Hui. 2003. *China's New Order*. Ed. Theodore Huters. Cambridge, MA: Harvard University Press.

Wang, Jing. 2008. *Brand New China*. Cambridge, MA: Harvard University Press.

Watson, James L. 1984a. "Introduction." Pp. 1–15 in *Class and Social Stratification in Post-Revolutionary China*, ed. J. L. Watson. Cambridge: Cambridge University Press.

Watson, James L., ed. 1984b. *Class and Social Stratification in Post-Revolutionary China*. Cambridge: Cambridge University Press.

Wenhui. 2008. "The Gradual Revealing of Problems with Publishing Motivational Works and Their Entry into the Winter" (*Lizhi lei tushu wenti xianxian jianjian buru dongtian*). *Wenhui Book Review*, Feb. 6.

White, Gordon. 1978–1979. "Politics and Social Status in China." *Pacific Affairs* 51 (4): 561–584.

White, Gordon. 1976. *The Politics of Class and Class Origin*. Canberra: The Australia National University.

Whyte, Martin King and William L. Parish. 1984. *Urban Life in Contemporary China*. Chicago: University of Chicago Press.

Xinmin Net. 2009. "Why Does the *Shenjia* of Liu Qian Exceed That of Chou Chieh-lun and Alexander Wang" (*Liu Qian Shenjia Ping Shenme Chao Zhou Jielun Wang Lihong*). March 23. http://news.xinmin.cn/rollnews/2009/03/23/1720226.html (accessed July 18, 2009).

Xu, Gary and Susan Feiner. 2007. "Meinu Jingji/China's Beauty Economy." *Feminist Economics* 13 (3/4): 307–23.

Xu, Haifeng. 2003. "Are You Already Middle Class?" (*Ni Zhongchan Le Ma?)* Beijing: Jingji Ribao Chubanshe (Economic Daily Press).

Yang, Mayfair. 1999. *Spaces of Their Own*. Minneapolis: University of Minnesota Press.

Yue, Xiao Dong and Chau-Kiu Cheung. 2000. "Selection of Favorite Idols and Models among Chinese Young People: A Comparative Study in Hong Kong and Nanjing." *International Journal of Behavioral Development* 24 (1): 91–98.

Zhang, Wei-Wei. 2000. *Transforming China: Economic Reform and Its Political Implications*. London, UK: Macmillan.

Zhao, Yuezhi. 2008. *Communication in China*. Lanham, MD: Rowman & Littlefield.

———. 1998. *Media, Market, and Democracy in China*. Champaign: University of Illinois Press.

Zhongguo xinwen chubanbao. 2009. "China Will Become the Fourth Largest Global Advertising Market" (*Zhongguo Jiang Cheng Quanqiu Disi Da Guanggao Shichang*). July 27. http://media.chuban.cc/zx/zh/200907/t20090727_51691.html (accessed Aug. 1, 2009).

Zhongguo Xinwen Wang. 2008. "The Societal Blue Book: 1.5 Million College Students Will Face Difficulties in Finding a Job" (*Shehui Lanpi Shu: Niandi Jiangyou 150 Wan Daxue Biyesheng Nanzhao Gongzuo*). Dec. 15. http://www.chinanews.com.cn/gn/news/2008/12-15/1487659.shtml (accessed July 17, 2009).

PART THREE

Branding and the Promotional Public Sphere

CHAPTER EIGHT

Activism, Branding, and the Promotional Public Sphere

Graham Knight

Introduction

In her analysis of sweatshop labor practices in the apparel industry, particularly in poorer developing countries of the global South, Collins (2006) identifies three major factors to account for the current growth of this type of labor process. In addition to the subcontracting system and the offshore relocation of product fabrication and assembly, she identifies the intensification of branding as a marketing and communication strategy. The intensification of branding speaks to two important developments in the organization of production and distribution characteristic of the current phase of globalization. The first is structural, namely the development of merchandisers like Nike who straddle the conventional distinction between manufacturer and retailer. In the conventional sense, Nike does not manufacture anything; it contracts out its production to manufacturers, based in newly industrializing countries like Korea and Taiwan, which situate their production facilities in low-wage countries such as China where environmental regulation and labor rights are weakly defined and poorly enforced. And while Nike does control some of its distribution network, the bulk of its sales occur through retail outlets that it does not own nor control. Branding is central to Nike's corporate identity and strategy as a merchandiser since it provides the virtual substance of what is otherwise a hollowed out organization whose products acquire the disproportionate share of their value from the symbolism conferred on them through the company's promotional practices—advertising, marketing, celebrity endorsements, event sponsorships, and other forms of affirmative communication—aimed at enhancing consumption.

This speaks directly to the second development. In a context where products are marked, at least in utilitarian terms, by parity or functional equivalence, branding has become an important mechanism of differentiation or distinction. The same contract factories that manufacture Nike's athletic shoes, clothing, and equipment often manufacture similar products for Nike's competitors. Although merchandisers retain control over product development and design and maintain quality control personnel in their contract factories, the products themselves tend to be more or less equivalent in terms of quality and performance. The brand name has become the principal signifier of difference, rather than the products themselves. The brand name, logo, and slogan have become a shorthand way of signifying the value of consumption as integral to social and personal identity and as a means for corporations to position themselves and their products distinctively in a competitive marketplace. Branding has become a technique for adding exchange value to both products (price) and corporations (stock value). Its effectiveness in achieving a value-added effect is indicated by the fact that large corporate retailers like Wal-Mart have increasingly developed their own in-house brands or private labels.

Product branding dates back to the structural transformation of industrial capitalism in the latter part of the nineteenth century that gave rise to corporate forms of organization, the development of monopolistic and oligopolistic markets, and the growth of advertising as a means to generate and sustain consumer demand. Branding represents the way that, under monopolistic and oligopolistic conditions, price competition is supplemented and/or supplanted by competition over product styling, design, packaging, imagery, and broader cultural and aesthetic associations (Baran and Sweezy 1966). With the growth of neoliberal economic ideology since the 1970s, branding has intensified further in a number of ways: organizational as well as product branding; the integration of branding and organizational communication generally; the branding of services in addition to goods; the globalization of branding; and the extension of branding to all manner of organizations, groups, and even individuals.

Branding adds value by means of communication. It is interwoven with the whole array of communicative practices in which organizations engage—advertising, public relations, social responsibility initiatives, celebrity endorsements, sponsorship, media relations, public reports, architecture, websites, vision and mission statements, internal memoranda, and so on. As one recent commentator on organizational identity and image has observed,

"The basic message here is that everything about an organization communicates. Everything" (Brønn 2002: 91). Much of this communication occurs in the public sphere where organizations undertake the process of securing and reproducing legitimacy. In democratic societies, however, the public sphere is an environment where legitimacy may be contested or threatened, as the example of anticorporate activism such as the movement against sweatshops demonstrates. In this respect, communication in the public sphere takes on a promotional aspect as it deals with the construction and circulation of identity and reputation in ways that are aimed at defending and enhancing organizational interests and autonomy. In this promotional public sphere any fixed or immutable distinction between the promotional signifier and signified breaks down; the two become mutually commutable. When Tiger Woods advertises Nike, Nike also advertises Tiger Woods; when Nike talks corporate social responsibility practices, talk of corporate social responsibility evokes Nike. There is no obvious way to distinguish between what is being promoted and what is doing the promoting in the "vortex of publicity" (Wernick 1991: 92).

The Promotional Public Sphere

The development of the promotional public sphere begins with what Habermas (1991) referred to as the "refeudalization" of the liberal bourgeois public sphere that occurred with the structural transformation of capitalism in the latter part of the nineteenth century. For Habermas, the political public sphere that had emerged in the seventeenth and eighteenth centuries was ideally an arena in which citizens gathered to debate issues of common interest in a critical and rational way, unadulterated by the play of private interests and competition for advantage. Though Habermas acknowledges that the public sphere was marked by a breach between an ideology of open participation and actual practices of widespread exclusion (of women and the proletariat in particular), he argues that the public sphere was an important aspect of the institutionalization of bourgeois democracy that allowed for the open expression of critical ideas at the boundary of political and civil society. According to Habermas, however, the transformation of liberal to corporate capitalism refeudalized the public sphere, turning it back into an arena for the public display of power, privilege, and prestige as it had been in the premodern era. The refeudalized public sphere became dominated by spectacle aimed at manipulating public opinion in line with powerful economic interests; it was increasingly characterized by affirmative rather than critical discourse as exemplified by an array of promotional communication—advertising, public relations, sensationalized journalism, and a media system geared to popular entertainment.

Habermas's initial formulation of the liberal bourgeois public sphere has been subject to extensive criticism (see *inter alia* the contributions to Calhoun 1992). Much of this has taken Habermas to task for overemphasizing the public sphere's critical, rational character and its immunity to manipulation by private interests and for paying insufficient attention to the way its exclusionary nature was central to its functioning by privileging a type of interest and rationality that were class- and gender-specific. Habermas assumes a unity of reason at work in the public sphere that not only allowed participants to set aside personal private interests in their debates but also provided the grounds to reach discursive consensus based on argumentation aimed at the common good, rather than bargaining or intimidation. Habermas's concept of the liberal bourgeois public sphere embodies the notion of *enlightened* self-interest. The development of the liberal bourgeois public sphere parallels the development of the bourgeois private sphere in which, economically, convention is gradually replaced by an instrumentally oriented self-interest represented by the accumulation of capital. The individual, male bourgeois is innovative and autonomous in both the private and public spheres. This means he is no longer automatically attached to existing practices or beliefs; he is free to experiment with new modes of thought and action, and capable of revising his behavior and opinions. Like property, ideas can be rationally assessed for their value and discarded when they are no longer profitable or effective. Thought and action become decisional, and neither is bound up with personal identity in a closed, self-reproducing way.

The paradox of Habermas's initial concept of the public sphere is not so much that he ignores its exclusionary character, but that he largely overlooks the implications of the fact that its refeudalization began to occur in the latter part of the nineteenth century—hand in hand with growing success on the part of women, the working class, and other excluded groups in achieving greater collective access and publicity. What happened historically was not only a structural transformation of the public sphere but also a substantive one, as new groups gained access to voice their issues and concerns and attempted to influence public opinion and political decision-making. The public sphere was not only transformed into an arena of economic or corporate promotionalism, it was also opened up to new political issues, problems, and perspectives in the form of collective action on the part of, for example, the organized labor movement, the women's (suffrage) movement, the antislavery movement, and the movements against cruelty to children and animals. In both respects, the unity of reason that was seen to allow male bourgeois citizens to set aside personal interests and reach consensus through argumentation was undermined. The affirmative promotional discourse of corporate interests was based on appeals to aesthetic and affective values. At the same time, the issues and problems that new groups brought into the public sphere for debate and resolution were structurally as well as substantively incommensurable. In theory, what enabled the individual bourgeois male to set aside private interests in the public sphere was that he shared in common with his peers the structural form on which these interests were based. Even if those interests were substantively competitive, they were nonetheless structurally uniform and commensurable since they shared a common basis in the privative character of property relations and the personality of possessive individualism that was its psychological and cultural correlate.

In response to critics of the English translation of *The Structural Transformation of the Public Sphere*, Habermas acknowledged the historical development of a plebian public sphere as a variant of the "hegemonic" bourgeois public sphere; the current loss of shared background convictions and the development of a "confused pluralism of competing and equally legitimate forms of life" beyond class interests; and the importance of voluntary associations in civil society to the contemporary public sphere (1992: 425, 445, 453). He did not, however, draw out the implications of these developments for the substantive functioning of the public sphere as a site of organized promotional and activist discourse. The assumption of a unity of reason and the goal of argumentative consensus central to the public sphere ideal becomes increasingly problematic in a public sphere in which issues are not framed solely in class terms but embrace multiple value spheres related to gender, religion, ethnicity, and so on. Once other groups organize and struggle to gain access to the public sphere, express their views, and participate in effective decision-making, the assumption of a common structural form of private interests no longer obtains. This not only undermines the assumption that private interests can be set aside in search of the common good (as represented for Habermas in the better argument), it also introduces the likelihood that the underlying frames of reference on which debate, argumentation, and consensus formation are based are no longer commensurable. Knowledge claims proliferate on the basis of different, often conflicting, worldviews and epistemologies. It can no longer be assumed even in theory that there is any unity of reason acting as the point of departure and destination for public discourse; the public sphere is flooded with uncertainty (Pellizzoni 2001, 2003). Public discourse is fragmented structurally and substantively as incommensurable forms of interest come into competitive play, and the public sphere becomes an arena of both economic promotion and what Ulrich Beck (1997) has called "subpolitics," social and political activism outside the institutionalized realm of party politics. The public sphere mediates a bilateral flow of communication between the system and the lifeworld. In its promotional form it functions as a conduit for what Habermas called the colonization of the lifeworld by system imperatives; in its subpolitical form it enables the infiltration of the system by lifeworld problems, concerns, and communicative frames of reference.

The dual character of a pluralistic, competitive public sphere characterized by promotionalism and activism means that consensus formation becomes more complex and difficult. This is compounded in a number of ways. In the first place, communication in the public sphere is increasingly mediated, and although the range of media is expanding with the spread of the Internet, large-scale media continue to play a central role in determining how information and debate are framed. This gives a distinct advantage to those with power, prestige, money, social ties, and organization in getting their message across and puts less well-resourced actors at a disadvantage. This inequality still allows power centers like governments and corporations to set the terms of debate, at least initially, and to do so in self-promotional ways. Dissenting voices often find that they have to conform to a promotional logic—branding and marketing themselves and their issues—in order to ensure media access, influence the terms of their public representation, and maximize public attention and political effect.

The relationship between promotionalism and activism is uneven, and the hegemony of promotional communication tends to accentuate the credibility of voices over the validity of their claims. The rationalization of decision-making and opinion formation makes identities the point of reference for assessing and evaluating ideas. Who speaks becomes a measure of the validity of what they say, particularly in a crowded public sphere where issues and interests have no obvious common denominator, and participants look for shorthand cues in order to take a stance on matters they may know little about otherwise. While the effect of this may be to accentuate the rhetorical power of speakers over arguments, it nonetheless reinforces a strong moral and ethical dimension to public discourse. Values play a central role in both promotional and subpolitical discourse, as is evident in both the communicative practices of a company like Nike and in the claims of its antisweatshop critics.

Growing emphasis on the identity and credibility of voices has had a number of implications. Firstly, the exclusionary divisions that characterized the liberal bourgeois public sphere have been increasingly replaced by internal lines of stratification and regionalization within the public sphere. Almost anyone can have a voice, but not everyone will be widely heard, let alone acknowledged. While problems of access have not disappeared, what is probably more at issue today is the relative positioning and durability of voices within the public sphere, especially with respect to center/periphery differences. The Internet, for example, has certainly enhanced the ability of critical, dissenting voices to speak, but the sheer scope of the medium means that many of these voices remain on the periphery in terms of how widely and effectively they resonate. Peripheral, alternative media remain dependent on an audience being made familiar with their existence, and their capacity to grow in size, credibility, and effect is constrained by their structural location within the public sphere. This may encourage many alternative media to address themselves mainly to the already converted, and seek to protect their niche within the public sphere in the face of challenges from rivals as well as opponents. Even for activists who are able to gain access to the mainstream media at the core of the public sphere, the terms of representation and the need for credibility are also restricted by these media's appetite for conflict, confrontation, and controversy. Mainstream media tend to dwell on the public activities of activists, especially when it is associated with violence or disruption, more than their message about the nature of and solutions to the problems they are voicing.

Exclusion is now not only more and more internal to the promotional public sphere, it is also increasingly strategic rather than conventional. Participants in a diversified public sphere come to see one another in terms of how qualified or not they are to have a say on a given topic by virtue of the identity or status background from which they enter the public sphere. Social qualifications, one's background, knowledge, and locus in the system or the lifeworld, begin to vie with and/or supplement critical rationality as the basis on which opinions and arguments are evaluated, accepted, or dismissed. In this respect, the public sphere comes to resemble more of a social field in Bourdieu's (1993) sense, i.e., an arena marked not only by a determinate range of practices (in this case debate, argumentation, and discursive interaction) but also by relations of status competition and power that determine the grounds on which hierarchies of value rationality are reproduced. Debate and argumentation function in competitive as well as cooperative terms, in terms of success and failure as well as better and worse. Silencing or marginalizing opponents by casting doubt on their credibility or legitimacy becomes a means of struggle for discursive success and the material and symbolic benefits this can bring.

As voices participate in the public sphere on the basis of incommensurable interests and issues, the distinction between strategic and communicative action that was fundamental to Habermas's critical theory begins to break down. The promotional public sphere becomes used more and more for strategic reasons as participants focus their energies on promoting their ideas and opinions, and on establishing their own topics, issues, and discursive frames as the most pressing, urgent, and important. Topics and issues arising from particularistic interests and concerns vie with one another for general consideration and universal relevance, and this generates a constant oscillation between the promotion of ethically and emotionally oriented rhetoric on the one hand, and a pragmatic resort to reflexive values as the basis for provisional consensus formation on the other. At the same time, strategic action geared to competitive success comes to depend more and more on communicative practices to secure consent and legitimacy on the part of those who may be put at a disadvantage by such action. The successfulness of strategic action rests on ethical as well as legal legitimacy, and this is secured communicatively within the boundaries of civil society whose problems, issues, and disagreements resonate throughout the public sphere.

The central issue confronting the liberal bourgeois public sphere was the problem of controlling the power of the state in the interests of a private sphere based on property and patriarchal authority. The promotional public sphere, on the other hand, is one in which activist voices are seeking to mobilize and deploy political power in the interests of civil society rather than curtail it. The counterpart to the promotional public sphere is a fractured private sphere rife with problems and conflicts, prominent among which are the inequities stemming from property relations and patriarchal power. In response to critics of his original conceptualization of the public sphere, Habermas recognized the historical development of a plebian public sphere as a variant of the "hegemonic" bourgeois public sphere; the loss of shared background convictions and the development of a "confused pluralism of competing and equally legitimate forms of life" beyond class interests; and the importance of voluntary associations in civil society to the contemporary public sphere (1992: 425, 445, 453). In a subsequent reformulation of the public sphere, he acknowledges not only the possibility of new forms of critical activism but also the way that the public sphere acts as a forum for the framing and dramatization of lifeworld problems and concerns and as a conduit for communicating these problems to the political system (primarily) for remedial action (Habermas 1998). The import of this, however, is that fashioning practicable solutions, rather than reaching argumentative consensus, has become the chief political task of the public sphere.

Activism and Branding

The development of the promotional public sphere in which the credibility of voices becomes as important, if not more so, as the validity of what they say reveals the importance of belief over knowledge as the critical determinant of resonance and rhetorical effect. Publics normally do not have the resources—time, expertise, money, or even dedication—necessary to evaluate competing and conflicting knowledge claims. The knowledge or information society is also a society of belief. The accentuated role of credibility and belief makes the professionalization of identity formation, through the growing role of experts and consultants in message and image design, more important as a communicative resource (Mayhew 1997). The growth of professionalized communication practices reflects not only the increasingly rationalized, reflexive nature of strategic communication but also the centrality of actor identity to such communication.

Branding plays an especially important role in professionalized communication and identity formation. Branding represents the way that communicative action has been subsumed by strategic action but in a way that makes communication itself more and more central to the design and implementation of strategy. This is particularly so for profit-driven organizations which rely on publicity to add value to their products. Branding becomes critical not only to overly promotional practices such as marketing, advertising, celebrity endorsements, and event sponsorships, but also to the broader array of practices associated with organizational communication management including public relations, issues management practices, and corporate social responsibility initiatives. Communication management and brand identity are oriented to the public at large as well as to actors whose stake in the organization is more proximate and determinate, such as employees, shareholders, suppliers, distributors, and retailers (Christensen and Cheney 2000). The brand identity becomes a way of traversing different contexts and levels of interest and relevance and of transferring qualitatively different kinds of value between them.

The commercial success of identity branding lies in a number of functions that branding can fulfill. Late modernity has been characterized as a social environment in which roles, identities, relationships, and interaction practices have become increasingly fluid, detached from their conventional structural moorings, individualized and detraditionalized (*inter alia* Baumann 2000; Beck and Beck-Gernsheim 2002). The growing importance of consumption over work and occupation as a source of identity and the rise of "new" social movement activism oriented toward identity normalization, status recognition, social rights, and risks point to the growing field of social contingency in which conventional meaning and action orientations are no longer necessary or even possible (except as a rationalistic means to avoid further decision-making). When the social field is in flux, branding offers a way to re-anchor identity and manage uncertainty while pursuing comparative advantage and competitive success—if only in the minimalist sense of self-preservation. Branding is also a way to associate with an imagined community of like-minded people, other consumers of the same brands, and enjoy the reassurance of their combined wisdom (can so many people be mistaken)?

A branded identity need not mean a singular, unitary meaning or content. Part of Nike's success as the leading global sportswear merchandiser consists in the way that the company has been able to fashion a multifaceted brand identity, simultaneously ironic and earnest, aesthetically stylish and technologically serious, "cool" and socially responsible (Goldman and Papson 1998; Knight and Greenberg 2002). Through a multifaceted marketing strategy the Nike brand conveys a personality of its own, and the company's identity comes to consist in the way these different poses coalesce smoothly and seamlessly. As Lury (2004) stresses, the brand is an object and a medium in its own right. Its familiarity, continuity, and visible ubiquity turn it into a kind of relief mechanism representing reliability, trust, and improvement that frees the consumer from the necessity of determining and assessing the terms of her or his decision-making. As a stable reference point in a world of flux, the brand neutralizes time, or rather the open-ended, contingent nature of time, by providing a reassuring sense of origin and permanence.

The promotional public sphere is also a sphere of surveillance where prominence can translate into critical scrutiny. By the late 1990s, for example, Nike had acquired a new—and from the company's perspective unwanted—dimension to its identity, that of sweatshop employer. As well as being a cultural icon, Nike was now for many consumers in the global North a political reference point for the worst forms of labor exploitation made possible by globalization. The growth of a transnational antisweatshop movement was part of a broader activist challenge to the corporate power resulting from the enhancement of market mechanisms and the retrenchment of state-centered regulatory capacities. Anticorporate activism in particular often took the form of "logo campaigns" targeting prominent brand name companies for their deficient performance in areas spanning labor conditions, gender and racial inequalities, environmental degradation, and the adverse impact on local communities (Bennett and Lagos 2007; Klein 2000).

In anti-logo campaigns, such as antisweatshop activism targeted specifically against Nike, the brand acted not only as a device for managing and positioning the full range of corporate products and services but also as a convenient target for activists' grievances and demands. As professional corporate communicators began to recognize, the brand signified not only the organization's preferred public identity but also its actual public image. Forced into responding publicly about their good intentions and ethical concerns, targeted companies like Nike subsequently handed social movement activists a second string to their bow. Activists were able to level criticism not only at unethical or harmful corporate performance but also at corporate hypocrisy for espousing one thing while doing the opposite. Given the importance of reliability and trustworthiness to claims-making in the promotional public sphere, allegations about the corporate credibility gap are a potentially more important tactic for influencing public opinion and introducing risk into the corporate environment than claims about harmful or unethical performance alone (Knight 2007).

Anti-logo activism is communicational; it relies on public expressions of protest and challenge where promotional tactics geared to publicizing not only the cause but also the activist organization or movement itself are used to confront and undermine corporate promotional strategy. The appeal of branding as a major feature of promotionalism lies in the need to establish and sustain a distinctive identity in an environment full of rivals as well as adversaries, potential allies, professional observers like the media, and ordinary bystanders. Although mergers do occur between activist groups and organizations, the recent trend has been towards an ever-greater differentiation and extension of the social movement field rather than consolidation and concentration. The expansion and ongoing differentiation of the public sphere provide an opportunity for new groups and organizations to voice their concerns just as changing forms of social problematization generate new risks, grievances, and the motivation to challenge the political and economic systems.

At the same time, as the theory of organizational isomorphism argues, actors occupying an organizational field also tend to resemble one another structurally due to interacting pressures that are both competitive and institutional (DiMaggio and Powell 1983). Most activist organizations acquire some degree of self-branding once they begin to institutionalize and professionalize their activities. This self-branding involves the adoption of various practices ranging from the symbolic, such as the organization's name and logo or image, to an assortment of organizational activities whose strategic significance also lies in their relationship to communication and the need for organizational credibility. These practices include permanent campaigning; a flexible, network form of internal coordination and affinity with other organizations; a concern with publicity in mainstream as well as alternative media; reliance on computer-mediated communication for coordination and information dissemination; issue-related R&D and assessment of the public response to specific issues; celebrity endorsements and event sponsorship; the use of communication experts and consultants to help frame, publicize, and promote the message; and even the development of "niche" issues and activism (*inter alia* Bennett 2003; Mayhew 1997; Greenberg et al. 2009; Lahusen 1996; Levitsky 2007).

The appeal of branding as a technique is not only that it helps sharpen and stabilize identity but that it also enhances what is known in the social movement literature as resource mobilization—the accumulation and deployment of money, time, human energy, commitment, reputation, and other forms of cultural and social capital. Resource mobilization is especially challenging for "new" social movements that are oriented primarily to issues of social recognition, rights, and risks. These movements do not have the same kind of structurally inbuilt membership and resource bases that were characteristic of the labor movement in which membership hinges on shared material conditions and interests, for example (though these do not automatically translate into successful mobilization). "New" social movements tend to attract participants, constituents, and sympathizers on the basis of subjective interests whose primary rationality is often ethical rather than material. Ethically framed issues have a strong emotional aspect, which accentuates their social resonance. Particularly for social movement organizations that address "distant" issues, developing and promoting a distinctive organizational identity that reflects this rationality becomes an important way to achieve recognition and acts as a means to mobilize resources. Distant issues are problems that are removed geographically, socially, and culturally from the movement's frontline participants who are normally acting on behalf of the objective interests of others elsewhere (Rucht 2000). The modern antisweatshop movement in the global North, for example, is primarily a distant issue movement whose membership mobilizes on behalf of industrial and agricultural workers in the global South by politicizing consumption as the means to bridge the social and economic divide between the two worlds. The branding of activist identity in ethically rational terms—framing and explaining the issues and the cause in terms of social justice, security, and well-being—becomes a means to reduce the distance of distant issues by generating ethical and emotional lines of identification.

The branding of activist identity becomes an important technique when issues, like commercial products, are subject to frequent turnover and fluctuation in terms of their meaning, relevance, and salience. A long-held view in research on social movements is that issue activism is subject to cycles of attention and contention. Issue attention tends to fluctuate primarily in relation to public response, especially to the perceived costs and complexities of remedial action and issue resolution, and to the emergence of new, competing issues in the media and on public agendas (Downs 1972). Issue contention, on the other hand, varies cyclically in line with the escalation and eventual exhaustion of activist responses. As an issue grows in prominence, more activist groups and organizations are attracted into the field of contention, heightening competition for resources and opportunities. This competition leads to more confrontational and disruptive forms of action that result in the demise of the movement and fading of the issues (Tarrow 1989, 1998). For both the attention and contention cycles the downward turn results from prior growth and momentum; decline is the side effect of previous success.

Organizational branding offers a way to offset these cyclical patterns by providing a more or less stable point of reference in terms of which issue turnover and fluctuations in issue identity can be controlled and understood. Just as corporations use their brand to organize the marketing of a diverse and ever-changing range of differentially branded products, so do many social movement organizations use their brand to manage and integrate an array of different issues whose own identities may be in flux. A promotional relationship between organization and issue or product is the corollary of this branding process: the organization promotes the product or issue, and the product or issue promotes the organization, putting it in a position to introduce new products and issues in a credible and trusted way later on. In a sense, organizational branding allows social movement organizations the opportunity to internalize the issue attention and contention cycles. As an issue or the tactics used to promote it begin to wane in significance or effect, the organization can move on to focus on other issues or adopt new tactics under the umbrella of a more or less stable brand identity. An example of this is Global Exchange, an organization active in the broad human rights movement that is representative of what Bennett (2003) refers to as "move on" activism. It played a leading role in promoting the antisweatshop movement in the late 1990s, but after conflicting with other organizations over its more conciliatory stance towards Nike, it moved on to other issues and causes. Its most recent initiatives include collective action for a sustainable, "green" economy and its association with Code Pink, a women's organization opposed to the Iraq war and occupation as well as the recent bailout of the American financial system.

Because the promotional public sphere is noisy and competitive, however, this virtuous circle of organizational branding is constantly interrupted and disrupted. The salience and all-encompassing scope of Nike's corporate brand, for example, gave antisweatshop activists an enlarged target for their criticisms about working conditions and labor practices in the company's contract factories in the global South. This was a movement aimed at Nike and other sportswear companies, not just at particular products. Organizational branding facilitates the attribution of responsibility on the part of diverse stakeholders, which complicates communication management by making conflicts of interest and power more transparent, and intensifying pressure on the organization to react quickly to resolve competing demands. When the organization as a whole is being criticized and held responsible, the reflex is to deny, displace blame, become defensive and secretive, reassert one's innocence, and attack one's critics in turn—the classic model of short-term crisis management. As Nike discovered in the mid-1990s when it responded in this way to growing allegations of sweatshop conditions in its factories, the strategy can easily backfire and serve only to amplify criticisms and enhance the prominence of critics.

For social movement organizations, on the other hand, the main problems of organizational branding concern relationships with members, constituents, and sympathizers rather than outside critics. Social movement organizations face the dilemma of representing the interests of their constituents at the same time as influencing significant others—the media, policymakers, corporate decision-makers, general public opinion—that are not only outside their organizational boundaries but also likely to be indifferent or hostile to social movement actions. Dissent and challenge are central to the meaning of social movements, but this complicates their relationship to societal power structures as well as their own constituents. Forming coalitions and alliances with similar organizations is one way to try to reconcile this dilemma. Alliances and coalitions enlarge the critical mass of opinion and energy behind a cause and heighten its public salience and significance. At the same time, the effects of isomorphism may predispose social movement organizations towards operational centralization and a weakening of the importance of grassroots involvement and mass mobilization. The pressure of both competitive and institutional isomorphism fosters the functional rationalization of organizational structures and practices, resulting in tendencies towards the differentiation, formalization, and professionalization of social roles. These are conducive to the development of exclusionary decision-making practices based on expertise and other forms of authority that marginalize and undermine participation and accountability at the grassroots level. When this happens, the relationship between organizational cadres and participants and supporters becomes instrumentalized, and the democratic ethos that social movements normally espouse becomes constrained and compromised in the interests of organizational elites seeking to preserve their power internally by enhancing their influence externally.

Marginalizing the role and power of the grassroots can allow social movement cadres and elites the opportunity to maneuver more flexibly and shift focus from one issue or issue aspect to another in response to the interests of external points of influence and power such as the media, policymakers, and public opinion. But this flexibility and breadth of interest come at a price as the participation of constituents becomes either reduced in scope and influence or organized on a controlled basis. With the widespread use of computer-mediated communication, grassroots participation can easily become more administered, distanced, and narrowly channeled to appeal to the particular concerns of sub-segments of the movement's constituency. Narrowcasting issue frames and participation appeals is an increasingly common byproduct of the use of the Internet that speaks to the growing influence of a marketing logic on politics (Bimber 2003; Howard 2006). By logging onto the website of Human Rights Watch, for example, the sympathetic citizen can discover that his or her role consists in only three things: donating to the organization, staying informed of the issues through subscribing to email alerts and reading reports, and taking action by cyber-signing an existing letter of concern about the issue(s) of his or her choice and sending it, with a click of the mouse, to the appropriate authorities. Even organizations that attempt to provide greater opportunities for grassroots participation nonetheless tend to organize this according to an administrative model designed to ensure control. Global Exchange, for example, encourages sympathizers to organize their own local chapter of the organization but provides a 20-page guide, the *Global Exchange Chapters Toolkit*, with detailed instructions and advice, including contact information for the Chapters Program Coordinator, on how to do so (Global Exchange 2009). What the guide does not do is ask its users to give critical feedback or provide their own suggestions and experiences.

Social movement organizations are tertiary sector organizations; they provide services rather than produce goods. From a branding and marketing perspective, services should ideally be promoted in a different way from physical goods. For many years the dominant marketing paradigm for goods was the marketing mix management or transactional approach. Consumption comprised the successful completion of purchasing as a self-contained event or transaction, albeit one that was hopefully performed on a continuing, serial basis. Services, on the other hand, are consumed on a continuous basis. In fact there is often no distinction between the moments or locations of production, distribution, and consumption; the three are simultaneous and copresent. The economy of services implies an ongoing relationship between producer, distributor, and consumer to the extent that the roles themselves tend to conflate: the consumer becomes something of a partner or coproducer of the brand under which the product is subsumed. It is, therefore, the management of relationships rather than transactions that is critical to the marketing and branding of services (Johansen 2005). As the economies of the advanced, affluent societies of the global North have come to consist more and more in the provision of services, the marketing of goods has also assumed a more service-oriented, relationship management aspect. As Lury (2004) notes, Ford no longer markets cars; it markets a relationship to cars and to travel and movement generally.

From the perspective of service promotion, the development of branding and marketing strategies on the part of noncommercial actors like social movement organizations and political parties is paradoxical inasmuch as it often resembles the transaction rather than relationship management model. As Johansen (2005) argues with respect to political parties, the growth of political marketing practices that rely on mediated rather than direct forms of communication and engagement has increased the distance between party elites and professional cadres on the one hand and the grassroots membership on the other. The adoption of transaction management techniques—polling, focus groups, maximizing favorable media hits, policy trial balloons, ensuring everyone stays on message, spin control, etc.—marginalize and alienate the grassroots. This has contributed to the declining levels of party membership and trust in party politics, a process that, ironically, has benefited social movements as disaffected citizens turn to more unconventional political channels to register their concerns. Yet there is ground on which to argue that successful social movement organizations may be treading the same path if they also eschew the slow, laborious work of direct, face-to-face communication for the speed and spread of mediated messaging and networking.

Accounts of the impact of the Internet on social movement mobilization and organization tend to emphasize the benefits, such as the ways that computer-mediated communication improves the agility with which activists can respond to issues, function across national borders, coordinate better and share information with one another, and develop new tactics such as virtual forms of protest and civic engagement (*inter alia* Bennett 2003; della Porta et al. 2006). Offsetting this is the way that networked media open up new avenues for official surveillance as well as pose the problem of securing depth and durability of commitment on the part of constituents who may not be asked to go much further than reaching for their checkbooks and pens and attending the occasional meeting or protest. The recent growth and popularity of social networking media may provide an opportunity to combine the instrumental benefits of mediated communication with the emotional solidarity and trust building effects of embodied interaction.

Yet as research by Gillan et al. (2008) suggests, even activists who embrace interactive media also recognize that the latter tend to increase emotional distance and that interactivity can militate against the cooperative development of complex or sensitive ideas by fostering polarization in terms of the loudest and most persistent voices.

If digitized social relations are relieved of the weight of sacrifice, struggle, doubt, and responsibility that real-world sociality entails, their capacity to generate any depth of affiliation becomes problematic. Networks, after all, are flexible and agile precisely because they generate often thinly embedded structures of normative expectation and obligation. Flexibility entails a reduction of commitment—in all directions. While this may enhance information flow and responsiveness, it may also lead to ephemerality and new forms of marginalization—who and what are left behind when "move on" activism moves on? As the use of technologically mediated forms of political communication becomes normalized, it increasingly dominates the social context in which all forms of political communication take place. Even activist use of direct, unmediated communication is now being rationalized along transactional rather than relationship management lines. In her study of a professional canvassing organization that works on behalf of progressive causes, Fisher (2006) demonstrates how even the conventional mobilizing technique of face-to-face interaction on the street or the doorstep has become aimed primarily at securing donations and signatures rather than developing deep knowledge of, engagement with, and commitment to issues and struggles.

Conclusion

Identity branding offers social movement organizations definite advantages for managing their relationships with powerful actors in an external environment. A branded identity is a way to acquire prominence in a public sphere crowded with noisy, competing actors using the techniques of promotional communication to enhance their status, reach, and impact. Branding stabilizes organizational identity as a reference point to which others can orient and against which they can position themselves. It acts as an umbrella under which shifting issues can be articulated, administered in a more orderly and coherent fashion by allowing activist organizations flexibility in how they respond strategically to the actions of their allies, rivals, adversaries, and audiences. Branding is a component of the internal issues management process that social movement organizations undertake in relation to the cycles of issue attention and contention. In these respects, branding functions for activist organizations in a similar way as for business corporations.

If branding offers activist organizations external benefits, these benefits come at a potential price internally with respect to relationships with constituents and supporters. Unlike corporate or governmental organizations, activist organizations represent the critical impulse that was and remains crucial to the functioning of the public sphere and its role in the institutionalization of democratic accountability and decision-making. Social movements typically internalize this democratic ethos in their own structures and goals and strive to realize it through self-exemplification. Identity branding clashes with this to the extent that it is associated with organizational and communicative practices that foster functional rationalization and internal distance within activist organizations between cadres and constituents. Branding intensifies strategic investment in the protection and maintenance of identity as both an outcome of organizational action and a resource for further action. And when the protection and reproduction of identity become paramount, grassroots participation is vulnerable to top-down administrative control or marginalization. The problem is not that the promotional public sphere excludes the expression of critical dissent and challenge. It is, rather, that the diverse, competitive, and incommensurable nature of the issues promoted in the public sphere tends to reify the identities of participants as a primary medium, i.e., relief mechanism, of communication. If the liberal public sphere offered its participants the illusory prospect of freeing themselves from their identities, then the promotional public sphere offers its participants the all too realistic prospect of binding themselves ever more tightly to theirs.

References

Baran, Paul, and Paul Sweezy. 1966. *Monopoly Capital: An Essay on the American Economic and Social Order*. Boston: Monthly Review Press.

Baumann, Zygmunt. 2000. *Liquid Modernity*. Cambridge: Polity Press.

Beck, Ulrich. 1997. *The Reinvention of Politics: Rethinking Modernity in the Global Social Order*. Cambridge: Polity Press.

Beck, Ulrich, and Elizabeth Beck-Gernsheim. 2002. *Individualization: Institutionalized Individualism and Its Social and Political Consequences*. London: Sage.

Bennett, W. Lance. 2003. "Communicating Global Activism: Strengths and Vulnerabilities of Networked Politics." *Information, Communication & Society* 6 (2): 143–168.

Bennett, W. Lance. 2003. "Communicating Global Activism: Strengths and Vulnerabilities of Networked Politics." *Information, Communication & Society* 6 (2): 143–168.

Bennett, W. Lance, and Taso Lagos. 2007. "Logo Logic: The Ups and Downs of Branded Political Communication." *Annals of the American Academy of Political and Social Science* 611: 193–206.

Bimber, Bruce. 2003. *Information and American Democracy: Technology in the Evolution of Political Power*. Cambridge: Cambridge University Press.

Bourdieu, Pierre. 1993. *The Field of Cultural Production: Essays on Art and Literature*. New York: Columbia University Press.

Brønn, Peggy S. 2002. "Corporate Communication and the Corporate Brand." Pp. 91–105 in *Corporate Communication: A Strategic Approach to Building Reputation*, ed. Peggy S. Brønn and Roberta Wiig Berg. Oslo: Gyldendal.

Calhoun, Craig, ed. 1992. *Habermas and the Public Sphere*. Cambridge, Mass.: The M.I.T. Press.

Christensen, Lars, and George Cheney. 2000. "Self-Absorption and Self-Seduction in the Corporate Identity Game." Pp. 246–270 in *The Expressive Organization: Linking Identity, Reputation and the Corporate Brand*, ed. Majken Schultz, Mary Jo Hatch, and Mogens Holten. Larsen, Oxford: Oxford University Press.

Collins, Jane. 2006. "Redefining the Boundaries of Work: Apparel Workers and Community Unionism in the Global Economy." *Identities: Global Studies in Culture and Power* 13: 9–31.

Della Porta, Donatella, Massimiliano Andretta, Lorenzo Mosca, and Herbert Reiter. 2006. *Globalization from Below: Transnational Activists and Protest Networks*. Minneapolis: University of Minnesota Press.

DiMaggio, Paul, and Walter Powell. 1983. "The Iron Cage Revisited: Institutional Isomorphism and Collective Rationality in Organizational Fields." *American Sociological Review* 48 (2): 147–160.

Downs, Anthony. 1972. "Up and Down with Ecology: The 'Issue Attention' Cycle." *The Public Interest* (Summer): 38–50.

Fisher, Dana. 2006. *Activism Inc.: How the Outsourcing of Grassroots Campaigns Is Strangling Progressive Politics in America*. Stanford: Stanford University Press.

Gillan, Kevin, Jenny Pickerill, and Frank Webster. 2008. *Anti-War Activism: New Media and Protest in the Information Age*. London: Palgrave Macmillan.

Global Exchange. 2009. *Global Exchange Chapters Toolkit*. Global Exchange. http://www.globalexchange.org/getInvolved/gxchapters.html.

Goldman, Robert, and Stephen Papson. 1998. *Nike Culture: The Sign of the Swoosh*. London: Sage.

Greenberg, Josh, Elizabeth Westersund, and Graham Knight. 2009. Smog and Mirrors: Public Relations and the Climate Change Debate in Canada. Unpublished manuscript. Ottawa: Carleton University, School of Journalism & Communication.

Habermas, Jurgen. 1998. *Between Facts and Norms: Contributions to a Discourse Theory of Law and Democracy*. Trans. William Rehg. Cambridge, MA: M.I.T. Press.

———. 1992. "Further Reflections on the Public Sphere." Pp. 421–461 in *Habermas and the Public Sphere*, ed. Craig Calhoun. Trans. Thomas Burger. Cambridge, MA: M.I.T. Press.

———. 1991. *The Structural Transformation of the Public Sphere: An Inquiry into a Category of Bourgeois Society*. Trans. Thomas Burger. Cambridge, MA: M.I.T. Press.

Howard, Philip. 2006. *New Media Campaigns and the Managed Citizen*. Cambridge: Cambridge University Press.

Johansen, Helene. 2005. "Political Marketing: More than Persuasive Techniques, an Organizational Perspective." *Journal of Political Marketing* 4 (4): 85–105.

Klein, Naomi. 2000. *No Logo: Taking Aim at the Brand Bullies.* Toronto: Knopf Canada.

Knight, Graham. 2007. "Activism, Risk and Communicational Politics: Nike and the Sweatshop Problem." Pp. 305–318 in *The Debate over Corporate Social Responsibility*, ed. Steve May, George Cheney, and Juliet Roper. Oxford: Oxford University Press.

Knight, Graham, and Josh Greenberg. 2002. "Promotionalism and Subpolitics: Nike and Its Labor Critics." *Management Communication Quarterly* 15 (4): 541–570.

Lahusen, Christian. 1996. *The Rhetoric of Moral Protest: Public Campaigns, Celebrity Endorsement and Political Mobilization.* Berlin and New York: de Gruyter.

Levitsky, Sandra. 2007. "Niche Activism: Constructing a Unified Movement Identity in a Heterogeneous Organizational Field." *Mobilization: An International Quarterly Review* 12 (3): 271–286.

Lury, Celia. 2004. *Brands: The Logos of the Global Economy.* London: Routledge.

Mayhew, Leon. 1997. *The New Public: Professional Communication and the Means of Social Influence.* Cambridge: Cambridge University Press.

Pellizzoni, Luigi. 2001. "The Myths of the Best Argument: Power, Deliberation and Reason." *British Journal of Sociology* 52 (1): 59–86.

Pellizzoni, Luigi. 2003. "Knowledge, Uncertainty and the Transformation of the Public Sphere." *European Journal of Social Theory* 6 (3): 327–355.

Rucht, Dieter. 2000. "Distant Issue Movements in Germany: Empirical Description and Theoretical Reflections. Pp. 76–107 in *Globalizations and Social Movements: Culture, Power and the Transnational Public Sphere*, ed. John Guidry, Michael Kennedy, and Mayer Zald. Ann Arbor: University of Michigan Press.

Tarrow, Sidney. 1998. *Power in Movement: Social Movements and Contentious Politics.* Second edition. Cambridge: Cambridge University Press.

———. 1989. *Democracy and Disorder: Protest and Politics in Italy 1965–1975.* Oxford: Clarendon Press.

Wernick, Andrew. 1991. *Promotional Culture: Advertising, Ideology and Symbolic Expression.* London: Sage.

CHAPTER NINE

"Through the Looking Glass"

The Promotional University 2.0

Alison Hearn

In 2006, a group of students at Cornell University formed an "image committee." Spurred by the lack of "cool hats [and] hoodies" at a Cornell–Yale football game, the committee's goal was to exert pressure on administrators to increase the university's branding efforts and raise its standing in the *U.S. News and World Report* rankings. Founder Peter Cohl expressed the committee's sentiment clearly: if the university's reputation and ranking drop, his "value as a human being feels like it's dropping" (Finder 2006). Meanwhile, north of the border in Canada, students at Trent University were aggressively demonstrating against the implementation of a new, expensive marketing campaign with the unfortunate slogan, "The world belongs to those who understand it"; not only was the slogan presumptuous and condescending, argued the students, but the campaign wasted precious university resources at a time when tuition fees were rising rapidly (Swerdlyk 2005). These examples illustrate two very different responses to the now firmly entrenched processes of university promotion, marketing, and branding around the globe.

It was a scant 19 years ago, in 1991, that Andrew Wernick published his groundbreaking volume, *Promotional Culture: Advertising, Ideology and Symbolic Expression*, which included a chapter on the rise of what he named "the promotional university." In this chapter, Wernick (a professor of cultural studies at Trent University as it happens) noted the ways in which North American universities were increasingly "entrepreneurial, public relations oriented, and engrossed in the search for funds" (Wernick 1991: 156). Certainly, Wernick was not alone in noting these developments, but he was singularly prescient in recognizing the centrality of branding and promotion, not only to the university's struggle for continued cultural relevance and financial survival but to the development of postindustrial capitalism itself. This chapter updates and builds upon Wernick's exploration of the promotional university. It will provide a brief historical overview of the paradoxical, yet generative, mission of the university in the West, and will examine the ways in which the contemporary context of advanced post-Fordist, neoliberal, "branded" capitalism has intensified the processes of promotionalism within universities identified by Wernick almost two decades ago.

The two examples described above illustrate that promotional activities and practices, even as they are central features of post-Fordist capitalist culture, can never completely contain or predict their effects; as they have come to profoundly condition self-conception and cultural understanding in some, they produce active and inventive resistance in others. This resistance can, but does not always, feed back into promotional representations. Indeed, this dynamic duality of containment and resistance resonates deeply with the paradoxical mission of the university itself. The university has historically been both a source of socially useful training and research in tune to the outside forces of government and industry and a site for the production of responsible, moral citizens, and social critique, which requires critical distance from those same forces. There can be no doubt, however, that over the last decade, one side of this dualism has become dominant while the other has struggled for survival. What happens to this centuries-old dual, and often paradoxical, mission of the university in an increasingly mediated, technologized, and globalized world, where aggregated reputation, generated by branding and promotion online and off, threatens to displace all other forms of value?

A (Very) Brief History of the Paradoxical University

The university has always been a contradictory, radically heterogeneous site, deeply conflicted at its core, continually in the process of interrogating its various responsibilities. Society requires the university to serve it, but this service requires the university's detachment and freedom from external social determinations. The university enacts this paradox, asking for authorization from outside social agents (government, industry) in order to reflect upon, criticize, or challenge them (Derrida 1983: 19). Jacques Derrida invokes the metaphor of "mochlos" or lever to describe this contradiction: the quest for academic freedom and the need for an outside source to authorize that quest push against each other, functioning as a generative and productive lever propelling the university forward through history. The contradiction, or conflict, between the university's need for authorization from external interests and its internally generated need for autonomy from those interests has been expressed and performed in myriad ways throughout the institution's long history.

The Earliest Universities

In its earliest incarnations, during the Middle Ages in Bologna and Paris, the university embodied conflict between external interests—church, state, commerce—and internal radical opposition to them. This tension existed between the *studia generalia*—the free association of students and teachers that made up the earliest universities—and both the sites and contexts of their associations (towns and businesses) and the content of their study (vocational orientations such as law, medicine, and theology, which required external authorization). The first *universitas* of students organized as a group in order to protect themselves from the price-gouging activities of the townspeople. These unions of students, once incorporated, found themselves able to make other kinds of demands, most notably of their teachers. Contrary to popular belief, then, the term "universitas" does not refer to a universality of knowledge but rather to "the totality of a group, whether of barbers, carpenters, or students" (Haskins 1957: 9), which "manages its own affairs and conducts business for itself" (Kane 1999: 3).

The model of the southern university emerged as the result of struggles between students, teachers, merchants, and city officials. In Northern Europe, however, the universities emerged out of struggles between teaching masters and the Church. Northern universities, such as the University of Paris, had their start as cathedral schools and were initially controlled by the bishop's secretary, the chancellor, who hired masters to teach and controlled who and what was taught. The newly formed College of the Masters of Paris eventually contested the power of the chancellor after a period of student riots and unrest. Some of these riots were precipitated by the radical teachings of scholars such as Peter Abelard, who dared to subject Church dogma to the formal structures of Greek reasoning. Teachers took to the streets, teaching in "ramshackle houses on the Petit-Pont that linked the island with the Left Bank of the Seine" (Kane 1999: 8). Students turned away from the chancellor's university and "made up a student city in the middle of the city" (Kane 1999: 9). Eventually, the contestation of the power of the Church by the masters of Paris ended in a royal charter and Papal Bull allowing the masters to incorporate the university as an independent body with the power to elect its own proctor to represent them to the king and the Church (Kane 1999; Haskins 1957). In its earliest incarnations, then, the university was the site of conflict and expressed its conflicted origins plainly. While it was subject to external determining agents for its curriculum and its context (after all, these universities had no buildings but were dependent on private halls, churches, and the street), it insisted at the same time on its independence in terms of internal arrangements and curricular decisions.

The Conflict of the Faculties

This paradox of the university, expressed as a tension between academic freedom and instrumental or administered knowledge, appears again in 1798, famously, in Immanuel Kant's *The Conflict of the Faculties.* In this essay, Kant dutifully and repeatedly recognizes the university's indebtedness to its political context and makes a case for the university as a site for social and government training and public service. At the same time, however, he argues for the university as a site for freedom of thought and inquiry. Kant attempts to defend both the academic freedom embodied by the lower faculty of philosophy, and the "usefulness" of knowledge imparted by the higher faculties—law, medicine, and theology. The higher faculties have the job of caring for men's civil, physical, and spiritual well-being and are necessarily under the influence and sway of the government. The lower faculty of philosophy has the job of policing truth and illuminating reason and requires autonomy from outside influence.

With this model, Kant asserts a view of the academy as simultaneously inside and outside the direct influence of external political or economic forces. But, perhaps more importantly, he restates the paradox of the university through a discussion of the organization of the disciplines. His model admits to a necessary element of usefulness and instrumentality at the same time as it advocates that thought and research be free from social and political pressures:

> It is absolutely essential that the learned community at the university also contain a faculty that is independent of the government's command with regard to its teachings, one that, having no commands to give, is free to evaluate everything and concerns itself with the interests of...truth; one in which reason is authorized to speak

> out publicly. For without a faculty of this kind the truth would not come to light (and this would be to the government's own detriment) (1979: 27–29).

This is Kant's "system of justification" (Derrida 1992: 6) for the university, one that might successfully navigate its internally generated mission of reason and its externally authorized mission of usefulness. This system is based on the regulatory ideal of reason as the final arbiter of action and thought. With Kant, reason is instituted as the "reason for" the university's necessary autonomy and its exemplary role and is structured in opposition to, or set apart from, the instrumental or technical ends of knowledge.

The "Cresthomatic" University

The central tension between the usefulness of the university to its society on the one hand and its need for academic freedom from external interests on the other is in evidence again in the university reform movements of the nineteenth century. It is best exemplified in the establishment of the University of London in 1825 and in the reforms foisted upon Oxford and Cambridge a decade earlier. At this time, Oxford and Cambridge were taken to task, most notably by Adam Smith and the Reverend Sydney Smith, for their exclusion of men not affiliated with the Church of England, their apparently nonexistent teaching practices, and their curriculum, which came under attack for its dreamy pursuit of "truth" and useless study of the classics. The Reverend Smith put forward a particularly potent argument for useful knowledge made available to the bourgeois classes and in so doing instated a covert class politic into debates about higher education that continues to this day:

> What other measure is there of dignity in intellectual Labour, but usefulness? And what ought the term University to mean, but a place where every science is taught which is liberal, and at the same time useful to mankind. Nothing would so much tend to bring classical literature within proper bounds, as a steady and invariable appeal to utility in our appreciation of all human knowledge (qtd. in Sanderson 1975: 35–36).

The dons at Oxford and Cambridge responded to these criticisms, arguing for the pursuit of useless knowledge. They linked the quest for high truth with spiritual practice and the Church and pitted the standard of "quality of mind" against a debased and vulgar notion of direct utility. Edward Copleston, provost of Oriel College, responded to Smith:

> To make necessity the standard of what is praiseworthy or honourable [sic] is against the uniform judgment of mankind. There must be surely a cultivation of

> mind, which is itself, a good: a good of the highest order; without any immediate reference to bodily appetites, or wants of any kind (qtd. in Sanderson 1975: 37–38).

The founding of the University of London in 1826 broke the Church's monopoly on higher education and established what would become generally accepted arguments for socially useful education. The informing spirit of the University of London emanated from the work of Jeremy Bentham, especially his notion of "chrestomathia," meaning "conducive to useful learning" (Young 1992: 105), a theory of pedagogy based on the qualities of efficiency and discipline. The University of London, along with the reformed German and American universities, offered a comprehensive range of useful subjects—medicine, engineering, mathematics, political economy, law—and focused purposefully on the utility of research and knowledge for outside interests (Sanderson 1975). These universities embodied in concrete form a politicized alternative to the class-based practices of open inquiry and "useless" literary education offered at Oxford and Cambridge.

During this time of university reform in the mid-nineteenth century, the disciplinary structures of knowledge and teaching with which we are now familiar began to solidify. These structures were clearly conditioned by outside economic, cultural, and political interests. The rise of industrialization and technology, the growth of the natural and social sciences, and the rise of a professional bourgeois class, for example, not only helped to determine the structure and delineation of the disciplines but also permeated the administrative structures and ideologies of the university itself. New modes of inquiry such as psychiatry, evolutionary biology, and sociology articulated what Michel Foucault has termed the "dividing practices" demanded by the "useful" university (1982: 208). Faculties competed against each other for internal and external funding and recognition. Thus, they came to function in relative isolation from each other. Bentham's model of education as panopticon set into motion a practice of disciplinarity as a "distinct form of power which trains the body and soul, by systematically observing and distinguishing its subjects" (Messer-Davidow and Shumway 1991: 212).

We can see in the emergence of the "cresthomatic" university a concomitant movement toward social conformity and political docility. Although in its earliest expression the useful university was intended to democratize education and to contribute to an informed national citizenry, the structural formulas for disciplinary efficiency worked instead to generate useful and productive social subjects. The discourses of university disciplinarity as we understand them today emerged at the same time as industrialization and the growth of market logic.

The Rise of Corporate U

The tension between the university's utilitarian and cultural/critical pedagogical and research missions, and between its dependence upon, and desired autonomy from, government and outside interests, continued to drive universities forward during the first half of the twentieth century. Although, given the slow extension of higher education to the masses and the growth of industrialization and increased demand for white-collar workers, the balance slowly began to shift toward utilitarian concerns and active, explicit collaboration with government and industry. Indeed, universities began to be seen as central to a nation's economic prospects, providing "human capital" in the form of a credentialized workforce and, at the same time, ideologically reinforcing the hegemony and perceived inevitability of liberal–pluralist capitalism.

The latter half of the twentieth century saw the mass expansion of higher education throughout North America and Europe. Higher education participation rates grew from five percent in the early part of the twentieth century to 50 percent today (Wernick 2006b: 561). This expansionist push, which emerged culturally and politically in the late 1950s and 1960s, was originally motivated by liberal ideals of democratic access. In the 1970s, however, these liberal ideals were increasingly challenged, as university enrollment slowed, the service-oriented workforce and its attendant disciplinary demands became dominant, and fiscal pressures, including unemployment, grew (Axelrod 1982; Newson and Buchbinder 1988). At the same time, public faith in the need for universities as purveyors of culture and training ground for good citizens, tentative at best, began to wane. Canada, for example, saw a 40 percent decline in support for higher education funding between 1965 and 1971 (Axelrod 1982: 146). At this time, government officials began to demand increased fiscal accountability on the part of universities, or "more scholar for the dollar" (Axelrod 1982: 147).

This shift in public opinion and political priorities with regard to the university must be understood in the context of the post-Fordist mode of capitalist production and neoliberal governmental policies (Wernick 1991). Post-Fordism, which took root during the 1970s and was firmly established by the 1980s, is marked by the rise of service and white-collar work, an emphasis on consumption over production, and the processes of "flexible accumulation," which include strategies of permanent innovation, mobility and change, subcontracting, and just-in-time, decentralized production (Harvey 1990). Flexible accumulation is heavily dependent on communication networks, high technology, and lateral flows of information and production, as opposed to hierarchical ones, and tends to emphasize the production and consumption of knowledge and symbolic products—including packaging, image design, branding, and marketing—over concrete material production (Goldman and Papson 2006; Harvey 1990). Under post-Fordism, the practices of marketing and branding become increasingly central to processes of capital accumulation (Harvey 2005; Holt 2006).

Neoliberalism is the political economic theory and mode of governmentality that accompanies these economic developments. Simply put, neoliberalism "proposes that human well-being can best be advanced by liberating individual entrepreneurial freedoms and skills within an institutional framework characterized by strong property rights, free markets and free trade" (Harvey 2005: 2). The role of the state is to advance and protect these freedoms through deregulation, privatization, and reduced social welfare benefits. Individual responsibility and autonomy is stressed, while communitarian or state-run social or cultural initiatives are discouraged. Perhaps most importantly, under neoliberalism, market exchange is seen as "an ethic in itself, capable of acting as a guide to all human action, and substituting for all previously held ethical beliefs" (Harvey 2005: 3).

Against this backdrop of post-Fordist capitalism and neoliberalism in the 1980s and 1990s, universities have begun to redefine themselves, as the external influences of government and industry and the ubiquity of market discourses combine to seriously threaten the university's orienting paradox. As governments attempt to cut costs, publicly funded universities are pushed into the arms of the private sector and external corporate sponsorship, while private universities, also hungry for funds, stake out strategic private partnerships of their own. Corporate presence is felt across campuses in the form of named buildings and stadiums, food courts and shopping malls, the imposition of restricted forms of technology and software, and the corporate sponsorship of university sports teams, to name only a handful of examples (Slaughter and Rhoades 2004). Sets of quantitative metrics drawn from industry emerge to measure university performance in the name of public accountability and efficiency. As external corporate influence grows, the university shifts its research and pedagogical emphasis to those fields likely to produce the highest monetary yield—business, the sciences, computer technology, and engineering—and the humanities are left to wither. Through established granting programs and new initiatives, governments push industry-defined, "mission-oriented," commercializable research. Interstitial organizations, such as patent and licensing offices, proliferate in order to broker relations between university researchers and private interests (Slaughter and Rhoades 2004). Meanwhile, academic labor and tenure are threatened, as university administrators hire larger and larger numbers of flexible, low paid, contract teachers to staff undergraduate service courses. Many students, influenced by the consumer culture around them, increasingly come to see the university as a service provider and their education as a zero-sum game where they should "get what they pay for"; this, in turn, results in increased pressure on the professoriate to inflate grades in order to meet student/consumer demand (Coté and Allahar 2007; Newson 2004; Brulé 2004; Edmundson 1997). At the same time, top-down corporate models of governance come to replace the long-established systems of bicameral university governance across North America; with administrative staff and bureaucratic systems on the rise, faculty and students are increasingly marginalized in decision-making processes (Hearn 2006; Newson and Buchbinder 1988; Gould 2003; Bok 2003). Finally, as a result of the infiltration of market logic, universities begin to brand, market, and promote themselves in earnest.

1991: Promotional Culture and the Promotional University 1.0

While forms of university advertising have been around since the eighteenth century, it was not until the early twentieth century that universities in the United States installed formal public relations offices. In response to this, and as early as 1903, conservative critics were bemoaning "the trend towards the commercialization of our institutions and learning" (Cutlip 1970: 23). By the 1970s, universities had actively begun to import marketing strategies from business in spite of vocal dissent amongst the professoriate (Fram 1973; Barton and Treadwell 1978). By the 1980s, university marketers had formed their own professional associations, consortiums, and conferences, as textbooks and an academic journal about marketing for higher education also emerged (Carrocci 2009: 7). By 1991, the year in which

Wernick published *Promotional Culture*, the practices of marketing and promotion by universities were widely accepted.

In *Promotional Culture*, Wernick defines promotionalism as the dominant symbolic language and mode of expression of advanced post-Fordist capitalism and neoliberal modes of governmentality: it names the extension of market values and commodity relations into all areas of life. Breaking with traditional views of advertising, which see production and consumption as conceptually distinct areas of consumer culture, Wernick insists that the commodity form cannot be separated from its promotional form and that consumption activity is bound to the production of promotional meanings and brands. Echoing the work of other poststructuralist theorists, such as Jean Baudrillard, Wernick argues that a promotional message comprises a unique mode of communication; it is a "complex of significations which at once represents (moves in place of), advocates (moves on behalf of) and anticipates (moves ahead of) the circulating entity…to which it refers" (Wernick 1991: 182). Promotion entails a rearrangement of the relation between sign and referent. The sign comes to displace the material object to which it refers and, in this way, acquires a kind of agency: "In this integrated system of production/promotion, the commodity and its double—the commodity sign and the promotional sign—are deployed together in a mutually referring and self-confirming way" (Wernick 1991: 16). Goods come to be designed less for their direct usefulness and more for the meanings and myths they are able to mobilize and represent. As a result, consumers do not simply buy for utility but rather "buy into" access to cultural meaning and status.

For Wernick, promotion is a speech act and, as such, is performative—a "mode of communication, a species of rhetoric… defined not by what it says but by what it does" (Wernick 1991: 184). Promotionalism works to perpetually persuade and to represent determinate sets of interests; as a result, it is always-already political. A culture marked by the ubiquity of promotional discourse is a truly postmodern one, signaled by a lack of trust in language. Here what matters most is not "meaning" per se, or "truth" or "reason," but "winning"—attention, emotional allegiance, and market share. Promotionalism, as a foundational component of commodity exchange and of most contemporary social discourse, is thoroughly instrumental, functioning to bring about some form of "self-advantaging exchange" (Wernick 1991: 181). Goods, services, corporations, people, and universities are all implicated in the logic of promotion.

The figure of the "brand" is the apotheosis and central representative figure of a promotional culture. Indeed, the finely calibrated practices of corporate branding express the self-advantaging values of capital most pointedly, inscribing these values directly into our experience. The communicative practices of promotionalism in the form of branding, then, comprise the deep commodification of culture, whereby our values and commonly used symbols are colonized by the market and put to work to sell. As a result, even though it might be semiotically complex, promotionalism is a homogenizing cultural force, which flattens distinctions between people, social relationships, and things, and delimits the terms within which to constitute our senses of self, community, relationships, and values. While marketers work to produce uniqueness and distinctiveness for individual commodities in and through branding and advertising, as the culturally dominant form of signification, these practices become the medium through which culture "impresses the same stamp on everything" (Adorno and Horkheimer 1999: 32).

In his chapter on the promotional university, Wernick examines the ways in which universities have been drawn into promotional logic, focusing specifically on student recruitment, accreditation, faculty career advancement, and academic publishing. Responding to the corporate influences described above, Wernick notes:

> For universities, as for late capitalist society as a whole, penetration by the price-system has been accompanied (and anticipated) by the extension of competitive exchange in general...the markets in which the university has become involved are not only those mediated by money. Like promotional politics, the promotional university is a site which brings together the market for commodities in the ordinary sense with other forms of competition (for status, for example) of a more purely symbolic kind (Wernick 1991: 158).

In the era of growing corporate influence, universities perpetually strive to accumulate "promotional capital" in the form of reputation and rankings in magazines such as *U.S. News and World Report*. They do so to such an extent that often the pursuit of rank and reputation completely displaces any internally generated ideals regarding independent cultural critique and pedagogical rigor; indeed, in a clear case of the tail wagging the dog, most universities explicitly use the categories for university adjudication established by these external publications as blueprints for their future. For Wernick, universities in the thrall of corporate capital and promotional logic lose sight of the university's dual and paradoxical mission, allowing themselves to go "through the looking glass. Rather than just evolving, each university's collective identity becomes a matter of obsessive definition, becoming in the end a wholly artificial construct" (Wernick 1991: 157).

The Promotional University 2.0

The conditions of the corporate university have only intensified since Wernick wrote *Promotional Culture* in 1991. Recognizing that the university occupies a privileged place in relation to the knowledge economy and that knowledge is now a form of venture capital, universities have begun to situate themselves at the intersection of the state and the market, enthusiastic participants in the blurring of boundaries between public and private sectors. Indeed, universities are now "actors initiating academic capitalism, not just players being 'corporatized'" (Slaughter and Rhoades 2004: 12). Their orienting contradiction seriously eroded, universities are now in the business of "doing" business. In Canada, there has been a push for "market-ready" industry-driven education in the form of specialized colleges, and, in the U.S., there has been a rise in for-profit universities. It is now possible "to find universities listed on stock exchanges as far flung as Johannesburg, Bombay, and New York" (Mount and Belanger 2004: 130). These developments have been accompanied by the solidification of post-Fordism and neoliberalism (no matter how crisis-ridden), and an increase in the degree to which image, reputation, and branding play a central role in the generation of capital. As the Internet and other forms of new communication technology have become commonplace, the drive for visibility and perpetual connectivity increases, and the generation of symbolic capital, via reputation building and image management, becomes a central concern for individuals and institutions (Hearn 2008). As Bill Readings presciently argued in 1996, the contemporary university no longer has a clear "regulatory ideal," such as citizenship or serving the public good. Instead, it has become "dereferentialized," driven by empty rhetoric and marketing logic, with no other watchword than the empty signifier "excellence" (Readings 1996); the university has become thoroughly promotionalized.

Brand U

As noted above, branding is a core activity of promotional capitalism. The goal is to deploy established cultural images and symbols in order to advance the interests of a particular product or service. Branders "are addicted to borrowed equity" (Goldman and Papson 2006: 329); they steal images, stories, and language to constitute brand identities. The goal of branding is not necessarily to accurately reflect the actual qualities of the particular product or service but simply to distinguish it, in a positive way, from its competitors. Branders trade in abstract, symbolic values in order to generate or enhance reputation. Branders also work to construct a community of loyal followers out of disparate interest groups and work to create a "virtual context" for consumption (Arvidsson 2005: 244).

Since the year 2000, the amount of money spent on marketing and communications by colleges and universities in the U.S. has risen more than 50 percent (Luettger 2008). As the market for students is likely to get more competitive due to projected reduced enrollment, much of this expense involves branding campaigns designed to create a unique institutional identity that will help a university stand out from among its many competitors. This new brand image must be scrupulously maintained across all promotional material, with consistency in the deployment of logo, motto, tone, and look (Porter 2008). Branding campaigns are not simply designed to help universities compete for the top students but to raise their profile in the public consciousness, bring in corporate sponsorship, research dollars and endowment funds, and communicate effectively with local communities and governments. Branding campaigns are expensive and can take years to establish; universities may try out several new mottos and logos before one sticks. In universities across the West, "tired looking logos are being redesigned… courses are being shaped and reshaped to sell" (Rothblatt 2008: 29), and marketers from the private sector have been brought in to oversee these changes.

While competition between universities is nothing new and reputation has always been central to the university's survival, what is new is "the self-consciousness with which a university's corporate image has come to be managed, the administrative prominence this task assumes, and the objectification, and indeed monetization, of academic reputation itself as a brand" (Wernick 2006b: 566).

UCLA spent $1.25 million on its last campaign, while the University of Maryland spent $5.1 million (Miley 2009: 6). For universities with less established reputations or promotional capital, branding practices are needed to establish their identity. For well-established universities, branding is a simpler exercise, since they can simply convert their reputation into a capitalizable brand. Indeed, older, established universities, such as Harvard or

Oxford, often convert their reputation and accumulated brand value into "rentable property"; a copyrighted school name can be licensed to any number of other business enterprises (Wernick 2006a; Grynbaum 2009). University branding campaigns now work across media platforms, from newspaper and television ads to promotional videos on YouTube and fan groups on Facebook (Miley 2009: 6). Recent university branding campaigns often replace traditional mottos with pithy slogans. Some of these include "A Legacy of Leading" (University of Idaho); "Redefine the Possible" (York University); "Inspiring Minds" (Dalhousie University); "Inspiring Innovation and Discovery" (McMaster University); "Open Minds, Creating Futures" (Ohio Dominican University); "Grasp the Forces Driving the Change" (Stanford University); "Knowledge to Go Places" (Colorado State University); "Investing in Knowledge" (University of Liverpool); and "Wisdom. Applied." (Ryerson University).[1]

In these slogans we see the designated themes and branding ideas of the corporatized, post-Fordist university expressed over and over again: knowledge as currency, celebration of the future, and innovation. As these themes are also common features in the marketing campaigns of many transnational corporations, they are of a piece with the work of corporate branding in general, which is to produce highly aestheticized modes of justification for life under capitalism (Goldman and Papson 2006). Here, we clearly see the limiting, homogenizing, and flattening effects of promotional discourse described by Wernick. These branding practices work to abstract a heterogeneous and complex institution into an image, which is then deployed and exchanged as a commodity on the reputational marketplace in the form of rankings and other quantitative forms of measurement. "The end result," as Chang and Osborn (2005) write, "is a spectacular economy of education, in which abstract rankings become images of educational institutions and the exchange values of these spectacular images replace the use values of the institutions themselves" (340).

The implications of the branded university are far-reaching. As Wernick insists, promotional discourse not only homogenizes, it heteronomizes, governing the day-to-day operations of the university from the outside by creating simplified abstractions of those operations; eventually, the "projected brand image feeds back into both product and its style of presentation" (Wernick 2006a: 566). As universities increasingly "fall through the looking glass," falling in love with an image that has been crafted to generate market share only, faculty, staff, and students are incorporated into the brand's promotional logic, often unwillingly. The centralization of a university's communicative processes in marketing departments leads to the imposition of strict rules for all university communication. Boston University, for example, recently issued a 67-page manual specifying the "look, tone, and feel" of appropriate university communication (Porter 2008). These practices of "message discipline" seriously limit the autonomy of departments and individuals within the university, thereby infringing on their academic freedom. Within the promotional university, dissent and dialogue are "replaced with dissemination" (Berland and Hanke 2006: 5). In addition, the self-advantaging rhetoric of promotionalism "encourages participation in consumer culture, rather than reflection on it" and works to "integrate students into a particular version of higher education" (Carrocci 2009: 84), that of the post-Fordist promotional university.

"Major in Yourself"

The corporate, promotional university also speaks in the neoliberal language of personal responsibility and the primacy of the individual. It occupies a privileged position in relation to the formation of selfhood, geared as it is towards young people poised on the verge of adulthood. Certainly, universities in the last several decades have occupied an "ambiguous position" as "youth corrals...and also as places of competitively driven (social and self) investment in 'human capital'" (Wernick 2006b: 561). Students are simultaneously courted and exploited in the corporate, promotional university.

Students arrive on the scene already deeply steeped in the ontological insecurity and material instability of post-Fordist consumer capitalism. Anthony Giddens argues that, in the absence of more traditional and secure forms of sociality and community and larger frames of meaning, perpetual attention to the construction of "self" through the processes of consumption provides the only remaining continuity or through-line in our lives. Selfhood, under these conditions, becomes a "self-reflexive project," a work in progress, a compelling, outer-directed narrative or biography, with consumption at the center. Here, "self-actualisation [is] packaged and distributed according to market criteria" (Giddens 1991: 198). As Wernick outlines, the self that emerges from these processes is a "persona produced for public consumption...which continually produces itself for competitive circulation" (Wernick 1991: 192): a promotional, or branded, self (Hearn 2008).

Many students perceive a university education and credentials as ways to enhance individual reputation and, given their cultural context within consumer capitalism, tend to believe an education is something that can be easily purchased. The consumerist mentality on the part of students can be seen to be a major factor in the current ranking obsession now gripping higher education. Within this framework, the university becomes a service provider, and the pedagogical aim of cultivating communities of "knowers and learners" is replaced with the neoliberal configuration of the student as an "autonomous chooser" (Newson 2004: 229). As mentioned earlier, students increasingly perceive education as a zero-sum game, where they get (in the form of grades) what they pay for (in the form of capital). The student consumer sees little point in contributing to the community of the university itself; rather, "they are accountable primarily to themselves and proceed through educational institutions on the basis of individual achievement and demonstrations of mastery over whatever body of knowledge they 'choose' to learn" (Newson 2004: 230; Edmundson 1997).

But, while students may feel they are in control as customers to be served, universities under academic capitalism perceive students as captive markets to be leveraged for corporate resources and manipulated by admissions officers to maximize the university's long-term yield. Students as built-in markets are the basis for universities' lucrative deals with a variety of corporate interests, such as Coke or Starbucks, who pay top dollar for exclusivity rights to campuses. As more and more university space is colonized by private enterprises and covered in advertising for those same interests, students cannot escape their interpellation within consumer capitalism. For example, York University recently solicited corporations to place their logos on York's online course sites for $10,000 each, and "student IDs are now adorned with MasterCard and Visa logos, providing students who may have few assets with an instant line of credit and an identity as full-time consumers" (Giroux 2008: 149). In addition to selling students to corporate interests, universities increasingly focus on the actual "production" of student markets through the strategic use of financial aid. While tuition fees have increased exponentially over the past 30 years, only a small percentage of the money is spent on improving student services or on research; the majority goes back into financial aid and merit packages designed to entice high functioning and potentially "high yield" students to the school. New admissions policies are intended to "craft a class" who will pay "immediate and long term dividends to the prestige and revenue interests of the institution"

(Slaughter and Rhoades 2004: 292–293). University financial aid officers no longer see student aid as a charitable operation but rather as a "strategic tool that (can) be used to manage both the quality of the class and the net revenue of the class" (Slaughter and Rhoades 2004: 294). As a result of this new "yield management strategy," the university moves away from its stated mission of providing access to historically marginalized populations and towards a new mission, which speaks only to "narrow institutional aspirations and economic interests, and the interests of already relatively privileged students" (Slaughter and Rhoades 2004: 297).

In the corporate university, these "narrow institutional aspirations" are economic interests and are bolstered and reflected in the branding and marketing campaigns aimed at students. In these campaigns, students are "rhetorically positioned as the subjects of transformation" (Carrocci 2009: 93) and are sold the idea that university experiences and credentials will add to their potential as highly individuated, promotional selves. The university experience is configured as a lifestyle choice, where brochures brag of retail and food courts, great social and sports events, and plentiful student services, so students will not have to compromise their already well-established consumer lifestyles (Carrocci 2009: 100). Of course, the responsibility for the outcome of that choice is firmly placed at the feet of the student, as the university configures itself as mere service provider. Students are encouraged to be "architects of their own destiny" (Coté and Allahar 2007: 110); a branding campaign at the University of Western Ontario tells a potential student, "Major in yourself!" (Carrocci 2009: 108). Graduating students at Columbia University are offered seminars to help them "brand" themselves,[2] and a regular column in the widely circulated Canadian higher education journal *University Affairs* perkily advises the same (Steele 2009).

The promotional university's embrace and perpetuation of the neoliberal student consumer can only be understood as evidence of cynical self-interest. Surely no real concern about pedagogical mission, critical reflexivity, or academic freedom is being expressed here. How is it possible to successfully teach students to think critically about their consumerist environment, for example, when they are sitting in a classroom named after a corporation? How can students learn to create a meaningful community of debate and respectful tolerance for difference when even the doors of their bathroom stalls are covered with homogenizing ads for beauty products and condoms? As Janice Newson argues, "How is it possible to develop and activate a reflexive consciousness among students about the role they should play in their own learning, if they do not hold, embrace, or enact a meaningful *political* status within institutions where they present themselves as learners?" (Newson 2004: 230–231, emphasis in original).

As students are increasingly interpellated as autonomous consumers, their understanding of what constitutes education shifts profoundly. This has definite implications not only for the students who lose out on the possibility for a life-changing education but for professors as well. Students regularly "use consumerist arguments to contest curricular objectives and teaching practices...even to the extent of using such grounds to trump their obligation to practice academic honesty" (Newson 2004: 231). As a result, professors are perpetually on the defensive; afraid of deviating from the requirements expressed on their syllabi for fear of litigious students and constantly pressed to reassure students as to how the class will produce career-getting "deliverables," professorial authority is regularly displaced by students' assertion of their sovereignty as consumers.

Promotional Research

Faculty research, the site of knowledge production, has also fallen prey to the logic of promotionalism and neoliberal individualism, and in ways that are potentially life-threatening. Faculty members are encouraged to see themselves as knowledge entrepreneurs; university licensing and technological transfer offices work to monetize their research as "venture capitalists scour colleges and universities in search of big profits to be made through licensing agreements, the control of intellectual property rights and investing in university spinoff companies" (Giroux 2008: 150). In Canada, a federally commissioned "expert panel" suggests that "innovation" be added to the traditional duties of the professoriate, alongside teaching, service, and research, and that a professor's ability to commercialize and monetize their research should be considered in decisions about tenure (Carrocci 2009: 35). Professors are regularly pitted against each other for outside grants and private sponsorships, undermining collegiality, and tenured professors routinely ignore the exploitative conditions under which their junior colleagues are forced to labor. Academic "stars" are those who generate grant money, regularly commercialize their research, or publish work that receives widespread recognition and enhances the reputational capital of the university.

The conditions of entrepreneurial knowledge work have a deep impact on the kinds of knowledge that are produced. Private corporate interests who regularly fund university research retain control of the results of that research; there are many frightening stories of scholars who have been asked to suppress or ignore research results because releasing them might threaten the corporate bottom line. In most cases, administrators of the promotional university have not supported researchers' rights to academic freedom (Washburn 2005).

The research situation at the promotional university is far direr than simple corporate influence on research questions or results. In the case of psychopharmaceutical research, for example, independent marketing agencies are routinely hired by pharmaceutical companies to ghost write scientific "studies, review articles, abstracts, journal supplements, product monographs, expert commentaries, and textbook chapters" (Healy 2004: 62). These agencies claim to "deliver scientifically accurate information strategically developed for target audiences" (Healy 2004: 61). The articles produced have the names of prominent medical researchers and academics attached to them; these researchers, in turn, accumulate reputational capital without having to actually do the work. This form of promotional ghost writing happens in the most prestigious journals in medicine and makes up approximately 50 percent of articles on therapeutic drugs in major medical journals. As critic David Healy convincingly argues, "This is not a scientific literature aimed at addressing scientific questions. It is a set of infomercials that have the appearance of scientific articles" (Healy 2004: 65). Nonetheless, much of this literature functions to establish consensus in the field. While your psychiatrist claims to be reading the literature and making up her own mind about certain drugs, the "scientific studies" meant to inform her, which ostensibly emerge from free and unfettered academic inquiry, have already been heavily doctored. In a true case of promotional inversion, the pharmaceutical companies create the problem, design and implement its study, disseminate the findings, and offer and collect profit from the cure.[3] This example demonstrates the power of promotional interests and rhetoric to actively create and define academic research, shaping the very parameters of our culture.

Conclusion

There can be no doubt that the corporate promotional university is a long, long way from the earliest days of the university in Bologna and Paris. Indeed, it is fair to argue that it no longer bears any resemblance whatsoever to the paradoxical institution Kant worked to explain and justify in the eighteenth century. One component of Derrida's "lever" appears to have been completely destroyed by the other; broken and branded, the remnants of the traditional ivory tower exist only in the glossy, ivy-covered viewbooks produced by marketing departments in contemporary universities. The university as a space free from external social pressures, where learning and thinking can happen in community, has become nothing more than a cynically deployed marketing tagline, pressed into the rhetorical service of academic capitalism. Those of us who still yearn for some regulatory ideal of the university beyond profit and accountability peer out longingly from the other side of the looking glass, trapped within the increasingly instrumentalized, promotional university.

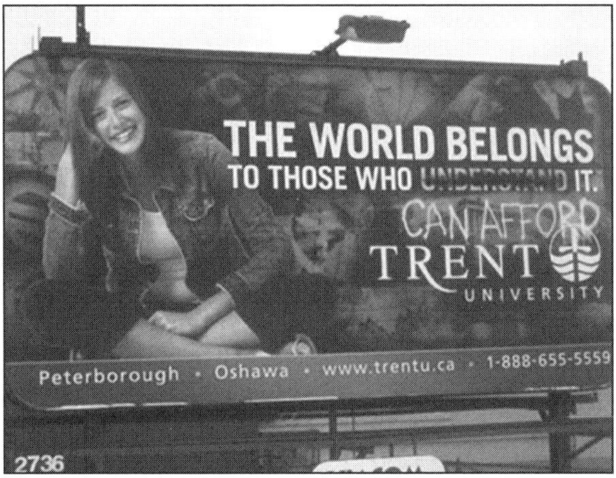

Figure 9.1 "The World Belongs..." *Source:* Ken Brown.

And yet, among the spaces of the "ruined" institution (Readings 1996), the university's paradox can still be glimpsed. In the actions of Trent students, who successfully scuttle their university's branding campaign by "writing over" it; in the work of students and alumni at Antioch College, who fight the college's closure and win[4]; or the students at Macalester College in Minneapolis, who establish their own alternative college based on a communitarian vision of social change,[5] we can see the power of collective thinking and the unfettered pursuit of knowledge assert themselves again and again. In spite of the degree of external corporate pressure, students and faculty around the globe continue the long tradition of the university as a site for radical social critique by continuing to stage protests against corporatization and globalization on campus and in society at large.[6] In the face of the hypercommodified promotional university, one truth from the era of the earliest universities remains. While the university, as a formal, administrated social institution, has always served the interests of those in power, a "universitas" of thinkers is an idea, process, or experience, not founded but fluid (Derrida 1992). As such, the potential always exists for resistance to the foreclosure of the university meanings by outside interests; academic freedom may need to be re-imagined and rethought, but the power of imaginative thinking remains. In the end, no matter how deeply entrenched the forces of commodification and promotionalism, they can always be countered—by exercising a critical imagination, posing questions of the place, asking over and over again: "Whose university is it?"

Notes

1. A variety of current university slogans can be found here: http://www.textart.ru/ advertising/slogans/education/university-slogans.html.
2. The "Build Your Unique Brand Identity" seminar was advertised in the March 2009 alumni newsletter for Columbia University's Fu Foundation School of Engineering and Applied Science. See http://www.clean.cise.columbia.edu/news/seas-news/ seas-news-martch-2009.
3. See Mary Ebeling's chapter in this volume for further discussion of these issues.
4. Find the full story here: http://recordonline.org/.
5. See: http://www.excotc.org/.
6. For information about forms of student activism now occurring in Canada and the U.S. see: http://www.campusactivism.org/. For a history of student activism around the globe, see Boren (2001).

References

Adorno, Theodor, and Max Horkheimer. 1999. "The Culture Industry: Enlightenment as Mass Deception." Pp. 31–41 in *The Cultural Studies Reader*, 2nd Edition, ed. S. During. London: Routledge.

Arvidsson, Adam. 2005. "Brands: A Critical Perspective." *Journal of Consumer Culture* 5 (2): 235–258.

Axelrod, Paul. 1982. *Scholars for Dollars: Politics, Economics and the Universities of Ontario 1945–1980.* Toronto: University of Toronto Press.

Barton, David, and David Treadwell. 1978. "Marketing: A Synthesis of Institutional Soul-Searching and Aggressiveness." Pp. 77–84 in *Marketing Higher Education*, ed. D. Barton, Jr. San Francisco: Jossey-Bass.

Berland, Jody, and Bob Hanke. 2006. "Against Profile Fetishization: University Marketing and Communication in the Age of Academic Capitalism." Paper presented at the Conference of the Union for Democratic Communication, May 18–21, in Boca Raton, Florida.

Bok, Derek. 2003. *Universities in the Marketplace.* Princeton: Princeton University Press.

Boren, Mark E. 2001. *Student Resistance: A History of the Unruly Subject.* New York: Routledge.
Brulé, Elizabeth. 2004. "Going to Market: Neoliberalism and the Social Construction of the University Student as an Autonomous Consumer." Pp. 247–264 in *Inside Corporate U: Women in the Academy Speak Out*, ed. Marilee Reimer. Toronto: Sumach Press.
Carrocci, Lindsay. 2009. Representing the Promotional University: Undergraduate Student Recruitment Strategies in Ontario 1997–2007. M.A. Thesis, University of Western Ontario.
Chang, Gordon, and J. R. Osborn. 2005. "Spectacular Colleges and Spectacular Rankings." *Journal of Consumer Culture* 5 (1): 338–364.
Coté, James and Anton Allahar. 2007. *Ivory Tower Blues: A University System in Crisis.* Toronto: University of Toronto Press.
Cutlip, Scott. 1970. "Advertising Higher Education: The Early Years of College Public Relations (Part 1)." *College and University Journal* (Fall): 21–28.
Derrida, Jacques. 1992. "Mochlos or the Conflict of the Faculties." Pp. 3–34 in *Logomachia: The Conflict of the Faculties*, ed. R. Rand. Lincoln, NE: University of Nebraska Press.
———. 1983. "The Principle of Reason: The University in the Eyes of its Pupils." *Diacritics* 13: 3–20.
Edmundson, Mark. 1997. "On the Uses of a Liberal Education: Part 1—As Light Entertainment for Bored College Students." *Harper's Magazine* (September), 39–49.
Finder, Alan. 2006. "Cornell's Image Patrol Wraps Itself in Ivy." *New York Times*, April 22. Section B. Metropolitan Desk.
Foucault, Michel. 1982. "Afterword: The Subject and Power." Pp. 208–226 in *Michel Foucault: Beyond Structuralism and Hermeneutics*, ed. H. L. Dreyfus and P. Rabinow. Chicago: University of Chicago Press.
Fram, Eugene. 1973. "Positive Steps for Marketing Higher Education." Pp. 56–67 in *The Future in the Making: Current Issues in Higher Education*, ed. D. W. Vermilye. San Francisco: Jossey-Bass.
Giddens, Anthony. 1991. *Modernity and Self-identity: Self and Society in the Late Modern Age.* Cambridge: Polity Press.
Giroux, Henry. 2008. "Marketing the University: Corporate Power and the Social Factory." *Our Schools, Our Selves* 17 (3): 147–165.
Goldman, Robert, and Stephen Papson. 2006. "Capital's Brandscapes." *Journal of Consumer Culture* 6 (3): 327–353.
Gould, Eric. 2003. *The University in a Corporate Culture.* New Haven: Yale University Press.
Grynbaum, Michael. 2009. "Crimson and Green." *New York Times*, September 4.
Harvey, David. 2005. *A Brief History of Neoliberalism.* Oxford: Oxford UniversityPress.
———. 1990. *The Condition of Postmodernity.* Cambridge, Oxford: Blackwell.
Haskins, Charles Homer. 1957. *The Rise of the Universities.* London: Oxford University Press.
Healy, David. 2004. "You Have No Right to Present this Research." Pp. 53–73 in *Disciplining Dissent: The Curbing of Free Expression in Academia and the Media*, ed. W. Bruneau and J. Turk. Toronto: James Lorimer and Company.
Hearn, Alison. 2008. "'Meat, Mask, Burden': Probing the Contours of the Branded Self." *Journal of Consumer Culture* 8 (2): 197–218.
———. 2006. "Money on the Brain: Narratives of the Corporate U." *Topia: Canadian Journal of Cultural Studies* 16: 109–122.
Holt, Douglas. 2006. "Toward a Sociology of Branding." *Journal of Consumer Culture* 6 (3): 299–302.

Kane, Sean. 1999. "Why Is a University?" Unpublished paper.

Kant, Immanuel. 1979. *The Conflict of the Faculties.* Trans. M. Gregor. New York: Abaris Books.

Luettger, Laura. 2008. "Brands Speak Beyond Images; Reflect Lifestyle, Students." *Rochester Business Journal* 24 (18): 22.

Messer-Davidow, Ellen, and David Shumway. 1991. "Disciplinarity." *Poetics Today* 12 (1): 201–225.

Miley, Melissa. 2009. "Universities Finally Espousing Branding." *Advertising Age* 80 (20): 6.

Mount, Joan, and Charles Belanger. 2004. "Entrepreneurship and Image Management in Higher Education: Pillars of Massification." *The Canadian Journal of Higher Education* 34 (2): 125–140.

Newson, Janice. 2004. "Disrupting the 'Student as Consumer' Model: The New Emancipatory Project." *International Relations* 18 (2): 227–239.

Newson, Janice and Howard Buchbinder. 1988. *The University Means Business.* Toronto: Garamond Press.

Porter, Jane. 2008. "Brand U: Marketing the Alma Mater." *BusinessWeek Online.* August 6. http://www.businessweek.com/bschools/content/aug2008/bs2008085_ 851921.htm (accessed September 1, 2009).

Readings, Bill. 1996. *The University in Ruins.* Cambridge, Mass.: Harvard University Press.

Rothblatt, Sheldon. 2008. "Global Branding and the Celebrity University." *Liberal Education* 94 (4): 26–33.

Sanderson, Michael, ed. 1975. *The Universities in the Nineteenth Century.* London: Routledge and Kegan Paul.

Slaughter, Sheila and Gary Rhoades. 2004. *Academic Capitalism and the New Economy: Markets, State and Education.* Baltimore: Johns Hopkins Press.

Steele, Carolyn. 2009. "Personal Branding in Academe—Believe It!" *University Affairs,* September 3. http://www.universityaffairs.ca/career-sense/personal-branding-in-academe-believe-it (accessed September 13, 2009).

Swerdlyk, Sara. 2005. "No Longer Outstanding, Small, Trent Promotes New Image." *Arthur: The Trent University Student Newspaper.* October 30.

Washburn, Jennifer. 2005. *University Inc.: The Corporate Corruption of Higher Education.* New York: Basic Books.

Wernick, Andrew. 2006a. "Rebranding Harvard." *Theory, Culture and Society* 23 (2–3): 566–567.

———. 2006b. "University." *Theory, Culture and Society* 23 (2–3): 557–563.

———. 1991. *Promotional Culture: Advertising, Ideology and Symbolic Expression.* New York: Sage Publications.

Young, Robert. 1992. "The Idea of a Chrestomathic University." Pp. 97–126 in *Logomachia: The Conflict of the Faculties,* ed. R. Rand. Lincoln, NE: University of Nebraska Press.

CHAPTER TEN

Silvio Berlusconi, One Man Brand

Gabriele Cosentino & Waddick Doyle

"Politics is like the drinks market. On the one hand you have liquor. On the other you have sweet drinks. But in between you have an immense space for people who drink Coke or Pepsi." –Silvio Berlusconi[1]

Introduction

Italy's current prime minister, Silvio Berlusconi, is a figure who has attracted much attention in the global media and who has become—for better or worse—a protagonist of contemporary Italian history. Berlusconi's unprecedented fusion of media, sports, and politics, his provocative statements and antics, and his sexual and financial scandals have brought him constant attention within national and international politics. He is also Italy's second wealthiest man, having built a fortune through media, retailing, finance, and sports before entering politics. In this chapter, we will examine how Berlusconi has innovatively used branding in his transition from business to politics and how in the process he has become a unique type of political brand that increases its force through the interconnection of formerly separate social and cultural domains.

Arvidsson (2006) claims that branding has become a central part of contemporary economic, social, and cultural systems. He contends that brands are to this century what factories were to the previous century, the fundamental form of social organization. Hence this study of Berlusconi as a brand is not exclusively focused on how Berlusconi won elections using branding techniques. Rather, it is a reflection on how power relations between communications and politics in Italy have changed over the past two decades, and how they are currently centered on brands as instruments of social organization. Likewise, Berlusconi's power has not simply been a product of the fact that he controlled a large number of television outlets and hence was able to prevent opposing points of view from being heard; while definitely important, this repressive power was not central to his success. In Foucault's sense of "productive power" (Haugaard 1997), we focus on Berlusconi's capacity to produce and frame discourses—an ability that stems in large part from his success in managing consumer brands, such as his television network and his soccer team, and the centrality of his persona to that management. This success eventually generated allegiance to Berlusconi's public persona as the incarnation of different values—entrepreneurship, sportsmanship, family values, self-realization—allowing him to personify the economic, social, and political transformations that Italy has undertaken since the late 1970s.

The period of Berlusconi's rise to power is linked to the transformation of Italy from an industrial and agricultural economy with strong government participation to a free market economy based on services and mass consumption. The collapse of the Italian party system in the early 1990s and the decline of the Catholic and Marxist ideological pillars that sustained the post-fascist period constituted the backdrop for Berlusconi's rise as a new type of politician: not only a central figure of the new type of political and social organization which emerged during Italy's transition into the twenty-first century but also the all-encompassing "brand" that structured it. As he moved across and among the different realms and discourses, he promoted a deeply capitalist ideology of desire fulfillment, which he both offered to the masses through television and personally realized by ostentatiously obtaining what he desired. His brand thus came to connote success and wealth that could be transferred from his companies to his person and eventually to his voters.

Central to Berlusconi's success—and the launching pad for all his other activities—was his earlier success in television, which Doyle (1990) has argued arose from his aptitude for building differentiated brand images for his various networks, resulting in distinct communities of audiences. Berlusconi utilized television as a means to extend his brand to these communities, creating discrete manifestations of branded identification among them as well as establishing himself as the common thread uniting them. Beyond this use of television content, he also used television as a structure through which to realize his political aspirations. It is not incidental that Berlusconi used the organizational structure of his advertising firm Publitalia—Italy's largest media buying company—as the basis for creating his political party Forza Italia (Poli 2001). The interconnection of different domains—segmented audiences for sports and entertainment television, electoral politics, and corporate enterprise—helped legitimize the transfer of power from the private sphere to the public sphere, and vice versa, further strengthening the identification between Berlusconi and the nation as a whole.

Yet as Arvidsson (2006) and Walker (2008) rightly point out, the designed communities that congregate around brands also actively participate in a brand's evolution, often by challenging the brand message. As crises and scandals broke around him between 2005 and 2009, Berlusconi's brand became subject to precisely this kind of challenge, prompting publics to question his brand's reliability. As we will discuss in the conclusion of this chapter, it remains to be seen whether the scandals recently endured by Berlusconi have resulted in an irreparable crisis or will instead generate further transformation of his brand and of the values associated with it.

We begin by recounting Berlusconi's rise to political power, followed by two sections dedicated respectively to the theorization of his brand and to an analysis of the circulation of values and symbols across different social domains.

Berlusconi's Rise to Power

In the winter months between 1993 and 1994, giant pictures of smiling toddlers appeared on billboards all around Italy. Underneath the pictures, the cryptic caption read "Fozza Itaia," a playful reference to the way a young child would pronounce the words "Forza Italia" ("Go Italy!"). It was later revealed to be a teaser for the upcoming electoral campaign of Forza Italia, a new political party founded by television and soccer entrepreneur Silvio Berlusconi (Muscau 1994). Confounding most expectations, Forza Italia won the Italian general elections on March 27, 1994. Since that landmark campaign, which introduced a new political party in a manner similar to how a new branded product might be launched, the direct inclusion of the logic of branding has irreversibly changed Italian politics. The protagonist of this revolution in the style and the substance of doing politics in Italy was Silvio Berlusconi, who has since been elected Prime Minister three times.

A law school graduate with some early successful experience in the real estate business, Berlusconi rose to prominence in the early 1980s with the development of the first national commercial television network in Italy. Starting from a small cable station in Milan, Berlusconi's channel, Canale 5, emerged as an innovative force in the chaotic private sector in Italy, which had been liberalized by the Constitutional Court in the late 1970s. Using semi-legal means to circumvent the court-ordered regulation of national broadcasting, by the end of the 1980s Canale 5 had developed into a full-fledged national commercial network, thus creating a new major venue for advertising and investments in Italy (Doyle 1990). Entertainment-based programming and innovative scheduling techniques, the acquisition of well-known television talents and the availability of significant—and controversial—amounts of capital put Canale 5 in the position to take over the rest of the competition in a short period of time.[2] The result was the creation of the Fininvest network which, under the political patronage of the then-prominent Italian Socialist Party (PSI), became the monopolistic force in commercial television, able to mount a very effective competition against the public service television network RAI.

The key to Fininvest's success in commercial television was its synergy with the advertising agency Publitalia, also owned by Berlusconi, which introduced a set of important innovations in television advertising. Due to nearly thirty years of state monopoly over broadcasting, television advertising in Italy was a largely underdeveloped sector compared to the United States or to other European countries. Publitalia entered the market with a well-trained sales force and with an unmatched ability to sell air time, virtually creating a whole new business sector. As a consequence, television advertising spending in Italy rose significantly throughout the 1980s, contributing to a period of economic growth for the country, which in some regions had evolved from the agricultural–industrial phase to a post-industrial, service-based economy (Ginsborg 1990). Consumer brands—from fashion to food products—became permanent fixtures of the Italian cultural landscape, largely thanks to the exposure provided by Berlusconi's networks. By 1987, the year ratings company Auditel was introduced, Fininvest controlled more than 60 percent of Italy's television advertising market (Grasso 2004).

In 1986, Berlusconi purchased the then-ailing soccer team AC Milan, which in a short period of time—thanks to innovative management and the acquisition of prized soccer stars—produced a series of striking victories both nationally and internationally. This contributed significantly to the rise in general awareness of Berlusconi as a public figure, given the sport's national popularity. Beyond real estate, television, and soccer, Berlusconi diversified his business activities by acquiring stakes in insurance, finance, film distribution, and retail, turning Fininvest into the major financial holding in Italy and himself into one of the country's richest persons ("Fininvest—The Group"). The successful style of business of Fininvest, mixing entertainment, sports, and service, became a hallmark of a rapidly modernizing Italy.

From a larger sociopolitical perspective, Berlusconi's channels helped the country transition from the 1970s—a decade plagued by terrorism and political unrest[3]—to the more stable and prosperous 1980s. The alignment between television and politics, which under RAI had strictly followed the party lines of the two major ideological currents, the Catholic and the Communist, eventually evolved under the cultural and economic effects produced by the private television sector. While seemingly steering clear of the model of politicized media typical of the Italian tradition, Berlusconi's channels had an important role in the evolution of political communication in Italy nonetheless. The very language of politics on commercial television had evolved, adopting most of the stylistic features of the medium, such as the emphasis on the visual qualities of the candidates, simplification of discourse, and the hybridization of different genres (Novelli 1995).

Buoyed by the economic success of his multiple enterprises, later in the 1980s Berlusconi concluded two controversial business deals which, coupled with Fininvest's growing indebtedness, soon put the company at risk of bankruptcy. The first was the acquisition of the Standa chain of department stores in an attempt to vertically integrate the entire chain of product distribution from advertising to large-scale retail. Standa proved to be an unsuccessful investment, however, and it was later sold. The second was the acquisition of the publishing company Mondadori, linked to the attempt to acquire a majority stake in the popular left-leaning newspaper *La Repubblica*. This maneuver had a number of legal implications—some are ongoing. But most importantly, the move revealed Berlusconi's intentions to use the media to influence the balance of power in Italian politics (Ottone 2009).

In the early 1990s, the Italian political class was almost entirely wiped out by the largest corruption scandal of the postwar period. The investigations brought to an end forty years of political domination by the Christian Democrats (DC) and interrupted the growth of the PSI party, Berlusconi's main political ally. The scandal led to the most severe institutional crisis in Italy since the issues of terrorism in the 1970s and created the conditions for drastic political changes. Accelerating the political transformations, a new "majoritarian" electoral system was put in place in 1993, effectively changing the traditional consensual dynamics into a winner-takes-all scenario. With the demise of the old ideological pillars, the DC and the Italian Communist Party (PCI)—the latter largely unaffected by the scandal but still deeply traumatized by the fall of the Berlin Wall—new political cultures started to emerge. In the Northern regions, the party Lega Nord had risen to prominence with an aggressive federalist message, expressing popular discontent with the centralized and unaccountable Roman government (Gold 2003).

It was against this backdrop of profound economic and social change, Fininvest's financial crisis, and the waning protection of the Socialist party that Berlusconi decided to enter politics. The most logical, and perhaps inevitable, means of doing this was to create his own political party. Combining his personal experience and skills with the help of pollsters, focus groups, and creative talents, the brand new Forza Italia party was a post-ideological, flexible organization that could offer a liberal agenda, attention to the core values of Italian society, and the ability to engender a renewed sense of national belonging in the simplified, catchy language of television—by then the preferred medium for political communications. Nearly twenty years of experience with television, advertising, and the marketing of consumer products qualified Berlusconi as the most suitable candidate to win the consensus of the Italian electorate. This is the brand of politics that the majority of Italians have since chosen for three terms, most recently in 2008.

Theorizing Berlusconi as a Brand

Berlusconi's success in politics wasn't simply the product of his control of media outlets and his capacity to persuade audiences of his opinions or suppress opposing points of view. If his ownership of television networks was useful to him, it was because television provided a model for changing habits and engendering beliefs in a society where media are increasingly central to social and cultural participation—managing what Davenport and Beck (2001) call the "attention economy." Such knowledge of the functioning of the media translated into a striking capacity to generate and manage belief around his brand across multiple markets, from television to soccer, and eventually into the political sphere. Rather than attempting to rationally persuade the Italian electorate of the validity of his positions, Berlusconi developed an innovative and relentless branding strategy to unify his political project.

Following Arvidsson's suggestion that the value of a brand is essentially linked to the notion of "consumer attention" (2006: 7), we understand Berlusconi's main political innovation as resting on his capacity to generate and maintain public attention with an innovative use of language, the strategic use of visibility, and the capacity to move across multiple social domains. Closely related to this, Muniz and O'Guinn (2001) argue that brands create communities and identities. In this vein, television audiences created by Berlusconi's networks, AC Milan fan groups, and other forms of mediated identities functioned as vital centers of public attention for Berlusconi's political strategy. Furthermore, Lury (2004) argues that brands are no longer simply signs that allow consumers to identify products but rather objects of value in their own right, which are in turn able to generate value for utterly different kinds of objects. A well-known example is the *Virgin* brand, which has moved from music retail to airlines, soft drinks, and even insurance. Just as the *Virgin* CEO Richard Branson was a key figure in shifting brand allegiance from one product to another within the same brand universe, Berlusconi used his image as a successful television tycoon to move audiences and publics from television to soccer and into the political domain. Berlusconi thus acted as a kind of meta-sign, an embodiment, in Lury's sense, of certain beliefs and practices that circulate from one domain to another.

Not only did Berlusconi become a brand; he also persuaded much of the Italian public that promoting mass consumption through branding and marketing was a political strategy that could resolve Italy's problems. He achieved this by selling himself as a personification of the consumer economy, as the person who had satisfied his own desires, achieved wealth and celebrity, and as Prime Minister could do the same for Italy. While outside Italy Berlusconi is often portrayed as a *commedia dell'arte* type of buffoon (Saubaber and Luksic 2009), Italian public opinion tends to perceive him as a person who overcomes the hypocrisy of Italian politics by speaking directly about what he wants. In this regard Berlusconi has compared himself to Casanova: "Casanova said the man who desires something, if he really desires it, can even become king. Let's take him as our model" (qtd. in RCS 2000). Berlusconi has thus branded himself as the personification of the successful satisfaction of desires.

Berlusconi also ruptured the Italian political tradition by marketing himself as if he were marketing a new product, targeting specific audience segments susceptible to vote for his brand and unabashedly characterizing himself as a type of "political Coke." Just as his television networks during the 1980s encouraged the exposure of media-friendly political personalities and discourses, he produced a simulacrum of himself for public consumption. After using his media empire and vast resources to change cultural and then political habits, he now tried to institute a new ritual among Italian voters: to "consume" Silvio Berlusconi, the entrepreneur, the soccer personality, and the would-be politician.

In the Berlusconi brand of politics, appearance matters and the capacity to manipulate appearance is a virtue rather than a fault. As evidence of this, Publitalia held casting sessions to choose candidates for the new party, often selecting candidates for their looks as much as for their politics (Schwarz 2001). This ideology resonates with a society where value is produced less through material labor than through forms of mediated communication whose main output is the production of communities and identities. Berlusconi consciously encouraged the formation—or fabrication—of these new types of political subjects, conforming to Arvidsson's (2006) claim that brands function as resources for the construction of the self.

Circulation of Forms between Private and Public Spheres

One of the distinctive elements of Berlusconi's political language is his constant use of metaphors drawn from soccer, religion, and business, often mixed together, which disrupt Italian political discourse with symbols and sentiments generated in other domains. Soccer references were particularly frequent in the early phase of Berlusconi's political career, allowing him to harness their affective power. When he decided to enter politics he famously used the words "*Scendo in campo*" (Italian for "I am going to run onto the football [soccer] field"). The reference to the sport also functioned as a metaphor for the reformed electoral system, which encouraged competition between two poles with a clear winner and a clear loser. Remarking on this communicative strategy in 2001, *The Economist* observed:

> Even now that it is in government, Mr. Berlusconi's party, Forza Italia, feels rather like a cross between a football club and an advertising agency. The mood in its offices is cheery, slick, and businesslike. [...] As a former Forza Italia senator who previously worked for Mr. Berlusconi's advertising company blithely put it: "We saw a market niche and decided to fill it" (2001).

The adoption of forms from the soccer domain does not simply occur discursively but also organizationally (Russo 2001). If Berlusconi's campaign machine and candidates were from Publitalia and its logic from television programming, his new party structure was largely built from the network of existing AC Milan soccer fan clubs. The main function of such a structure was to connect communities of fans rather than build political activists. This encouraged the emergence of a new political culture where the forms of popular culture were translated into the world of politics—penetrating even to the symbol of the Forza Italia, an Italian flag on a blue background that resembled the national football symbol. Again, *The Economist* explained it well:

> Like many Italians, Mr. Berlusconi adores football [...] Forza Italia's name comes from the words Italians use to cheer on their national football team, known as "gli Azzurri," the Blues—just what Mr. Berlusconi likes to call his own political team. He sees himself as the player–manager (2001).

In 1994, on the same night the Senate voted to accept Berlusconi's first government, AC Milan beat Barcelona and won the Champions League. That very night, his network Italia Uno screened a summary newscast, showing footage illustrating the Senate's confidence in the new government interspersed with that of his soccer team running around the field in triumph (Rodotà 1994). This tableau illustrates how thoroughly sports and politics had been fused, bringing together different audiences in ways rational persuasion might not.

Another set of metaphors Berlusconi often uses are derived from religion. As Semino and Masci (1996) have argued, his use of phrases such as "I believe in the Italian miracle" when announcing his entrance into politics coded the move in religious terms. Semino and Masci likewise argue that his entry into politics maps neatly onto a "good Samaritan" narrative, where Berlusconi heroically came to the aid of an Italy in distress. In addition to alluding to himself as a political prophet, Berlusconi has said at least once that he was chosen by the people and anointed by the Lord; he occasionally refers to his assistants as disciples (*La Stampa* 2009). In 2006, referencing legal troubles he was experiencing at the time, he likened the situation to persecution, saying "I am the Jesus Christ of politics, a victim, patient, putting up with everything and sacrificing myself for everybody" (qtd. in *La Stampa* 2009). On other occasions he has conflated religious metaphors with sports. When speaking at the Vatican, for instance, he compared the Pope to his football team, saying, "Your Holiness, let me say that you resemble my team Milan. You, like us, go around the world to announce a winning idea, God" (qtd. in Maltese 2001).

In a further example of combining metaphors from different domains, Berlusconi once compared the Holy Roman Catholic church to a faith business (Fiori 1995) and has expressed his wish to "spiritualize" capitalism (Musso 2003). Indeed, the third set of metaphors Berlusconi draws upon emerges from the world of business. Guided by what is termed *aziendalismo*, the idea that the principal business of government is to govern affairs, Berlusconi promotes the notion that politics is simply economic management—allowing him to translate his success as an entrepreneur to the political world, as have other contemporary business figures-cum-politicians (see, for example, Greenberg in this volume). It comes as no surprise that he announced during his 1994 campaign that he would be the "CEO of Italy" (qtd. in Musso 2008: 75). That this business success is at times infused with religiosity functions to give some sense of saintliness to material success, which was certainly never the case in Catholic Italy.

As we have been arguing, Berlusconi's managerial and political success is related to the ability of stories to travel from one context to another: television shows into sports, soccer stories into politics, his private life into the public sphere. Berlusconi's meaning is not fixed but changes constantly as he shifts from one genre of discourse to another. As Italian scholar Federico Boni has argued, "Berlusconi is a superhero without characteristics. Like a comic book figure, he can assume any shape: football coach, messiah, sex-crazed monster and family man, national leader and nightclub pianist [...]" (qtd. in Smoltczyck 2009). It is precisely Berlusconi's capacity to move between genres, to mutate from one form to another, and to appeal to different groups that constitute the essence of his brand. Following Gaonkar and Povinelli (2003), we argue that this circulation of forms is central to the construction of value and meaning for Berlusconi's branded politics.

This rhetorical strategy also has the capacity to change the relationship between private and public domains. Musso (2003) offers the example of how Berlusconi built his campaign around an image of himself as successful entrepreneur, family man, and celebrity, as illustrated by the biography he distributed to 12 million households in 2001 as a kind of electoral brochure. The glossy booklet was called *Una Storia Italiana*, which literally means "an Italian story," but it is also evocative of "*La Storia Italiana*," or Italian history. Berlusconi thus presented himself as a sort of synecdoche of Italy which, according to Musso, fundamentally realigned the definitions of private and public, in which the private life of Berlusconi the political celebrity becomes the ideal representation of national identity.

The Brand in Crisis: Soccer Fiascos

On the evening of May 25, 2005, Berlusconi's successful combination of television, soccer, and politics came to an unprecedented climax. In Istanbul, AC Milan was leading 3-0 in the Champions League final against Liverpool. Berlusconi, in the double role of AC Milan president/owner and Prime Minister, was at the stadium. Canale 5, his television channel, was showing a live broadcast of the game. The network's cameras often zoomed in to reveal his glowing expression. The TV commentator could hardly maintain a neutral tone, overwhelmed as he was by the excitement of being part of such a mighty assembly of powers. The Berlusconi brand was in full display and about to be rewarded with an all-round triumph. Then the unexpected happened. In the now infamous "six minutes of folly," Liverpool tied and then won the game during the penalty shots. The Milan players were in a state of disbelief; the fans were shocked. Berlusconi, visibly disappointed, commented: "[s]occer is like politics. You think you've won, but instead..." (qtd. in RCS 2005). In hindsight, the impromptu comment is revealing: for the first time, Berlusconi had experienced a soccer defeat from a political perspective.

For a decade Berlusconi had been developing an entire political strategy based on establishing synergy between soccer and politics—a connection that was structural, rhetorical, and ultimately political (Russo 2001). By maintaining the AC Milan presidency while prime minister, he continued to leverage the popularity of the team for political purposes—a fact that led Italian pollster Luigi Cresp, a former Berlusconi communication consultant, to comment that the destinies of AC Milan and Berlusconi were inseparable (Ceccarelli 2006). The Istanbul fiasco inaugurated a period of crisis, not only for the AC Milan brand but for Berlusconi as well. Such a spectacular defeat had tarnished AC Milan's aura of invincibility, halting nearly two decades of expansion and success. To make matters worse, the following spring AC Milan and other leading Italian soccer teams underwent investigation for match-rigging charges, resulting in severe penalties in the following season. Over the next two years, Berlusconi embarked on a campaign to revamp the AC Milan brand, purchasing several well-known but aging players, including British footballer and pop icon David Beckham. Commentators speculated that Berlusconi was managing AC Milan mostly as a show business enterprise, rather than as a soccer team demanding technical improvement (Bocca 2009); one argued that the purchase of star players "responds more to the logic of marketing than to that of soccer: [the goal is] to increase the value of Milan's brand" (Tito 2009).

The crisis of AC Milan, and Berlusconi's unsuccessful attempts to counter it, revealed unexpected fissures in the association of sports and politics. As Berlusconi was to discover, such an innovative synthesis could also yield negative effects. An image-based politics tied to the success of a soccer team could backfire if the team did not win enough or if the team conduct was tainted by scandals. The realities of Italian soccer, pressured by aggressive financial operations, competition for television rights, and rising costs for acquiring talents, had finally caught up with the dream of an undefeatable AC Milan and an ever-victorious Berlusconi. In the spring of 2009, the team's management announced its intention to sell the fans' beloved Brazilian player, Kakà—a move meant to provide AC Milan with a prompt injection of cash in the wake of growing financial problems (*Corriere dello Sport* 2009). As a journalist observed in the months leading to the player's transfer, "The romantic veil of Milan as a family team that treasures its champions has fallen" (Currò 2009). Fans vehemently protested, some even going so far as to write Kakà's name on the ballot for local elections in the city of Milan (Sorrentino 2009)—arguably an explicit reference to Berlusconi's use of soccer for political ends. The Milan brand was perceived as having been "desacralized," tainted by worldly ailments such as corruption and poor finances. Consequently, the ability of soccer to provide Berlusconi's brand of politics with symbolic capital had been drastically diminished. Berlusconi himself commented that Kakà's sale had cost him "at least two percent of the votes in the [2009] European Elections" (qtd. in Tito 2009).

After the Istanbul debacle, Berlusconi lost the 2006 political elections to center-left candidate Romano Prodi. While there is no available study linking the political results to Berlusconi's soccer-related setbacks, it is worth pointing out that during the pre-election debates Berlusconi adopted a unexpectedly sober and statesman-like attitude, distancing himself from the image of the entertainer and sports personality he had so often embodied on public occasions. During the second debate in particular, Berlusconi centered his rhetorical strategy on the reiteration of figures and statistics trumpeting the accomplishments of his administration. The following summer, Italy won the soccer World Cup, and Prodi celebrated the victory in

Rome with the players, among them several top AC Milan players. Berlusconi reportedly complained that Prodi had used the victory as an advertisement for the government, and that Berlusconi himself should have been the one celebrating the World Cup victory (Bocca 2006). One might argue that Berlusconi felt betrayed by the very game he had helped to create. While the "soccer as politics" metaphor continued to circulate within the Italian political sphere, it had become harder for Berlusconi to retain full control over it.

The Berlusconi Brand, Up Close and Personal

The soccer-related setbacks and the defeat in the 2006 presidential elections dented not only Berlusconi's brand but also his self-esteem (Bei 2007). In one of his first post-election public appearances, he distanced himself from the unsuccessful domain of soccer, choosing a much more familiar trope of "community" with which to ally himself. Yet his well-crafted brand would soon endure another critical transformation. During an appearance at the 2007 Telegatti television awards, broadcast by Canale 5, Berlusconi flirted with several women, including Mara Carfagna, former television starlet (later appointed Minister of Equal Opportunity in the fourth Berlusconi government). A few days later, Berlusconi's wife, Veronica Lario, wrote a letter to *La Repubblica* deploring his disrespectful behavior and exhorting that "from a public man, I demand public apologies" (Lario 2007). The incident was the first of a series that began to tarnish his image over the next few years. Throughout his career as a public figure, Berlusconi had often revealed a macho penchant for acts of gallantry and appreciation of feminine beauty (Amato 2007); nonetheless, he had usually attempted to temper this with an image as family man, loving father, and devoted husband. The electoral booklet "Una Storia Italiana," for instance, was a celebration of both his entrepreneurial success and his strong belief in family values, personified by his five children—albeit by two different marriages—and his publicly declared fondness for his mother. In the brochure, the divorce from his first wife in the early 1980s was presented as unfortunate incident in a history of otherwise morally impeccable conduct.

What began to surface in the aftermath of the Telegatti episode was a much less romantic picture of a powerful man with a promiscuous lifestyle. Reports emerged that he had used his position to lure women into sexual relations, often under the pretense of professional advancement. Berlusconi seemed at first unprepared to address the breach of trust opened by his public flirtations with other women. When first challenged by his wife in 2007, for instance, he immediately responded with a letter of apology to the same newspaper. Shortly afterwards, however, pictures of him in his summer residence with three young women appeared on the cover of a popular Italian tabloid magazine (Rizzo 2007). The cover ran the title, "Berlusconi's Harem," a term that was repeated in subsequent journalistic accounts of Berlusconi's private life. Indeed, the Italian media, particularly the newspapers that did not support Berlusconi, seemed eager to dive into the details of his private life. In late 2007, several Italian newspapers published the transcripts of wiretappings from an investigation for possible corruption charges against Berlusconi and RAI executive Agostino Saccà (D'Avanzo 2007). The wiretappings revealed, among other things, that Berlusconi was pressuring Saccà to hire a number of female acquaintances to work in important television productions. In the summer of 2008, a politician revealed to the press the existence of an unpublished wiretapping that allegedly contained explicit reference to sexual intercourse between Berlusconi and Mara Carfagna, who was by then serving as Minister of Equal Opportunity (Lopapa 2008). Berlusconi's television networks tended not to cover such scandals, signaling a mounting apprehension around the exposure of information about his private life.

Despite the surfacing scandals, in 2008 Berlusconi won the presidential elections with a very large majority, possibly because of the poor performance of the center-left administration led by Prodi. However, in late April 2009, nearly a month prior to the elections for the European Parliament, Berlusconi's wife publicly denounced the recruitment criteria his party had adopted. She insisted that a number of female candidates in Berlusconi's party shared a background in television or entertainment and were chosen more for their physical appeal than their political credentials. Lario dismissed them as "shameless trash" (Gruppo Espresso 2009), and the candidates were promptly removed from the electoral lists. Then, upon discovering that Berlusconi had attended the eighteenth birthday of Noemi Letizia, an aspiring showgirl from Naples, Lario accused her husband of "consorting with minors" (Cresto-Dina 2009). A few days later she filed for divorce. Though previously the Italian press had tended to ignore the private lives of politicians, Berlusconi's sex scandals were reported in major Italian newspapers, signaling that the increasing publicity of politicians' private spheres had over time given a whole new dimension to the political battle in Italy.

The final episodes of this difficult period came from two unexpected sources. The first involved the revelations of escort Patrizia D'Addario, who handed to Italian prosecutors the audiovisual recordings of two encounters she had had in Berlusconi's residence in Rome, one involving sexual intercourse (Bonini 2009). In the second, paparazzo Antonello Zappadu took pictures of Berlusconi's private mansion in Sardinia, which showed scantily clad young girls entertaining him and famous guests, including an entirely naked Mirek Topolanek, former Czech prime minister (Bisso 2009).

In a 2009 article written for *The Guardian*, editor-in-chief of *La Repubblica* Ezio Mauro commented that Berlusconi's "potent mixture of the personal and political has become his undoing." What Mauro saw as "the most ambitious experiment in modern populism that the West has known"—based on the constant "consecration of the leader before his people" and the removal of "every barrier between the public and the private"—was coming to an end. Just as with the crisis of the AC Milan brand, Berlusconi's brand as a public figure and politician began to fray.

We argued in previous sections that Berlusconi's brand of politics operates according to a logic of seduction rather than according to a more traditional model based on rational persuasion. Sports victories, picture-perfect families, luxurious homes, and tanned and attractive bodies are the tenets of a "new dimension of leadership," in which both physical and fictional appearances "are used to build consensus" (Ceccarelli 2009). In Italy, as in other contemporary liberal democracies, the media exposure of politicians has increasingly contributed to the politicization of their private spheres and to their transformation into mediated celebrities. Coming from advertising and television, Berlusconi was a pioneer in this process of "celebrification" of politics (Turner 2004). By seamlessly moving from soccer to television in order to maximize the exposure of his own brand, Berlusconi contributed to the erosion of the distinction between private and public. This has facilitated the aggregation of different communities of public and audiences around the same brand and the circulation of values among genres. But negative stories can circulate as well, simultaneously affecting multiple domains.

The exposure of the private sphere has over time generated an increase in the supply of personal information that cannot always be monitored and controlled by the gatekeeping function of the traditional media, often creating the conditions for critical information to be released and for scandals to arise.[4] Giuseppe D'Avanzo, Italian political journalist, commented that Berlusconi's politics "has been so far an effective consensus machine" based on a "powerful psychological weaponry… and on the full control of the entertainment industry that creates myths, lifestyle, desires and spells." However, by the spring of 2009 Berlusconi was "tied to an agenda that he hasn't written… He is forced to chase a 'reality' that he can't remove from public attention" (D'Avanzo 2009). The brand has been first extensively exposed and then challenged by its public. What remains to be seen is whether continued exposure will cause the brand to enter an irreversible crisis, or instead create the conditions for transformation.

Political Brands in the New Media Milieu: Risks and Opportunities

Berlusconi is said to have once claimed that "with the housewives I freed, I could become Prime Minister" (qtd. in Wolff 2009). He was most likely referring to how his private networks had engaged the "housewife" demographic with targeted programming and tailored advertising, giving this segment of the population both cultural representation and a steady flow of entertainment to facilitate their daily chores. The claim sums up Berlusconi's vision that demographics segmented for marketing purposes can develop into cultural identities and in turn into political ones. The economic and cultural operations required to achieve such innovative political strategy demanded the creation of a sophisticated seductive apparatus that started with his television network, evolved via the creation of the Forza Italia party, and culminated with the celebration of the persona and body of Berlusconi himself. As a result, Berlusconi now maintains an electoral base consisting of voters who engage in a relationship with him based on trust and affection. Berlusconi's celebrity-based brand of politics functions particularly well as a source of identification between a leader and the public. Although he is a billionaire with political and financial ties to the world's elites, Berlusconi's supporters perceive him as a relatable "people's man" with whom they can connect emotionally. This type of media-centered populism works by dispersing itself into the private spheres of identity and affection—what Musso (2008) calls the management of emotions—and by focusing on the bonds of trust that the personal qualities of leaders can elicit.

In this context, the recent scandals could produce two potential outcomes. On the one hand, the breach of reputation suffered by Berlusconi's brand of politics can have a detrimental effect not only in a moral sense—as recently expressed by the Catholic Church's criticism of Berlusconi's conduct[5]—but also, more importantly, in the political realm. In the most recent European elections, Berlusconi's party did not perform as well as expected, possibly as a consequence of his impending divorce and extramarital affairs (Fiammeri 2009). The scandals revealed that the border separating the allure of Berlusconi's physical and symbolic persona and "political porn," as one commentator aptly defined it, can be very thin.[6] The recent revelations about Berlusconi's extramarital affairs, his abuses of power, and the allegations about his consorting with minors have affected the stability of his brand as a family man. Patrizia D'Addario has emerged as the most vocal representative of what a Spanish newspaper has called "the revolt of *veline*" (Mora 2009)—the challenging of Berlusconi's dynamics of power by some of the very instruments of his show business politics, the attractive young starlets. Such issues ignite a critical reaction both from within and from outside his private sphere. Just as managing AC Milan as a show-business operation upset fans and players alike, so did his image-obsessed political strategy meet with mounting criticism and backlash.

These episodes reveal the inherent instability of Berlusconi's political project. His type of branded politics is increasingly difficult to sustain within a mediated environment where the potential for access to and dissemination of private information has multiplied. It is telling that Berlusconi has pushed aggressively for a law restricting the spreading of information obtained through wiretappings during criminal investigations (Galluzzo 2008). Yet in the media-saturated space of contemporary society, an image-based politics increasingly exposes itself to breaches and interferences not only by means of prosecutors but also by uncontrolled sources of information such as the ubiquitous paparazzi or even regular citizens.

On the other hand, the Berlusconi brand has proven its ability to constantly transform itself. It is possible that this period of crisis can be seized upon to evolve into new directions. As Fiske has argued, scandals as media events are "moments of visibility and turbulence," when elites and publics negotiate the definition of the border between public and private spheres (1994: 7). In the aftermath of the scandals, Berlusconi dismissed the accusations, admitting to "not being a saint" (qtd. in RCS 2009). From the religious tones used in his political debut to the more mundane tones of recent public appearances, Berlusconi has demonstrated an uncanny ability to constantly navigate among different genres and types of discourse. As a result, he has tended to maintain his "fan" communities. Even after the recent scandals, Berlusconi retained solid approval ratings in Italy; he remains one of Europe's most popular political figures. Thanks to his media empire and his ability to connect with public sentiment, Berlusconi has also been able to remain at the center of media attention. In a political sphere based on the economy of attention, what seems to be essential is the ability to attract and maintain interest in the brand. It could be argued that Berlusconi's scandals fit into a framework of desire satisfaction that can strengthen a sense of identification among some segments of the voting population. It is in this sense that crisis can be turned into opportunity.

Here is one opportunity: Berlusconi's latest mutation is into a rock star. In November 2009, the Italian edition of *Rolling Stone* declared him "rock star of the year" on the basis of his celebrity and sexual exploits (Reguly 2009). Berlusconi's brand has now become that of a libertine celebrity, a transgressor of norms. In the new media milieu of reality television, saturated by individualism and narcissistic self-exposure, Berlusconi the "one-man brand" may still be the ideal representative of his public.

Notes

1. Quoted in Guarino and Ruggeri (1987).
2. See Guarino and Ruggeri (1987).
3. See Ginsborg (1990).
4. For example, see Delli Carpini and Williams (2004).
5. For example, see La Rocca (2009).
6. See Hourihane (2009).

References

Amato, Rosaria. 2007. "Berlusconi e le donne, battute e gaffe tra Veronica, Aida e le altre." *La Repubblica.it*, January 31. http://www.repubblica.it/2007/01/sezioni/politica/lettera-veronica/berlusconi-donne/berlusconi-donne.html (accessed August 14, 2009).

Arvidsson, Adam. 2006. *Brands: Meaning and Value in Media Culture*. London: Routledge.

Bei, Francesco. 2007. "Come sono stato depresso, il Capo consolato da Yespica." *La Repubblica.it*, January 27. http://ricerca.repubblica.it/repubblica/archivio/repubblica/2007/01/27/come-sono-stato-depresso-il-capo-consolato.html (accessed August 4, 2009).

Bisso, Marino. 2009. "Feste a Villa Certosa, foto sequestrate." *La Repubblica.it*, May 31. http://ricerca.repubblica.it/repubblica/archivio/repubblica/2009/05/31/feste-villa-certosa-foto-sequestrate-violata-la.html (accessed August 5, 2009).

Bocca, Fabrizio. 2006. "Berlusconi: che insulto lo spot di Prodi." *La Repubblica.it*, July 11. http://ricerca.repubblica.it/repubblica/archivio/repubblica/2006/07/11/ berlusconi-che-insulto-lo-spot-di-prodi.html (accessed August 5, 2009).

———. 2009. "E' finito il tempo dello show." *La Repubblica.it*, June 3. http://ricerca.repubblica.it/repubblica/archivio/repubblica/2009/06/03/finito-il-tempo-dello-show.html (accessed August 4, 2009).

Bonini, Carlo. 2009. "Ecco le registrazioni di Patrizia." *La Repubblica.it*, June 20. http://ricerca.repubblica.it/repubblica/archivio/repubblica/2009/06/20/ecco-le-registrazioni-di-patrizia.html (accessed August 7, 2009).

Ceccarelli, Filippo. 2006. "Da Lauro a Pertini a Berlusconi la politica al ritmo del Pallone." *La Repubblica it*, July 10. http://ricerca.repubblica.it/repubblica/archivio/repubblica/2006/07/10/da-lauro-pertini-berlusconi-la-politica-al.html (accessed August 4, 2009).

———. 2009. "La Rossa, la Bionda e la Vocalist da Piano Bar Ecco le Bellissime alla Corte di Re Silvio." *La Repubblica.it*, April 28. http://ricerca.repubblica.it/repubblica/archivio/repubblica/2009/04/28/la-rossa-la-bionda-la-vocalist-da.html (accessed August 4, 2009).

Corriere dello Sport. 2009. "Braida: Kakà non è Stato Ceduto." January 18. http://www.corrieredellosport.it/Notizie/Calcio/55394/Braida:+%C2%ABKak%C3%A0+non+%C3%A8+stato+ceduto%C2%BB (accessed August 5, 2009).

Cresto-Dina, Dario. 2009. "Veronica, addio a Berlusconi, Ho deciso, chiedo il divorzio." *La Repubblica.it*, May 3. http://www.repubblica.it/2009/04/sezioni/ politica/elezioni-2009-2/veronica-divorzio/veronica-divorzio.html (accessed August 14, 2009).

Currò, Enrico. 2009. "Milan, un' azienda in crisi." *La Repubblica.it*, March 2. http://ricerca.repubblica.it/repubblica/archivio/repubblica/2009/03/02/milan-un-azienda-in-crisi-berlusconi-peccato.html (accessed August 5, 2009).

D'Avanzo, Giuseppe. 2007. "Inchiesta Berlusconi 'Saccà va sospeso.'" *La Repubblica.it*, December 13. http://www.repubblica.it/2007/12/sezioni/politica/berlusconi-indagato/berlusconi-regime/berlusconi-regime.html (accessed August 5, 2009).

———. 2009. "L'isolamento dello stregone." *La Repubblica.it*, June 20. http:// www.repubblica.it/2009/06/sezioni/politica/berlusconi-divorzio-9/isolamento-stregone/isolamento-stregone.html (accessed August 4, 2009).

Davenport, Thomas, and John Beck. 2001. *The Attention Economy: Understanding the New Currency of Business*. Harvard Business School Press.

Delli Carpini, Michael, and Bruce Williams. 2004. "The Collapse of Gatekeeping and Agenda Setting in the New Media Environment." *American Behavioral Scientist* (47) 9: 1208–1230.

Doyle, Waddick. 1990. *From Deregulation to Monopoly: A Cultural Analysis of the Formation of a Private Television Monopoly in Italy*. Ph.D. Dissertation, Griffith University.

Economist. 2001. "The Triumph of Populism." July 7. http://www.economist.com/node/682010 (accessed October 20, 2009).

Fiammeri, Barbara. 2009. "Dell'Utri:'Sì, un effetto-Noemi c'è stato.'" *Il Sole 24 Ore*, June 9. http://www.ilsole24ore.com/art/SoleOnLine4/dossier/Italia/2009/elezioni-europee/italia/berlusconi-effetto-noemi.shtml?uuid=a5c7c952-54c4-11de-85a9-3ff48dbd43f8&DocRulesView=Libero (accessed August 14, 2009).

Fininvest. "Fininvest—The Group." http://www.fininvest.com/_eng/gruppo/

Fiori, Giuseppe. 1995. *Il venditore*. Milano: Garzanti.

Fiske, John. 1994. *Media Matters*. Minneapolis: University of Minnesota Press.

Galluzzo, Marco. 2008. "Berlusconi: un decreto sulle intercettazioni." *Corriere.it*, July 2. http://archiviostorico.corriere.it/2008/luglio/02/Berlusconi_decreto_sulle_intercettazioni _spieghero_co_9_080702006.shtml (accessed August 8, 2009).

Gaonkar, Parameshwar, and Elizabeth Povinelli. 2003. "Technologies of Public Forms: Circulation, Transfiguration, Recognition." *Public Culture* 15 (3): 386.

Ginsborg, Paul. 1990. *A History of Contemporary Italy.* London: Penguin.

Gold, Thomas. 2003. *The Lega Nord and Contemporary Politics in Italy.* New York: Palgrave Macmillan.

Grasso, Aldo. 2004. *Storia della Televisione Italiana.* Milano: Garzanti.

Gruppo Espresso. 2009. "Veronica Lario: 'Le veline candidate? Ciarpame senza pudore per il potere.'" *La Repubblica.it,* April 28. http://www.repubblica.it/2009/04/sezioni/politica/elezioni-2009-1/veronica-lario-arrabbiata/veronica-lario-arrabbiata.html (accessed August 14, 2009).

Guarino, Mario and Giovanni Ruggeri. 1987. *Berlusconi: Inchiesta sul signor TV.* Rome: Editori Riuniti.

Haugaard, Mark. 1997. *The Constitution of Power.* Manchester: Manchester University Press.

Hourihane, Anne Marie. 2009. "Putin's Posings a Classic Example of Political Porn." *Irish Times.com,* August 10. http://www.irishtimes.com/newspaper/opinion/ 2009/0810/1224252314324.html (accessed August 10, 2009).

La Rocca, Orazio. 2009. "Bagnasco la morale dei politici Occorre coerenza di comportamenti." *La Repubblica.it,* May 30. http://ricerca.repubblica.it/ repubblica/ (accessed August 14, 2009). archivio/repubblica/2009/05/30/bagnasco-la-morale-dei-politici-occorre-coerenza. html

La Stampa.it. 2009. "Da unto del Signore a non sono santo. Quando Berlusconi parla di Santità." July 22. http://www.lastampa.it/redazione/cmsSezioni/politica/ 200907articoli/45766girata.asp (accessed November 20, 2009).

Lario, Veronica. 2007. "Veronica Berlusconi, lettera a Repubblica: 'Mio marito mi deve pubbliche scuse.'" *La Repubblica.it,* January 31. http://www.repubblica.it/2007/01/sezioni/politica/lettera-veronica/lettera-veronica/lettera-veronica.html (accessed August 7, 2009).

Lopapa, Carmelo. 2008. "Quelle telefonate stanno per uscire. Alla Camera l' incubo Grande Fratello." *La Repubblica.it,* July 2. http://ricerca.repubblica.it/repubblica/ archivio/repubblica/2008/07/02/quelle-telefonate-stanno-per-uscire-alla-camera.html (accessed August 14, 2009).

Lury, Celia. 2004. *Brands: The Logos of the Global Economy.* London: Routledge.

Maltese, Curzio. 2001. "Berlusconi, Marketing e Fede." *La Repubblica.it,* July 4. http://www.repubblica.it/online/ventirighe/cruna/cruna/cruna.html (accessed January 10, 2010).

Mauro, Ezio. 2009. "He Saw Himself as a Modern Caesar. Now His Decline Is Epic." *The Guardian,* June 21. http://www.guardian.co.uk/world/2009/jun/21/silvio-berlusconi-italy (accessed June 22, 2009).

Mora, Miguel. 2009. "La rebelión de las 'velinas' cerca a Berlusconi." *El Pais.com,* June 21. http://www.elpais.com/articulo/internacional/rebelion/velinas/cerca/Berlusconi/elpepiint/20090621elpepiint_6/Tes (accessed August 11, 2009).

Muniz, Albert and Thomas O'Guinn. 2001. "Brand Community." *Journal of Consumer Research* 27 (4): 412–432.

Muscau, Costantino. 1994. "Fozza Itaia e Berlusconi vinse." *Corriere.it,* April 19. http://archiviostorico.corriere.it/1994/aprile/19/Fozza_Itaia_Berlusconi_vinse__co_0_940419322.shtml (accessed August 3, 2009).

Musso, Pierre. 2003. *Berlusconi, le Nouveau Prince.* Paris: Editions de l'Aube.

———. 2008. *Le Sarko-berlusconisme.* Paris: Editions de l'Aube.

Novelli, Edoardo. 1995. *Dalla TV di partito al partito della TV.* Firenze: La Nuova Italia.

Ottone, Piero. 2009. *La Guerra della Rosa.* Milano: Longanesi.

Poli, Emanuela. 2001. *Forza Italia: strutture, leadership e radicamento territoriale.* Il Mulino: Bologna.

RCS. 2000. "Il leader azzurro 'arruola' Casanova: anch' io fui un discreto dongiovanni." *Corriere.it,* May 13. http://archiviostorico.corriere.it/2000/maggio/13/leader_azzurro_arruola_Casanova_anch_co_0_0005136863.shtml (accessed January 10, 2010).

RCS. 2005. "Ancelotti: 'Sei minuti di follia inspiegabile.'" *Corriere.it*, May 25. http://www.corriere.it/Primo_Piano/Sport/2005/05_Maggio/25/champ_reazioni.sh tml (accessed August 4, 2009).

RCS. 2009. "Berlusconi: 'Non sono un santo.'" *Corriere.it*, July 22. http://www.corriere.it/politica/09_luglio_22/berlusconi_non_sono_un_santo_6731ad64-76ae-11de-829e-00144f02aabc.shtml (accessed August 9, 2009).

Reguly, Eric. 2009. "Berlusconi: On the Cover ... And under Them." *Globe and Mail,* November 23. http://www.theglobeandmail.com/blogs/reguly-in-europe/berlusconi-on-the-cover-and-under-them/article1373860/ (accessed November 23, 2009).

Rizzo, Roberto. 2007. "Berlusconi e 5 ragazze, foto su Oggi." *Corriere.it*, April 17. http://www.corriere.it/Primo_Piano/Politica/2007/04_Aprile/17/rizzo.shtml (accessed August 5, 2009).

Rodotà, Stefano. 1994. "Berlusconi e la tecnopolitica." *MicroMega* (3): 85–96.

Russo, Pippo. 2001. "Berlusconi and Other Matters: the Era of 'Football-Politics.'" *Journal of Modern Italian Studies* (5) 3: 348–370.

Saubaber, Delphine and Vanja Luksic. 2009. "Berlusconi, le bouffon de l'Europe." *L'Express,* July 8. http://www.lexpress.fr/actualite/monde/europe/commentaire.asp?id=773074&discom=1 (accessed November 19, 2009).

Schwarz, Peter. 2001. "Italy's Berlusconi and His 'House of Freedoms'—A New Dimension in the Development of the Right Wing in Europe." *World Socialist Website*, May 7. http://www.wsws.org/articles/2001/may2001/ital-m07.shtm (accessed January 3, 2010).

Semino, Elena and Michela Masci. 1996. "Politics Is Football: Metaphor in the Discourse of Silvio Berlusconi in Italy." *Discourse & Society* 7: 243–269.

Smoltczyck, Alexander. 2009. "How Berlusconi became Italy's Superman." *Der Spiegel*, May 12. http:// www.spiegel.de/international/europe/0,1518,612909,00.html (accessed August 21, 2009).

Sorrentino, Andrea. 2009. "La rabbia dei tifosi, anche Kakà irritato." *La Repubblica.it*, June 5. http://ricerca.repubblica.it/repubblica/archivio/repubblica/2009/06/ 05/larabbia-dei-tifosi-anche-kaka-irritato.html (accessed August 5, 2009).

Tito, Claudio. 2009. "Gheddafi, vuoi comprare il Milan?" *La Repubblica.it*, September 4.http://ricerca.repubblica.it/repubblica/archivio/repubblica/2009/09/04/gheddafi-vuoi-comprare-il-milan.html (accessed August 10, 2009).

Turner, Graeme. 2004. *Understanding Celebrity.* London: Sage.

Walker, Rob. 2008. *Buying In.* New York: Random House.

Wolff, Michael. 2009. "All Broads Lead to Rome." *Vanity Fair*, September. http://www.vanityfair.com/politics/features/2009/09/wolff200909?currentPage=1 (accessed August 10, 2009).

CHAPTER ELEVEN

Marketing Chimeras

The Biovalue of Branded Medical Devices

Mary Ebeling

"Never Stop Moving™" —Slogan for DePuy Orthopaedics Inc.

In 1929 President Herbert Hoover praised advertising executives, saying to them, "You have taken over the job of creating desire and have transformed people into constantly moving happiness machines, machines which have become the key to economic progress" (qtd. in Curtis 2002). Though these words were spoken decades ago, at an earlier stage of capitalist development, the statement remains apposite to the circumstances of advanced, late capitalism in which we currently live. It captures well a belief that marketing, supported by a corporatized state, constitutes the citizen as a consumer, pliable to manufactured desire that transforms individuals into engines of wealth creation for the corporations that market to them (Ewen 1996). Accordingly, we produce the surplus value that can be captured not only out of our purchasing behavior but, as I will explore here, out of our relationships both intimate and public, and out of our bodies, our tissues, our genetic material (Waldby and Mitchell 2006; Healy 2004). Through the branding of drugs and medical devices, we are transformed from citizens into consumers and into productive subjects of capital.

Since the U.S. Food and Drug Administration (FDA) substantially lifted regulations on drug promotion directly to patients in 1997, much public attention and concern has been directed toward how far the pharmaceutical industry can push its marketing tactics. Concerns about the proliferation of drug advertisements and their role in inspiring patients to think of themselves as consumers comprise part of a much larger debate about the role of the "medical–industrial complex" and the commercialized biomedicalization of society (Petersen 2008; Conrad 2007; Mansfield 2005; Moynihan and Cassels 2005; Greene 2004; Lakoff 2005; Clarke et al. 2003; Scott and

Ferner 1994; Ehrenreich and Ehrenreich 1971). In 2004, the FDA also loosened regulations on direct-to-consumer marketing of medical devices, and since then, device makers have significantly increased their marketing and branding efforts to patients (U.S. Food and Drug Administration 2004). While there are ongoing, contentious debates and lobbying efforts to deregulate direct-to-consumer pharmaceutical marketing in the United Kingdom and the European Union, at the time of this writing the United States and New Zealand are the only two countries in the world that permit direct-to-consumer marketing communications for drugs and devices.[1]

With the deregulation of direct-to-consumer drug and device marketing, a productive field for broadcast commercials and other marketing activities emerged to bypass doctors who prescribe drugs and communicate directly with patients who use them. Drug direct-to-consumer marketing has now become highly sophisticated. Pharmaceutical companies use direct-to-consumer marketing to recoup the enormous resource investments that go into bringing a new drug to market.

While medical devices represent a much smaller fraction of the biomedical market than pharmaceuticals do, the marketing and branding techniques that have proven so successful for drugs are now increasingly deployed for devices. Yet, unlike drugs, many advertised medical devices—such as stents, defibrillators, hip replacements, and injectable fillers—require at least minimal surgery and often invasive implantation directly into the patient's body by a surgeon. Why is the branding of medical devices necessary? How, exactly, would a patient enact the brand identity of the defibrillator implanted into her heart?

In an effort to answer these questions, this chapter will explore how branding contributes to the wider commercialization of medicine and the changed relationship between medicine, capital, and the body. After a brief theoretical discussion, I will explore the case of Pandia, an injectable medical device originally approved as part of an HIV-treatment regime.[2] This case is based on ethnographic fieldwork I conducted at one of the U.S.-based offices of a European advertising firm in 2007. Over the course of a month, I observed the firm's strategic planners tasked with building a marketing campaign to brand the medical device for use in cosmetic applications, especially facial reconstruction. As I will discuss in-depth below, such use is considered "off-label," or not FDA approved. As advertising and marketing strategies encourage new cosmetic uses for this device, what was once medically necessary becomes a matter of "lifestyle choice." This case of branding constitutes a transformative process that renders patients consumers who quite literally embody the brand and, through that embodiment, produce brand value. Through this exploration, the activities of off-label use promotion, direct-to-consumer marketing, and branding can also be understood within the broader theoretical frameworks that address the parallel rise of biotechnologies and biocapitalism as well as the political economies of biomedicine.

Branding and the Production of Biovalue

Brands are more than an arbitrary attachment of certain emotions or attributes to a consumer product—they are "social currency" through which people are able to perform particular meanings and values (Lury 2004: 10). Brands and consumers are necessarily co-constitutive; when marketers are tasked with building a brand for a product, they must also identify a consumer base and build a profile of the potential customer, and they hope that the targeted consumer will recognize herself in the brand's identity. This process primarily occurs through the work of strategic planners—the marketing professionals working within branding firms—who develop a consumer profile from segmentation studies, data from focus groups, and interviews with consumers, and use this profile to construct a branding strategy. A brand's attributes are directly informed by the consumer profiles that strategic planners develop, and the brand's immaterial qualities—the emotions and ideas that are fastened to a product that have little to do with its physical properties—are materialized, or fleshed out, through the consumer.

A brand's meaning exists in a feedback loop between the brand and the consumer: marketing constructs and suggests the meaning of a brand; the consumer recognizes and derives this meaning; at the same time, the consumer imbues the brand with her own meaning; marketing activities then return that meaning to the brand (Lury 2004). The brand is a dynamic new media object, which "has its own (recursive) logic or performativity through which is organized a two-way, dynamic, selective and asymmetrical communication…between producers and consumers" (Lury 2004: 7–8). During fieldwork at the marketing firm Avanté, this recursive logic was well articulated by Bill, a strategic planner, who noted that branding is

> about creating advocates, and movements of advocates, creating emotional harmonization with brands and consumers…as a brand you have to stand out, connect

> on a different level. It is not about what the product can do, but what values the brand shares with the consumer…it is about a relationship.

Within this brand-mediated complex of relationships between producers, products, and people, consumers operate in a "context of consumption" where, through their enactment of the brand's intended identity well beyond the point of purchase, they are productive of value for the brand (Arvidsson 2005: 244). The emergence of the brand as a site of the social coproduction of value in late capitalism has been well established by scholars of consumer culture (Arvidsson 2008, 2005; Douglas and Isherwood 1996; Ewen 2001; Lury 2004; Miller 1998; Slater 1997). Through a network of highly mediated relationships between people and things, the immateriality and socially produced significance of an object generates value above the material and labor costs of its production, exchange value which extends well beyond the material object itself (Marx [1867] 1992). When considering brand value, Arvidsson notes that brands "figure as immaterial capital" or equity that is derived from the "subjective meanings" invested in them; brand equity is placed on a company's balance sheet as an asset that generates value (Arvidsson 2005: 239).

The same late capitalist society that gave rise to the brand also produced the conditions of a biocapital society, where the basic building blocks of life, genetic material and tissues, are capitalized upon, commodified, submitted to intellectual property rights, and publicly traded through value chains. Within biocapitalism, a reformulation of Foucault's conception of biopower to include notions of value is essential to understanding the subjective positions within these emerging circuits; as Rose argues, when "the plethora in which vitality itself has become a potential source of value," the result is biovalue, or "the value to be extracted from the vital properties of living processes" (2007: 32). As Foucault originally conceived, the power over life constitutes the human body in two ways. First, the body may be treated as a machine to be disciplined and optimized to increase its capacities, while at the same time made docile so as to integrate it within a political–economic system. The body is constructed, secondly, as a site of biological processes and the "mechanics of life," that is supervised and submitted to regulatory controls and interventions, particularly medical interventions (Foucault 1984: 261–262). Just as Foucault showed that biopower was fundamental to the development of early industrial capitalism, where power was no longer an external, coercive force but an internalized and a productive one (1984: 263), biovalue is essential to the development of biocapitalism. Biovalue produces a "new kind of laboring body" (Harvey 2000: 104). As branding increasingly harnesses the immateriality of consumer practices and exploits consumers' coproduction of the brand's assets (Arvidsson 2005: 239–243), it is necessary to understand how the marketing of branded medical devices also captures this surfeit of biovalue.

Making Chimeras: Rebranding Devices and Transforming Patients

In order to guarantee the revenue streams necessary to recoup the long and very expensive process of bringing a drug or a device to market—generally seven to nine years at a cost of around $800 million—it is essential for drug and device companies to target patients as consumers of branded biomedical goods (Newburger 2006). Virtually every pharmaceutical company invests significantly more in the marketing and promotion of products than in research and development; it can be argued that such companies are more accurately thought of as biomedical marketing companies rather than biomedical innovators (Ismail 2005).

Only a few years after pharmaceutical direct-to-consumer marketing was deregulated by the FDA, an article on branding medical conditions appeared in the trade journal *Medical Marketing & Media*. Written by marketing veteran Vince Parry, the article laid out how "condition branding" opened up new pathways for establishing a drug on the market:

> Typically, when marketers talk about branding, they are referring to the unique identity of a product or service that enables customers to distinguish it from competitors. However, within the pharmaceutical industry, marketing professionals have increasingly taken branding to the next level by branding the disease or condition that a particular product is capable of treating. The idea behind "condition branding" is simple: If you can define a particular condition and its associated symptoms in the minds of physicians and patients, you can also predicate the best treatment for that condition (Parry 2003: 43).

Condition branding, and the drug branding and rebranding that arise from it, have proven to be highly effective marketing strategies for drug companies to protect markets, drug patents, and the potential productive value of patients' "new laboring bodies" (Harvey 2000). For example, the rebranding of pharmaceutical giant Eli Lilly's top-selling antidepressant Prozac as Sarafem demonstrates that the process required the creation of a new condition for which Sarafem would be the appropriate treatment. In the process, a patient who has medical needs may be reconceptualized as a consumer with culturally significant desires, so that drug companies may build brand constituencies through which they can extract value, both financial and otherwise, for the brand.

Prozac and Sarafem are chemically identical but differ in how they are packaged (Prozac has a yellow and green coating, Sarafem's is pink and purple), who the target patient is, and what each is FDA-approved to treat. Under the brand name Prozac, the chemical is used as a remedy for symptoms associated with depression, while Sarafem is used to treat a highly contested and little recognized condition known as premenstrual dysphoric disorder (PMDD) (Ebeling 2008; Mintzes 2006; Greenslit 2005). More than a remedy for a nebulous medical condition, however, Sarafem also treated looming financial problems for Eli Lilly, since the company faced the prospect of competition from generic alternatives as its patent on Prozac was due to expire in 2001. In an effort to preserve its blockbuster drug, Eli Lilly launched a marketing campaign for Sarafem in 1999, well ahead of the expiration date for its Prozac patent, and sought FDA re-approval for the treatment of a "new" set of symptoms as well as a new set of patients who would potentially act as advocates for the "new" drug.

The rebranding of Prozac as Sarafem highlights how drug branding encourages a patient to become an active consumer who can advocate for the marketed benefits of the branded drug to her doctor. This is a process that is largely hidden from potential patients: for instance, advertisements for Sarafem did not mention its chemical similarity to Prozac, opting instead to describe the vague symptoms that could be treated (Greenslit 2005; Ebeling 2008). Eli Lilly was also careful to distinguish PMDD as a physical disorder, rather than a disease of the mind; the company thus emphasized that Sarafem treated a physical malady while Prozac treated a psychological condition, distinctions fraught with gendered notions of a mind/body split.[3] Not only was a new disease created through rebranding, but a new identity was also created for those who suffered from the disease and were treated by the drug. In his extensive study of the use of Sarafem by pre-operative transgendered men for the treatment of PMDD and by nontransgendered men for symptoms of depression, Greenslit showed that all of the study participants were uncomfortable at the thought of using Sarafem, since the drug was branded *for* women as well as treating a disease *of* women, which directly contrasted not only with their gender identities but also with how they identified their disease states (Greenslit 2002, 2005). The Sarafem consumer, a woman who suffers from a physical ailment, did not fit the identity of the Prozac consumer, a person of any gender identity suffering from clinical depression. The rebranding story of Sarafem can also be illustrative more generally of how medical devices—from contact lenses to artificial hips and breast implants—are undergoing similar efforts in order to create new advocates for branded devices.

Unlike branded drugs, the branding and rebranding of medical devices is a peculiar phenomenon, where a patient is directly marketed a product she is not qualified to implant into her body: the product, by necessity, must be administered by a doctor. What value, then, would a device maker see in spending promotional budgets on directly marketing to patients? Moreover, medical devices have a comparatively shorter market life due to constant innovations of functionality and design, which impacts their regulatory timeline as well as potential revenue—both of which are significantly less when compared with pharmaceuticals. In 2007, the medical device market was worth $50 billion in sales, compared with a drug market worth $320 billion (Steinberg 2007). Companies spent $200 million on advertising for medical devices in 2007, a small fraction of the more than $50.1 billion spent for direct-to-consumer drug promotions in 2007 alone (Gagnon and Lexchin 2008; Arnold 2009). The smaller market potential notwithstanding, device makers are replicating the promotional strategies for their goods that have already proven so successful for the drug industry.[4] Highly sophisticated marketing techniques are used to insinuate device companies' marketing messages seamlessly into news or entertainment content and construct a fertile context of consumption in which patients transmute into consumers; device makers can enroll consumer agency to make consumer choices and to be brand advocates (Moynihan and Cassels 2005).

Compounding this transformation of patients into consumers, within biocapitalism the distinction between the categories of producers and consumers collapses. Consumers become producers, and producers, consumers (Rajan 2006). This collapsing of categories is most pronounced in the biomedical industry, where a patient may benefit from surgery to remove diseased tissue and that tissue can be subsequently sold to a biotech company to develop a new product that will be marketed to other patients.[5] Biovalue is extracted directly from the bodies of both producers and consumers not only through the commodification of genetic material, tissues, and body parts, but also through the process of encouraging patients to act as consumers (Rajan 2006: 98). The patient's body both produces and consumes value and fits into larger regimes of capital flows of production and extraction—what Harvey calls "productive consumption" (Harvey 2000: 103–

106). No longer are patients merely persons in need of medical intervention; through the marketing and branding of biomedicine that is essential to sustaining biocapitalism, patients must comparison shop and make choices about the best medical care for themselves. In her examination of the cosmetic surgery industry, for example, Jones demonstrates that the ways in which cosmetic procedures are marketed to women suggest that the industry conceives of its patients as consumers; patients are often seen as "avid shopper(s): only willing to commit to a 'purchase' after perusing all options" (2008: 70). Rajan further notes that the production of biovalue is a discursive act, manifested through branding and advertising, which serves as a rationalization for aggressively marketing to patients. A patient is "empowered" with branded knowledge so that she can walk into her doctor's office and demand that a branded device or drug be prescribed (Rajan 2006: 57).

A patient cannot use a hip replacement in the same way that she may use a cold remedy or any other consumable product sold over the counter. The aim of these marketing campaigns is not to influence the patient's purchasing behavior but rather to transform her body into a productive site of financial value. The walls of her doctor's office are covered with glossy charts produced by Eli Lilly, the pen used to write a script is inscribed with the logo of GSK, the disease-awareness pamphlet her doctor gives her has been drafted in the PR offices of Wyeth, and when her surgeon implants a joint replacement, a sales representative from Johnson & Johnson will be there in the operating room guiding the doctor on the proper use of the device.[6] Direct-to-consumer marketing of branded medical devices that emphasizes consumer choice over medical expertise has goals similar to those of branded drugs: to insinuate the brand into the center of the relationship between a patient and her doctor, to recruit the patient in performing the immaterial and productive labor for the brand that ultimately influences the decision-making and medical judgment of the doctor, and to return that biovalue to the brand. As is the case with drugs, it is necessary to mount the most successful marketing campaign possible, branding the device and the disease state, as well as identifying new consumers for the device. This process starts with a FDA reclassification.

Regulating Devices and Their Off-Label Uses

The FDA regulates medical devices under its Center for Devices and Radiological Health. Under this rubric, the FDA groups devices within three regulatory classes depending on a device's safety and control factors. Devices with the highest safety risks, such as implantable devices, fall under Class II and Class III; both undergo either a Premarket Notification (PMN) review or the more rigorous Premarket Approval (PMA) review before they can be marketed (Nygaard 2008; Newburger 2006). When a device or a drug is FDA-approved, especially through the PMA, the approval only extends to the stated use or indications in the application process; any uses outside of those indications—such as uses of an approved device in patients for whom the device has not been tested, usage of the device in other areas of the body and, in the case of drugs, prescribing other than the permitted dosage or administering the drug to an unapproved class of patient—are all considered to be off-label uses. Since off-label uses are unapproved, this also means that the off-label uses have not been properly tested, or tested at all, in clinical trials. The FDA has no authority to regulate off-label uses, since its position is that such uses are part of sound medical practice with the potential to advance medical knowledge. They do, however, regulate the *promotion* of off-label uses, which is considered illegal (U.S. Food and Drug Administration 1998).[7] In order for device manufacturers to gain clearance to promote and market an off-label use for a device, they must resubmit an application for the new indications, and the device must undergo an Investigational Device Exemption (IDE). Only after gaining re-approval may a manufacturer legally market the device for the new indications.

Often without public awareness, marketers employ highly sophisticated, controversial, and at times illegal tactics to promote off-label usages of drugs and devices primarily to health practitioners, the group which represents the largest portion of marketing efforts. The industry spends on average only 14 percent of their promotional budgets on direct-to-consumer marketing, with the remaining 86 percent of efforts going into marketing to doctors (Kaiser Family Foundation 2003: 3). Since many off-label uses are untested and unproven, they can have dire consequences for patients. For example, the FDA issued public warnings concerning the off-label use of Recombinant Human Bone Morphogenetic Protein (rhBMP), a genetically engineered medical device injected into the lumbar spine; off-label use was potentially life-threatening, especially if rhBMP was injected into the cervical spine (U.S. FDA 2008). Several patients died as a direct result of such off-label use of the device, prompting an investigation by the Department of Justice. The DoJ found that the device maker, Medtronic Inc., had illegally promoted off-label usages of its rhBMP-based INFUSE bone grafting technology.

The widely promoted Botox is another branded medical device prone to illegal off-label abuses. After the FDA warned patients that off-label uses of Botox could lead to serious adverse side effects, including death, the regulatory body now requires that Botox and other injectables be labeled with "black-box warnings," similar to the warnings on cigarette packages (Ebeling 2008; Singer 2009). Despite the potential lawsuits and regulatory fines that a company can incur for illegally promoting off-use practices, the potential payoff of an untapped market of "new laboring bodies" of patients/consumers demanding off-label uses far outweighs the risks.

Marketing Chimeras: Promoting Off-Label Uses of Skin Fillers

"True Beauty Doesn't Lie...You Have the Power to Influence Your Appearance."
—From the website for Restylane, a cosmetic, injectable medical device.

Many of the new subdermal gels and fillers currently used for facial cosmetic procedures were initially developed and approved as devices for solely medical applications, such as in dissolvable sutures, to relieve joint pain, or to repair eye damage (Ebeling 2008). Most have undergone the branding process (including FDA re-approval for new uses) for cosmetic applications, essentially codifying off-label uses of these devices and making it legal to promote such uses. Two of the fillers continue to be regulated for medical applications only: Silikon 1000 for retinal treatments, and Sculptra to treat facial fat loss in HIV-positive patients on antiretroviral drug therapies. Both are marketed to consumers and doctors for off-label—that is, unapproved—cosmetic purposes.

The market for injectable fillers has mushroomed since 2003, when the FDA approved Restylane for use under the skin between the nose and mouth. Since then, at least 13 more injectable fillers have been brought to market, with several more in clinical trials. All are promoted as nonsurgical alternatives to facelifts or as longer-lasting wrinkle treatments compared with the injectable neurotoxin Botox. Injectable fillers are the second most popular cosmetic procedure, only behind Botox. The market potential for nonsurgical cosmetic procedures more generally is enormous and growing: in 2007, for the first time in 10 years, plastic surgeries decreased while nonsurgical procedures increased eightfold, representing 83 percent of the 11.5 million cosmetic procedures conducted annually in the United States (American Society for Aesthetic Plastic Surgery 2007). The financial benefits of branding to companies making these devices are obvious: the market potential for poly-L-lactic acid as an injectable, cosmetic filler for nonsurgical "facelifts" is greater than as a dissolvable suture.

During ethnographic fieldwork conducted at Avanté, a subsidiary European marketing and advertising firm of a multinational corporation, I observed some of the processes involved in rebranding a device through the promotion of off-label usages. I collected data from meetings with strategic planners working on an account for a device-making subsidiary of one of the world's leading pharmaceutical companies as well as collected data from print and web-based marketing campaigns the device maker developed to market the device to both health practitioners and patients.

Avanté strategic planners working on Project Buffy—the code name for the project on injectable skin filler Pandia for their client, medical device maker BMC Inc.—were tasked with developing a branding strategy for the device. A Class III medical device which had received FDA premarket approval in 2004, Pandia was a synthetic polymer used as an intradermal injection in HIV-positive patients to correct fat loss in the cheek area (called "lipoatrophy"), a condition caused by the use of antiretroviral therapy (ART) and an outward manifestation of a person's HIV-positive status. Avanté was retained to create a marketing, advertising, and public relations strategy to promote off-label usage of the device both to consumers and to doctors—namely, to promote the use of the device in HIV-negative patients for cosmetic purposes in the face and other parts of the body. This off-label use went beyond the FDA approval for injection of the device into areas such as directly below the eyes, on the forehead, and into hands. While the marketing campaign could not be launched until the device received an IDE—additional approval for the new indications—the strategizing to promote these off-label uses occurred while the device was still under review. If the client's device won an IDE for these new indications, legalizing the promotion of such practices, the marketing plan would be ready for immediate implementation.

The company was hopeful that the rebranding strategy might turn Pandia, a niche product, into its biggest-selling device. As mentioned above, since the device was indicated for use in HIV-positive people undergoing ART therapy and was only indicated for injection into the cheek area, its market was incredibly limited. But if the device could be remarketed as an elective cosmetic device for women between the ages of 35 and 50, the profit potential would be enormous. In anticipation of FDA re-approval for the new uses, the planners devised a complete marketing and communication campaign to target HIV-negative women aged 35 to 50 for cosmetic usage in the cheek area of the face. Based on extensive segmentation studies and data collected through focus groups, the "target" was an affluent, professional woman, who considers her looks as an asset and who would not opt for plastic surgery but would consider injectables such as fillers and Botox as attractive options. With the slogan, "For the woman who's redefining a new way to age," the strategic planners created a branding identity for this target, including a full narrative of her consumption habits and tastes, personal values, attitudes, and beliefs.

During an interview with Sara, one of the planners working on the account, she referred to comparative research on attitudes toward aging that had been conducted in several countries and was used to inform the campaign strategy. Citing the report, she noted that American cultural attitudes deem the ideal age for a woman to be 25 years, whereas in France the ideal age is 40. It was this finding, she told me, that helped to shape the "value proposition" for the rebranded device, which would enable women, as they age, to retain a cherished asset: a youthful appearance. Through this marketing campaign's interpellation of the patient's productive biovalue—her unlined face—not only was the filler transformed from a medical device into a cosmetic one, but the device also became productive of value from and for the bodies of the consumers of the rebranded device.

Although the strategic planners already had considerable knowledge about the approved uses of the injectable device, much discussion was focused on using the device in other areas of the face and in the hands, all off-label uses. These strategies were devised in anticipation of re-approval and were not made public, at least according to the official branding strategy. Yet these unregulated uses began to appear publicly nonetheless. For instance, while the U.S. website for the device emphasized the FDA-approved uses only, the use of "before" and "after" images of women within the target age group seemed to implicitly promote the nonmedical, cosmetic, off-label uses of the device. Another issue arose during the strategy meetings: it was unclear how strategic planners had learned about new uses for the device—for instance, whether the information came directly from meetings with the client, from meetings within the marketing firm, or from doctors, such as cosmetic surgeons, who had been engaging in off-label usage of a device. My concern was that some of the new, off-label uses were "workshopped" in marketing meetings based on the market potential that the strategic planners had determined from segmentation studies and focus groups and integrated into promotional strategies to doctors and to patients. Fishman produced similar findings in her ethnography of "continuing medical education" (CME) conferences organized by pharmaceutical companies on female sexual dysfunction and in-trial drugs used to treat the "disorder": the conferences were used during the re-approval process to "set the market" by suggesting the reapproved uses to medical practitioners in anticipation of the FDA approving the new uses (Fishman 2004: 197).

Until a device maker obtains FDA re-approval for the off-label uses it hopes to market, direct promotion and marketing of off-label uses by the company is illegal. While a broadcast advertisement for Restylane, the cosmetic filler mentioned earlier in this chapter, cannot mention its off-label applications, the line between legal direct-to-consumer communication and illegal promotion is often blurred. Marketing may tap into what Arvidsson calls the "productivity of contemporary consumer practices" by utilizing online social networking as part of the overall branding effort (Arvidsson 2005: 239). Restylane did this when it launched an online viral marketing campaign in 2007 on YouTube by creating a channel called "happybirthday4935" and posting a video that appeared to be created by a son at his mother's 50th birthday party. It is not until the end of the video that the viewer learns that it is a branded communication from Restylane, at which point the viewer is encouraged to "age gracefully."[8] The YouTube campaign was part of a much larger marketing effort that included a contest and reality show called *The Hottest Mom in America*, a summer 2007 production that brought thousands of women to New York in the hopes of winning a part in the show and receiving a year's worth of free injections of Restylane. The show also included a website where women could upload videos of themselves explaining why they should be considered the "Hottest Mom in America."

It is legal for doctors to promote off-label uses in interviews with journalists, so long as the doctor is not acting as an official spokesperson for the device maker. For instance, the December 2007 issues of the women's fashion magazines *Allure* and *Harper's Bazaar* both featured lengthy articles on nonsurgical cosmetic procedures now available on the market, including discussion of the array of injectable wrinkle fillers. Featured prominently in the *Bazaar* story was dermatologist and entrepreneur Dr. Patricia Wexler. Her remarks about each injectable device reflected the marketing language of the brands themselves (Ebeling 2008). When discussing Pandia's off-label uses, Wexler noted that the product acts as "a trellis on which the collagen can grow," a description I heard cited word for word during my observations at Avanté. Throughout the article, she recommended off-label, unregulated applications, such as using injectable fillers in the eye area, in the temples, in the jawline, on the cheekbones, and in the fine lines surrounding the mouth—uses the strategic planners that I interviewed claimed were awaiting FDA re-approval.

These articles clearly encourage off-label use of injectable fillers targeting the potential consumers of these products. As a practicing dermatologist, Dr. Wexler's opinions and promotions of off-label uses of injectable fillers are especially credible among the marketers' target audience, generally women of a certain income bracket and age group who can afford cosmetic procedures and are thus more receptive to these marketing messages. In regard to FDA regulated direct-to-consumer communications, these sorts of promotional activities for off-label uses constitute at the very least a gray area. At worst they are seriously questionable practices, both ethically and medically, on the part of the doctor and the device maker. Through these promotions of off-label uses, the context of consumption was set for Pandia as well as for the newly transformed consumer advocate for the brand.

The consumer of Pandia literally embodies the brand through her newly wrinkle-free face. That brand value becomes enhanced when she advocates for Pandia, despite the fact that the procedure was not medically necessary. This value, however, doesn't simply return to the brand; the consumer's youthful appearance also produces the social value for the consumer, value that she sought to capture (and embody) by undergoing the procedure. The branding of Pandia was predicated on this consumer embodiment of value. Rethinking the "laboring body" and its productive value is central to understanding how the branding of Pandia transforms individuals into consumers of medical devices rather than patients who benefit from biomedical innovations, such as this device's medical benefits for HIV-positive patients. It is also central to our understanding of how a consumer's body is enrolled to be a productive force of biovalue. In order for biocapitalism to flourish, access to productive bodies—what Haraway has variously called accumulative bodies or chimeras—is essential (Haraway 1990; Haraway and Harvey 1995). While biovalue is not directly extracted from the tissues of the consumer receiving an injection of Pandia, it is captured through her body by its chimerical transformation via biotechnological enhancement.

Conclusion

Direct-to-consumer advertising and promotional activities account for a fraction of the overall promotional activities that pharmaceutical companies and device makers employ in order to create new markets for their products. The majority of the effort goes into marketing directly to doctors and health care providers, as it is they whom companies can influence to write a prescription or make care decisions in regard to patient health. In 2000, the ten largest pharmaceutical companies spent $1.9 billion on promotional events for doctors. Typically, pharmaceutical companies will spend $8,290 per doctor on "detailing," or office visits by sales representatives, with the average doctor receiving 28 visits per week; companies will also provide her with free samples, explain new findings from company-sponsored drug trials, and demonstrate the latest product innovations (Consumers Union 2006). All of the direct-to-consumer promotional activities merely contribute to the ultimate goal of drug and device marketing: to influence a doctor's behavior to prescribe the company's device and to create the ripe conditions for an expandable market for the company's product. Favorable market conditions for a device include a marketing campaign that has the power to influence coverage decisions made by health insurers,[9] create strategies that "make it easier for healthcare professionals to recommend a device and/or answer patients' questions" about a device for which they have seen an advertisement, and build a critical mass attitude toward a device, so that no other option can be considered viable (Tausend 2004: 80; Paragamian 2008). While drug and device companies will argue that direct-to-consumer marketing is used to "empower" patients with information about a drug or device as well as about a disease state or condition, this stated motivation belies the real stakes of the process.

Ostensibly the FDA is charged to provide oversight on marketing practices; yet the agency often sides with corporate interests rather than providing rigorous oversight to protect consumers and patients.[10] While the FDA's official position on off-label uses of drugs and devices is to allow for spontaneous, observation-driven and innovative medical practice that expands medical knowledge and ultimately benefits patients, all too often in practice these off-label uses are advocated by pharmaceutical and medical device companies. Such marketing efforts not only blur the distinction between medical innovation and sales pitch but also profoundly disrupt the relationship between a patient and her doctor through the transformation of the patient into a consumer.

There is no doubt that certain procedures involving medical devices, such as hip replacements, provide profound benefits to patients suffering pain and disabilities from their conditions. In this chapter, my aim was not to critique the device or the surgery but rather to shed light on the promotional regimes that encourage patients to become consumers of medical devices. It is through those regimes that productive forces are at play directly upon the bodies and identities of patients. In the case of the illegal off-label promotion of devices, off-label is no longer within the purview of medical innovation but rather within marketing regimes of biopolitics where marketing actively seeks to transform the patient's body into one that dually labors and consumes for biocapital. The body thus becomes a site where biovalue can be extracted by transforming the patient's relationship to medicine, doctors, and her own body.

Notes

1. While branded television commercials are illegal in the United Kingdom and other parts of the European Union, other "unbranded" direct-to-consumer "disease-awareness campaigns" are allowed. In July 2008, for instance, Eli Lilly (UK) launched the first-ever patient education campaign on erectile dysfunction in younger men in the U.K. (Medical News Today 2008).
2. All names, including that of the product, the advertising agency, the client, and the strategic planners, are pseudonyms.
3. In his article on gender identity and Sarafem, Greenslit (2005) details how the battle included not only the gender identity of patients using either Sarafem or Prozac, but also the gendering of mental and physical conditions. He demonstrates that Eli Lilly tapped into the feminist arguments for and against biological determinism in order to market Prozac as Sarafem, by emphasizing that PMDD is a physical disorder, and not all in a woman's mind. This branding strategy stood in stark contrast to the branding of Prozac, a drug to treat a mental condition.
4. These strategies include but are not limited to ghost writing; detailing meetings where drug company sales reps visit doctors at their practices; "educational" conferences at resorts for doctors; and "unbranded" patient educational websites about disease states and conditions, such as www.knowmenopause.com or www.40over40.com.
5. A recent and often quoted example of this phenomenon is *Moore v. Regents of University of California*, a 1990 court case where John Moore underwent surgery to remove his

spleen. Genetics Institute, Inc. and Sandoz Pharmaceuticals Corp developed a patented cell line from Moore's removed organ without his informed consent.

6. In the United States, it is common practice for sales representatives for medical devices and equipment to be present in operating rooms. The surgeons are often guided by the sales reps on the use of the equipment, since the reps know more about the new equipment than the doctors.
7. In the largest healthcare fraud case in history, Pfizer was fined $1.2 billion for criminal misconduct as part of a larger $2.3 billion settlement action for illegally promoting off-label uses of four of its drugs to doctors (O'Reilly and Capaccio 2009).
8. To view the video go to: www.youtube.com/user/happybirthday4935. Restylane's "Hottest Mom in America" reality show and contest website can be viewed at: www.hottestmomonline.com.
9. As an example of this influence, when Viagra first hit the market in 1998, most health insurers covered the drug while only 15 percent of health plans covered contraceptives (Rauber 1998).
10. The FDA continues to undergo investigations into the effectiveness of its regulation of the pharmaceutical and device industry. In the most recent investigation of 118 new drug applications submitted to the FDA in 2007, the Department of Health and Human Services found that out of more than 29,000 clinical investigators listed on these applications, only 206 disclosed potential financial conflicts, which could indicate not only a conflict in terms of the potency, efficacy, and risks of a given drug but also virtually no regulatory oversight on the part of the FDA (Department of Health and Human Services 2009).

References

The American Society for Aesthetic Plastic Surgery. 2007. Cosmetic Surgery National Databank 2006. New York: The American Society for Aesthetic Plastic Surgery.

Arnold, Matthew. 2009. "Between Screens: A Shift in DTC." *Medical Marketing and Media* 44 (4): 40–44.

Arvidsson, Adam. 2008. "The Ethical Economy of Customer Coproduction." *Journal of Macromarketing* 28 (4): 326–338.

———. 2005. "Brands: A Critical Perspective." *Journal of Consumer Culture* 5 (2): 235–258.

Clarke, Adele E., Janet K. Shim, Laura Mamo, Jennifer Ruth Fosket, and Jennifer R. Fishman. 2003. "Biomedicalization: Technoscientific Transformations of Health, Illness, and U.S. Biomedicine." *American Sociological Review* 68 (2): 161–194.

Conrad, Peter. 2007. *The Medicalization of Society: On the Transformation of Human Conditions into Treatable Disorders.* Baltimore: The Johns Hopkins University Press.

Consumers Union. 2006. Prescription for Change: Detailing: The Consumers Union.

Curtis, Adam. 2002. "Episode 1: Happiness Machines." *Century of the Self.* Video Documentary. Directed by Adam Curtis. United Kingdom: British Broadcasting Corporation.

Department of Health and Human Services. 2009. *The Food and Drug Administration's Oversight of Clinical Investigators' Financial Information*, ed. D. R. Levinson. Washington, D.C.: Office of Inspector General, Health and Human Services.

Douglas, Mary, and Baron Isherwood. 1996. *The World of Goods: Towards an Anthropology of Consumption.* New York: Routledge.

Ebeling, Mary. 2008. "Beyond Advertising: The Pharmaceutical Industry's Hidden Marketing Tactics." *PR Watch*, February 21.

Ehrenreich, Barbara, and John Ehrenreich. 1971. *The American Health Empire: Power, Profits, and Politics.* New York: Vintage.

Ewen, Stuart. 2001. *Captains of Consciousness: Advertising and the Social Roots of the Consumer Culture.* New York: Basic Books.

———. 1996. *PR! A Social History of Spin.* New York: Basic Books.

Fishman, Jennifer R. 2004. "Manufacturing Desire: The Commodification of Female Sexual Dysfunction." *Social Studies of Science* 34 (2): 187–218.

Foucault, Michel. 1984. "Right of Death and Power over Life." In *The Foucault Reader*, ed. P. Rabinow. New York: Pantheon.

Gagnon, Marc-Andre, and Joel Lexchin. 2008. "The Cost of Pushing Pills: A New Estimate of Pharmaceutical Promotion Expenditures in the United States." *PLoS Medicine* 5 (1): 29–33.

Greene, Jeremy A. 2004. "Attention to 'Details': Etiquette and the Pharmaceutical Salesman in Postwar American." *Social Studies of Science* 34 (2): 271–292.

Greenslit, Nathan. 2002. "Pharmaceutical Branding: Identity, Individuality and Illness." *Molecular Interventions* 2 (6): 342–345.

———. 2005. "Dep®ession and Consum♀tion: Psychopharmaceuticals, Branding and New Identity Practices." *Culture, Medicine and Psychiatry* 29: 477–501.

Haraway, Donna. 1990. *Simians, Cyborgs, and Women: The Reinvention of Nature.* New York: Routledge.

Haraway, Donna, and David Harvey. 1995. "Nature, Politics, and Possibilities: A Debate and Discussion with David Harvey and Donna Haraway." *Environment and Planning D: Society and Space* 13 (5): 507–527.

Harvey, David. 2000. *Spaces of Hope.* Berkeley, CA: University of California Press.

Healy, David. 2004. "Shaping the Intimate: Influences on the Experience of Everyday Nerves." *Social Studies of Science* 34 (2): 219–245.

Ismail, M. Asif. 2005. "Drug Lobby Second to None: How the Pharmaceutical Industry Gets Its Way in Washington." Washington, D.C.: Center for Public Integrity.

Jones, Meredith. 2008. *Skintight: An Anatomy of Cosmetic Surgery.* Oxford: Berg.

The Kaiser Family Foundation. 2003. "Impact of Direct-to-Consumer Advertising on Prescription Drug Spending." Washington DC: The Henry J. Kaiser Family Foundation.

Lakoff, Andrew. 2005. *Pharmaceutical Reason: Knowledge and Value in Global Psychiatry.* Cambridge: Cambridge University Press.

Lury, Celia. 2004. *Brands: The Logos of the Global Economy.* New York: Routledge.

Mansfield, Peter R. 2005. "Banning All Drug Promotion Is the Best Option Pending Major Reforms." *Journal of Bioethical Inquiry* 2 (2): 75–81.

Marx, Karl. [1867] 1992. *Capital: A Critique of Political Economy, Vol. 1.* New York: Penguin Classics.

Medical News Today. 2008. "40Over40: A New Campaign to Tackle Low Awareness Of Erectile Dysfunction and Its Health Implications in Younger Men." *Medical News Today*, June 24.

Miller, Daniel. 1998. "Why Some Things Matter." Pp. 3–21 in *Material Cultures: Why Some Things Matter*, ed. Daniel Miller. Chicago: University of Chicago Press.

Mintzes, Barbara. 2006. "Disease Mongering in Drug Promotion: Do Governments Have a Regulatory Role?" *PLoS Medicine* 3 (4): 461–465.

Moynihan, Ray, and Alan Cassels. 2005. *Selling Sickness: How the World's Biggest Pharmaceutical Companies Are Turning Us All into Patients.* New York: Nation Books.

Newburger, Amy E. 2006. "Cosmetic Medical Devices and Their FDA Regulation." *Archives of Dermatology* 142 (2): 225–228.

Nygaard, Ingrid. 2008. "What Does 'FDA Approved' Mean for Medical Devices?" *Obstetrics & Gynecology* 111 (1): 4–6.

O'Reilly, Cary and Tony Capaccio. 2009. "Pfizer Agrees to Record Criminal Fine in Fraud Probe." *Bloomberg News*, September 3.

Paragamian, David. 2008. "Blueprint for Branding Devices." *Medical Marketing & Media* 43 (3): 47–49.

Parry, Vince. 2003. "The Art of Branding a Condition." *Medical Marketing & Media* 38 (5): 43–49.

Petersen, Melody. 2008. *Our Daily Meds: How the Pharmaceutical Companies Transformed Themselves into Slick Marketing Machines and Hooked the Nation on Prescription Drugs.* New York: Picador.

Rajan, Kaushik Sunder. 2006. *Biocapital: The Constitution of Postgenomic Life.* Durham: Duke University Press.

Rauber, Paul. 1998. "It's a Man's World: Female Contraception Often Not Covered by Insurance Companies." *Sierra*, September–October.

Rose, Nikolas. 2007. *Politics of Life Itself: Biomedicine, Power and Subjectivity in the Twenty-first Century.* Princeton: Princeton University Press.

Scott, D. K., and R. E. Ferner. 1994. "'The Strategy of Desire' and Rational Prescribing." *British Journal of Clinical Pharmacology* 37 (3): 217–219.

Singer, Natasha. 2009. "F.D.A. Orders Warning Label for Botox." *New York Times*, May 1, B2.

Slater, Don. 1997. *Consumer Culture and Modernity.* Malden, MA: Polity Press.

Steinberg, Brian. 2007. "New Medical-Device Ads; Old Concerns; Can a Knee Implant Be Sold This Way, And Should It Be?" *Wall Street Journal*, April 10.

Tausend, Kevin. 2004. "Devices Go DTC." *Medical Marketing & Media* 39 (11): 76–82.

U.S. Food and Drug Administration. 2008. FDA Public Health Notification: Life-threatening Complications Associated with Recombinant Human Bone Morphogenetic Protein in Cervical Spine Fusion. In *Public Health Notifications,* ed. D. Schultz. Washington, D.C.: U.S. Food and Drug Administration.

———. 2004. Draft Guidance for Industry and the FDA: Consumer-Directed Broadcast Advertising of Restricted Devices. Washington, D.C.: U.S. Food and Drug Administration.

———. 1998. "Information Sheets: 'Off-Label' and Investigational Use of Marketed Drugs, Biologics, and Medical Devices." Washington, D.C.: U.S. Food and Drug Administration.

Waldby, Catherine, and Robert Mitchell. 2006. *Tissue Economies: Blood, Organs, and Cell Lines in Late Capital.* Durham, NC: Duke University Press.

PART FOUR

Performing the Brand

Art, Entertainment, and Entrepreneurship

CHAPTER TWELVE

The Politics of Commerce

Shepard Fairey and the New Cultural Entrepreneurship

Sarah Banet-Weiser & Marita Sturken

In February 2009, cult graphic artist and cultural entrepreneur Shepard Fairey was arrested in Boston and accused of vandalism for illegally putting up posters on the street. This was not an exceptional situation, since Fairey had been arrested, by his own count, fourteen times before. However, the arrest happened to coincide with a major retrospective of Fairey's work at the Institute of Contemporary Art in Boston, thus garnering mainstream press attention. A month later, Fairey appeared in court in Boston with his lawyer to fight what the *New York Times* called a "cascade" of vandalism changes, prompting yet again a debate (one deliberately instigated by Fairey over the years) about the difference between street art, graffiti, and branding. "He's raising important issues about consent and who decides what we see in public spaces," Jill Medvedow, director of the Institute of Contemporary Art, told the *Times*. "It gives Boston an opportunity not just to engage but to help lead that debate" (Goodnough 2009). Fairey himself suggested he was being punished for advocating that public space "should be filled with more than just commercial advertising."

Yet Shepard Fairey is hardly a typical street-graffiti artist working against the corporate establishment of advertising and its colonization of the street. He is himself a brand. Emerging from the skateboarding scene in the mid-1990s, he achieved early cult status with his "Andre the Giant Has a Posse" sticker campaign, featuring images that depicted wrestler Andre the Giant underscored with the capitalized word "obey" as a way to both mock and critique the ubiquity of advertising. Through his Studio Number One, he produces not only political posters such as the now celebrated HOPE, PROGRESS, and CHANGE Barack Obama posters but also a line of hip skater-surfer inspired clothing under the label Obey Giant (sold with the slogan "manufacturing dissent since 1989") and advertising campaigns such as a recent Saks Fifth Avenue campaign that deploys Constructionist-style graphics to entreat shoppers to "Want It!" His 2009 endeavors include "re-branding" George Orwell's *Animal Farm* with a new illustrated cover and a poster art campaign for clean energy.

Fairey is emblematic of a new kind of cultural producer, at home with entrepreneurship and progressive cultural politics simultaneously. His marketing strategies for his clothing line, for instance, are a direct critique of the persuasive power of advertising while they simultaneously do the work of selling clothes. In his ad campaign for Saks, Fairey deliberately uses the codes of anticonsumerist socialist art. This play with art and commerce, and recoding of the language of capitalist critique into campaigns that are playfully yet directly about marketing consumerism, is a key characteristic of the new cultural entrepreneur. Fairey's creation of a recognizable "nonbrand" brand, one that resonates most prominently with a hip, (primarily) urban youth culture, exemplifies many aspects of contemporary brand culture, in which individuals create, experience, resist, and challenge identities through and within the visual and political culture of branding. Fairey is successful at negotiating these many roles—from the artist who is credentialed by his arrest record as retaining the authenticity of the "street" to the manager of a clothing brand who runs a factory in Los Angeles with a large number of employees, from the artist of weekly produced, quickly run political posters to an artist whose work is sold in limited editions and featured in museum retrospectives. Fairey's Obama political poster (at the time of this writing entangled in a copyright battle) was acquired by the Smithsonian; his style mixes political poses with brands in an unapologetic way, accompanied by a discourse that roams from Heidegger to code words like "flexibility." For instance, in his widely circulated Manifesto about the OBEY campaign, Fairey describes his OBEY sticker campaign as "an experiment in Phenomenology," referencing Heidegger's notion that phenomenology is "the process of letting things manifest themselves." He states, "The first aim of phenomenology is to reawaken a sense of wonder about one's environment. The OBEY sticker attempts to stimulate curiosity and bring people to question both the sticker and their relationship with their surroundings" (Fairey 1990). He aims, often quite successfully, to straddle both this artistic aim of reawakening a sense of wonder with the producers' aim of selling the dissemination of ideas and slogans through commodities.

We see Shepard Fairey as an icon of a new form of cultural entrepreneurship whose profile reveals the current relationship of brand culture, postmodern indie remix culture, and neoliberalism. We are particularly interested in the means by which neoliberal capitalism and its manifestation with the discourse of creative economies legitimates the role of the cultural entrepreneur within brand culture, and the implications this has, both positive and negative, on artistic production and on consumer and artistic relationships to brand culture. Cultural entrepreneurship has taken on new dimensions in the past two decades, with an increasing number of artists and musicians moving seamlessly between making art, creating brands, running small businesses, and selling their cultural capital, all while working to retain their status as radical (sometimes street) artists. In this context, alternative bands liberally sell their music to advertising agencies, artists are designing ad campaigns for mainstream brands, and the typical ad man is expected to have his own indie band on the side.

Fairey and others like him epitomize what has been called by Richard Florida and others the "creative economy." The creative economy is celebrated by public planner Elizabeth Currid as "a fluid economy that allows creative industries to collaborate with one another, review each other's products, and offer jobs that cross-fertilize and share skill sets, whether it is an artist who becomes creative director for a fashion house or a graffiti artist who works for an advertising agency" (Currid 2007: 7). This flow between art that continues to define itself on the margins and the global capital networks of cultural entrepreneurs tells us something about how, and in what ways, brand culture has a particular kind of value in a neoliberal context. The framework of cultural entrepreneurship can help us to understand the construction of cultural competencies (with art and brands playing key roles) in neoliberal global capitalism. Within the changing relationship of culture and commerce, consumer participation is not simply (or even most importantly) indicated by purchases made but is rather signaled as brand affiliation, a connection which links brands to lifestyles, to politics, and even to social activism. Brand culture not only shapes consumer habits but also all forms of political, social, and civic participation, so that in the contemporary era, brands have become, in Adam Arvidsson's words, "immaterial, informational objects...they are part of the propertied ambience of media culture in which life unfolds" (Arvidsson 2006: 13). The concept of brands as ambience, and the idea that branding is the primary context for everyday living, raises the issue of how brand culture can serve as a force for progressive social change (or not). If brands are part of culture in which "life unfolds," what then does this "life" look like? How is it manifest?

The "Rise" of the Creative Economy

The definition of art within creative and romantic terms has depended historically on the ideological and aesthetic separation of the cultural realms of artistic creativity and commerce. Traditionally, art was defined as an avenue toward enlightenment, transcendence, and the sublime, with commerce set up as its opposite, defined by instrumental goals, those of rational governance and profit. This ideological separation has never accurately defined the relationship of art and commerce since its origins; artists have always been involved in collaboration with those industries and organizations that finance, distribute, and sell their work, and artistic creativity has been imbricated throughout its history in commercial interests, from simpler relationships such as the artist as apprentice and that of artists and art dealers to the much more complex market for books, music, television, and film (Caves 2000). Yet, even the radical critiques of the modernist avant-garde retained an idealistic and ideological distinction between art and commerce and art and branding. At the same time, the domain of marketing and advertising has always borrowed liberally from the domain of art, with early ad agencies hiring illustrators to make ads, using paintings in ads, and over the years working to appropriate the cultural capital of art into the world of branding. The signature of art has been a primary value that brand managers have strived for in the post-1960s era of advertising styles. In the contemporary era of style management, design and aesthetics have achieved a much higher focus in brand culture.

It goes without saying that in the contemporary moment, the traditional separation between art and commerce has not only been diminished but has lost its value. More importantly, one could argue that the strategies of brand culture have been easily incorporated into art in its postmodern phase, and that brand managers have successfully created the category of brand/ad as art. While the merging of brand culture and art has produced an increased ease with discourses of branding within the domain of art (as well as the constant reinvention of art forms at the margins), it has simultaneously dislodged, if not enabled, art's hold on the concept of creativity.

In the past twenty years, the idea of a creative economy has gained increasing visibility (and state validation). As both Nicholas Garnham and

David Hesmondhalgh have pointed out, in the United Kingdom there has been a move within government-funded institutions—marked in both vocabulary and directed resources—from the "cultural industries" to the "creative industries" (Garnham 2005; Hesmondhalgh 2007). In North America, Richard Florida's 2002 book *The Rise of the Creative Class* became a bestseller and a platform from which cities around the U.S. and Canada began new practices of urban planning that emphasized a "creative workforce," including an extensive process of gentrification and a celebration of those who productively channel their "innate creativity" as a line of work (Florida 2002). As many critics of this concept have noted, one result of the renewed focus on the creative class and industries has been the off-loading of state responsibilities to the individual, so that the state plays a smaller and smaller role in funding artistic and creative social services. This means that the state abdicates its role supporting wage-earning workers to focus instead on those "innately creative" individuals who effectively become "entrepreneurs" (and temporary laborers) in an economy that privileges individual self-employed and/or freelance labor.

In the creative economy, charting and measuring creativity becomes paramount. "Creative consultants" and brand managers are hired by city planners to produce a more creative city, which ostensibly then increases the value of a city in terms of actual revenue, tourist dollars, and reputation (Florida and others have been hired to consult with city planners to rebrand cities such as Des Moines and Toronto as newly energized and creative) (Peck 2005). Creativity is quantified and measured on scales such as Florida's "gay index" which sees the demographic of gays and lesbians as evidence of an open city, tolerant of lifestyles and amenable to creativity as an economic force. In the spring of 2009, Elizabeth Currid and Sarah Williams produced a study, "The Geography of Buzz: Art, Culture, and the Social Milieu in Los Angeles and New York," that "locates hot spots based on the frequency and draw of cultural happenings: film and television screenings, concerts, fashion shows, gallery and theater openings" (Ryzik 2009). The study used a "buzz-o-meter" to be able to "quantify and understand, visually and spatially, how this creative cultural scene really worked" (Ryzik 2009; Currid and Williams 2010). Creative autonomy, long considered historically to be in opposition to (and thus threatened by) market forces, is, within this economy, effectively organized and managed by market forces. This is especially salient in a creative economy that valorizes those works that are "buzz-worthy" due to media presence and attention. As Richard

Caves points out, "No wonder that a 'buzz'—a critical mass of favorable, or at least involved, discussion—is treasured among those who promote the sale of creative goods. It is also a check on them, because it mobilizes many involved persons' judgments on the worth of creative works that are the subject of serious promotional investments" (Caves 2000: 181). The value of "buzz"' is certainly not new to the contemporary era, but the shifting labor and organizational practices around creativity that characterize this era mean that "buzz" is no longer mundane gossip or overhyped opinions but a key factor in the exchange value and distribution of creative products.

For Florida, creativity means a whole range of activities and identities that intersect and relate to create a highly energized, productive economy: those who work in science and engineering are unproblematically positioned in Florida's work alongside artists, musicians, and other "culturally creative" people. Many scholars and cultural critics have critiqued Florida's concepts of the creative class and creative economy, arguing that it is simply a justification for bourgeois gentrification, rendering invisible the labor of immigrants and the working class within the fabric of contemporary cities (Peck 2005). Florida's bold proclamation that the "creative class" is rising is not theorized in terms of material or cultural inequalities, shifting labor relations or practices, or an increasingly immigrant service labor force.

In this context, creativity is essentially a brand; it is reified and transformed into an object that is marketed, distributed, and exchanged within the contemporary economy, and takes on a particular "value" as a lifestyle, policy, or set of politics. When creativity is itself organized as a kind of brand, it is effectively reconfigured through commodity fetishism so that its relationship to labor is effaced, and it is allied with broader social concepts and desires. In marketing expert Douglas Holt's account of "iconic brands," he insists that the most successful brands are those that connect with a particular social and cultural myth rather than attempt to connect with an individual consumer's desires: the successful, iconic brand, he argues, "is a historical entity whose desirability comes from myths that address the most important social tensions of a nation" (Holt 2004: 38). The concept of creativity as a brand addresses these kinds of tensions within contemporary culture. While "creativity" historically has represented something intangible, a unique property of particular individuals that cannot be exchanged on the marketplace like a can of soda or a pair of jeans, in the current political and cultural economy brands are no longer necessarily attached to specific commodities. Shepard Fairey as a creative brand, one that signifies street culture, savvy word play, and a pastiche of graphic image styles that signal dissent, packages a particular kind of creativity into market items for both art-world consumers and youthful skateboarders.

Creativity thus becomes something reconfigured and packaged as a way to accumulate profit. In the plans for creative cities, neighborhoods are designed around indexes of creativity, so that art galleries, coffee houses, theaters, and well-kept walkways indicate not only a safe neighborhood, but one where creativity attracts a particular class of people (namely, those who have the cultural and economic capital to visit art galleries and museums, spend time at coffee houses, etc.). It is worth noting that, in the context of the recent financial crisis, the really new creative city might be Detroit, where artists have (like generations of artists in other cities before them) begun to move into neighborhoods with foreclosed homes—cheap real estate being a key incentive to low-paid artistic production. This is one of the ironies of the Richard Florida model: cities which are successful in fostering creative bourgeois economies tend to be too expensive for all but the most successful artists to live and thus quickly become environments where creativity is signaled by branding and marketing, but actual artistic production is in short supply.

Creative Laborers, Entrepreneurs, and Neoliberal Capital

Brand culture and creative economies are both supported and maintained by the ethos of neoliberal capital. Indeed, Florida's notion of the creative class is an outgrowth of neoliberal capitalism and the discourse of the free-agent economy. In many ways, the idea of the "creative class" rejuvenates—and rebrands—the historical notion of a meritocracy, where those who are the most "creative" will find a place in this economy. The "merit" element of this rebranded meritocracy no longer relies so intimately on the familiar Horatio Alger-inspired narrative of hard work and unique intelligence; the contemporary meritocracy is instead predicated on how well one can "channel" one's innate creativity (with the assumption that all people are "creative"). However, the same constraints that shaped traditional notions of meritocracy, in which identity characteristics such as class, race, and gender were rendered invisible as determining factors in achieving "success," continue to shape the creative meritocracy. In her work on the contemporary art and fashion industries in London, Angela McRobbie argues that the transition from the cultural industries to the creative industries has meant, among other things, a "miserable hierarchy, which comprises of corporate winners at the top, artist-teachers in the middle, and all the others at the bottom, putting together a patchwork of careers." Laborers in the creative economy rely only or primarily on their individual talents; absent of any state or federal support for "creativity," with creative labor romanticized as "cool" and "artistic," creative laborers are designated as "agents of the neo-liberal order" (McRobbie 2004: 194).

Neoliberalism, according to David Harvey, is a reorganization not only of the state's role in the economy but also of other capitalist practices, such as the emergence of global markets for goods and services, the global networks of production that sustain these markets, and the various ways in which new technologies have been applied to every stage of the economic process, including manufacturing, financing, distribution, and exchange. This has resulted in not only the decentralization of production, but also in the reorganization of labor and markets, including changing labor patterns (such as the normalization of the itinerant laborer, flexible production, and a multiskilled labor force) (Harvey 2007; Schiller 2007). Within this economic context, postindustrial capitalist practices develop systems of production and distribution that respond to smaller niche groups of consumers in order to maximize profit and which are framed within a discourse of "individualism," "creativity," and "freedoms." The fact that these ideals continue to be shaped and defined by advertising and branding strategies is not considered problematic; rather, politics and consumerism, advertising and art, individualism and cultural entrepreneurship become the contours of culture. Shepard Fairey's artistic endeavors are a kind of logical outgrowth from this context; his skill at placing cultural critique, branding, and art dynamically side by side is not conceived of nor understood as an act of "culture jamming" or anticapitalist activism. Rather, his brand of rebellious creativity is precisely the kind nurtured by the restructuring of markets and culture within neoliberalism.

Thus, neoliberalism has required a re-imagining of not just economic transactions and resources but also of those practices and institutions that had traditionally not been considered in economic terms, such as social and individual relations, emotion, social action, and creativity. It is not simply that neoliberalism has "taken over" these realms of life that hitherto had been understood in noncapitalist terms or in noncapitalist spaces, but that society and culture are reorganized under neoliberalism, so that "the social good will be maximized by maximizing the reach and frequency of market transactions, and it seeks to bring all human action into the domain of the market" (Harvey 2007: 3). This, of course, includes creativity—evidenced by the "outsourcing" of Florida's and other consultants' and managers' labor in rebranding cities and their denizens as creative.

If creativity is a resource and a commodity within neoliberal creative economies, who then is the creative laborer of neoliberalism? The neoliberal creative economy, with its "flexible" workforce and increasingly itinerant laborers, obfuscates divisions of labor—especially in terms of those who remain in low-paid service jobs. Celebratory rhetoric about the "new" consumer who is also a creative producer (rhetoric that comes not only from advertising and marketing but also from intellectuals who see new possibilities in a changing technoscape) needs to be interrogated: what, exactly, is the consumer producing? As Jamie Peck argues,

> Both the script and the nascent practices of urban creativity are peculiarly well suited to entrepreneurialized and neoliberalized urban landscapes. They provide a means to intensify and publicly subsidize urban consumption systems for a circulating class of gentrifiers, whose lack of commitment to place and whose weak community ties are perversely celebrated... this amounts to a process of public validation for favored forms of consumption and for a privileged class of consumers (Peck 2005: 764).

It is the case, of course, that the creative *laborer* seems to be missing from the "creative class," except as a glorified, highly stylized "entrepreneur" like Shepard Fairey. Indeed, the "laborer," historically defined as someone who works for wages, or as an unskilled person who does work for skilled workers in a particular trade, is dependent on an organized system of labor, revolving around state-defined wages, trade unions, and so on. The entrepreneur, in contrast, is understood as an ambitious individual, dependent on no one but him/herself, a person who "owns" his or her own labor and is thus accountable for not only profit but risks accumulated by this labor. Fairey, not only through his creative artistic productions but also in his position as someone who takes on the risks of "bucking the system" —or at least the system's policies on the use of public space—occupies the subject position of the creative laborer. His multiple arrests, his play with politics and art, and his audacious, independent, "street" attitude read as a well-crafted script for the cultural entrepreneur. The entrepreneur is at the center of the creative economy, indicating, as Peck argues, that only a particular, privileged class of consumers/producers has a place within the creative economy. This creative entrepreneur is celebrated and romanticized because of the kind of work ostensibly produced: no gritty, industrial products that workers care nothing about (but which are, of course, still necessary for all capitalist industries), but rather artistic and innovative expressions of inner creativity, products which workers care intensely about, with passion driving the production process rather than a mind-numbing need for minimum wage.

Andrew Ross sees this creative class as the "precariat," comprised of workers whose precarious and itinerant labor is romanticized and needs to be understood within the context of the market and compensated labor, rather than mystified as outside the market (and thus denied the rights within it) (Ross 2009). As McRobbie notes about the transition from the "cultural industries" to the "creative industries," "creativity" is mobilized as a particular kind of incentive that works to lessen government's role in social and cultural services. That is, self-employment is romanticized as a lucrative career option: "Set up your own business. Be free to do your own thing. Live and work like an artist…We can now extend this to suggest that artists' ways of earning a living become a model for livelihoods, as well as lifestyle. This is the logic of 'everyone is creative'" (McRobbie 2004: 189).

The brand culture that sustains the creative class and produces creativity as a brand thus has as its signature a retooled producer/consumer relationship. Within this relationship, consumers become producers in a context that is given both ideological and material support through "new" technological formats and market forces. The creative class is comprised not only of professionals who are paid for their creative labor but also of "creative amateurs," encouraged to be "empowered" by the flexibility and openness of new technological formats and expanded markets. Capitalist practices have been retooled in efforts to reach these new creative amateurs, involving shifted marketing strategies of engagement, authenticity, and creativity. This retooling has led to, among other things, an intensified practice of "stealth advertising," guerilla marketing tactics (including practices like street art), and a focus on user-generated content, where consumers participate in the development of a brand through online competitions, creating videos and advertising for television and other media on personal web pages on social networking sites. Thus, YouTube culture allows anyone with access to the web to disseminate their "amateur" videos to potentially wide audiences and thousands spend countless (unpaid) hours doing so; do-it-yourself (DIY) production has created networks of crafts and other workers who sell their handmade wares through the web, and consumers can even insert their own picture into Fairey's HOPE poster on the Obamicon.me web site, to create their own personal poster and brand (and, not incidentally, to personalize an iconic image in an era in which the personalized commodity is a key marketing device).

Garnham argues that we need to interrogate the policy decisions that mobilized this shift: the shift from state to market in the U.K. is "a reinforcement of 'economic' and 'managerial' language and patterns of thought within cultural and media policy" (Garnham 2005: 16). Garnham's point, along with Ross's, is that it is not so much that "creativity" is lauded and rewarded in new ways in the contemporary political economy but rather that the economic practices that have characterized more traditional forms of labor, such as the denial of labor rights and managerial policies, have shifted to incorporate an expanded realm of creative labor. Yet, the ideological dimensions of creativity—as a passionate pursuit of innovation, as an innate individual characteristic, or as a skill that is somehow outside the field of commerce—continue to define the process of creative labor, resulting in a relentlessly individualist kind of work, absent of any kind of state governance, such as workplace protection, job security, healthcare, and so on. A familiar mystique thus surrounds the creative laborer, even as neoliberal infrastructures precisely provide the context for the creation and nurturing of this mystique. Peck critiques: "As Florida counsels: 'We cannot know in advance who the next Andy Warhol, Billie Holiday, Paul Allen, or Jimi Hendrix will be, or where he or she will come from'; yet it would appear to be a racing certainty that these as-yet unborn supercreatives will want to live in Austin, TX, or somewhere very much like it. And they will likely ride into town by mountain bike" (Peck 2005: 762). One could easily add Shepard Fairey to Florida's list of creatives as an artist whose individualism and promiscuity within cultural realms add to a broader romantic construction of the creative entrepreneur.

Most creative laborers do not uncritically embrace the intersections and collapses between creativity and commerce. Rather, as Hesmondhalgh argues, many creative workers emphasize an attitude of "ambivalence" toward creative work; the historical opposition between creativity and commerce is maintained, but creative labor is how creative workers make a living, so there must be compromises. As Hesmondhalgh shows, there is a great deal of anxiety and insecurity about pay in the creative economy—the romantic construction of "living on the edge" doesn't go too far in paying bills, particularly in the midst of an economic downturn (Hesmondhalgh 2007). The ostensible autonomy of creative labor—that one can, in Florida's concept, channel innate human creativity to make a living doing what one loves and be intellectually fulfilled—is seen here as a kind of control mechanism, in which the overly romanticized notion of "creative autonomy" and the cultural entrepreneur obfuscates the actual material realities of neoliberal capitalism.

Shepard Fairey—and his success as an artist—can be understood within this economy, as the practices and logics that comprise current notions of "creativity" mobilize his identity as a cultural entrepreneur. Fairey epitomizes this intersection of the marketing-inspired "creative class," and the creative laborer—a street artist who has successfully branded himself, sells his brand as commodities, and regularly does commercial ad campaigns while using his brand for various political causes such as environmentalism and human rights. These different components of Fairey's creative labor do not stand in contrast or opposition to each other—some political, others commercial—but rather form complementary elements of the overall "brand" of Shepard Fairey. As he has stated, "I think to have these very impractical delineations between art, design, what's keeping it real, and what's commercial, is not very psychologically healthy for most artists and designers…it's just a reality that rather than being apologetic about it, we've put together a group of people who actually thrive on that overlap" (Beer 2008).

Fairey's success is evidence of the ways that cultural capital trickles upward in the neoliberal creative economy, in which the cultural capital of the street (and being arrested on the street is defined as a badge of marginal status that has market value) is invaluable in the world of mainstream branding. Yet Fairey's negotiation of these potential contradictions demonstrates a discourse that is decidedly different from the tortured defenses that artists once used to claim they weren't selling out. He subtitles his massive coffee-table book "Supply and Demand," he remakes dollar bills, and he talks constantly of flexibility, a key buzz word of the neoliberal creative economy and its redefinition of work. Indeed, his continued work in support of Barack Obama demonstrates how he negotiates these potential contradictions: the August 20, 2009, cover of *Rolling Stone* magazine features a new Shepard Fairey portrait of Obama, a more sober and ambivalent depiction than his HOPE posters. Using the same red, white, and blue color palette as the HOPE poster, Obama is shown on the *Rolling Stone* cover looking stern and determined, surrounded by what appears to be a halo of stars and the question: "Will he take bold action or compromise too easily?" Fairey claims his inspiration for the illustration was in part Gilbert Stuart's portrait of George Washington, which became the basis for the engraving on the dollar bill, situating Obama among other significant U.S. presidents (as well as the connection with presidents and official forms of currency), and also "to say the jury's still out on whether this President will live up to his promise" (Kennedy 2009).

This play between validating mainstream politics and policy while simultaneously using art to ask questions about those politics and policy is a hallmark of Fairey's work. When Fairey argues for the right to poster the streets with his Obey Giant poster messages, he does so not through a radical discourse about the street as a public space that should be decommercialized but rather through the discourse of a taxpayer's rights: "I became active as a street artist because I felt public space was the only option for free speech and expression without bureaucracy...I also found the whole idea that you could be arrested for stickering or postering as something I wanted to rebel against. In my opinion, the taxpayers are the bosses of the government. I'm a taxpayer—why can't I use public space for my imagery when corporations can use it for theirs?" (Heller 2009: 94). Though Fairey likes to refer to his relationship to corporate capitalism as an "inside/outside strategy" with a "Robin Hood effect," and, as we noted, his reputation as an artist of the street is crucial to his value as an artist, he also stakes out the position that "capitalism is a way for hard work to yield rewards" (Heller 2009: 97). It is precisely the context of creative economies and neoliberalism that allows such comments to seem complementary rather than contradictory. It is also the case that Fairey's style has been enormously effective in creating these boundary-crossings between the street and the mainstream.

Postmodern Style and Creative Copyright

The intersection of the ethos of a neoliberal economy with the ethos of a creative economy is a key feature of a current brand culture that thrives not only on the fluid and flexible relationship of branding processes and cultural production but also on a postmodern aesthetics of remix, mashup, and pastiche culture. Style is a key feature of brand culture, and the dislodging of style from content (in particular, political content) is a key aspect of postmodern style. This raises interesting questions about the relationship of postmodern style in both art and branding to neoliberalism, a context in which Fairey's work can be seen as emblematic. Fairey's work as cultural entrepreneur cannot be separated from this aesthetic (or style), one that resonated so powerfully in the case of his Obama poster that it can be seen as indicating a new kind of national aesthetic in the United States (Sturken 2009).

Of all of Fairey's work, the Obama poster has had the most influence and been the most successful at circulating in cultural domains beyond branding and street art. The poster has been phenomenally popular, spawning not only many imitators but also a significant number of second-generation references. For instance, during the 2009 upheavals protesting the Iranian election, images of the young woman Neda Agha-Soltan, whose on-camera death created a martyr and icon of the struggle, were remade in the style of Fairey's poster and circulated on the Web. The Fairey poster uses many conventions of U.S. political advocacy, deploying the cliché of celebrity and political affirmation in its image of a leader looking off toward an imagined horizon. Yet, the poster effectively recodes its political discourse in a way that aims to interpellate viewers who are adept at reading style as a form of reference. It thus marks a dramatic shift in American political aesthetics. The colors of the image reference the red, white, and blue of American patriotism (each color is slightly off the traditional patriotic palette), thus playing with the codes of the flag. The image evokes the patterned lines of newsprint that signify Bolshevik agitprop political posters run off a modern press. The poster, in fact, signals in all its aspects a reference to a previous style and plays with the conventional codes of political postering at all levels. The original poster was created by Fairey to advocate for the campaign; it was then transformed into several official campaign versions with different slogans and was later adapted by Fairey into a White House–sanctioned Inauguration Day poster. One version of the poster formed the template for a Fairey-produced *Time* magazine cover, and the HOPE poster was then acquired by the Smithsonian for the National Portrait Gallery. That a new kind of cultural aesthetic could infiltrate official national culture so quickly was one of the most remarkable aspects of the poster's trajectory (it's worth remembering that most U.S. political aesthetics have been within the realm of kitsch and that the Bush White House's aesthetic was decidedly cowboy kitsch). Fairey's accomplishment in creating a poster that exemplifies a contemporary postmodern aesthetic of pastiche that always operates at more than one level was not remarkable within the context of street postering and branding that he normally occupies. Yet, its movement into the much more conventional political context was.

Fairey has a much longer history of playing with the codes of political posters. He creates posters quickly, often producing many versions of images and posting weekly versions on his website for his fan base. This can create a sense of repetition (and the critique that he is redundant, however Warholesque he may be) when his work is seen in museum retrospectives and fine art catalogues. Much of this poster work has deployed pastiche and remake as strategies. Fairey produced a series of posters of political figures such as Angela Davis, Che Guevara, and Lenin (as well as posters of cultural figures like Sid Vicious, Jimi Hendrix, and Bob Marley) by remaking famous images in a mix of historical poster styles. Here, Fairey can easily be situated in the broader context of postmodern remix-remash culture, much of which combines the work of professionals (mashup music) and the so-called amateurs of YouTube culture. It is important to note here the potential disconnection between style and political effect that such work can produce. Fairey plays loosely with the images of political figures and, more importantly, with styles associated with political art, in ways that have sometimes prompted criticism. It could be fairly argued that his use of Soviet styles of graphic postering for much of his work reduces such styles to mere graphics in ways that render their political form into free-floating signifiers easily attached to brands. Again, the "manifesto" for Fairey's Obey Giant company references this kind of free-floating signifier, insisting on the consumer's semiotic labor: "The [OBEY] sticker has no meaning but exists only to cause people to react, to contemplate and search for meaning in the sticker. Because OBEY has no actual meaning, the various reactions and interpretations of those who view it reflect their personality and the nature of their sensibilities" (Fairey 2009).

Fairey is not unique in playing with those graphic styles that rose out of Marxism. Constructionist graphic styles have a long history of appropriation (prompting art critic Hal Foster to criticize the "fetishizing of Constructivism" in the 1980s) (Burgoyne 2008). Even the *Communist Manifesto* itself was repackaged and rebranded on its 150th anniversary into a stylish version designed by Komar and Melamid, one that, it was quipped at the time, could easily be tucked into a Prada purse. However, Fairey has been particularly successful in using these styles to marry brand culture and progressive political positions with a dose of irony. Fairey's 2009 Saks Fifth Avenue campaign features a model with a raised fist evoking Socialist Realist art (and the slogan "Arm yourself with a slouchy bag") and shopping bags emblazoned with "Want It!" all designed with a Rodchenko-style Constructionist aesthetic of red and black. It's worth noting that Fairey has quite effectively deployed the modern reproductive media of stickers and screen printing as means to produce large numbers of posters, which he releases regularly in limited editions to his fans. The styles he borrows and venues he uses have thus been largely modern—billboards, screen printing—rather than digital.

This style is thus one that defines itself through its derivative quality. Fairey's work thrives on the repetitive, redundant effect of modern posters run off a press and uses style as both shaping mechanism and reference. The reference to the original style is its defining feature. Fairey's appropriative strategies, which have been particularly effective examples of this style, show us the ways that brand culture is itself a space of ongoing recirculating appropriation, to the extent to which the derivative can be seen as the essential quality of postmodern branding strategies. The network and circulation are what matter rather than the uniqueness of the thing itself.

In remix pastiche culture with its borrowing, citing, and intertextual meaning, copyright and the ownership of images and ideas are often read as old economy rather than new. In the context of postmodern style and within the context of an open source–creative commons ethos of new media, ownership is a contradictory status of shifting positions. In brand culture, similarly, it is possible for consumers to easily see themselves as brands and for them to have highly affective relationships to brands—less within the terms of the ownership of a commodity and more within the terms of identification and incorporation. The integration of postmodern styles into brand culture, ironically, fits neatly with the discourse of creative commons and open source on the Web and with the discourses of the creative economy flexibility that define creative labor as potentially free and open.

Shepard Fairey's struggles with the ownership of public spaces, which have resulted in his constant arrest, have also extended to his appropriative imaging techniques. In the art world, this has produced the criticism of his style as too derivative to be rewarded museum-world status. In the context of political postering, it produced the now well-known lawsuit in which the Associated Press sued Fairey in February 2009 for copyright infringement. Until recently, Fairey had always claimed that he did not know the original source of the photograph that he used as the image template for his Obama poster, one of thousands that were taken of the then-candidate and countless campaign events. It affirms Fairey's position that it took many months for someone to track the image down. To add to the messiness and complicated tensions involved in contemporary copyright and fair use legal battles, at the time of writing, Fairey has now admitted that he was "mistaken" about which photograph he actually used for reference in the HOPE poster and has released a public statement in which he admits that "he sent false images and deleted other images to conceal his mistake" (this admission has added an even more dramatic element to the ongoing fair use legal battle between Fairey and the Associated Press, and the outcome of the case has yet to be determined) (Ng 2009). Regardless of recent changes in the fair use case, AP filed the case after the poster demonstrated significant success in the market: it became a hot commodity, selling out of all copies, with a commemorative edition acquired by the National Portrait Gallery. AP claimed that Fairey had unfairly used a photograph taken by Manny Garcia, a photographer who was contracted to AP at the time he took the image; Garcia responded by stating that he was honored by Fairey's use of the image and that it was not covered by his AP contract. Fairey responded by claiming "fair use" of the original photograph and countersuing AP. He stated:

> I am fighting the AP to protect the rights of all artists, especially those with a desire to make art with social commentary. This is about artistic freedom and basic rights of free expression, which need to be available to all, whether they have money and lawyers or not. I created the Obama image as a grassroots tool solely to help Obama get elected president. The image worked due to many complex variables. If I could do it all over again, I would not change anything about the process, because that could change the outcome (Fairey 2009).

Fairey is basing his case on the way in which his poster is a "transformative" work of the original photograph, which was taken as one of many hundreds of news photos of the candidate. As Jonathan Melber has written, Fairey "set out to make an image for a political campaign: something that would inspire people to support a presidential candidate and symbolize their hope. He was creating something aspirational, not descriptive; his message was subjective opinion, not objective fact" (Melber 2009). Initially, Fairey was represented by the Stanford Law School's Fair Use Project, founded by Lawrence Lessig, organizer of Creative Commons, and directed by Tony Falzone.

The AP case and its focus on copyright and the ownership of a particular image represent one of the ways that Fairey's creativity and postmodern style can be thought of as a kind of brand. The case revolves around issues of private property—who has rights to a particular image, who owns it, and who can profit from it (Edelman 1979)? Creativity, in this context, is an object within the law, susceptible to appropriation, sale, and contracts. In this same context, however, it also symbolizes the creative autonomy of an artist, something much less tangible, ostensibly not intended for profit and the logics of merchandising. The contradictions contained within the branding of creativity are demonstrated by Fairey's response to AP: Fairey's legal team issued a response to AP's accusations in April 2009, which denied most of the claims made by AP and included several photographs and art works (including Fairey's own as well as some by Jeff Koons, Banksy, and Keith Haring) found on the AP website, claiming that AP did not have permission to use those images. While Fairey maintains that he did not include those images to charge AP with a violation but simply to point out the inconsistency in the case, the back-and-forth between AP and Fairey raises some important issues for creative labor in the creative economy (Fairey 2009). In particular, the Fairey "fair use" case signals residual tensions between a historical opposition between commerce and creativity (or, more specifically, art) that are obfuscated within the contemporary creative economy. Fairey has in the past sent "cease and desist" letters to artists producing work with the "OBEY" slogan, notably to the CafePress store about a work by Larkin Werner entitled Steelerbaby (Sherwin 2009). Obey Giant contended that the merchandise involving the word "obey" was an infringement on his trademark. (Werner claims that his use of "obey" was not inspired by Shepard Fairey; since the letters were exposed in the blogosphere and Fairey filed his AP lawsuit, they have been rescinded.) While such skirmishes have created an active blogosphere discussion, they raise broader issues related to creative labor and creative commons values.

The ethos that defines creative workers as anyone with the know-how to channel their inner creativity is thus supported and legitimated by labor practices that are characteristic of the neoliberal era, practices that suggest the coexistence of and intersection between creative activity and exploitation, as Marc Andrejevic (2008: 25) observes. These claims of copyright infringement, fair use, and trademark violation are complex and contradictory precisely because of this environment. If creative workers all espouse an ethos of creative commons and open source, who will pay the bills? As Peck argues:

> Discourses of urban creativity seek to normalize flexible labor-market conditions, lionizing a class of workers that can not only cope with, but positively revel in, this environment of persistent insecurity and intense, atomized competition, just as they

> enforce modes of creative governmentality based on compulsory individualism, compulsory innovation, compulsory performativity and productiveness, compulsory valorization of the putatively new (Peck 2005: 764–65).

In one sense, Shepard Fairey and the rise of the creative, cultural entrepreneur can be understood as part of a larger commercial endeavor, where the branding of creativity demonstrates some of the latest business maneuvers in an increasingly competitive urban youth market. However, Fairey's work, and its enthusiastic reception, also prompt questions about how and in what ways branding strategies have expanded beyond conventional marketing and into lifestyles, identities, and culture. Moreover, beyond merely encroaching into new domains, they suggest reshaping and reimagining of these domains such that it is more accurate to think not of branding expanding into culture but of branding *as* culture itself.

In an era when the "Obama brand" is part of everyday parlance due in no small part to Fairey's work, debates over the line between art and advertising or authenticity and commercialism seem tired and passé. It becomes pressing instead to ask questions about what cultural and critical significance the brand has in contemporary capitalism. Shepard Fairey's body of work demonstrates the importance of taking into account the complexities of consumer identity, affect, and desire when discussing alternative systems of consumption. We are less interested in the contradictions at work in Shepard Fairey the artist than we are in what he represents about the complex contradictions of cultural entrepreneurship at large: both the potential for social activism to thrive under the guise of consumerism and for artists and workers to be incorporated in new yet similarly disabling ways into the workplaces and work lives fostered by neoliberalism. Fairey's model of anti-consumerist cultural entrepreneurship rejects the discourse of Naomi Klein's *No Logo* with its binary of consumerism and social activism and thus makes a kind of sense within a neoliberal context. Fairey's success in maintaining a pose of rebellion while working the marketplace, the art world, and the street can be seen in a different light than, for instance, the success of corporations such as Nike in selling themselves as rebels while dominating the marketplace. In his aesthetic of the derivative, his playful negotiation of capital, he exemplifies a creative generation that has effectively created a new meaning of the brand.

It is easy to critique Fairey's position; the challenge is to take its implications seriously. Indeed, interrogating the relationships between politics, individual identity, and consumer culture seems particularly urgent in the U.S.

today, where questions include: What is it about the contemporary neoliberal context that makes Fairey and his body of artwork not only intelligible, but perfectly logical? What are the conceptual, institutional, and economic apparatuses that have been advanced, embraced, and made normative in the contemporary cultural economy—the "creative" economy—that appeal to our intuitions and affect, that tap into desire, that simultaneously re-imagine and re-affirm values? How does brand culture support and legitimate these conceptual apparatuses? And, if nothing else, a focus on Fairey's Obama poster and the power it achieved should remind us of the potential of these new forms of cultural entrepreneurship to inspire new ways of thinking. This poster has, in essence, changed the aesthetic of American political and patriotic culture. That is no small thing.

References

Andrejevic, Marc. 2008. "Watching Television Without Pity: The Productivity of Online Fans." *Television & New Media* 9 (1): 24–46.

Arvidsson, Adam. 2006. *Brands: Meaning and Value in Media Culture.* New York: Routledge.

Beer, Jeff. 2008. "Shepard Fairey Has a Posse." *Creativity*, November.

Burgoyne, Patrick. 2008. "Constructivism: The Ism That Just Keeps Givin'." August 7. http://www.creativereview.co.uk/crblog/constructivism-the-ism-that-just-keeps-givin/

Caves, Richard E. 2000. *Creative Industries: Contracts Between Art and Commerce.* Cambridge, MA: Harvard University Press.

Currid, Elizabeth. 2007. *The Warhol Economy: How Fashion, Art, and Music Drive New York City.* Princeton, NJ: Princeton University Press.

Currid, Elizabeth, and Sarah Williams. 2010. "The Geography of Buzz: Art, Culture and the Social Milieu in Los Angeles and New York." *Journal of Economic Geography* 10 (3): 423–451.

Edelman, Bernard. 1979. *Ownership of the Image: Elements for a Marxist Theory of Law.* London: Routledge.

Fairey, Shepard. 1990. "Manifesto." http://obeygiant.com/articles/manifesto

———. 2009. "Shepard Fairey vs Associated Press." http://obeygiant.com/headlines/ the-ap-obama-referencing

Florida, Richard. 2002. *The Rise of the Creative Class and How It's Transforming Work, Leisure, Community, and Everyday Life.* New York: Basic Books.

Garnham, Nicholas. 2005. "From Cultural to Creative Industries." *International Journal of Cultural Policy* 11 (1): 15–29.

Goodnough, Abby. 2009. "Boston Vandalism Charges Stir Debate on Art's Place," *New York Times*, March 12. http://www.nytimes.com/2009/03/12/arts/design/12boston.html?_r=1&scp=9&sq=shepard+fairey&st=nyt

Harvey, David. 2007. *A Brief Introduction to Neoliberalism.* New York: Oxford University Press.

Heller, Steven. 2009. "Still Obeying after All These Years: Steven Heller Interviews Shepard Fairey." In Shepard Fairey et al., *Obey: Supply and Demand—The Art of Shepard Fairey.* 2nd Edition. Berkeley, CA: Gingko Press.

Hesmondhalgh, David. 2007. *The Cultural Industries*, 2nd Edition. London: Sage.
Holt, Douglas B. 2004. *How Brands Become Icons: The Principles of Cultural Branding*. Cambridge, MA: Harvard Business School Press.
Kennedy, Helen. 2009. "Shepard Fairey-designed Obama Portrait on Cover of *Rolling Stone* Deifies, Questions President." *New York Daily News*, August 6.
McRobbie, Angela. 2004. "'Everyone is Creative': Artists as Pioneers of the New Economy?" Pp. 186–199 in *Contemporary Culture and Everyday Life*, ed. Elizabeth Silva and Tony Bennett. New York: Routledge.
Melber, Jonathan. 2009. "The AP Has No Case against Shepard Fairey." *Huffington Post*, February 8. http://www.huffingtonpost.com/jonathan-melber/the-ap-hase-no-case-again_b_165068.html
Ng, David. 2009. "AP Accuses Shepard Fairey of More Lying." *Los Angeles Times*, October 20. http://LATimesblogs.latimes.com/culturemonster/2009/10/ap-accuses -shepard-fairey-of-purposeful-deception.html
Peck, Jamie. 2005. "Struggling with the Creative Class." *International Journal of Urban and Regional Research* 29 (4): 740–770.
Ross, Andrew. 2009. *Nice Work If You Can Get It: Life and Labor in Precarious Times*. New York: New York University Press.
Ryzik, Melena. 2009. "Mapping the Cultural Buzz: How Cool Is That?" *New York Times*, April 6.
Schiller, Dan. 2007. *How to Think About Information*. Champaign: University of Illinois Press.
Sherwin, Brian. 2009. "Disobey Shepard Fairey." *Myartspace.com*, March 8. http://www.myartspace.com/blog/2009/03/disobey-shepard-fairey.html
Sturken, Marita. 2009. "The New Aesthetics of Patriotism." *Journal of Visual Culture* 8 (2): 10–14.

CHAPTER THIRTEEN

Strange Powers

The Branded Sensorium and the Intrigue of Musical Sound[1]

Devon Powers

One of the standout pairings of music and advertising in recent years occurred when Apple—a company that has been called the "Oprah Winfrey" of independent music (Lee 2008)—featured in a 2007 iPod commercial the song "1-2-3-4" by the little-known Canadian artist Leslie Feist. The song relies on the reedy warmth of Feist's voice, which dots the melody like a pointillist applying paint to a canvas; a growing cascade of instruments, clapping hands, and other voices enliven the tune's delightfully rich hues. In the commercial, the song's video plays on the screen of an iPod Nano, and when a hand reaches into the frame to snatch it away, another iPod in a different color takes its place. Again and again, multiracial hands remove multicolored iPods, as Feist sings on, the lilt of the melody played out in a sweet choreography of colorfully clad backup dancers. When the ad ends with the tagline, "A Little Video for Everyone," it's difficult not to feel cheered. Adorable song, adorable commercial, adorable device: a triumph for all in what, to all appearances, seemed to be an exquisite union.

Just how exquisite? That would become apparent in the ensuing months. Consecrated by Apple via its ad agency, TBWA/Media Arts Lab—by that time lauded for striking visuals and hip musical choices—the commercial proved to be a brilliant promotional vehicle for the singer, exposing her to a massive audience. In the wake of the commercial's debut, Nielsen's BuzzMetrics noted an increase of "triple digit percentages" in discussions about Feist online, with single sales of the song jumping a whopping 586 percent (Paoletta 2007; High and Sutherland 2008). An April 2008 feature in the U.K's *Guardian* newspaper noted that the commercial "turned the '1-2-3-4' video into a global phenomenon," which by then had logged more than eight million YouTube views (Petridis 2008). Popular enthusiasm merged with critical praise when "1-2-3-4" landed in the top five of the *Village Voice's* long-running year-end critics' poll; by spring 2008, the singer had received four American Grammy nominations and won five Canadian Juno awards (Stevenson 2008; Lederman 2008). *Advertising Age* also named "1-2-3-4" the best ad song of 2007, declaring that "with corporate radio more irrelevant than ever...Apple was nimble enough to pluck this one up first" (Moran 2007).

Considered from the vantage point of music/advertising partnerships, Feist's success might be exceptional, but it is far from anomalous. As artists increasingly seek out television as a new avenue for exposure in a cacophonous and competitive musical marketplace, those who might once have forbidden the licensing of their music for advertisements have come to embrace such agreements (Elliot 2009; Taylor 2007; Klein 2009; Wyman 2007; see also Banet-Weiser and Sturken in this volume). At the same time, as the Feist/Apple example clearly demonstrates, brands that take risks on undiscovered artists have much to gain, since thoughtful choices can provide priceless publicity and credible, organic brand equity. If it is true that advertising is "the new radio" (Barhard and Rutledge 2009), we must keep in mind that radio has a dual purpose: it broadcasts music to would-be consumers and organizes those listeners into demographics. When advertising takes on radio's functions, another goal joins these traditional purposes—to imbue the experiences and emotional associations of music with brand awareness. As Taylor (2007) suggests, this is also a promotional act for the agency and its client, since if advertising can make "an obscure band into a hit, their taste and perspicacity would make them look good to their potential customers" (241).[2]

More than the shrewd selection of an up-and-coming artist, Apple's use of Feist also signaled a faith in the mnemonic promise of "1-2-3-4" and the fit of Feist's sound with Apple and its Nano. Though the song deviates somewhat from the standard verse-chorus form that has dominated pop music since the early twentieth century (Suisman 2009: 50), it is a departure that arguably reinforces, rather than undermines, its memorability. After the introduction, three distinct musical sections of four bars each repeat over the course of the song, building as the song moves towards its close. Its structure can be described like this:

Intro A B C A' B' C A" A" (8 bars each) C C Outro

At the moderate pace of about 116 beats per second, each section is rather short, about eight seconds. The 30-second iPod spot skips the intro to move directly through sections A, B, and C, so that by the end, a listener has gotten a taste of the entire song. The A section (with the lyrics "one two three four/ tell me that you love me more/ sleepless, long nights/ that was what my youth was for") uses only two notes; the B and C sections follow a straightforward, D major scale. Thanks to careful editing, the song announces its title twice during the commercial (once in the opening line quoted above, and again in the last line she sings before the commercial ends) and its theme, romantic relationships, is safe, common, and relatable. It's hardly a wonder, then, that music journalists regularly commented that this concoction proved tremendously catchy, likening the song to a "nursery rhyme" (Tyrangiel 2007) or describing it variously as "three minutes of summery euphoria" (Banks 2007); "about as captivating as pop music can get" (Petridis 2008); and a "mind [sticker]" that was an "addictively bouncy nugget" (Stevens 2007). Apple agreed: to wit, the company followed the "1-2-3-4" spot with a MacBook ad in January 2008 that featured Yael Naim's "New Soul," which one journalist identified as "another bit of winsome, sing-song pop sung by a sultry-voiced young songbird who sounds suspiciously like Feist" (Rayner 2008). Apple has continued to use bubbly, major-key pop songs by unknown bands with female vocalists in its Nano commercials, including "Bruises" by Chairlift in 2008 and "Bourgeois Shangri-La" by Miss Li in 2009—a testament to the fact that Feist's irresistible sonic appeal aided Apple not just in moving product but also in clarifying its sonic identity.

These points bring me to my central argument: While the increasing intimacy between popular music and advertising has been discussed in scholarly literature in terms of whether it augments or depletes the value of music as art or culture (Klein 2008, 2009; Allan 2005; Frank 1998), less frequently discussed is what it indicates for music *as sound*—that is, music as a medium founded on aurality rather than visuality. Music's aural elements make it more than simply another commodity; instead, music holds unique sensory qualities that are consumed by the ear, implicating the physical sense of hearing as well the social act of listening. As branding is increasingly directed beyond promotional activities such as advertising, marketing, and design to encompass experience itself (Moor 2003, 2007), the significance of music within branding demands an understanding of why music is endowed with the power to brand.

Music is deeply ingrained in the phenomenology of consumerism, both as an affective component of the experience of consumption but also as a "space" in which consumption happens. In her analysis of "new marketing" techniques and the assimilation of consumer experience as "both the object and the medium of brand activity" (2003: 42), Moor identifies musical events such as sponsored concerts as essential sites where brand managers attempt to steep their clients' products in emotion-rich experiences. Further, she notes that "the addition of music to the mundane can move us beyond the here-and-now into a space of private fantasy or nostalgia; like the brand itself, it can move us backwards or forwards in time, coordinating the activities of the present with those of an imagined past or future" (Moor 2003: 54). Likewise, in his ethnomusicology of malls, Sterne (1997) asserts that "the idea of music pervading quasi-public commercial spaces is the height of banality," since music is taken for granted among the "flows" that manifest spaces of capitalist activity; a retail space such as a mall or a store may use music to reflect its character as well as to attract sought-after consumers and pace their buying (23, 25, 29–32). Music, then, has the capacity not only to create and sustain brand meaning but also to serve as a metaphor for brand activity itself. Arvidsson (2006) writes that the brand is "a kind of platform that anticipates certain kinds of actions and attachments" and "part of the propertied ambience of media culture in which life unfolds" (7–8; 13); the same observations hold true for music.

I argue in this chapter that the rise of sonic branding and, specifically, the use of music as a core element extends music more deeply into consumerism's phenomenology; to do so, it relies on a number of interlocking, longstanding assumptions about the power of musical sound[3] and the physiology of hearing. The first assumption is that musical sound is a natural, universal language that trades on bodily, rather than mental, experience. The second assumption follows closely: the sounds of music are a vector of pure affect, a direct and untroubled way to access, trigger, and control emotional states. Third, music is a sonic "science," a code which can be unlocked and exploited. After a brief discussion of the historical foundations for these assumptions, I will showcase how this trio of assumptions is manifested within the discourse on sonic branding found in books, the trade press, and on sonic branding firm websites. Buoyed by (yet only partially inscribed within) neuroscientific, musicological, and philosophical discourses about the power of music, these notions suggest that sonic branders are attracted to music because it is heard uncritically—some might even say it *cannot* be heard critically. I argue that the union of these perspectives not only legitimates sonic branding as a new form of expertise for the management of musical sound but also has important implications for sensory experience.

This chapter seeks to expand upon inquiries into the experiential aspects of branding through identifying sound, specifically musical sound, as a major, underexamined aspect of a brand's identity. My perspective on these matters borrows from those of musicology, ethnomusicology, anthropology, and popular music studies to fit into what has come to be known as sound studies. Following Scott (2009) in his observations about sound studies, this move toward the sonic is "not about rejecting the visual in favor of the aural, but about recovering, recuperating, and incorporating neglected aurality" (Scott 2009: 2). The sound of a brand is not simply an addendum to its visuality but is rather a multifaceted terrain of value worthy of consideration on its own terms—a fact that brand advisers are increasingly recognizing as they move toward thinking of brands not just as multimedia but also as multisensory. If, as Howes (2005) argues, "consumer capitalism has...increasingly made it its business to engage as many senses as possible in its drive for product differentiation and the distraction/seduction of the consumer" (288), the sonic aspects of the emergent branded sensorium are worthy of increased scholarly attention and innovative critical practices.

Seductive Sounds and Wanting Ears

Oliver Sacks, famed neuropsychologist and author of a number of popular texts on neurology, has noted, "We have, as yet, scarcely touched the question of why music, for better or worse, has so much power. It is a question that goes to the heart of being human" (2006: 2532). Paradoxically, it is the innate humanity of music that evinces its animalism and Pavlovian potential. "The stirring or animating power of music entails emotional no less than motor arousal," he writes. "We turn to music, we need it, because of its ability to move us, to induce feelings and moods, states of mind" (2529).

Sacks is not alone in his quest to unravel the natural origins of music's intrigue; fields ranging from philosophy and psychology to cognitive neuroscience and biomusicology have pursued questions pertaining to the biological and/or mental dispositions underpinning human musicality (for instance, see Wallin, Merker, and Brown 2001; Peretz and Zatorre 2003;

Sloboda 2005; Dowling and Harwood 1986). The approaches and conclusions of these endeavors are diverse and sometimes conflicting, but what they often share is an interest in understanding how music may stimulate thought, action, and emotion, and a consideration of music as a prism for understanding the human brain in general. Dowling and Harwood have stated this general principle well:

> The study of musical patterns tells us something about the mind, and the study of the mind tells us something about the forms of music. Musical form illumines our understanding of the mind because all people everywhere seem always to have had music, and so music takes its place beside language as a basic and universal cultural pattern. Not only are the behaviors of singing and listening found worldwide, but music everywhere has structure. The variety of structure found in the world's musics provides some idea of the limits of human mental capacity—of possible mental organizations. That which is musically possible, which the ear can hear and the mind can grasp, is the province of cognitive psychology (1986: x).

These interests likewise have deep roots in human history, as awareness about the power of music can be traced to antiquity (Bicknell 2009; Adorno [1938] 1991; Attali 1985). Ancient Greek philosophers maintained that music could work "directly on the soul" (Bicknell 2009: 4); these views subsequently informed religious perspectives on the subject in both Christianity and Islam, which believed music to be by turns divine and dangerous (Bicknell 2009: 4, 8; Attali 1985: 22). The power of music was also a topic of the secular writings of the Enlightenment, as thinkers contemplated the nature of the aesthetic and the distinctions between science and the arts (Verba 2004: 313). Rousseau, for instance, philosophized that music could express emotion more powerfully than the other arts, while Kant, who conceived of hearing as the most disruptive of the five senses, resented music for "problematizing the division between nature and art" (Verba 2004: 314–315; Parrett 1998: 254).

The continuities between these diverse understandings of musical power suggest that emotion is commonly conceived as an aspect of music itself. While it is not my intent to discount these longstanding and/or contemporary empirical findings, I concur with Bicknell (2009) that music's emotional power ultimately cannot be divorced from specific musical consequence—that is, why music matters at any given time, in any given context, to any given person (21, 149). This means that the creation of music and the act of listening to it are distinct social activities that transpire within particular cultural, historical, and economic frameworks, rendering music much more than a stimulus to be deconstructed or a universal language to be decoded (Frith 1996: 100; Tagg 1993: 56; Sterne 1997: 19; Bicknell 2009: 81). At the extreme, to conceive of musical power as arising primarily from musical sound constructs a discourse with the potential not only to evacuate music of its sociality but also to govern the body, as such claims frequently rest on assumptions about how that music is heard—and, in turn, about the sense of hearing. As Connor (2004) notes, "Hearing provides intensity without specificity, which is why it has often been thought to be aligned more closely with feeling than with understanding" (157). This tendency to equate hearing and feeling puts it in opposition to sight; where vision is "a fallen sense [that] takes us out of the world" yet "also bathes us in the clear light of reason," hearing is thought of "as manifesting a kind of pure interiority," naturally situating us deeply within the world as well as our own bodies (Sterne 2003: 15). Taken together, these beliefs support what Jonathan Sterne (2003) calls the "audiovisual litany" (15)—the ideological premise of music and hearing as ahistorical, decontextualized, and atomized from other sensory activity.

To counter this, a growing body of scholarship has addressed the historical changes that resulted in an alteration of both music and hearing, with particular interest in the industrial period from the late nineteenth through mid-twentieth centuries. During that time, sound technologies such as radio, the phonograph and gramophone, and telephony emerged and became consumer objects, part of the panoply of mass media devices that would revolutionize modern life (Sterne 2003: 183–184; Douglas 2004: 7; Suisman 2009: 5; Millard 2005: 4–5). These devices would change how, when, and to what people listened, forge sonic connections between disparate groups, and construct a social sense of sonic fidelity, all the while creating the potential for deeply personal listening experiences (Sterne 2003; Douglas 2004; Millard 2005). They would also set the stage for new levels of musical commodification: moving from sheet music to live broadcast to recorded music, music would become something divorced from the time and space of its production, sold, reproduced, and broadcast to become more deeply intertwined in American life than ever before (Suisman 2009; Millard 2005).

As part of the growth of mass society and mass communications, the industrialization of music also facilitated its use as a tool of persuasion and social control. Just as visual technologies such as posters, photographs, and film would become instruments for influencing public opinion and behavior, at the turn of the twentieth century music began to be put to similar purposes, through a number of different avenues. On the most basic level, music advertised itself and thus could promote its own consumption; as evidenced in the promotional practices of a fledgling American music industry during the early 1900s, the best way to sell music was to make the hearing of it unavoidable (Suisman 2009: 11, 58–59). The industry, which came to be known as Tin Pan Alley, also displayed faith in music's persuasive powers from another direction, as its "science of songwriting and arranging" simplified and standardized musical qualities such as melody, structure, and theme to better anticipate a song's success (Jones and Schumacher 1992: 160; Suisman 2009: 44–48). The practices of Tin Pan Alley coincided historically with a growing interest among researchers in how music affected the human mind. Such research was being commissioned as early as the late 1800s and found application in the use of music as a "disciplinary technology" in factories a few decades later; music was meant to increase productivity and diminish the doldrums of repetitive work (Jones and Schumacher 1992: 158; Jones 2005: 727–731). Finally, beyond its use by the culture industries and other sectors, music also served instrumental purposes for the state. Music was used, for example, to reinforce the patriotic effort behind WWI (Suisman 2009: 197, 256–257; Jones and Schumacher 1992: 158; Tischler 1986: 165–166). It is also worth noting that the media effects tradition of communications research of the 1930s through the 1960s began with an interest in radio, as figures such as Paul Lazarsfeld obtained government funding to study audience attitudes and shape effective propaganda techniques—at least one of which, Voice of America, liberally employed music (Pooley 2008: 51–56; Simonson 2008: 300).

Given this background, it is perhaps unsurprising that Theodor Adorno—whose analysis of the culture industry in the 1940s has made him an invaluable resource for critical scholars to this day—devoted so much of his writing to a discussion of music. In his extensive writings on the subject, Adorno critiques the debasement of music under industrial capitalism as a tool of social control, an agent of false consciousness, and a catalyst of alienation (for example, see Horkheimer and Adorno [1944] 1997; Adorno [1932] 2002 and [1941] 2002; Attali 1985: 9). His essay, "On the Fetish Character in Music and the Regression of Listening," argues that industrialized music deadens its listeners rather than provokes contemplation or artistic appreciation, so that "the listener is converted, along his line of least resistance, into the acquiescent purchaser" (Adorno [1938] 1991: 32). This is due to formal qualities of the music as well as the conditions of its consumption. Evacuated of abstraction and avant-garde impulses—innovative instrumentation, bold structure and dynamics, or complex melodic lines, to name but a few—standardized music, mediated by radio and advertising, molds its listeners through ceaseless repetition, so much so that "to like [music] is almost the same thing as to recognize it" (30).

It is in this way that the strange powers of music seem to bewilder and intrigue its critics and converts alike. Adorno, and the members of the industry he scorns, share a conviction about music's seduction as well as skepticism regarding the capacity of audiences to resist it. Such views have persisted in much subsequent discourse about musical sound, making for paradoxical similarities between, for instance, the moral panics about rock and roll or rap music, the rapture about the same genres among music critics, and marketing literature that advocates the use of music to "condition" those who hear it. Within popular music studies, important scholarship has endowed musical audiences with the agency to make meaning and define themselves (for example, see DeNora 2006; Grossberg 1992; Frith 1981); but such work often stops at how music is an object of cultural meaning or a ritual, failing to adequately consider sound as a phenomenon or listening as a practice. Advocates of what Shank (2006) has termed "popular musicology" (11) have found ways to explain the structure of popular music and the meaning of sound and thus seek to augment deep, critical listening, but these sources, too, continue to regard music as representation rather than considering the social construction and political economies of listening (see McClary 2006, 2007a, 2007b; Middleton 2006). In an attempt to be mindful of both of these tendencies as well as the contributions of anthropology and cultural musicology/ethnomusicology (see Erlmann 2004; Howes 2005; Austern 2002), my focus here on the sonic aspects of music explores how discourses about sound and its sensory perception flow seamlessly toward support of the branded, cultural economy in which we reside. If "methods such as deep listening can augment critical faculties" (Scott 2009: 2), it is pressing to develop them as sonic branding comes to more thoroughly administer our sonic environment.

Branding Musical Sounds

Sonic branding refers to the use of sound to enhance brand awareness, appeal, and cohesion. First conceived in the 1980s, since the 1990s the field has grown both in number of firms and in scope, paralleling the heightened prominence of professional branding more generally (Parikh 2009: 53; Bronner and Hirt 2009; Jackson 2003: xv, xx; Moor 2007: 3; Klein 2000). Contributing to this growth is the "360-degree approach to branding" and "the spread of new media," which create opportunities to extend and cement brand identity across multiple platforms (Hein 2006). Though this chapter focuses on musical sounds, sonic branding encompasses much more than licensing music to commercials, retail spaces, and the like. It can also include the creation of original music for those same events, sonic logos (such as the NBC chime or Intel notes), sound design for a product in use (think of the slam of a car door or the whirr of an air conditioner), voice selection for customer service messages on a telephone, sounds delivered via websites or mobile phones, phonetics, and the acoustics of workspaces (Kilian 2009: 38; Lindstrom 2005: 65; Jackson 2003). Advances in sound media and acoustic technology likewise amplify sonic branding's potential.

In addition to the aggressive licensing of both original song renditions and covers, many sonic branding firms encourage the development of musical trademarks. Crafting original music or soundscapes brings the benefit of made-to-order sound that, unlike licensed sound, has no expiration date (Jackson 2003: xvii; Kurpiers 2009: 141; Lindstrom 2005: 12). Sonic branding thereby resonates with other contemporary practices that have vastly expanded the application of intellectual property laws to cover many more aspects of cultural exchange and sensory experience (Coombe 1998; Howes 2005: 288).

Cinema is a crucial point of inspiration for producers wishing to link sound and image. In one instance, U.S. television network NBC hired New York City–based sonic branding firm Audiobrain to craft a soundtrack for the 2008 Olympic Games, to which they held exclusive broadcast rights. The goal of the network was to use music to "conjure up believable cinematic moments" as a way of driving home the "Olympic story" (Conley 2008). Similarly, Dan Jackson, founder of British sonic branding firm SonicBrand,[4] draws parallels between sound branding and sound in films, noting that "the role of sound in films is to enhance the experience, make the action more believable and make it more memorable" (2003: 16). Sonic branding also grows out of the use of music in retail environments, musical jingles in advertisements, and corporate sponsored musical acts on early television and radio, all of which sought to interweave music with the act of consumption and shape customer relationships (Klein 2009: 17–19). In spite of these antecedents, sonic branding's buzz turns on its supposed novelty. In the trade press, newspapers, and books on the subject, the territories of sound are deemed widely uncharted, infrequently and haphazardly employed, and ripe for managed improvement. The Sound Agency founder Julian Treasure laments that although design has permeated almost every aspect of our visual environment, "almost nothing you hear has been designed by anyone" (Treasure 2007: 9); Brian Rupp, creative director of Rumblefish, argues that "'we all have ears, but most brands don't have voices'" (qtd. in Capps 2007). Insights like these among professional sonic branders suggest that they view sound as an incredible growth opportunity for bringing intentionality to the aural environment.

Sonic branding favors uses of sounds, including music, that are "strategic" or "systemic" rather than merely "creative" (Jackson 2003: 9; Franus 2007), confirming that under a regime of branding, "all elements of a company's symbolic and material culture become subject to the same degree of analysis and design-intensivity" (Moor 2007: 42). Where creativity suggests that sonic choices are made based on subjective criteria or without much forethought, strategy strives for objectivity and empirically driven premeditation. This functions to instantiate sonic branding as a type of cultural intermediation (see Negus 2002; Featherstone 1987; Bourdieu 1984), expert knowledge applied for the express purpose of implementing these strategies. Sonic branding likewise validates this expertise through "the quasi-academic knowledge that comes from both their own educational backgrounds and, increasingly, from specialist research institutions staffed by university graduates from a range of disciplines" (Moor 2007: 55). In what follows, I draw from sonic branding firm websites, books on the subject, and the trade press to document the reliance of sonic branding on three assumptions about sound: 1) that sound is a universal, natural language that works on the body; 2) that sound accesses "pure" emotion; and 3) that sound may be understood scientifically.

Sound as a Universal, Natural Language that Works on the Body

In a 2004 *Financial Times* article, Dan Jackson argues:

> If any brand wishes to communicate, control, coerce, or convince, it has to do so via one, or preferably more than one, of the senses. And while media choice may be more complex now than 20 years ago, human senses remain the same; smell, taste, touch, sight, and hearing. Each gathers information and the brain works out what it means and how we respond (Jackson 2004).

Though Marx and others have explored how the senses are objects of history and "a human accomplishment" (Stewart 2004: 59; Marx 1978: 89), sonic branding privileges the ahistoricity of the senses, its consistency within a complicated and capricious media landscape. This alleged timelessness means that sonic branders need only tap into tried-and-true sensory experiences in order to discover fresh brand strategies. To this point, Martin Lindstrom, in his book *BRANDsense*, argues that "the future of branding" will belong to brands that "adopt characteristics of religious sensory experience" (Lindstrom 2005: 7) and thus are able to convert their consumers into dedicated believers.

For the sense of hearing in particular, the pursuit of eternal sensory experience that may be modeled for contemporary ends suggests that sonic branding aspires to connect with sound's primeval, irrational nature. As Julian Treasure writes, "We are not so modern that a sudden sound does not cause an immediate release of adrenaline and cortisol, our fight/flight hormones" (Treasure 2007: 127)—a reflexive, bodily response. From this vantage, it follows that if sound has the potential to produce reactions that are automatic, it can also be put toward "influencing behaviors" (Franus 2007); further, music can be a "'a form of mind control'" (Mucha 2005). This allows music and other sounds to function as a kind of stimulus whose response can be conditioned (Lindstrom 2005: 10–11), a move that also conflates hearing, listening, and sound.

Sound and hearing are further collapsed in the sonic branding literature through the notion that hearing is a perpetually activated sense. Sonic branders are fond of noting that "we have no earlids" (Treasure 2007: 9), by which they mean that sound cannot be avoided. Hannes Raffaseder, in a chapter titled "Audio Brands and Brand Sounds: Relevance of Timbre in Audio Branding," explains that

> Unlike the eye, the ear cannot be simply closed. Also, as it is not fixed to a visual angle it receives all audio signals from its environment. Hence, the flow of acoustic information is generally much too complex to be consciously perceived and analysed in total... While acoustic perception always happens automatically, albeit often unconsciously, visual perception requires active looking (2009: 98).

Raffaseder's characterization constructs sound as enveloping in all senses of the word: not only does it surround completely, but it also encloses all who come in contact with it, precluding escape. We can also see here the return of the "audiovisual litany" mentioned above—sound's appeal is an outgrowth of its ability to skirt the critical faculties consumers have developed in the visual realm. If we cannot "turn off" our ears, then sonic communication must affect us; moreover, musical sound in particular then has direct access to our memories. As a senior vice president for music at Grey Global Group argues, "Music tattoos a permanent resonance in your brain...that's what branding should be—permanent resonance" (qtd. in Capps 2007).

Finally, sonic branders consider the universality of musical sound a necessary, cost-effective tool in a globalized environment. According to one, "'Music is the only byproduct of what is achieved in advertising that crosses all language barriers'" (qtd. in Altshuler 2007)—further argument that more planning should go into its selection. Likewise, U.K. firm SonicID claims on its website that "music, sound and voice transcend language for global brands that operate in multiple territories, markets or categories." If this is the case, sonic branding is, both literally and figuratively, a sound investment.

Sound Accesses "Pure" Emotion

Supported by the belief that sound communicates internationally and irrepressibly, sonic branding seeks to tap into the "collective unconscious and design emotional messages" (Jackson 2003: 32). This pertains to two activities simultaneously. On the one hand, there is a process of what one executive called "'reinforcing the emotional context of the brand'" (qtd. in Farinella 2009), which involves using sound to create a unique audio identity. The second usage, stemming from this, is a process of emotional suggestion—using musical sound to "[make] us feel particular emotions" we might not feel in absence of the sound (Fisher 2004). As the sonic branding firm Rumblefish writes on its website:

> We're all attuned to the "pre-language" of sound from a very early age, and we're quite adept at interpreting its meaning. It's the universal language of emotion, requiring no explanation or translation. And it affects us on a very personal level, stirring up meaningful associations and acting on our physiology to produce intense feelings.

The ability of sound to strike us within our emotional centers confirms once again that it is a useful mechanism in a marketplace where the consumer has learned to avoid marketing messages. A 2008 *Fast Company* article on sonic branding notes that "no matter how immune consumers may believe they are to these kinds of audio cues, they're not made out of wood" (Conley 2008)—suggesting that it would be inhuman to be unaffected in the presence of sonic stimulus. Sonic branders thus become something akin to the conductors of a symphony, aspiring to bring its audience to rapture, all for the benefit of the brand. In describing what they do on their website, SonicID claims that their work in sound "stirs emotions, influences behavior, strengthens perceptions and boosts brand value," while Dan Jackson claims that sonic branding is "all emotional manipulation...but it's completely legal" (Fisher 2004).[5]

Sound as Science

In a 1990 article entitled "Music, Mood, and Marketing," Bruner describes music as "not simply a generic sonic mass, but rather a complex chemistry of controllable elements" (Bruner 1990: 94). Though Bruner's article predates the growth in earnest of sonic branding by several years, it anticipates one of its most important premises: that sounds can be engineered to produce predictable outcomes. This suggests that despite the fact that branders seek to connect with complicated, "irrational" emotions, rational systems of knowledge can be created and deployed to cajole these reactions. Sonic branding thus participates in a practice common within other facets of advertising and marketing.

These systems of knowledge have two primary components. First, they make use of scientific understandings of sound drawn from ancillary disciplines such as psychology, physics, cognitive neuroscience, and biology, using technical terms to explain how sound works on the brain and body. For instance, sonic brander Stephen Arnold's website notes that "brands delivered sonically reach a place in the brain that visual branding alone doesn't approach. The tune lodges in the cerebral cortex forming a memory implant in the aural pathways to the brain." Jackson's *Sonic Branding* includes a chapter entitled "The Sciency Bit," that includes descriptions of sound waves, the range of frequencies audible to the human ear, characterizations of the left and right brain, and how music accesses memory. The website for The Sound Agency claims that "the science of psychoacoustics has made it possible to predict the effect of sound on human beings," corroborating the company's belief that "the better we understand sound, the more effectively we can control and make use of it" (Treasure 2007: 15).

The second component of these systems of knowledge are the models, often proprietary, developed by the firms themselves for auditing, analyzing, and adapting a brand's sound. In *Sound Business*, Treasure outlines his SoundFlow model, which uses three categories for describing a sound's components: the "drivers" of the sound, such as time, pitch, and dynamics; the "filters" which impact its employment, such as environment, function, and "brand/values"; and the "outcomes" desired from particular sounds, be they psychological, behavioral, or physiological (Treasure 2007: 115). This model can then be used to come up with an ideal BrandSound which is "all the intentional sound which communicates and/or reinforces the qualities, tones and values that are best aligned with the brand promise, and which enhances and amplifies the desirable aspects of the brand experience" (Treasure 2007: 142). Jackson and his team at SonicBrand (now part of CuttingEdge Commercial) suggest using a "sonic branding engine" to audit a brand. Among the many activities involved are research into how a brand has used sound in the past as well as how its competitors utilize sound; the development of a "moodboard" of songs that communicate the brand's core emotional values; and the development of specific "sonic guidelines" (Jackson 2003: 104–108, 115–117, 129). As part of his technique for coming up with a brand's sense identity, Lindstrom advocates the creation of a brand "sensogram" (2005: 18) to determine how a brand is currently utilizing each of the five senses, then systematically determining new ways to expand a brand in all five sensory directions.

These systems, meant to transmit empirical understandings, also convey cultural attitudes that carry political consequences. Consider, for instance, the following passage from Julian Treasure's *Sound Business*, where he notes that heavy metal and rap music

> ...are strongly suspected of creating unhealthy psychological and attitudinal states, including misogyny, aggressiveness, and depression, and of causing a range of anti-social and damaging behaviors such as violence, crime, self-harm, cult membership, and even suicide (Treasure 2007: 135).

Here, the culture surrounding these types of music, including any existing stereotypes, is coded in sonic terms—the *sound* of these types of music, and the sound alone, produces these reactions. Though not all sonic branders necessarily go as far (though Jackson makes a similar point about rap and heavy metal and mental distraction; see Jackson 2003: 37), such an extreme example highlights how sonic branding understands sound as a driver of culture: if the sound of rap music can be blamed for pushing its listeners to be violent, then brands should be cautious in associating their brands with it, making such a choice evidence of prudence rather than bias. Furthermore, if musical power and influence are aspects of music itself, sonic branders can determine that they are simply directing that power rather than taking an active role in its construction.

Conclusion

In "The Work of Art in the Age of Its Technological Reproducibility," Walter Benjamin famously wrote, "Just as the entire mode of existence of human collectives changes over long historical periods, so too does their mode of perception" ([1936] 2008: 23). Building on the suggestion that what it means to perceive is not a fixed quality but rather a function of shifting sensory realities, Benjamin locates the power of film in its multisensory, immersive nature—it is not just an "optical" technology but also a "tactile" one which uses multiple channels of perception to interact with its spectators and present a profound, even hyperreal, experience (40). Coupled with what those spectators bring to the cinematic event, film unlocks a profound potential for new ways of being, making it both singularly transgressive and uniquely pernicious.

We might use Benjamin's insights to draw a parallel between the world he lived in during the 1930s and the contemporary branded environment. As brand architecture extends into deeper levels of sensory activity in the pursuit of attention, value, and attachment, consumers are given the option to interact with brands with their whole bodies, at many levels of experience. As I have argued above in the case of musical sound, the drive toward this totalizing experience of the brand is not only to unify the various sites where a consumer may encounter a brand but also to penetrate into arenas of perception supposedly not accustomed—and therefore still vulnerable—to branded messages. As we have seen, sonic branders determine musical sound to be particularly handy for these kinds of uses, reflecting and reinforcing the prolific discourse that has long interpreted its sonic elements as uniquely alluring and the ear as wholly susceptible to that allure.

Sonic branding mobilizes and actualizes a particular kind of expertise meant to understand, interpret, and control both music as sound and hearing as a sense, then buttresses those ways of understanding as a means of creating and extracting value. What Kurpiers (2009) says about sound designers is also true of sonic branders: they "enact and concretize sonically ideas [and] cultural norms about social relations, behaviors, and ideologies [and] organize musical sounds in ways that convey meaning within a multilayered, sometimes thorny labyrinth of constituents, ideologies, and popular culture" (205). This is one level on which sonic branding has political consequences. Masquerading as "objective" knowledge that turns on a "systemic" use of "science," what it actually peddles is deeply subjective and highly social, and relies heavily on meaning that is culturally created.

The "scientific" character of its expertise likewise makes for parallels between sonic branding and other technologically driven projects such as the mapping of the "Music Genome" and the development of proprietary algorithms that analyze and predict musical success (Werde 2004; Walker 2009). Each participates in further disciplining the sonic environment by distilling its social elements into quantifiable categories, which can then be redeployed to create monetary and other kinds of values for the primary benefit of brand actors. This has the potential to invite and privilege some ways of listening and some kinds of music over others but does not, alone, determine those results. As R. Murray Schafer wrote in *The Soundscape* more than thirty years ago:

> The soundscape of the world is changing. Modern man is beginning to inhabit a world with an acoustic environment radically different from any he has hitherto known. These new sounds, which differ in quality and intensity from those of the past, have alerted many researchers to the dangers of an indiscriminate and imperialistic spread of more and larger sounds into every corner of man's life. Noise pollution is now a world problem. It would seem that the world soundscape has reached an apex of vulgarity in our time, and many experts have predicted universal deafness as the ultimate consequence unless the problem can be brought quickly under control (Schafer 1977: 3).

That Schafer's prescient work has come to the attention of sonic branding firms[6] but has been lost on many in media studies is both ironic and worrisome. The new media literacy that promotional culture requires must begin to consider the impact and implications of the world of sound. As the brand continues to develop its aurality, we should be listening carefully.

Notes

1. Special thanks to James Rodgers for his help in the musical description of Feist's song "1-2-3-4," and to D. Travers Scott for reading this article in draft form.
2. Taylor's article focuses on Moby and his 1999 album, *Play*—frequently recognized as a key turning point in the licensing of independent music to advertising.
3. Within this chapter, I often use the terms music, musical sound, and sound interchangeably, although I acknowledge that there are important distinctions. Following Bicknell (2009), I define music as "humanly organized sound" that is "organized for the purpose of enriching or intensifying experience through active engagement" and is "regarded primarily, or in significant measure, as sounds" (11). This marks a distinction be-

tween music and other auralities, such as delivered speech or noise. That the boundaries between music, noise, and sound are continually challenged supports my argument that sonic branding relies problematically on the constancy of music, sound, and the sense of hearing.

4. At the time of this writing, SonicBrand had been merged with a firm known as CuttingEdgeCommercial, though it was independent at the time Jackson published *Sonic Branding* in 2003.
5. I would like to briefly mention that these appeals to irrational emotional responses corroborate gender biases. Julian Treasure, for instance, notes that hearing is "clearly more feminine" than sight because it is "passive, receiving, always open" (Treasure 2007: 73). This is only the most direct statement of what is a more subtle gendering of the listener as female and sound as male, evident in the sonic branding literature not only in the omnipresent mind/body split but it also in how sound is endowed with the ability to aggressively "enter" its listener against her will. How gender in particular and identities in general are constructed through sonic branding is worth additional research.
6. See Bronner and Hirt (2009).

References

Adorno, Theodor. [1941] 2002. "On Popular Music." Pp. 437–469 in *Essays on Music,* ed. R. Leppert. Berkeley, CA: University of California Press.

———. [1932] 2002. "On the Social Situation of Music." Pp. 391–436 in *Essays on Music,* ed. R. Leppert. Berkeley, CA: University of California Press.

———. [1938] 1991. "On the Fetish Character in Music and the Regression of Listening." Pp. 29–60 in *The Culture Industry,* ed. J. M. Bernstein. New York: Routledge.

Allan, David. 2005. "An Essay on Popular Music in Advertising: The Bankruptcy of Culture or the Marriage of Art and Commerce?" *Advertising and Society Review.* http://muse.jhu.edu/journals/asr/v006/6.1allan.html

Altshuler, Marc. 2007. "Effective and Sustainable Branding Starts with Music." *Advertising Age,* November 5.

Arvidsson, Adam. 2006. *Brands: Meaning and Value in Media Culture.* London: Routledge.

Attali, Jacques. 1985. *Noise: The Political Economy of Music.* Minneapolis: University of Minnesota Press.

Austern, Linda Phyllis, ed. 2002. *Music, Sensation, and Sensuality.* New York: Routledge.

Banks, Richard. 2007. "In Short: The Girl Done Good, Yet Again." BBC.co.uk, 19 April. http://www.bbc.co.uk/music/reviews/6r3n (accessed January 10, 2010).

Barhard, Rachel, and Jack Rutledge. 2009. "Music + Ads: Advertising Is the New Radio." Adweek.com, June 5. http://www.adweek.com/aw/content_display/news/agency/e3if23ea57e4d01ad14116494ef49f3985d (accessed January 10, 2010).

Benjamin, Walter. [1936] 2008. "The Work of Art in the Age of Its Technological Reproducibility." Pp. 19–55 in *The Work of Art in the Age of Its Technological Reproducibility and Other Writings on Media,* ed. M. W. Jennings, B. Doherty, and T. Y. Levin. Cambridge, MA: Belknap/Harvard University Press.

Bicknell, Jeanette. 2009. *Why Music Moves Us.* New York: Palgrave Macmillan.

Bourdieu, Pierre. 1984. *Distinction: A Social Critique of the Judgement of Taste.* Cambridge, MA: Harvard University Press.

Bronner, Kai, and Rainer Hirt, eds. 2009. *Audio Branding: Brands, Sound and Communication*. Baden-Baden, Germany: Nomos Verlagsgesellschaft.
Bruner, Gordon C. 1990. "Music, Mood, and Marketing." *Journal of Marketing* 54 (4): 94–104.
Capps, Brooke. 2007. "More Than Just Jingles: One Shop Uses Sound to Give Brands Voices." *Advertising Age,* April 16.
Conley, Lucas. 2008. "Strike Up the Band." *Fast Company,* June.
Connor, Steven. 2004. "Edison's Teeth: Touching Hearing." Pp. 153–172 in *Hearing Cultures: Essays on Sound, Listening, and Modernity,* ed. V. Erlmann. New York: Berg.
Coombe, Rosemary. 1998. *The Cultural Life of Intellectual Properties: Authorship, Appropriation, and the Law*. Durham, NC: Duke University Press.
DeNora, Tia. 2006. "Music and Self-Identity." Pp. 141–147 in *The Popular Music Studies Reader,* ed. A. Bennett, B. Shank, and J. Toynbee. New York: Routledge.
Douglas, Susan. [1999] 2004. *Listening In: Radio and the American Imagination*. Minneapolis: University of Minnesota Press.
Dowling, W. Jay, and Dane Harwood. 1986. *Music Cognition*. New York: Academic Press, Inc.
Elliot, Stuart. 2009. "Commercials and Musicians Share the Need to Be Heard." *New York Times,* 6 February.
Erlmann, Veit. 2004. *Hearing Cultures: Essays on Sound, Listening, and Modernity*. New York: Berg.
Farinella, David John. 2009. "Companies Seek Signature Sound." *Variety,* 4 December.
Featherstone, Michael. 1987. "Lifestyle and Consumer Culture." *Theory, Culture & Society* 4: 55–70.
Fisher, Alice. 2004. "Tills Are Alive with the Sound of Music." *Sunday Telegraph,* December 26.
Frank, Thomas. 1998. *The Conquest of Cool: Business Culture, Counterculture, and the Rise of Hip Consumerism*. Chicago: University of Chicago Press.
Franus, Noel. 2007. "Building Brand Value Through the Strategic Use of Sound." AIGA.org. http://www.aiga.org/content.cfm/building-brand-value-through-sound (accessed January 10, 2010).
Frith, Simon. 1996. *Performing Rites: On the Value of Popular Music*. Cambridge, MA: Harvard University Press.
———. 1981. *Sound Effects: Youth, Leisure, and the Politics of Rock 'n' Roll*. New York: Pantheon Books.
Grossberg, Lawrence. 1992. "Is There a Fan in the House? The Affective Sensibility of Fandom." Pp. 50–65 in *Adoring Audience: Fan Culture and Popular Media,* ed. L. A. Lewis. New York: Routledge.
Hein, Kenneth. 2006. "Sonic Branding Firms get Increase in Sales Volume." *Brandweek,* 3 April.
High, Kamau, and Mark Sutherland. 2008. "Ad Rock." *Billboard*, 10 May.
Horkheimer, Max and Adorno, Theodor W. [1944] 1997. "The Culture Industry: Enlightenment as Mass Deception." Pp. 120–167 in *Dialectic of Enlightenment*. New York: Continuum.
Howes, David. 2005. "Hyperesthesia, Or, the Sensual Logic of Late Capitalism." Pp. 281–303 in *Empire of the Senses: The Sensual Culture Reader,* ed. D. Howes. New York: Berg.
Jackson, Daniel. 2004. "Listen Carefully." *Financial Times,* 28 September.
———. 2003. *Sonic Branding: An Introduction*. New York: Palgrave Macmillan.

Jones, Keith. 2005. "Music in Factories: A 20th Century Technique for Control of the Productive Self." *Social and Cultural Geography* 6 (5): 723–744.

Jones, Simon, and Thomas Schumacher. 1992. "Muzak: On Functional Music and Power." *Critical Studies in Mass Communication* 9 (2): 156–169.

Kilian, Karsten. 2009. "From Brand Identity to Audio Branding." Pp. 35–48 in *Audio Branding: Brands, Sound and Communication*, ed. K. Bronner and R. Hirt. Baden-Baden, Germany: Nomos Verlagsgesellschaft.

Klein, Bethany. 2009. *As Heard on TV: Popular Music in Advertising*. Surrey: Ashgate.

———. 2008. "In Perfect Harmony: Popular Music and Cola Advertising." *Popular Music and Society* 31 (1): 1–20.

Klein, Naomi. 2000. *No Logo: Taking Aim at the Brand Bullies*. New York: Picador.

Kurpiers, Joyce. 2009. Reality by Design: Advertising Image, Music and Sound Design in the Production of Culture. Ph.D. diss., Duke University.

Lederman, Marsha. 2008. "High Five for Feist." *Globe and Mail*, April 7.

Lee, Jennifer 8. 2008. "Is Apple the Oprah for Indie Bands?" *New York Times*, October 3.

Lindstrom, Martin. 2005. *BRANDsense: Build Powerful Brands through Touch, Taste, Smell, Sight, and Sound*. London: Free Press.

Lury, Celia. 2004. *Brands: The Logos of the Global Economy*. New York: Routledge.

Marx, Karl. 1978. "Economic and Philosophic Manuscripts of 1844." Pp. 66–125 in *The Marx-Engels Reader*, ed. R. D. Tucker. New York: W.W. Norton.

McClary, Susan. 2007a. "Constructions of Subjectivity in Schubert's Music." Pp. 169–197 in *Reading Music*. Burlington, VT: Ashgate.

———. 2007b. "Living To Tell: Madonna's Resurrection of the Fleshly." Pp. 213–238 in *Reading Music*. Burlington, VT: Ashgate.

———. 2006. "This Is Not a Story My People Tell: Musical Time and Space According to Laurie Anderson." Pp. 21–28 in *The Popular Music Studies Reader*, ed. A. Bennett, B. Shank, and J. Toynbee. New York: Routledge.

Middleton, Richard. 2006. "In the Groove or Blowing Your Mind?: The Pleasures of Musical Repetition." Pp. 15–20 in *The Popular Music Studies Reader*, ed. A. Bennett, B. Shank, and J. Toynbee. New York: Routledge.

Millard, Andre. 2005. *America on Record: A History of Recorded Sound*. New York: Cambridge University Press.

Moor, Liz. 2007. *The Rise of Brands*. New York: Berg.

———. 2003. "Branded Spaces: The Scope of 'New Marketing.'" *Journal of Consumer Culture* 3: 39–60.

Moran, Charlie. 2007. "2007's Best Ad Songs." *Advertising Age*, 17 December.

Mucha, Thomas. 2005. "The New Sounds of Selling." *Business 2.0*, May.

Negus, Keith. 2002. "The Work of Cultural Intermediaries and the Enduring Distance Between Production and Consumption." *Cultural Studies* 16 (4): 501–515.

Paoletta, Michael. 2007. "The Apple of Feist's Eye." *Billboard*, October 6.

Parikh, Rayan. 2009. "Finding the Rhythm: Elias Arts and the Pioneering of Audio Identity." Pp. 53–60 in *Audio Branding: Brands, Sound and Communication*, ed. K. Bronner and R. Hirt. Baden-Baden, Germany: Nomos Verlagsgesellschaft.

Parrett, Herman. 1998. "Kant on Music and the Hierarchy of the Arts." *The Journal of Aesthetics and Art Criticism* 56 (3): 251–264.

Peretz, Isabelle, and Robert Zatorre. 2003. *The Cognitive Neuroscience of Music*. Oxford: Oxford University Press.

Petridis, Alex. 2008. "Headed for the Top." *The Guardian*, April 26.

Pooley, Jefferson. 2008. "The New History of Mass Communication Research." Pp. 43–69 in *The History of Media and Communication Research: Contested Memories*, ed. D. W. Park and J. Pooley. New York: Peter Lang.

Raffaseder, Hannes. 2009. "Audio Brands and Brand Sounds: Relevance of Timbre in Audio Branding." Pp. 95–108 in *Audio Branding: Brands, Sound and Communication*. Baden-Baden, Germany: Nomos Verlagsgesellschaft.

Rayner, Ben. 2008. "Apparently, Feist Sells iPods." *Toronto Star*, 9 February.

Sacks, Oliver. 2006. "The Power of Music." *Brain* 129 (10): 2528–2532.

Schafer, R. Murray. 1977. *The Soundscape: Our Sonic Environment and the Tuning of the World*. Rochester, VT: Destiny Books.

Scott, D. Travers. 2009. "The Utility of Sound Studies' Theory and Method for Histories of New Media and Communication Technologies." Paper presented at The Future is Prologue Pre-Conference for the International Communication Association, Chicago, IL, 21 May.

Shank, Barry. 2006. "Introduction to Part One." Pp. 11–14 in *The Popular Music Studies Reader*, ed. A. Bennett, B. Shank, and J. Toynbee. New York: Routledge.

Simonson, Peter. 2008. "Writing Figures into the Field: William McPhee and the Parts Played by People in Our Histories of Media Research." Pp. 291–320 in *The History of Media and Communication Research: Contested Memories*, ed. D. W. Park and J. Pooley. New York: Peter Lang.

Sloboda, John. 2005. "Empirical Studies of Emotional Response to Music." Pp. 203–214 in *Exploring the Musical Mind: Cognition, Emotion, Ability, Function*. New York: Oxford University Press.

Sterne, Jonathan. 2003. *The Audible Past: Cultural Origins of Sound Reproduction*. Durham, NC: Duke University Press.

———. 1997. "Sounds Like the Mall of America: Programmed Music and the Architectonics of Commercial Space." *Ethnomusicology* 41(1): 22–50.

Stevens, Darcie. 2007. "Phases & Stages." *Austin Chronicle*, 27 April.

Stevenson, Jane. 2008. "1 2 3 4; Not Only Is This Feist's Biggest Hit, It's Also the Number of Grammys Our Musical Ambassador Could Win." *Globe and Mail*, February 10.

Stewart, Susan. 2004. "Remembering the Senses." Pp. 59–69 in *Empire of the Senses: The Sensual Culture Reader*, ed. D. Howes. New York: Berg.

Suisman, David. 2009. *Selling Sounds: The Commercial Revolution in American Music*. Cambridge, MA: Harvard University Press.

Tagg, Philip. 1993. "'Universal' Music and the Case of Death." *The Critical Quarterly* 35 (2): 54–85.

Taylor, Timothy D. 2007. "The Changing Shape of the Culture Industry; Or, How Did Electronic Music Get into Television Commercials?" *Television and New Media* 8 (3): 235–258.

Tischler, Barbara. 1986. "One Hundred Percent Americanism and Music in Boston during World War I." *American Music* 4 (2): 164–176.

Treasure, Julian. 2007. *Sound Business*.Gloucestershire, UK: Management Books 2000 Ltd.

Tyrangiel, Josh. 2007. "Top 10 Songs." Time.com. http://www.time.com/time/specials/2007/top10/article/0,30583,1686204_1686244_1690619,00.html (accessed 10 January 2010).

Verba, Cynthia. 2004. "Music and the Enlightenment." Pp. 301–322 in *The Enlightenment World*, ed. M. Fitzpatrick. New York: Routledge.

Walker, Rob. 2009. "The Song Decoders." *New York Times*, October 14.

Wallin, Nils, Bjorn Merker, and Steven Brown, eds. 2001. *The Origins of Music*. Cambridge, MA: MIT Press.

Werde, Bill. 2004. "We've Got Algorithm, but How About Soul?" *New York Times,* March 21.

Wyman, Bill. 2007. "How to Calculate Musical Sellouts." *Washington Post*, 14 October.

CHAPTER FOURTEEN

Texts That Sell

The Culture in Promotional Culture

Jonathan Gray

When discussing promotional culture, especially in passing, we as cultural critics too often reduce it to being exploitative, propagandistic, and the essence of superficiality.[1] It is "only so much hype," the media equivalent of the used car salesman who annoyingly hounds us around the car lot. Just when we might wish to lose ourselves in a television program and its sentiment, for instance, promotions can remind us of the depressing reality that ultimately the show we're watching is there to move product as much as, or more than, it is to enlighten, engage, or amuse us. As such, to teach media literacy, to make our students more aware of advertisers' tricks, and to study how promotions work as semiotic and economic entities can be ways of fighting back. I do not wish to challenge such moves. However, it is my contention that amidst our training as practitioners of cultural jujitsu, we rarely examine promotional culture as *culture*—as reflective, artistic, worthy of engagement, and as perhaps contributing positively to the mediasphere. Granted, cultural criticism will often focus on how promotions tap into popular culture to find the images and text most likely to provoke an affective response, or we will acknowledge it as an *imposed* culture, one that makes us spend, eat, and smoke more, yet think less. Important exceptions exist of course, and such exceptions may gradually be becoming the rule, as the other chapters in this collection suggest through their sophistication. But the bulk of published work still rarely considers ads as contributing much aesthetically, unless the aesthetics are a means to a cash-grab end. Ads, though, do not just produce profits, dupes, and the ills of capitalism; they also produce engagement, reflection, interest, meanings, and interpretive introductions to much of the culture that advertising's staunchest critics generally regard as more legitimate, artistic, uplifting, and hence worthy of aesthetic analysis.

In the realm of film and television, promotional culture is often a key and indistinguishable part of the artistic product. Behind corporate conglomerates' horizontal and vertical integration and plans for synergistic conquest of the audience are frequently videogames, posters, ad campaigns, merchandise lines, toys, and trailers that are active sites for the creation, consumption, and enjoyment of the narrative. Many of these "spinoffs," "extratextuals," and "peripherals" surround film and television texts with hype, generating revenue themselves at times but also serving the larger goal of directing audiences to the film, show, or franchise. Comparatively little has been written about them, even though they command an inordinately large amount of public space. Bus stops and subways are regular homes to movie posters, almost every television ad break includes at least one ad for another show or for a film, and increasingly they will include URLs directing us to a website for further promotional information. Toy, clothing, game, and souvenir stores teem with licensed merchandise. Amusement parks offer us spinoff rides, iTunes offers us podcasts, and daily emails come to us from Amazon telling us of many deals on DVDs with bonus materials and CDs soundtracks. And so on. Promoting film and television is a huge industry even if academia rarely pays attention to it.[2] The average Hollywood film budgets $36 million for marketing, regularly a third or more of its budget (Friend 2009: 41, 46). Television networks hold back on selling all available ad slots in order to promote their own wares. Amanda Lotz notes that network television annually foregoes over $4 billion worth of ad time to advertise its own programs, airing over 30,000 promos per year (Lotz 2007: 108–9). When not draining money, other forms of promotions can generate large revenues, as with DVD sales and rental figures that regularly eclipse box office receipts or as with the lucrative market in licensed toys and videogames.

Undoubtedly, these promotions have an economic effect on the success of the film or show, especially in a media-saturated environment in which promotions are required to let audiences know the film or show exists in the first place. We could and should also examine how such promotions employ the same techniques—and often the same questionable or outright objectionable techniques—that other ads do. But we must look at not only the ad but also the add—at what is added to the text by the promotions. After all, if someone is moved to watch a certain movie by a trailer, that trailer will need to have done more than insist that the film be watched; rather, it will need to have constructed a series of meanings, themes, and/or characters to which the audience responds. Similarly, if children play with a licensed toy, it will need to have spoken to them in some way. And if someone spends time rifling through bonus materials on a DVD, watches ads for a television show and contributes to a fan site, and/or plays a licensed videogame, again, something is needed to hook them. In all such cases, the promotional and/or spinoff material will need to use textual hooks, if for no other reason than to differentiate itself from the thousands of other promotions vying for the audience's time and attention. The promotions need to create a text of their own, in other words, and thus the promotion becomes a text itself. Or, more specifically, it becomes a "paratext" (Genette 1997), a textual element appended and related to a larger text that nevertheless offers its own meanings. Add all these paratexts to their millions of images, narratives, and characters, and consider that a great deal of the meanings of film and television with which we interact—a great deal of the culture—comes to us from the paratexts and promotions.

To better understand the promotional culture that surrounds film and television, I argue, we cannot assume that such paratexts merely echo the meanings of the film or show. Surely, for instance, we have all seen spectacular trailers for what turn out to be awful movies and vice versa. Meaning often begins at the level of the promotion, and even after we have watched a film, or after a show is up and running, promotional materials can still change the text's meaning. In doing so, promotions and paratexts become viable parts of the text and, by extension, viable contributors to the aesthetics, thematics, and artistry associated with the text. In what follows, I will draw several examples from contemporary media culture to show how central promotional and paratextual materials in film and television become to the culture that surrounds the film and show.

In challenging the promotion/art binary, it is by no means my intention to serve as apologist for Madison Avenue; academic and popular critiques of promotional culture are often well founded and necessary. Thus, I am not arguing that cultural critics give up their day jobs. Instead, I would like us to do more. My purpose is to interrogate the ways in which we delineate often too crudely between culture that "matters" and that is worthy of study as a site for engagement and the creation of meaning, and culture that is "just" advertising. Focusing on how this duality works with promotional culture surrounding film and television properties, the chapter studies how promotional culture and art are merging and how the work of art is often performed, albeit to varying levels of success, by promotional culture.

Branding Textuality

Before looking at specific examples, though, I will first argue that branding is a process that creates textuality and therefore that ads are often as much textual as they are promotional.

Madison Avenue has, of course, long since moved on from the days in which ads would calmly and verbosely describe a product; rather, today's advertiser needs to create an image to append to that product. In the process, as Sut Jhally writes, ads regularly assume a *tabula rasa*, seeing the product as an empty slate with no prior meaning or history. Next, "once the real meaning has been systematically *emptied* out of commodities…advertising then *refills* this void with its own symbols" (1987: 51, emphasis in original). Much advertising, then, aims to sell products by creating brand identity, and by promising value-added—product and metaphysics.

Take the Mac vs. PC advertising war in 2008–2009, for instance. Mac drew first blood with its ads featuring comedians Justin Long and John Hodgman. Hodgman represents the PC, an uptight, often smug, unfunny, nerdy, pudgy, and out-of-touch middle-aged man with few social skills yet many an ugly suit, while Long as the Mac is handsome, cool, confident, funny, relaxed, hip, and casually dressed. The ads occasionally offered nominal information about the two computers but largely worked by textualizing the two entities, authoring the Mac as the computer of now and the PC as dumpy and ineffective. They added qualities that cannot objectively belong to a computer—how can a laptop be confident or funny, or nerdy and pudgy for that matter? In doing so, therefore, the relative *actual* qualities for the computers proved almost completely irrelevant. Then, PC struck back with its smart "I'm a PC" campaign, offering many diverse individuals declaring that they are a PC. Unwilling to let Mac's advertisers author their client's "text," PC's advertisers tried to outdo their competitor by suggesting that PCs are special precisely because no one person can represent them—their text, they suggested instead, is limitless and open. As Judith Williamson explains, everything in an ad works as a gestalt and condensation of the product (1978: 79), and these ads worked to create a story, history, and character for each computer.

As Gillian Dyer notes of the semiotics of advertising, in ads "[t]he meaning of one *thing* is transferred to or made interchangeable with another *quality*, whose value attaches itself to the *product*," as elaborate semiotic chains are created to tie a product as blank slate to a theme, purpose, and identity—a text (1982: 116–7, emphasis in original). Branding is about surrounding a product with layers of symbolism in an attempt to give it a meaning both for those new to the product and, as value added, to those already owning the product (and, it is hoped, likely to be return customers). No guarantee exists that customers will buy into this textuality and symbolism, but at least in intent, ads aim to make products into texts and into popular culture.

If we turn to ads for films or television shows, the situation becomes slightly more complex, though, since now the film or television show is itself a text. As I type away on my Mac, it offers no story of itself, and, as Jhally (1987) notes, most product manufacturers work hard to erase the production histories of their items for sale, so my Mac needs help in becoming a text, help that an ad is only too willing to provide. By contrast, a film or television show already offers a text, so the advertiser's role is now to produce a text for a text. The tension involved in such a process can often result in icy relations between directors and marketing teams, as discussed in a *New Yorker* article featuring Tim Palen, Lionsgate's co-president of theatrical marketing (Friend 2009). Writer Tad Friend charts how Palen will often create campaigns for films that the directors themselves hate, and regard as wholly unreflective of their work, simply because he feels his own text is likely to sell better than the director's. For example, Palen decided to market Oliver Stone's *W.* as a controversial, cheeky and irreverent look at President George W. Bush, even though Stone's film treats its subject as a tragic figure; Palen thought the irreverence would succeed at finding an audience better than the suggestion of a more measured, sympathetic approach, and thus he sold a different text. Surely, too, we have all been victims of trailers or ad campaigns that excited us about a film or television show, or that suggested a different genre or tone, only to be deeply disappointed when eventually watching what is basically a different text. Even when they are not radically augmenting texts, promotions will often amplify specific qualities of texts and downplay others, thereby subtly re-authoring the public record of the text. In all such instances, we see that even texts can be retextualized, and rebranded at the level of the promotion.

At the same time, it would be foolish to believe that initial textual constructions simply vanish upon watching a film. As numerous audience researchers have examined, a large part of consumption has to do with the hopes and expectations that one brings to the text, and if promotions have already surrounded a text with themes and meanings, these cannot simply be turned off upon viewing (e.g., Barker and Brooks 1998; Barker, Arthurs, and Harindranath 2001). Further, lest we make the mistake of thinking that only viewers of the film or television show contribute to that film or show's presence in popular culture, we should remember that millions of potential viewers see the promotions and then walk away without having seen the film or show, yet with a sense of why they won't see it, and hence with a sense of what it means. For such non-viewers, the promotions are the text. Thus, texts begin not with the film or show's consumption but with the paratext or promotion's consumption for both viewers and non-viewers. As such, to study the meanings created by paratexts, and the branding of the text, is to study more fully texts' lives away from the film or show.

Springfield Sprawl: *The Simpsons* beyond Television

To find the culture in promotional culture and to see the sprawling text in action, we could begin by turning to Exhibit A for promotional culture in today's media environment, a town of four-fingered, yellow residents called Springfield. While many readers might successfully identify Springfield as the home of the Simpson family, surely few readers regard Springfield as trapped solely within the television show, *The Simpsons.* Rather, Springfield and *The Simpsons* are seemingly everywhere, overflowing from television to comics, clothing, toys, videogames, a film, ads, books, DVDs, CDs, keychains, cell phone rings, and countless other platforms. One would struggle to find any other show in television history whose global presence has involved so many promotional tie-ins. Admittedly, many of these promotional spinoffs generate revenue in and of themselves, so they are not solely promotional, but they have rarely been considered as part of the text itself in academic studies. Instead they are more often classified as part of the show's promotional sphere. Here, however, by focusing on one particular instance of *Simpsons* overflow—the online ads for *The Simpsons Game*—I want to argue that the text, and the artistic object that is *The Simpsons*, exists in part in its promotional wing.

I choose the ads for *The Simpsons Game* in part to be perverse, since, as the ad for the videogame timed to be released following *The Simpsons Movie* based on the series, it is a promotion for a promotion timed to the release of another promotion of a show. As such, it would be easy to focus on it first and foremost as a hypercommercialized money-grab, as a synergistic attempt to squeeze as much money as possible from a successful media product. Ads for games of a movie of a television show rate low on most traditional scales of artistic value. However, upon closer examination of these ads, we can see a viable source of *The Simpsons* as text.

Should one have sought out *The Simpsons Game*'s website or been directed there by its ensuing viral popularity, one would have found a series of links to parodic trailers for supposed standalone videogames, each of which used *The Simpsons* to parody established and popular games or game genres (and each a level in the actual game). One of these—*Medal of Homer* (see Figure 14.1)—went on to win a Golden Trailer award for innovative videogame advertising, given that it deftly parodied both the *Medal of Honor* games specifically and war games and war films more generally. With a grave yet sweeping orchestral and choral soundtrack befitting the likes of *Saving Private Ryan*, the ad opened with a series of zoom-and-pan scratchy black and white war "photos" (drawn in *Simpsons* style), playing with the visual style of Ken Burns documentaries, and of *Medal of Honor*'s cut sequences. Title cards were interspersed throughout such photos, reading "In the Last Great Invasion" "Of the Last Great War" "They Gave Each Other the Strength" "To Make History." This reverent spectacle was interrupted following the third title card, though, as we cut to a shot of Homer scratching his behind. The irreverence then bubbled up further following the last title card, as a prancing Homer interrupted, "Oooh, I'm France, I'm a little girl. I don't want to be bombed and attacked." The ad continued to its conclusion, cutting between shots of, for instance, Homer belching flame or rolling around as a huge human blob and shots framed to mimic war movie trailers.

In short, many of the key ingredients of *The Simpsons* were in the ad: significant irreverence and bodily humor, especially from Homer; *The Simpsons'* signature brand of attractive animation; smart, brilliantly executed media parody that lampoons the seriousness with which war games, war films, and their soundtracks take themselves; and the snark for which the show is famous. All of this took place in a brief, 80-second clip, replicating the television show's style of offering short bursts of media parody. One was not just watching an ad for the game of the show, in other words: one was getting *The Simpsons* itself. As with much comedy, *The Simpsons* television show is often broken down into smaller segments, each of which can work independently, and here the online ad offered a similar segment, just as rich with Simpsonesque humor and style as anything one might find in the television show. As an ad, the clip may be seen by some as less authentic, as simply hawking its wares, and as purely secondary to the primary text that is the *Simpsons* television show. But it produced and continued the text of *The Simpsons* with considerable skill. This paratext, in other words, is part of the text, having become a site not only of the production of the text but also of engagement with the text. The ad was as much a part of the artistic object that is *The Simpsons* as is an amusing sequence from an episode on television.

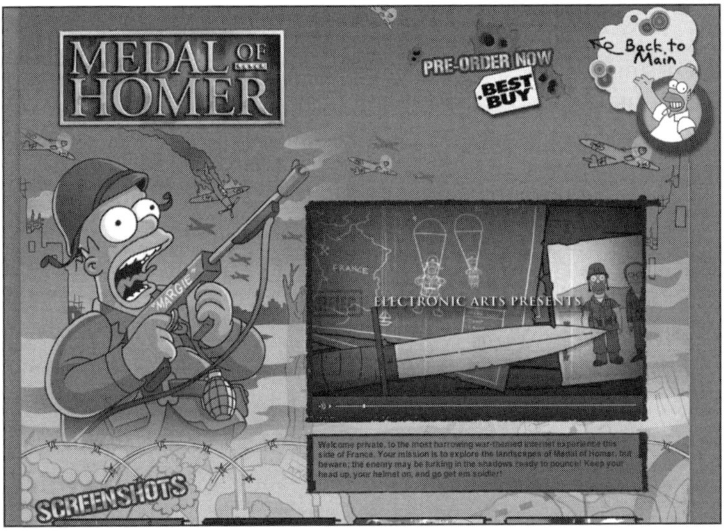

Figure 14.1 The *Medal of Homer* page on *The Simpson Game*'s website.

Nor was it alone in this regard. *The Simpsons*' history, and many of its public meanings, have often relied heavily upon its paratexts and promotions. While producers and authors play a role in creating art and while I have suggested that the ad's producers and authors contributed to this production, art is also created by consumers, and an artistic object's place in society will always rely as much on its audience as on the object itself. For a notable example of audiences authoring *The Simpsons* and determining its place in popular culture at the level of the promotion and the paratext, we could rewind the clock to its early days on air and especially to the Bart

Simpson T-shirt craze of the early 1990s. A furor surrounded the show in its early years, a furor directed at Bart as irreverent youth, but one that centered on—and was in many ways ignited by—the mass popularity of Bart T-shirts labeling Bart an "Underachiever," while he responds, "And Proud of It, Man." Many parents, teachers, principals, and pundits around the United States worried about children learning a slacker attitude from the T-shirt's sentiment, and as a result, many schools banned the T-shirts, and conservative rhetoric and complaints swarmed around the show (see Glynn 1996; Parisi 1993). This rhetoric completely failed to realize the sly message in the T-shirt: as Laurie Schulze notes, "Bart has managed to turn the tables on the system that's devalued him and say, 'In your face. I'm not worthless, insignificant, or stupid. If you want to label me an underachiever, I'll turn that into a badge of courage and say I'm proud of it'" (qtd. in Brook 2004: 178). Nevertheless, as paratext, the T-shirt created an image for many Americans of *The Simpsons* as a show of little to no values, intent on corrupting children's minds.

In 1992, at the Republican National Convention, President George H. W. Bush sealed this image of the show when he insisted that the U.S. needed more families like the Waltons and fewer like the Simpsons. In doing so, Bush confirmed *The Simpsons*' role as a front in the nation's culture wars between conservative America and liberal America. While *The Simpsons* was infused with Matt Groening's anti-establishment beliefs, sly satiric edge, and irreverence, the T-shirt controversy and the Bush speech suddenly amplified these qualities. Now, to watch *The Simpsons*, and/or to wear the T-shirt, was to posit oneself proudly against Bush's neo-conservatism, while to dislike the show, and/or to ban one's children from seeing it, was to publicly declare one's allegiance to those ideals. The promotional material made the show considerably more controversial, edgy, and anti-establishment than many of its episodes did. Certainly, in England, where the T-shirt controversy never bubbled up to the same degree, and where Bush's comments received considerably less attention, the show was often seen as endearingly *pro*-family values, to the point that Archbishop of Canterbury Rowan Williams has often proudly and unflinchingly sided with Bart over Bush, claiming that *The Simpsons* is "on the side of the angels" (BBC 2004).

To understand why paratexts and promotions are so powerful, we might reframe the issue as one of time and space. At the time of this writing, *The Simpsons* airs in the U.S. on the FOX network on Sundays at 8 p.m, and usually at several other half-hour slots during the day in syndication. Thus, the show itself is strictly contained by time and space. However, *The Simpsons*' paratexts allow Springfield to exist well beyond those boundaries. Echoes of Springfield are found in most shopping malls, throughout cyberspace, in countless souvenir stores worldwide, in games and electronics stores, on newsstands, in comic stores and bookstores, in TV specials, lying on the floor of many a child's room, in Burger King and MasterCard ads, on many an adult collector's shelf, on people's chests and heads, and in countless other venues. Such is FOX's strategy of synergy: that people will not be able to escape Springfield. But when Springfield is seemingly everywhere, a sprawling suburb that knows no bounds, many people will only experience Springfield outside of the television show, as suburbanites who never visit the city of the show itself. Even many of those who regularly watch the show at its scheduled time and space will also experience Springfield in countless other locales. *The Simpsons*, therefore, often exists in the paratexts and promotions, and those paratexts and promotions are fostering many of its meanings and its fans', non-fans', and anti-fans' reactions.

The Many Planets of *Star Wars*: The Toys and Their Films

If *The Simpsons* has proven to be a franchise par excellence for television, a filmic counterpart is the phenomenally successful *Star Wars*. *Star Wars* still has arguably the most voluminous paratextual entourage in entertainment history. Writing in 1992, before the franchise's proliferation of videogames, and before the second trilogy opened the floodgates for yet more merchandise sales, Stephen Sansweet noted that *Star Wars* had earned over $2.5 billion from merchandise alone (1992: 14). Spearheading *Star Wars*' early merchandising efforts were its action figures, with 42 million selling for a profit of $100 million to toy company Kenner in 1977 alone, and with 250 million selling by the early 1990s (Sansweet 1992: 71). It is such success that has often placed *Star Wars* in the crosshairs for cultural critics who see it as responsible for kicking off the host-selling era of 1980s television, with *My Little Pony*, *Strawberry Shortcake*, *The Transformers*, and colleagues taking over toy stores and Saturday morning television-watching in a well-coordinated effort in part modeled on *Star Wars*' success. Again, rather than see *Star Wars*' promotional culture and merchandising solely as a strategy to dupe kids into pledging allegiance to The Force, we might examine what meanings the toys added to the franchise, and the degree to which they helped shape common conceptions of and enjoyment of the *Star Wars* text.

Licensed toys have traditionally provoked the ire of cultural critics more than an attempt to understand their complexities (e.g., Englehardt 1986; Kline 1989). Thus, we know them to help profits, but little has been said of their textual role. A rare, and more nuanced, analysis of licensed toys can be found in Dan Fleming's *Powerplay: Toys as Popular Culture.* Rejecting the notion that licensed toys are simply spinoffs of other properties, Fleming instead argues that they generate their own textuality, as events in an ongoing process of textual phenomenology (1996: 11). "There may be a great deal going on," he notes, "when a child plays with the [licensed] toy, for which a TV programme cannot be held responsible" (1996: 15). Such toys, he argues, continue the story from a film or television program, but also provide a space in which meanings can be worked through, and in which questions and ambiguities in the film or program can be answered. Turning specifically to the *Star Wars* films and toys, Fleming notes first that central character Luke Skywalker is "a rather softly defined character," thereby allowing children playing with the toys to give the film's apparent hero a more resolute character in their play, or to identify with any of the other characters/toys instead. Similarly, he regards the toys as providing a relatively open field of play for children, resulting in a "deliberate generation of complexity" for the *Star Wars* text and an "ultimate refusal of narrative closure" (1996: 96, 102). Where the films required set plots, themes, and endings that would in turn aim for resolution, the toys allowed children to play up or down established themes, and to make their own substantial imprint on the *Star Wars* universe. Thus Fleming sees the toys as variously able to strengthen or to weaken established meanings in the films. In particular, for instance, he notes that with a "softly defined" hero surrounded by a motley crew of aliens, creatures, ships, and weapons:

> Perhaps unwittingly, what Kenner had tapped into with their original range of ninety-two small *Star Wars* figures (with more for the succeeding films) was precisely those contexts in which the original character of Luke Skywalker had been meaningful. The little plastic version of Luke seems very much at home surrounded by his menagerie of odd associates. And fitting him neatly into a plastic spacecraft with lots of opening panels, movable bits and quirky shapes was precisely the point—the technological environment was being adapted to offer a human "fit" and qualities of human variety (1996: 99).

The toys, in other words, may have accentuated the films' narrative of a youngster coming to terms with the difference and all the technologies that surround him. Luke's mastery of this environment grows throughout the films, but with all the figures under his or her control, the individual child's control would have been significantly more assured, hence strengthening the theme of the growing up narrative.

If we take Fleming's lead to examine the phenomenology of not just the toys but the entire *Star Wars* text, we find that the toys held the potential to play a sizeable role in the development of that text. For while Springfield must move out from the television show into its paratexts between 8:30 p.m. Sunday and 8:00 p.m. on the following Sunday, *Star Wars*' galaxy far, far away has lived via its toys and spinoff promotions and merchandise for much of its time in the universe. *Star Wars* fans had to wait for three years between films, stringing each trilogy out over six years. Between 1977 and 1983 in particular, before the ubiquitous presence of VHS in Western homes, if *Star Wars* was to live, it had to enter the body of paratexts. Toys became ways to keep the series alive. Between 1980's *Empire Strikes Back* and 1983's *Return of the Jedi*, young fans were left with multiple questions (Is Darth Vader Luke's father? Will the Rebellion rise again? What's happened to Han Solo? Will Luke become a Jedi?) that necessitated a transference of text to toy/paratext for many young fans. What happened during those years, as Fleming suggests, is that *Star Wars* invited young fans to take over to a certain degree. With the backdrop of a cosmic battle between good and evil, as Fleming states (here of the *GI Joe* toy line), "what perpetuates the whole line in all its interrelated forms, is perhaps the child's endless pursuit of the story within the story, of what is really going on while the aggression rages" (1996: 107). Fans were being asked to fill in the spaces that existed just off screen. A grand, protracted war of mythic proportions had been set up, an army of figures and vehicles sold, and the individual child was left in charge, becoming, in play, part of the battle, balancing right and wrong. The child was asked to bring all sorts of concepts together—good and evil, science and nature, rationality and intuition, childhood and adulthood, power and responsibility, familiarity and otherness—to provide synthesis.

Interestingly, too, many of the figures are of characters who prove entirely peripheral in the films. Characters who walk across the screen as alien extras become full-fledged figures, and many characters are named only as toys. To take one example, "Hammerhead" appears briefly in *Star Wars: A New Hope* sitting in the Cantina. S/he has no lines, nobody references him/her, and we learn nothing about him/her. Thus, when faced with the toy, the playing child can assign Hammerhead a gender, can make him/her a "good guy," yet another Imperial, or something altogether different, and can perpetuate his/her peripheral status or assign Hammerhead new importance. To the individual playing, Hammerhead could have been a traveling salesman, Admiral Ackbar's lover, an ace Rebel fighter pilot, and/or Mos Eisley's town drunk.[3] In no small way, then, these toys allow children to feed meanings back into the proscribed narratives. Here we can draw parallels with what many commentators have noted of fan fiction's expansive capacities (e.g., Bacon-Smith 1992; Jenkins 1992; Penley 1997; Brooker 2003), except a key difference is that the toys are licensed, as is play, and so no six-year-old received cease and desist letters from Lucasfilm's lawyers for acting out stories in the school yard.

With such examples, we see how the toys not only intensified several themes of the film—the focus on the cosmic battle, and the voyage of personal discovery especially[4]—but also allowed children to personalize these themes, situating themselves in the middle and as active participants, not just as distanced spectators. And they kept those meanings and the text itself alive and thriving. The toys worked to ensure *Star Wars* and its meanings stayed relevant, and kept circulating, added to, and being refreshed. It is perhaps no coincidence that in the mid-1990s, as Lucas announced his intention to make another trilogy, new toys (and, now, videogames) were sent forward as minions to throw coals on *Star Wars* fans' old flames. The toys, in other words, have never merely been profit-makers: they have played a vital role in, and have become a vital *part of*, the primary text and its unrivalled success.

So successful were the toys that to some critics, they may appear to be the actual show, and the films the promotions. Writing of Disney's films' relationship to the Disney videos and merchandise, for example, Robert Allen suggests that the films are simply "the inedible part of a Happy Meal" and the "movie on the lunchbox" (1999: 119, 123). Allen's proclamation may alarm us if we see promotional culture as entirely debased of meanings other than shifty, devious pleas to purchase, and empty superficialities designed to get us to the purchase, but we might instead see it as a mere reflection that promotions are often vibrant parts of an artistic object, not inherently different, distinct, and removed entities. Certainly, a closer look at the *Star Wars* figures would reveal many other ways in which they accentuate the films' themes, in particular clarifying the story into a grand battle of good and evil, and into a family saga. I examine both meanings in greater detail elsewhere, also exploring the degree to which the toys gendered the text (Gray 2010), but here I want to underline that the toys have become inseparable from the public understanding and appreciation of *Star Wars*. To many of its fans, *Star Wars* has not only extended itself but at times resided in toys/paratexts.

The toys have also played a large role in communicating *Star Wars* to non-fans, and even to non-watchers. After all, if one considers the ubiquity of *Star Wars* toys in Western society particularly in the late 1970s and throughout the 1980s, then the toys can still be seen as having played an important role in determining what *Star Wars* is and means to society as a whole. Children need not have played with the toys, and adults need neither have bought them nor been implored to buy them, for the toys to register as central to popular culture. Given the near-omnipresence of the army of *Star Wars* merchandise, many non-fans will likely have experienced more *Star Wars* through their run-ins with its paratexts and promotional entourage, and through their meanings, than with the films themselves. When Springfield or a galaxy far, far away overflow into public space, non-fans are more likely to experience the text at the level of the overflow, raising their own messages, themes, and narratives to primary status in the public understanding of a text.

Heroes and Sidekicks: Telling Stories with Promotions

Star Wars had many followers, and while it was hardly the first media property to realize the goldmine that exists in merchandising, with Disney in particular already an accomplished transmedia marketer, its success certainly seems to have been responsible for kicking in a new era of transmediality, one to which entities such as *Transformers*, *Pokemon*, and *Harry Potter* are indebted. However, not only did it propose a relatively new business model to a rapidly converging and conglomerating media industry; it also proposed a relatively new way to create stories and characters to a generation of writers who grew up with it. For example, when discussing transmedia with me at the 2008 Disney Studios and International Radio and Television Seminar's Digital Media Summit, *Lost* showrunner Damon Lindelof began by explaining the history of *Star Wars*' Boba Fett, a character whose cult popularity was established as a toy. Lindelof drew inspiration from *Star Wars*' act of telling its story across media including films, toys, comics, novels, and videogames, and felt that he and *Lost* had learned a great deal from this transmedia narrative style. Likewise, former *Heroes* co-executive producer and writer Jesse Alexander was clear in an interview with me that *Star Wars* showed him that transmedia storytelling was not only possible but the way to go.

With this in mind, we could examine *Heroes* and its use of transmedia storytelling—or, to rephrase, its use of promotional material to tell a story. Shows such as *Lost*, *Heroes*, and a growing number of others are written either across multiple media venues—television show and website, film, and comic book—or at the least with other media venues in mind. *Heroes* was 2008's Emmy Award winner for Outstanding Interactive Media Programming, as the story overflowed into various websites and MySpace pages set within the fictional frame of the show, into novels that covered gaps in the television narrative, into an elaborate text message-based game, into online competitions to create a new hero, and into an online graphic novel. It is to this graphic novel that I wish to turn.

The online graphic novel was a free comic that cleverly weaved in and out of the television narrative of *Heroes*, at times following and repeating actions from the show, at times offering fuller context or background, at times penning entirely new material and episodes. *Heroes* the television show often adopts a comic book aesthetic, visually in filming angles and in opening frames that offer titles in comic book style, and thematically in its interest in superheroes. Moreover, several characters have obtained the ability to see the future and draw it in comic book style, and another comic-book loving, time-traveling character has often sought guidance from a comic series called *9th Wonders*, penned by one of the aforementioned clairvoyants. The inclusion of a comic book in the show's transmedia arsenal was almost to be expected. Undoubtedly, NBC also looked upon the comic book as a way to draw in the comic reading demographic; as a free spinoff, the comic would need to have been justified to the network as promotional by nature. Nevertheless, it is also rich with narrative and often beautifully penned.

The comic book is visually evocative, drawn by numerous well established comic book artists, including Michael Turner, Phil Jimenez, Micah Gunnell, and Marcus To. It is written by a collection of *Heroes* writers, moreover, and thus was not "farmed out" to another company. And rather than simply transpose elements from the show into the comic book, it introduced an entirely new character, Hana Gitelman (aka "Wireless"), who similarly exists across many of the show's other transmedia venues. After enough episodes had been penned to be collected in print, the *Heroes* staff bound them with two alternate covers drawn by famed comic book artists

Jim Lee and Alex Ross. The comics can be read independently of the series, albeit with difficulty, or as a supplement that adds extra information and narrative. In this regard, they are promotions but also viable sources of diegesis. Whereas *The Simpsons* has no discernible developing narrative, thereby rendering its various transmedia venues "in world" but not contributors to an ongoing narrative per se, and whereas *Star Wars* toys and videogames allow fans to add their own imprint on the universe yet not in canonical fashion, *Heroes*' comic book is an instance wherein the narrative continues and is expanded upon, canonically, in a "promotional" venue.

Pizza as Text? A Conclusion

In these various examples, I have illustrated how promotion and text, or ad and art, are merging, with no clear line between them. However, cultural criticism has often proven to be heavily invested in the existence of a firm line, frequently suggesting that being promotional obviates being artistic or contributing to the meaning of a text, and that being promotional is always and only about being promotional. For instance, writing of "alternate reality games" (ARGs) that surround some films and shows, drawing audiences into the diegetic frame to solve puzzles, much as *Heroes* has done with its comics and other transmedia, Henrik Örnebring exhibits frustration with how "there is relatively little academic concern with how ARGs function as *marketing tools*." He reiterates further that "[t]heir primary purpose is not to create new opportunities for interaction, networking and audience participation in mediated narratives, but simply to create an enjoyable experience that will build the franchise brand in the minds of media audiences" (2007: 449, 450). He is correct, of course, to point out that most ARGS are designed to advertise and to create buzz, like the *Heroes* comic book and *The Simpsons Game*'s online ads; many are allowed to exist because they brand the text. But as I have been arguing, Örnebring's hard and fast division between marketing and branding on one side, and interaction, networking, and audience participation on the other, ultimately cannot hold. Branding is the process of making a product into a text, and thus when the product is itself a text, branding in and of itself need not mean anything more than adding sites of construction for that text. What Örnebring calls the ARG's "simple" task "to create an enjoyable experience that will build the franchise brand in the minds of media audiences" will quite often *require* that the ARG works "to create new opportunities for interaction, networking and audience participation in mediated narratives." His division, as such, folds back on itself, illustrating the degree to which many promotions confuse the industry's and academia's binary of marketing and creativity.

Örnebring's criticism offers something of a red herring. Of course the profit imperative of an ARG may dictate the course of the story and may considerably hamper the scope of the narrative. But this is a problem endemic to all commercial media, and hence to films and television programs too, not just promotional material. In the case of film and television, the profit imperative is bound tightly to the narrative impulse, but this does not necessarily overwhelm that impulse. David Simon and HBO needed to make money with *The Wire*, as did RKO and Orson Welles with *Citizen Kane*, but this does not debase either text. By no means do I suggest that we should drop our concern with rampant commercialism and with the problematic nature of stories that aim to sell, but once more this is an issue endemic to film, television, and popular culture as a whole, not just to ARGs, spinoff toys, online ads, and other promotions.

Paratexts can confound and disturb many of our hierarchies and binaries of what matters and what does not in the media world, especially the long-held notion that marketing and creativity are or could be distinct from one another. In doing so, some invite us to study promotions not only as *commercial* culture—though of course we should still do so—but also as commercial *culture*.

Admittedly, some promotions serve only to annoy consumers. But hype and promos are likely to do so only when the consumer does not care about (or actively dislikes) the related text, when the promos contribute nothing or take away from the text, and hence when they do not make the leap from being just a promo to being something more. Take, for instance, a promotion for Domino's *Dark Knight*-related "Gotham City pizza." As critics touted the film's dark aesthetic, I found myself wondering what a pepperoni pizza was supposed to add to *The Dark Knight* as text. The pizza's and the ad's sole contribution was to signal the size of the film ("it even has a pizza named after it"). This move was wholly unnecessary, given the scale of the advertising campaign, and it was trumped by the pizza's and ad's act of taking away from the film, making it seem, well, cheesy. The paratexts were wholly unincorporated, therefore, not a problem because they were an ad and a pizza, but a problem because they were an ad and a pizza that contributed nothing meaningful to the text or its narrative, storyworld, characters, or style. By contrast, such a promotion may have fit *Spider-Man*, given alter ego Peter Parker's stint as delivery man, or *Teenage Mutant Ninja Turtles*, given the characters' love of pizza. For *The Dark Knight*, they were only ads and pizzas.

Alongside the Gotham City pizza, we can place countless other examples of promotional material that fails to add anything substantive to the storyworld, or even to sample that world for would-be viewers. We could also point to cases when the promo's meanings clash with those of the text, as for instance when a show is sold as one genre when it is in fact another. Such moments may cause confusion as to what the text is actually about. Let me be clear, then, in stating that I am not arguing that all promotions contribute meaningfully to the artistic object. Nor am I suggesting that those that do contribute should be exempt from criticism for their promotional aspects. Rather, I am arguing that it is wholly insufficient to regard "promotion" or "advertisement" as totems that ward all artistry or meaning away from a text.

Nevertheless, cultural criticism has often taken promotional culture as such a totem, and the consequences for the state of media and cultural criticism have been severe, as we have tended subsequently either to ignore ads in our work, or to study them only insofar as they are purveyors of rampant consumerism. We have forgotten to look at the culture in promotional culture. It has been beyond the scope of this chapter to discuss the multiple benefits of art and of narrative, and their value to society, but I hope it is safe to assume these benefits and values as read; if so, we must conclude that film and television promotions can serve an aesthetic function and an important cultural function in society. They are not just leading us further into a spiral of consumerism based on debased values—although at times they may certainly be doing that as well. Rather, they do the work of art.

Hollywood has long since recognized the importance of promotional material, channeling large portions of budgets into creating it. Increasingly, too, some of the industry's most talented individuals are working in its promotional wings, and many of its big name writers and directors are crossing over to ensure that their ARGs, spinoffs, tie-ins, and promos synch up with the text they're creating. In the course of researching my book *Show Sold Separately*, I interviewed numerous producers of DVD bonus materials, licensed videogames, ARGS, and web extras, and all approached their work as artists. A quick browse through fan sites, moreover, will confirm that many audiences consider such promos viable parts of the artistic object. Even in the field of labor relations, the 2008 WGA strike proved that the line between creation and promotion is being challenged within Hollywood, as one of the writers' (unmet) demands was to be fairly compensated for creating webisodes and other promos that traditionally the industry has regarded as merely promotional. What I am posing, then, is that it is high time that we in academia catch up. While producers, fans, writers, and budgets have been operating with implicit acknowledgment of the importance of promotions, we have often kept our eyes steadfastly on the film or show itself. In doing so, multiple meanings have eluded us. If close reading, production analysis, audience ethnography, and critical theory of films and television shows have long been in our toolkit, we must now apply the same analytical tools to promotions.

Notes

1. This article draws in large part from Gray (2010). Thanks are extended to NYU Press for allowing me to reprint occasional passages and case studies.
2. For a particularly notable exception, see Kernan (2004).
3. A later toy moved to shut down some of these meanings by giving Hammerhead a gender and a name, Momaw Nadon, and by labeling him as a gardener. Nevertheless, by this point, undoubtedly many toy owners had invented their own canon regarding Hammerhead.
4. For more, see Gray (2010).

References

Allen, Robert C. 1999. "Home Alone Together: Hollywood and the 'Family Film.'" In *Identifying Hollywood's Audiences: Cultural Identity and the Movies*, ed. M. Stokes and R. Maltby. London: BFI.

Bacon-Smith, Camille. 1992. *Enterprising Women: Television Fandom and the Creation of Popular Myth.* Philadelphia: University of Pennsylvania Press.

Barker, Martin, and Kate Brooks. 1998. *Knowing Audiences: Judge Dredd, Its Friends, Fans and Foes.* Luton: University of Luton Press.

Barker, Martin, Jane Arthurs, and Ramaswami Harindranath. 2001. *The Crash Controversy: Censorship and Film Reception.* London: Wallflower.

BBC. 2004. "Archbishop 'May Star in Simpsons,'" *BBC News*, June 20. http://news.bbc.co.uk/1/hi/entertainment/tv_and_radio/3823541.stm.

Brook, Vincent. 2004. "Myth or Consequences: Ideological Fault Lines in *The Simpsons.*" Pp. 172–196 in *Leaving Springfield: The Simpsons and the Possibility of Oppositional Culture*, ed. J. Alberti. Detroit: Wayne State University Press.

Brooker, Will. 2003. *Using the Force: Creativity, Community and Star Wars Fans.* New York: Continuum.

Dyer, Gillian. 1982. *Advertising as Communication.* New York: Routledge.

Englehardt, Tom. 1986. "The Strawberry Shortcake Strategy." Pp. 68–110 in *Watching Television*, ed. Todd Gitlin. New York: Pantheon.

Fleming, Dan. 1996. *Powerplay: Toys as Popular Culture.* Manchester: Manchester University Press.
Friend, Tad. 2009. "The Cobra: Inside a Movie Marketer's Playbook." *The New Yorker,* January 19: 41–46.
Genette, Gerard. 1997. *Paratexts: Thresholds of Interpretation.* Trans. Jane E. Lewin. Cambridge: Cambridge University Press.
Glynn, Kevin. 1996. "Bartmania: The Social Reception of an Unruly Image." *Camera Obscura: Feminism, Culture, and Media Studies* 38: 61–91.
Gray, Jonathan. 2010. *Show Sold Separately: Promos, Spoilers, and Other Media Paratexts.* New York: New York University Press.
Jenkins, Henry. 1992. *Textual Poachers: Television Fans and Participatory Culture.* New York: Routledge.
Jhally, Sut. 1987. *The Codes of Advertising: Fetishism and the Political Economy of Meaning in the Consumer Society.* New York: Routledge.
Kernan, Lisa. 2004. *Coming Attractions: Reading American Movie Trailers.* Austin, TX: University of Texas Press.
Kline, Stephen. 1989. "Limits to the Imagination: Marketing and Children's Culture." Pp. 299–316 in *Cultural Politics in Contemporary America,* ed. Ian Angus and Sut Jhally.
New York: Routledge.
Lotz, Amanda. 2007. *The Television Will Be Revolutionized.* New York: New York University Press.
Örnebring, Henrik. 2007. "Alternate Reality Gaming and Convergence Culture: The Case of *Alias.*" *International Journal of Cultural Studies* 10 (4): 445–462.
Parisi, Peter. 1993. "'Black Bart' Simpson: Appropriation and Revitalization in Commodity Culture." *Journal of Popular Culture* 27 (1): 125–142.
Penley, Constance. 1997. *NASA/TREK: Popular Science and Sex in America.* London: Verso.
Sansweet, Stephen. 1992. *Star Wars: From Concept to Screen to Collectible.* San Francisco: Chronicle.
Williamson, Judith. 1978. *Decoding Advertisements: Ideology and Meaning.* London: Marion Boyars.

NOTES ON CONTRIBUTORS

Melissa Aronczyk is Assistant Professor in the School of Journalism and Communication at Carleton University, Canada. Her current research explores the phenomenon of nation branding and its implications for national space, the production of value and problems of identity in a global context. She is currently revising her monograph on the topic, *Branding the Nation*, for Oxford University Press.

Sarah Banet-Weiser is Associate Professor of Communication and American Studies and Ethnicity at the University of Southern California. She is the author of *The Most Beautiful Girl in the World: Beauty Pageants and National Identity* (University of California Press, 1999) and *Kids Rule! Nickelodeon and Consumer Citizenship* (Duke, 2007), and the co-editor of *Cable Visions: Television Beyond Broadcasting* (NYU Press, 2007). She is currently working on a book about brand culture, neoliberalism, and political possibility entitled *Authentic™: Political Possibility in a Brand Culture* (New York University Press, forthcoming).

John Corner is currently Visiting Professor in the Institute for Communication Studies at the University of Leeds and an Emeritus Professor of the University of Liverpool. His major works include *Television Form and Public Address* (Arnold, 1995), *The Art of Record* (Manchester, 1996) and *Critical Ideas in Television Studies* (Oxford, 1999). Recent publications include the edited collection *Media and the Restyling of Politics* (with Dick Pels, Sage, 2003) and the authored volume *Public Issue Television* (with Peter Goddard and Kay Richardson, Manchester, 2007). His current research includes inquiry into aspects of documentary form and the changing nature of the relationship between media and political culture.

Gabriele Cosentino is a PhD candidate in the Department of Media, Culture and Communication at New York University. His writings on the intersections between popular culture, media and politics have been published in various edited collections.

Arlene Davila is Professor of Anthropology and American Studies at New York University. Her most recent book is *Latino Spin: Public Image and the Whitewashing of Race* (New York University Press, 2008). She writes and teaches on issues of consumption, media, urban studies, the political economy, and the global circulation of media, focusing in particular on U.S. Latinos.

Waddick Doyle is the founder and chair of the Department of International Communications and founder and director of the Masters in Global Communications program at the American University of Paris. He has published on what he calls the sacralization of brands and reality television and on media and belief. Doyle is presently writing a book about the rise to power of the Italian political, media and advertising tycoon, Silvio Berlusconi.

Mary Ebeling is Assistant Professor of Sociology at Drexel University. She studies the political economies of emerging technologies. Her current research is focused on the development and marketing of translational medicine and nanobiotechnologies in postindustrial settings in Italy and the United States. Her work has appeared in *Science Communication, Sociological Research Online, PR Watch,* and *Radical History Review.*

Jonathan Gray is Associate Professor of Media and Cultural Studies at the University of Wisconsin, Madison. He is author of *Show Sold Separately: Promos, Spoilers, and Other Media Paratexts* (NYU, 2010), *Television Entertainment* (Routledge, 2008), and *Watching with The Simpsons: Television, Parody, and Intertextuality* (Routledge, 2006), and co-editor of *Satire TV: Politics and Comedy in the Post-Network Era* (NYU, 2009), *Battleground: The Media* (Greenwood, 2008), and *Fandom: Identities and Communities in a Mediated World* (NYU, 2007). He also co-edits *Popular Communication: The International Journal of Media and Culture.*

Miriam Greenberg is Assistant Professor of Sociology at the University of California Santa Cruz. Greenberg's work lies at the intersection of urban sociology, media and cultural studies, and political economy. She studies the rise of urban branding in the U.S. and globally; urban representation in the media; and the role of media, marketing, and the symbolic economy in urbanization and restructuring. She is the author of *Branding New York: How a City in Crisis Was Sold to the World* (Routledge, 2008) and *Crisis Cities:*

Framing Disaster and Redevelopment in New York and New Orleans, with Kevin Fox Gotham (Oxford University Press, forthcoming).

Alison Hearn is Associate Professor in the Faculty of Information & Media Studies at the University of Western Ontario. With Liora Salter, she is co-author of *Outside the Lines: Issues in Interdisciplinary Research* (MQUP, 1996), which explores the possibilities of critical thinking and cultural commentary both within and beyond the setting of the university. She is currently working on a book about reality television entitled *Real Incorporated: Explorations in Reality Television and Contemporary Visual Culture.*

Graham Knight is Professor in the Department of Communication Studies and Multimedia at McMaster University in Canada. His teaching and research interests lie mainly in the areas of contemporary social theory, political sociology, and media sociology. He has published widely in the areas of promotionalism, particularly on corporate public relations.

Hongmei Li is Assistant Professor of Communication at Georgia State University and George Gerbner Postdoctoral Fellow at the Annenberg School for Communication, University of Pennsylvania for 2008–2010. She obtained her PhD from the Annenberg School for Communication, University of Southern California. Her research interests center on advertising and consumer culture, nation branding, nationalism, cultural identity, gender and sexuality, globalization, and the Internet in Chinese society. She has published in *Critical Studies in Media Communication*, *Public Relations Review*, and *International Journal of Communication.*

Celia Lury is Professor in the Department of Sociology at Goldsmiths, University of London. She has published extensively in the area of sociology of culture, including *Brands: the Logos of the Global Economy* (Routledge, 2004); *Global Culture Industry: The Mediation of Things*, with S. Lash (Polity, 2007); and *Inventive Life: Towards the New Vitalism*, edited with M. Fraser and S. Kember (Sage, 2006). Her edited volume *Inventive Methods*, edited with N. Wakeford, is forthcoming from Routledge.

Liz Moor is Senior Lecturer in Media and Communications at Goldsmiths, University of London. Her research interests are in the area of consumer culture, material culture, design, and branding. She is the author of *The Rise* *of Brands* (Berg, 2007) and the co-editor (with Guy Julier) of *Design and Creativity: Policy, Management and Practice* (Berg, 2009).

Jefferson Pooley is Assistant Professor of Media and Communication at Muhlenberg College in Allentown, Pennsylvania. He is co-editor, with David W. Park, of *The History of Media & Communication Research* (Peter Lang, 2008). His research centers on the history of communication studies, as the field's emergence has intersected with the twentieth century rise of the other social sciences. His particular interest is in the field's memories of itself. He also writes about celebrity, consumer culture, and media policy.

Devon Powers is Assistant Professor in the Department of Culture and Communication at Drexel University. Her research focuses on twentieth century popular music, cultural intermediation, and cultural circulation. She is currently completing her book, *Sounding Off:* The Village Voice *and Rock Criticism* (University of Massachusetts Press, forthcoming) about rock criticism as a form of public intellectualism. She has published articles in *Journalism History*, *Journalism Studies*, and *Popular Music and Society*.

Marita Sturken is Professor and Chair in the Department of Media, Culture, and Communication at New York University where she teaches courses in visual culture, cultural studies, cultural memory, and consumerism. She is the author of several books, including *Tangled Memories: The Vietnam War, the AIDS Epidemic, and the Politics of Remembering* (University of California, 1997) and *Practices of Looking: An Introduction to Visual Culture* (with Lisa Cartwright, Oxford University Press, 2001, Second Edition 2009), and *Tourists of History: Memory, Kitsch, and Consumerism from Oklahoma City to Ground Zero* (Duke University Press, 2007).

INDEX